Democracy and
Judicial Independence

The hum of their voices and movements came back upon the steady draft which blew through the door. The air entered the open windows and blew over the heads and back to Horace in the door, laden with smells of tobacco and stale sweat and the earth and with that unmistakable odor of courtrooms; that musty odor of spent lusts and greeds and bickerings and bitterness, and withal a certain clumsy stability in lieu of anything better.

—William Faulkner, *Sanctuary*

Democracy and Judicial Independence

A HISTORY OF THE FEDERAL COURTS OF ALABAMA, 1820–1994

Tony Freyer & Timothy Dixon

CARLSON
Publishing Inc

BROOKLYN, NEW YORK, 1995

Research for this book was made possible, in part, through the generous support of the Eleventh Circuit Historical Society.

Library of Congress Cataloging-in-Publication Data
   Freyer, Tony Allan.
      Democracy and judicial independence : a history of the federal
   courts of Alabama, 1820–1994 / Tony Freyer & Timothy Dixon.
         p.   cm.
      Includes bibliographical references and index.
      ISBN 0-926019-86-4 (hardback : alk. paper)
      1. District courts—Alabama—History.   2. District courts—United
   States—History.   I. Dixon, Timothy J., 1958–   .   II. Title.
   KFA515.F74   1995
   347.761'02—dc20
   [347.61072]   95-35314

Typographic design: Julian Waters

Typeface: Adobe Janson Text

Index prepared by Scholars Editorial Services, Inc., Madison, Wisconsin, using NL Cindex, a scholarly indexing program from the Newberry Library.

Printed on acid-free, 250-year-life paper.

Manufactured in the United States of America.

To the federal judges from Alabama,
past and present,
and Charles W. Gamble.

Contents

Illustrations

Preface

The federal judiciary in Alabama often tested the relationship between judicial independence and American democracy. The state joined the Union in 1819 as part of a territorial expansion that aggravated the struggle over slavery and led eventually to the Civil War. From the beginning, the routine litigation and major constitutional suits that arose in Alabama had significant implications for the national economy and political conflicts: struggles over the freedman's rights during and after Reconstruction; controversies involving regulation of the railroads and then leading New Deal agencies; numerous confrontations during the civil rights struggle that followed the Second World War; and efforts since the 1970s to include previously excluded groups in the democratic process. Federal judges repeatedly decided the limits of constitutional separation and democracy. Moreover, the Constitution established judicial independence, but the conflicts inherent in the division of powers and checks and balances often required judges to exercise discretion in order to settle disputes.

The Constitution's Article III established the basic jurisdiction of the Supreme Court and the lower federal tribunals but left it to Congress to determine the system's structure and responsibility. In Alabama, from the beginning federal judges employed changing jurisprudential assumptions and local institutions to broaden their powers and strengthen their independence. The Judiciary Act of 1789 attempted to balance the third branch's constitutional separation and dependence on state law. Throughout the period before the Civil War, a local federal courtroom culture emerged, however, which reduced the state's power over judges' decision making. Constitutional amendments and laws enacted during Reconstruction strengthened this local institutional culture. Then the gradual yet steady growth of federal legislation, culminating in the New Deal, broadened national power without significantly weakening local autonomy.

The Second World War marked a further turning point in the character of federal judicial independence. The Supreme Court responded to the rise of totalitarian dictatorships during the 1930s and 1940s with a new presumption favoring democracy and a freer exercise of civil rights and liberties.

The Court's decisions facilitated the gradual emergence of a national consensus supporting the principle if not the substance of rights claims. The struggle of African Americans to fulfill this democratic promise engendered the Court's decision in *Brown v. Board of Education* (1954), the South's massive resistance to its implementation, and the civil rights movement's eventual overcoming of this defiance, particularly through the Civil Rights Act of 1964 and the Voting Rights Act of 1965. At the center of this struggle were the federal courts in Alabama.

The federal judiciary's expansion of America's rights consciousness also increased centralization of the national judicial establishment. As a result, judicial independence depended more on national institutional autonomy than a local courtroom culture. During the closing decades of the twentieth century, federal courts in Alabama used this independence to strengthen the bond between individual rights and American democracy.

In recent years, scholars have given increased attention to the lower federal courts. In different ways this work addresses institutional change to explain and evaluate the relationship between judicial independence and the democratic process.[1] Kermit Hall and Lawrence Friedman have done more than anyone to integrate these issues into the broader themes of American legal history.[2] Edward A. Purcell, Jr., has employed sociological theory to study the subject systemically, while Tony Freyer has attempted to explore the relationships between institutional change and the economy on the one hand and civil rights on the other.[3] There is also a growing number of studies of federal district and circuit courts within particular states or regions, as well as works on individual federal judges.[4] Our history of the federal courts in Alabama seeks to make a useful contribution to this literature. We also hope to tell an interesting story.

The authors are grateful to many individuals and institutions for assistance. The Eleventh Circuit Historical Society, through the leadership of Thomas C. MacDonald, Jr., president, Thomas Reese, the Society's former executive director, and Honorable John C. Godbold, provided the primary initiative for the project. Without their interest, and the support of the Society's anonymous benefactor, this book would not have been written. The support of the Judicial Conference of the United States, Committee on the Bicentennial of the Constitution, was also important.

The personnel and resources of the University of Alabama School of Law facilitated in many ways the book's completion. We wish to thank particularly former Deans Charles W. Gamble and Nathaniel Hansford, and current Dean Kenneth C. Randall, and to acknowledge the support of the Alabama Law School Foundation and the Edward Brett Randolph Fund. For preparation of the endless drafts, we benefited from the expertise of Lori Hall, Patty Nelson, and most recently Alesia Darling. Anderson Wynn of the Duplicating Center also gave useful assistance. The Law Library's Dr. Paul M. Pruitt aided our search for sources with persistent, expert, and friendly diligence. Kyra L. Weinberg, Peter Wonders, and Erby Fischer rendered excellent service as research assistants. Rufus Bealle, the university's former chief counsel and member of the Law School class of 1942, provided certain important insights, as did Professor Wythe Holt.

The offices of the clerk of the court for the U.S. Court for the Northern, Middle, and Southern districts were always helpful. We wish to thank especially Charles T. Cliver, former clerk of the court for the Northern District, who provided us with a valuable collection of documents, and Robin Holeb-Ableman, librarian, U.S. District Court, Southern District of Alabama. Virginia Hare, the Northern District Court's law librarian, was also most helpful. At different times the clerks of the court and the librarians of the Eleventh and Fifth Circuit Court of Appeals also provided useful information. Professor Freyer is grateful to each of the judges, who over the years consented to interviews, and to the judges' clerks and staffs for their friendly welcome. The authors, the federal bench and bar of the state of Alabama, and the Eleventh Circuit Historical Society are indebted to Mary Ann Hawkins for organizing and making available to the public the manuscript files, dockets, and records of Alabama's federal courts, included in Record Group 21 at the National Archives, Southeast Region, East Point, Georgia. We wish to thank, too, Reginald T. Hamner, executive director, Alabama State Bar, Edwin C. Bridges, director, Alabama Department of Archives and History, and Norwood Kerr, head, Archives Reference.

Professor Freyer wrote the narrative of the book, and Mr. Dixon prepared the appendixes and did much of the editing. The authors wish to thank Ellen and Forrest McDonald for insights and encouragement. We dedicate the fruits of our study to Charles W. Gamble and the federal judges from Alabama, past and present.

Tony Freyer
Timothy Dixon

Tuscaloosa
July 1994

Democracy and
Judicial Independence

I

The Paradox of Federal Judicial Power in Antebellum Alabama

INTRODUCTION

"Federal judges almost always alone decide those questions," wrote Alexis de Tocqueville, "that touch the government of the country most closely."[1] Tocqueville's assessment, even after a hundred and seventy years, remains true. Yet the reasons why federal courts have exercised such influence throughout the nation's history are not obvious, in part because the federal judge's nonelective and good-behavior position seems at odds with American democratic traditions. Complicating the issue is the subordinate status of federal tribunals below the Supreme Court. Moreover, in many cases state law binds the lower federal courts. Ironically, this apparent dependence rarely prevents federal judges from exercising sufficient discretion to achieve an independent power in American democracy.[2]

The lower federal judiciary's operation before the Civil War suggested how dependency and discretion might be reconciled. The states, rather than the federal government, exercised "real power" during the antebellum years, Tocqueville said. Nevertheless, Americans accepted that "it was almost impossible that the execution of a new [state] law should not injure some private interest." The Constitution relied on "private interest to attack the legislative measure of which the Union might have complained," and it was that interest to which the federal courts "offer[ed] protection." Thus, while federal justice and state sovereignty were "at odds," the federal courts "attack[ed] only indirectly ... strik[ing] at the consequences of the law, not at its principle; it does not abolish but enervates it." The courts intervened, Tocqueville concluded, "in public affairs only by chance, but the chance recurs daily."[3] The overriding constitutional command that federal judges protect individuals—particularly residents of different states—compelled repeated consideration and interpretation of the limits and meaning of state and federal law and the Constitution itself.[4]

The need for interpretation and the discretion it implied had significant implications for the judicial selection process. Since the nation's earliest years, politicians had noted the connection between the political party someone belonged to and his chances of becoming a judge. The broad issues dominating the federal judicial selection process during the antebellum years involved the influence of political parties and the extent to which previously powerful groups had surrendered influence to party operatives. The second two-party system, which emerged during the 1820s, linked the president, Congress, and state officials and imposed a certain coherence on this network of commitments. To some extent these relationships reflected simple partisan patronage. At the same time, personal contacts, kinship relations, individual ambition, the North-South sectional conflict, slavery, and various economic interests transcended mere party politics. The persistence of these traditional factors reflected the decentralized character of antebellum party organization.[5]

Andrew Jackson's election in 1828 promised wider democratic political involvement.[6] But when it came to selecting federal judges, both Democrats and Whigs chose nominees who were at least socially prominent, if not elite. The influence of social criteria on judicial discretion was ambiguous. Education, family background, personal connections, economic opportunity, and social standing determined status. The judicial selection process assumed that party membership was an effective measure of a federal judge's values because the party was "an important socializing institution" representing "a collection of likeminded persons (especially among political activists)."[7] This recognized the political motivations of the appointing president and home-state national representatives (especially senators). Also significant were state-based factors such as legal education, the socialization that occurs between new and old judges within a jurisdiction, and the state's geographic location.[8]

These factors interacted with formal legal institutions and values. The strength of precedent, whether an issue was routine or new, the quality of the evidence and lawyer's arguments, the clarity of the Supreme Court's previous rulings, and the local setting in which a case occurred shaped the scope or limits of a federal judge's discretionary authority. What characterized the decision-making process was a continuum: Grouped at one end were the judge's instincts and experience; at the other end were the formal institutional arrangements. The more routine a case, the greater the likelihood that formal institutional considerations shaped the judge's decision. Where the arguments of both sides were equally compelling, however, the room for the influence of the externals increased.[9]

Lawyers, too, shaped judicial decision-making. The jurisdiction of the federal district and circuit courts, and ultimately the Supreme Court, represented the federal "market" for legal services. The uses to which federal judges put their jurisdiction—including the exercise of discretion—defined the opportunity of lawyers and their clients. Even so, formal jurisdictional boundaries defined only the outer limits of this opportunity. Within those boundaries the range of private interests that Tocqueville identified was sufficiently broad to test fully the scope of the judge's discretionary authority.

The distinct nature of the lawyer's role also was important. In part, lawyers symbolized abstract knowledge and lofty institutions. No less important, however, was the lawyer's broker role. In this "transactional relationship," lawyers served as intermediaries "bringing together distributors and recipients of aid in transfers of information, money, property, and the like." The relationship was sufficiently routine that lawyers generally relied on what might be characterized as "insider" knowledge, such as the "going rates for particular injuries . . . , recent trends in jury verdicts for particular kinds of cases, the attitudes of trial judges as related to the situations of a lawyer's clients, and the style and experience of the opposing party's lawyer." The lawyer's broker role and his informal legal knowledge and networks depended on a "courtroom work group," including judges, clerks and magistrates, and other attorneys.[10]

The broker role epitomized the interactional nature of factors shaping judicial discretion. Notwithstanding formal institutional arrangements and personal background, federal judges were members of the courtroom's working culture. In addition, they usually had been part of it as lawyers before being appointed. It was in this culture that both judges and lawyers viewed cases arising from the wider society. This meant that factors remote from the local courtroom culture could exert a dominant influence on judicial discretion only in exceptional cases.

From entering the Union in 1819 to becoming the home of the Confederate capital in 1860, Alabama occupied a central place in the American constitutional order. Two Supreme Court justices came from the state. And despite national partisan politics, when selecting candidates for the federal courts, presidents usually deferred to local interests. Generally, then, before the Civil War a locally oriented courtroom culture combined with formal, informal, and institutional factors to shape the exercise of judicial discretion in Alabama.[11]

The federal courts' operation and decisions provided one measure of judicial discretion. From 1820 on, Alabama's federal litigation steadily increased, until by the 1840s the state had three separate federal district courts. Congress, however, left the administration of all three courts to a single judge. Similarly, the litigation arising from Alabama's federal circuit courts grew apace. Yet despite repeated appeals, Congress gave only modest relief to the one Supreme Court justice and the district judge responsible for administering this growing workload.[12] In addition, relatively few lawyers handled the litigation, and combined with the two federal judges constituted a small, fairly cohesive working courtroom culture.[13] Shared jurisprudential assumptions enabled bench and bar to pack statutes and constitutional provisions with "extratextual" meanings. The interplay of local factors and this flexible jurisprudence expedited the courts' handling of the expanding workload. Even so, Alabama's federal judges had to balance local and national policy imperatives.[14]

Political and social factors provided a context within which the local legal culture operated. The appointment process was the most conspicuous point at which explicit partisan considerations influenced the state's federal bench. Still, in selection of the four federal district judges, tensions between the state's northern and southern sections generally determined the appointment. These substate pressures were only slightly less significant for the appointment of the two Supreme Court justices. Mitigating further the strength of strictly partisan politics was the expectation shared by both Democrat and Whig presidents that federal judges would "maintain federal authority, respect state rights, further the development of the state . . . economy, and sustain major administrative policies." Although slavery and sectionalism intruded on the judicial selection process in Alabama as elsewhere by the 1850s, the old consensus continued to have an impact up to 1860. Over the long term, each judge's social standing and the socioeconomic health of Alabama's two sections, more than partisan politics alone, influenced the decisions reached within the local legal culture.[15]

The operation of federal judicial power in antebellum America was paradoxical. As Tocqueville noted, the federal courts and state sovereignty generally were at odds. In Alabama and elsewhere, federal courts provided nonresidents a forum that was comparatively independent of the states' protectionist policies. The foundation of this independence, however, was a specialized federal judicial culture based in each state.

EXTERNAL FACTORS INFLUENCING JUDICIAL DECISION MAKING

Both national and local factors influenced Alabama's federal judges. The most conspicuous pressures involved slavery and other struggles that divided the entire nation. At the same time, local political and social tensions between north and south Alabama were significant. Whether national or local factors were of greater importance depended in part on the relationship between the district and circuit federal courts. Most litigation reaching both courts involved routine commercial and property issues having primarily local implications, rather than major constitutional controversies affecting the nation. As the judicial selection process suggested, the social and political background of the district judges and the justices' views of both constitutional or routine litigation tended to be determined by local experience. Of course, national conflicts periodically exerted pressure, but generally local factors prevailed.

Federal District Judges' Selection and State Sectional Pressures

Sectional political pressures within Alabama influenced the appointment of federal district judges. Broadly, the conflict was between the state's northern and southern sections. Market factors associated with water and land routes converging on Mobile made that city the center of factional politics in south Alabama. A similar interplay between economic and political interests in the Tennessee Valley resulted in Huntsville becoming a political center of north Alabama. Also, because the State Constitution of 1819 liberally incorporated the principle of white manhood suffrage, it was the elected representatives of the people in the legislature who exercised the most political influence. The legislature, of course, elected the state's two United States senators, who confirmed or rejected federal appointees, including federal judges and other federal judicial officials. Nevertheless, state sectional pressures lessened the impact of national party partisanship while heightening the importance of personal connections and local tensions.[16]

The appointment of Charles Tait, Alabama's first federal judge, reflected these sectional pressures. As a United States senator from Georgia, Tait had worked closely with fellow Georgian, Secretary of the Treasury William H. Crawford to win statehood for Alabama. After the triumph, Tait left the Senate and moved to the new state's southern section, making his home in Clairborne in what became ultimately Wilcox County. Crawford intended initially that Tait would return to Washington as one of Alabama's senators, but political pressures required the election of someone from the northern section. Tait's second choice for position was the new federal district judgeship. However, there were two other candidates for that office, also from south Alabama: the former federal territorial judge Harry Toulmin and William Crawford (no relation to Secretary of the Treasury Crawford). Toulmin was a confidant of President James Monroe, while the Alabama Crawford was a political ally of Governor William Wyatt Bibb. In the end, political dynamics forced Crawford to withdraw his name, and Monroe chose Tait over Toulmin. In a letter to Toulmin, Monroe indicated that Treasury Secretary Crawford's influence and the state's sectional divisions had given Tait the victory.[17]

7

State sectional tensions also were more important than narrow party divisions in the selection of Tait's successor. Turning his attention to his plantation, Tait resigned from the federal district court in 1826. By then, Andrew Jackson's new Democratic Party organization had begun to influence the factional clashes between north and south Alabama. Still, the Jacksonian party structure was superimposed on the entrenched pattern of sectional strife. With Tait's departure, the political dynamics that had led to his earlier expeditious withdrawal now resulted in William Crawford becoming President John Quincy Adams's appointment to the federal district court. Crawford was closer to the Jeffersonian Republicans than to the Jacksonians. Yet as an active politician from the Mobile area, Crawford represented the second triumph of the southern section in the selection of the state's federal district judge.[18]

When Crawford died in 1849, similar political factors determined his successor. During the intervening two decades, Alabama had developed a vigorous two-party system, though the Democrats usually prevailed over the Whigs. Still, the Whig Zachary Taylor was president, and his party influenced both the state legislature and Alabama's two United States senators. Growing economic tensions aggravated the state's traditional sectional conflicts. Cotton merchants, shippers, insurers, and planters from south Alabama initiated most federal litigation in Mobile. Most of the cases arising in the northern section, by contrast, were civil and criminal cases concerning land. The Panic of 1837 and the ensuing depression created so much new litigation that Congress added a second district court headquartered at Huntsville. But even though north Alabama now had its own clerk, federal attorney, and marshal, Congress declined to fund a new judge. Thus, Crawford and his successor were required to hold annual terms in Mobile and Huntsville.[19]

Alabama's northern Whigs demanded that Taylor appoint a judge from their part of the state. Taylor listened, however, to the state's southern Whigs, who favored candidates from Montgomery and Mobile, and ultimately chose the popular former Jacksonian-Democratic governor, John Gayle. During his thirty-year political career, Gayle had moved from the Democrats to the Whigs, who elected him a presidential elector and then a state court judge. Finally, his popularity was such that a predominately Democratic Mobile elected him to Congress. Although himself a Whig, Taylor acceded to the wishes of the state's overwhelmingly Democratic congressional delegation, which heavily favored Gayle.[20]

Throughout the 1850s, the sectional struggles on the national level over the extension of slavery into the territories and the handling of fugitive

John Gayle (1792–1859), U.S. District Court Judge from 1849 to 1859; Whig.
Alabama Department of Archives and History

slaves permeated grassroots politics. In Alabama, the conflict manifested itself in controversies involving federal slave-trade legislation. These laws required prosecution in federal court of anyone who imported slaves into the United States. Democratic President James Buchanan supported vigorous prosecution, and on circuit in Mobile, Justice John A. Campbell did not disappoint him, despite considerable popular resistance.[21]

John Gayle died in July 1859, and Buchanan's selection of a new federal district judge for the state was politically explosive. The clash between Alabama's northern and southern sections had become extreme because radical states' rights Democrats favoring secession were dominant. United States senator Clement C. Clay, Jr., a leader of north Alabama's radicals, recommended to Buchanan a fellow radical, Huntsville lawyer and former state court judge Leroy P. Walker. Walker had attacked Campbell's slave-trade decisions as an "unconstitutional exercise of federal power." The state's other Democratic senator, Benjamin F. Fitzpatrick from south Alabama, nominated George W. Goldthwaite, a Montgomery lawyer and chief justice of the Alabama Supreme Court. Goldthwaite was also Justice Campbell's brother-in-law.[22]

Not surprisingly, Campbell supported Goldthwaite. But he assured Buchanan's attorney general, Jeremiah S. Black, that the overriding consideration was whether the nominee was independent of the radicals. Throughout Alabama's two sections there were "tens of thousands" of potential jurors, Campbell wrote, "who did not appreciate the moral and religious arguments against the slave trade" and who therefore looked on the "importation of Africans" as a "missionary enterprise." Because the federal district court conducted "most of the federal legal business in Alabama," Campbell urged, the president "should not select a candidate who supports the measures that I have condemned."[23]

Buchanan rejected Walker because of "his absurd opinion on the subject of the slave trade." The family connection between Campbell and Goldthwaite made the latter unacceptable. So Buchanan finally chose William Giles Jones of Mobile, a Whig-turned-Democrat recognized as Alabama's foremost authority on insurance, maritime, and admiralty law. In addition, observed Congressman Sydenham Moore, no one had "labored more zealously or actively for Mr. Buchanan in the last election." Still, the long-standing state sectional tensions, though politicized by the slave-trade issue, influenced the president's decision. "I selected Mr. Jones," Buchanan said, "because he enjoyed an eminent reputation as a lawyer, and resided at Mobile where nearly all the business of the court must be dispatched."[24]

From 1820 to 1860, four presidents had appointed four different federal district judges in Alabama. Although national party partisanship became increasingly important throughout the period, it was never the dominant consideration. The determining factor in each instance was the tension between north and south Alabama. When Monroe and Adams appointed Tait and Crawford, respectively, traditional personal connections and state sectional conflicts were more important than party. The impact of party was more ambiguous in Taylor's choice of Gayle. However, the prevailing influence of south Alabama, a district controlled by Democrats, and Gayle's personal connections and popularity among old Democrat allies there, were the deciding factors. Buchanan's selection of Jones against the background of the national sectional struggle involved party politics more directly than the other three appointments. The rejection of Campbell's brother-in-law suggested, moreover, the denial of personal ties. Nevertheless, Buchanan himself stated that it was the connection between national and state sectionalism that caused him to choose someone from south Alabama.[25]

Underlying the state's sectional conflicts were social and economic tensions. The economic growth of the state's southern section steadily eclipsed that of north Alabama. Accordingly, the comparatively healthier economic conditions in the south influenced the four men's law practices, political careers, and tenure as federal judges. This local orientation was consistent with Tait's and Crawford's belonging to the commercial wing of the Jeffersonian-Republican Party. It also suggested why Gayle and Jones, despite involvement in Democratic politics, were committed for longer periods to the Whig Party. Each judge came from a socially prominent family; the political contacts he had established in Virginia, Georgia, or South Carolina permitted him to maintain this social status in Alabama. Even so, social and political preeminence were rooted in the economic order of south Alabama. Procommercial values shaped by local rather than national tensions guided the constitutional and legal interpretations of each judge.[26]

The population distribution and corresponding economic growth of each section further influenced the selection of federal district judges. During the 1820s, when first Tait and then Crawford were appointed, Madison County, including Huntsville, its leading residential center, had a white and slave population totaling 17,481. Mobile County's total white and slave population was 2,672. By 1849, when Gayle became the state's federal district judge, Mobile County's total population had grown to 27,600, exceeding Madison's 26,427. More significantly, the white population of the southern county was 17,303, whereas that of Madison was just 11,937. In 1859, when Jones was appointed,

11

the disparity in white population had become even more pronounced: 28,559 to 11,685. Thus twenty years after statehood the port city and its hinterland were growing faster than its northern rival. As a result, the northern plea for a federal judge could not overcome the handicap of a static business environment.[27]

These economic and demographic realities shaped the values of Alabama's federal district judges. Even when they held court terms in the Northern District, the experience of local economic growth of the south likely influenced their decisions. Moreover, Tait, Crawford, Gayle, and Jones had active legal practices in south Alabama, where debtor-creditor relations constituted the bulk of their work. In addition, each judge belonged to the procommercial wing of his party. Tait and Crawford were Jeffersonian Republicans whose commercial interests placed them closer to what became Whig rather than to Jacksonian economic policies. Gayle and Jones at different times were Democrats, yet the longest-held party affiliation of both was Whig. Finally, all four lived in comparatively urban communities, which reenforced their predominately commercial orientation.[28]

Each judge's social background reenforced his economic and political values. Tait, Jones, and Crawford had been born in Virginia; Gayle, in South Carolina. All four experienced the rigors, uncertainties, and opportunities of immigration to Alabama. Unlike the great majority of their fellow immigrants, however, Tait, Gayle, and Jones had received a college education before embarking on a career in law. Each one, moreover, enjoyed extensive political contacts prior to and during his residence in the state. A firm ally of William H. Crawford, Tait belonged to a powerful Georgia faction including planters, professionals, and former Virginians, which opposed the Yazoo land sales. Moving to Alabama, he became a successful planter and a noted scholar whose scientific inquiries won membership in the American Philosophical Society and the Academy of Natural Sciences of Philadelphia. The Alabama Crawford possessed less conspicuous though nonetheless useful political contacts, which led to appointment as territorial federal district attorney in 1817 and election the next year to the presidency of a bank in his hometown of St. Stephens. Defeated in the race for United States Senate, Crawford was elected in 1825 to the state legislature, representing the southern counties of Washington, Mobile, and Baldwin. For four years he was also a trustee of the University of Alabama.[29]

The political experience of Gayle and Jones rivaled that of Tait. Arriving in Alabama on the eve of statehood, Gayle enjoyed remarkable success as a lawyer and an elected official. During his first fifteen years in the state, he held a succession of offices, including county solicitor, state legislator, circuit judge, justice of the supreme court, and finally governor, to which he was elected

12

for a second term without opposition. As governor, Gayle firmly rejected John C. Calhoun's and South Carolina's nullification theories. Shortly thereafter, however, he successfully used states' rights arguments to justify the removal of the Creek Indians from their land and its cession to Alabama. Disillusioned with Jackson, Gayle moved to Mobile, where he established a thriving law practice and became a partisan Whig. Before coming to Alabama in 1834, Jones studied law under a prominent Virginia politician. This contact facilitated Jones's appointment to the land office in Demopolis and fostered a successful law practice in north Alabama. He was elected representative from a county in that section but moved to Mobile in 1849 where again he served in the legislature. In Mobile, Jones, like Gayle, achieved noteworthy success as a lawyer. He became a Democrat during the 1850s only after Alabama's Whig Party collapsed.[30]

The political division between Alabama's Democrats and Whigs translated into differing views toward constitutional interpretation. In part, the constitutional principles of the state parties mirrored those of the national party platforms. The national Whigs' support of a national bank, internal improvements, the tariff, and liberal land distribution rested on a loose construction of the Constitution. The Democrats either opposed outright or accepted a much more moderate version of each of these policies, arguing strict construction. How both local parties applied these principles to specific issues within the state varied, of course. Concerning abolitionism, particularly, south Alabama Whigs certainly opposed freedom for slaves, but less adamantly than did the Democrats. The Democrats continually maintained that the Whigs' loose constitutional construction aided the abolitionist cause. By the 1850s, the issue so consumed both national and local politics that most of the state's former Whigs became Democrats. The contentiousness surrounding Buchanan's rejection of Walker, the Huntsville states' rights Democrat, in favor of the Whig-turned-Democrat Jones indicated, however, the extent to which relative moderation on the slavery issue persisted throughout south Alabama even on the eve of secession.[31]

Uneven economic growth and long-standing political and social pressures exacerbated sectional tensions within Alabama. Like so many Americans of the period, Tait, Crawford, Gayle, and Jones achieved success in life after settling in a new place. The four started, however, with social and political advantages most of their contemporaries lacked. Sooner or later, moreover, all cultivated these advantages in the state's southern section, linking their own individual success to local opportunities. As a result, it was not surprising that as federal judges they supported the sort of commercial values associated with the Whig Party. Yet these values reflected a local, more than a national, experience, and very probably the local experience exercised the greater influence on each judge's decisions.

Federal Circuit Judges and Sectional Conflict

In addition to the four federal district judges, two Supreme Court justices came from Alabama. During the antebellum years, Alabama was central to the national rise and dominance of Jacksonian Democracy. In 1837, near the end of Jackson's second term, Congress enacted legislation enlarging the Supreme Court's membership from seven to nine and increasing the number of circuits. Martin Van Buren and his successors maintained sectional balance on the Court by appointing first John McKinley and then John A. Campbell from Alabama. Contemporaries considered a justice's circuit court duties as important as his service in Washington. So the organization of the circuits aroused perennial controversy involving not only substantive jurisdictional issues but increasingly the larger sectional struggle between slave and free labor. Although the free states' population and corresponding legal business were growing faster, the slave states nonetheless controlled five out of nine circuits. Thus national as well as local political tensions influenced the circuit duties of McKinley and Campbell.[32]

The social and professional experience of the two justices was similar to that of their district court colleagues. McKinley was born in Virginia and grew up in Kentucky before moving to Huntsville in 1818. Born in Georgia, Campbell was admitted to the state's bar in 1829 at the age of eighteen; the next year he moved to Montgomery, married, and after seven years moved on to Mobile. Although both men's fathers were professionals, the senior Campbell was one of Georgia's more distinguished lawyers and politicians. McKinley did not attend college; Campbell graduated with honors from the University of Georgia and then attended West Point, compiling an unremarkable record. McKinley was not a prominent attorney, but he attained considerable success as a loyal and partisan Jacksonian Democrat, elected twice to the Senate, once to the House of Representatives, and several times to the state assembly from north Alabama. Campbell, by contrast, was said to be Alabama's most brilliant lawyer, establishing a national reputation arguing before the United States Supreme Court. He too was elected twice as a Democratic representative to the state legislature. During the Nashville Convention, just before the compromise of 1850, Campbell also supported the triumph of moderate resolutions defending slaveholders' rights but nonetheless opposing secession.[33]

National more than local political pressures determined each man's appointment to the Supreme Court. As soon as Congress enlarged the Court and expanded the circuits, Jackson increased the number of southerners by nominating John Catron of Tennessee and William Smith of Alabama. Just as Jackson's term ended, Catron accepted but Smith did not, leaving Van Buren the opportunity to choose another Alabamian. This time it was the Democratic loyalist McKinley. The legislation creating the new circuits favored Alabama and the other old southwestern states. Van Buren selected McKinley because he had the endorsement of various congressmen from these states. Ironically, the circuit duties proved so onerous that McKinley repeatedly pleaded for relief, and Congress eventually ameliorated the problem. His impact on the Court and the circuit was modest enough to justify Campbell's assessment that McKinley was "a feeble man—not much superior to a Methodist preacher."[34]

The national tensions bringing about Campbell's appointment were even more significant. When McKinley died in 1852, the sectional struggle over slavery loomed ever larger despite the compromise of 1850. To fill the vacancy, the lame duck Whig Millard Fillmore sent to the Democrat-controlled Senate three nominations, all of which were rejected. Once the responsibility passed to Democrat Franklin Pierce, Chief Justice Roger B. Taney took the unusual course of sending two justices, Catron of Tennessee and Benjamin R. Curtis of Massachusetts, to urge Pierce to appoint Campbell. Encouraging this remarkable endorsement was Campbell's comparative moderation within the Democratic Party at a time when southern Democrats were espousing secession. Campbell supported neither the Free Soilers' Wilmot Proviso nor many Southerners' demands for the acquisition of new territory from Mexico. "I regard the . . . acquisition of New Territory as it may affect the *balance* of power in the federal government," he wrote John C. Calhoun in 1847. "What will be the effect of any large acquisition? Will it be to preserve the balance of power as it now exists?" Campbell doubted this, because the new territories were "wholly unfit for a negro population." Amid increasingly unstable sectional politics, such views were sufficiently moderate that northern and southern Democratic senators confirmed Campbell.[35]

These considerations suggested other tensions that fueled the persistent conflict over the federal circuit courts. The Judiciary Act of 1789 had tied the justices of the Supreme Court to the states by requiring them to hold circuit. From the beginning the justices worked to end the system, but they were always disappointed.[36] McKinley declared that the office was "certainly the most onerous and laborious of any in the United States." He covered between six and ten thousand miles annually, much more than any other justice.[37]

Repeatedly McKinley petitioned Alabama's congressional representatives. "No physical strength could enable one individual to perform the extensive travel in the circuit and attend to the duties of the court," he pleaded. From the bar came "great complaints against the judge in consequence of the non-performance of the [circuit] duties." McKinley urged Congress to publish his petition so that the "lawyers and judges . . . [would] know the cause of the interruptions to the business of the courts." In his own defense he asked whether it was "proper" that any judge should be permitted "no time allowed . . . for attending to . . . private concerns? no time for relaxation? no time for reading and study?" Was it "just to suitors . . . to deprive them of the services of the judge, by requiring more of him than he can possibly perform?" Was it "just" to impose on him "as much service . . . as of four or five others of the judges."[38]

At stake in this controversy were wider tensions involving the entire nation. In Alabama as in other states, there existed a small but influential segment of the bar that represented important political and economic interests in the federal courts. To some extent these groups and their lawyers had a common interest in improving federal judicial administration. On a deeper level, however, the struggle was between those who favored ending the Supreme Court justices' circuit riding and those who did not.[39]

In 1855, Stephen A. Douglas of Illinois expressed the rationale of those seeking to maintain the basic system. It was "good for the country" and "good" for the Supreme Court, he said, that the justices "should be required to go into the country, hold courts in different localities, and mingle with the local judges and with the bar." If the members of the Court were "released from all duties outside the city of Washington, and stay[ed] here the whole year round, they w[ould] become . . . mere paper judges." As a result, he concluded, the justices would "lose the weight of authority in the country which they ought to have, just in proportion as they lose their knowledge of local legislation and of the practice and proceedings of the courts below."[40]

In Alabama as in the other states, it was the circuit rather than the district court dockets that were congested, causing delay. In Alabama and throughout the nation, moreover, it was the district judge who generally came to the aid of the Supreme Court justice. One remedy periodically proposed was to appoint separate circuit judges to sit with the district judge to form a circuit court. The Supreme Court's circuit riding would thus end. A second recurring proposal, the one favored by Douglas, was to give district judges the circuit jurisdiction while at the same time creating a new circuit court of appeals presided over by the district judges and a Supreme Court justice. From the southern states' point of view, however, both options potentially increased the number of circuits as well as the number of district courts. Throughout most of the antebellum period, the North's population and legal business were greater than those of the South's. Yet the South had one more circuit. Extensive alterations might easily generate political dynamics resulting in the South losing its advantage.[41]

At several other points federal judicial authority intersected with sectional tensions. During the antebellum period, the difference in each section's labor systems complicated what otherwise would have been prosaic legal issues. Procedural and substantive debtor-creditor issues involved technical problems of rights under commercial, admiralty, criminal, and property litigation. The substantive law of the states differed, requiring the federal courts repeatedly to prefer certain rules over others. Inevitably, such choices had different ramifications for slave or free economies. But as long as the South possessed an edge in the number of circuits, it could maintain its "peculiar institution." Also, the circuit advantage ensured that slaveholders would probably retain a majority on the Supreme Court, since justices from slave states rarely if ever rode circuit in free states and vice versa. From the 1830s on, the struggles involving slavery and personal liberty laws heightened the stakes of the South's control of a majority of the circuits and of the Supreme Court itself. Thus pressures for efficiency associated with the North's greater legal business gave way before the deeper sectional divisions.[42]

The degree to which national factors could supersede local ones was further limited by the circuit court's decisions concerning such important constitutional issues as slavery. Despite the fact that most litigation coming before the circuit as well as the district federal courts involved routine matters of commercial contracts and property titles, two external political and socioeconomic factors exerted pressure. One encompassed the sectional struggle within the whole Union. The other involved local sectional struggles that shaped the appointment and decisions of federal district judges. These district judges also frequently handled the circuit court's duties. Such considerations suggested that in routine litigation and even in certain constitutional cases, local rather than national pressures prevailed.[43]

INSTITUTIONAL FACTORS SHAPING DECISION MAKING

The informal working culture of the federal courts shaped the federal judge's discretion. The framers of the Constitution established the federal judiciary to give nonresident private interests an impartial forum for the trial of cases. Generally, however, Section 34 of the Judiciary Act and the Supreme Court justices' circuit riding tied federal judges to local law. The Supreme Court's review imposed counterpressures facilitating a broad reconciliation of local and national policy concerns.[44] In addition, various jurisprudential, procedural, and jurisdictional factors enhanced the significance of Alabama's lone district judge, and to a lesser extent the circuit-riding Supreme Court justice. The comparatively small number of lawyers practicing before the federal court, the routine nature of most litigation, and the inevitable need to choose among conflicting legal rules established flexible boundaries within which these two judges exercised discretion.[45]

Judicial Discretion and State Law

Certain assumptions shaped federal judges' exercise of discretion. During the antebellum years, the prevailing view was that judges found, discovered, or declared rather than made law. This theory seemed to confine judges to strict adherence to the formal language of statutes, previous common law cases, and the Constitution itself. Other principles, however, channeled the application of the theory into a search for first principles. This search required a scientific analysis that invited considerable flexibility in the interpretation of legal texts and permitted a corresponding general disregard of stare decisis. Thus more often than not the choice of law was dependent on discretion.[46]

Federal judges' efforts to balance dependence and discretion involved two jurisprudential issues. The first was the relationship between the federal and state governments within a constitutional structure based on fragmented sovereignty. This issue was central to the great national and states' rights struggles involving the Marshall and Taney courts, nullification, and the controversies over slavery that culminated in the Civil War. Periodically during the antebellum years, Alabama's federal courts confronted these major constitutional questions. More often, however, the state's federal judges wrestled with the second important jurisprudential issue: What were authoritative sources of law in the federal tribunals? Before Alabama joined the Union, the Supreme Court had rejected a federal criminal common law. The Court asserted nonetheless broad authority to formulate rules derived from state and federal statutes, international jurisprudence, a state's local law, English legal precedent, "general principles" common to "republican governments," and the constitutional text itself.[47] To decide cases, Tait and his successors chose among these sources of law.

These judges rarely felt bound by precedents or the principle of stare decisis. During the period, one view held that in law as in "every branch of human inquiry . . . the veneration of authority has been one of the principal barriers to human improvement." James Kent's *Commentaries on American Law* affirmed this point: "I wish not to . . . press too strongly the doctrine of *stare decisis*, when

I recollect there are more than one thousand cases to be pointed out in the English and American books of reports, which have been overruled, doubted, or limited in their application." Given these considerations, Kent urged the value of wise experimentation in judicial decision making. "It is probable that the records of many courts in this country are replete with hasty and crude decisions," he said. "Such cases ought to be examined without fear, and revised without reluctance, rather than to have the character of our laws impaired, and the beauty and harmony of the system destroyed by perpetuity of error. Even a series of decisions are not always conclusive evidence of what is law." The judge concluded that "the revision of a decision very often resolves itself into a mere question of expediency." Behind Kent's suspicion of reliance on precedent was perhaps a general conviction that law must be flexible to adapt to the constant change so characteristic of antebellum America.[48]

Still, a strain existed between legal precedents and universal principles shaping the limits of judicial discretion. A belief in universals reflected the assumption that fundamental laws associated with Newtonian physics and the will of God controlled human affairs. According to *Hunt's Merchants' Magazine*, judges should respect precedent "grounded upon principles of universal equity." They should "consult precedents established by their predecessors . . . extract from those precedents . . . ethical principles . . . and clearly . . . point them out in . . . opinions." There was "nothing more surprising," the writer continued, than the "admirable coincidence" existing between "ancient and modern judicial precedents . . . extending from . . . ancient Rome to . . . modern America constituting a uniform and perfect system of practical ethics." Accordingly, noted the *North American Review*, "So long as the struggle between precedent and reason shall continue, legal opinions . . . will depend more on the character and turn of mind of the judge, who is to decide it, than any general principle."[49]

Other assumptions shaped the judge's resolution of the two jurisprudential questions. Integral to the early nineteenth-century's belief in legal science was the distinction between written and unwritten law. The Constitution was the chief example of written law, though state and federal statutes were significant forms as well. Following the logic of science, judges and legal commentators such as Alabama's Benjamin F. Porter justified a liberal interpretation of constitutional and statutory phrases by presuming that they embodied certain first principles. Put another way, the scientific search for fundamental principles reflected a willingness to "pack" written constitutional or legal phraseology with "extratextual concepts, such as natural justice or the 'obvious' meanings or definitions of words." These scientific principles possessed no legal force of their own; used to interpret written law, however, they acquired a

19

working content. Accordingly, the specific texts bound the judge's interpretation, but the finding of first principles left him considerable freedom to determine the text's ultimate meaning.[50]

Similar reasoning explained why unwritten law could be viewed as legitimate. Antebellum Americans obeyed constitutions and statutes because they were the formal expression of the popular will or republican spirit. Through the search for scientific principles, judges reconciled their dependence on the text with their discretion to interpret it. But in the cases involving unwritten law, what held the judge accountable to republican values? Federal judges in Alabama and elsewhere responded to this question by considering whether the state's local common law or some other legal corpus was the appropriate source. Moreover, during the search for first principles, federal courts decided from what source the law came. "Thus while the principal inquiry testing the limits of judicial discretion in constitutional cases was whether a decision could justify departing from the constitutional text," wrote one commentator, "the principal inquiry testing the limits of judicial discretion in nonconstitutional cases was whether a decision could justify departing from state law."[51]

Existing jurisprudential assumptions had little meaning, however, until judges applied them in actual cases. Only rarely did federal courts address large constitutional questions. More often, and still in only comparatively few cases, the Supreme Court reviewed and overruled the lower federal court. The great bulk of federal cases was routine, involving the determination of and choices between state laws. The courts settled most of the growing case load expeditiously, with little more than a summary consideration. Throughout the period the average term held by either a federal district or circuit court remained about three days.[52] Neither judicial review by the Supreme Court nor the respect due state law retarded the freedom to choose and interpret legal principles according to prevailing jurisprudential assumptions. This suggested that the informal working legal culture established fairly clear expectations as to how federal judges would exercise discretion.[53]

This broad scope for independent action enhanced the status of state law in federal court. In a wide range of issues, federal statutes bound the federal judges to state law. These statutory provisions, however, left room for interpretation. The largest source of litigation in either the district or circuit court was diversity jurisdiction. One of the most important provisions governing these cases was Section 34 of the Judiciary Act of 1789, which required federal courts to follow state law in all instances where it applied. This language suggested that there were cases in which state law did not apply, and upon such a construction federal judges in Alabama and elsewhere gradually formulated a general commercial law identified with *Swift v. Tyson* (1842).[54]

Concerning something as basic as the jury trial there was also ample room for discretion. The judge's control over jury verdicts gradually increased throughout the nineteenth century. Rooted in the early common law's presumption that the jury decided both law and fact, the trend was toward strengthening the judge's authority to prescribe the law. In 1852, the Supreme Court described one dimension of the problem. Noting the differing practices among the states, the Court found that in certain states the "court neither sums up the evidence in a charge to the jury, nor expresses an opinion upon a question of fact." But in most states the courts adopted the "English usage" whereby the judge "always sums up the evidence and points out the conclusions, which in his opinion ought to be drawn from it; submitting them, however, to the consideration and judgment of the jury." Although either process facilitated the "purposes of justice," the practice of the federal courts "should conform, as nearly as practicable, to that of the state in which they are sitting, that mode of proceeding is perhaps to be preferred, which from long-established usage and practice has become the law of the courts of the state."[55]

In Alabama, on these and other points, the "practice" was unsettled. Prior to the Civil War, the leading authority on the state's law was Benjamin F. Porter. In numerous articles for national publications, Porter described a corpus of law founded partially on the "common and commercial law of England" and in "many instances" the civil law of continental Europe. At the same time, "statutory provisions" and "occasionally . . . local customs" created various "exceptions."[56] Porter applauded the code the Alabama legislature enacted in 1852. But he feared and expected that "under local influences, and demagogical power" the politicians would "modify" the code "by grafting upon it provisions . . . of every incongruous nature. This man will want an exemption, and that a repeal—this an alteration, and that a proviso; till it will become as ringed and striped as the Israelite's rods, wherewith he generated piebald sheep."[57] Regarding the relation between judge and jury, Porter described a mixed pattern of authority that was confirmed by the state courts' long vacillation.[58]

Alabama's federal judges handled their business with dispatch. In the Northern District from 1824 to 1860 there were usually two terms annually, each term generally lasting from two to five days. Yet the number of orders the judge issued increased steadily. In 1828 there were a 23 orders. By 1846 the number had grown to 1,557 on the law side and 27 in chancery. In 1860 the number increased to 43 chancery and 1,754 civil orders.[59] Federal no less than state judges thus followed the popular expectation that law was "an every-day,

practical, common-place, business-like affair. . . . Readiness, precision, plain-
ness, pertinency, knowledge of law, and a short-hand method of getting at and
getting through with a case, were the characteristics and desiderata of the
profession. There was no time for wasting words."[60]

The number, type, and outcome of cases filed suggest further dimensions of the federal judge's business. In the Southern District during seven
different years between 1822 and 1856, a sample drawn from docket books
included 818 motions filed. The types of motions were civil, criminal, and
admiralty; the outcomes were designated as judgment, dismissed, or continued.
Of the eleven criminal motions, there was a judgment in only one case; ten were
continued, and none was dismissed. The record was clearer concerning admiralty: overall there were 85 motions filed, with a judgment in 39, dismissals in
24, and continuances in 22. The most business was on the civil side, with 722
motions filed. The court gave judgment in 487, continued 204, and dismissed
26 motions.[61]

The average over these seven years was 117 motions filed annually. The
amount of business was thus noteworthy but not overwhelming, and there was
enough time for growing litigation. The type and outcome of motions filed and
the proportional mix reflected, moreover, the federal court's particular market
for legal services. Consistent with the lack of a federal criminal common law and
few federal criminal statutes, the criminal practice was insignificant. Given the
importance of the port of Mobile, it was not surprising that about 10 percent of
the motions filed were in admiralty. Clearly, though, the bulk of business
involved property and commercial contract issues arising on the civil side under
diversity jurisdiction. On the whole, the record supported the opinion of lawyers
like Josiah Bond and Joseph Baldwin that the federal courts primarily served
nonresidents in various select yet important categories of litigation.[62]

Still, perhaps the most notable point was that so few suits were
dismissed. In most instances of civil and admiralty litigation, the court arrived
at a judgment (526 out of 808), and in 226 there was a continuance. The court
dismissed only fifty suits. Even in the few criminal cases, the judge almost always
continued rather than dismissed. Although each court's term lasted only a few
days, the litigants knew that sooner or later some formal resolution was likely.
Thus nonresident property and commercial interests and the lawyers representing them could reasonably expect consideration from Alabama's federal district
courts.[63]

Dismissals were also rare in the federal circuit court. In the circuit court
for the Southern District during two terms of 1846 and one of 1857 there were
237 motions filed. Twenty-two were appeals from district courts within the

state, and four others were appeals from the District of Columbia. In these suits the court gave judgment in twelve, continued twelve others, and dismissed none. In all the other suits there were only four dismissals, and these occurred in criminal cases. Reflecting differences in jurisdiction, the case mix varied between the district and circuit courts. The circuit considered 39 motions in criminal suits and none in admiralty; a preponderance of the court's business was civil in nature (155, including the appellate cases). Compared to the district level, there were twice as many continuances in the circuit court. The two jurisdictions also had opposite records on the criminal side: The circuit judge gave judgment in 24 suits and ordered continuances in eleven. Finally, the circuit court was about as unwilling as the district court to dismiss a suit.[64]

While the federal court's workload grew, the number of Alabama's federal judges remained the same. The state's cotton economy and political significance fostered increasing litigation between local and nonresident private interests. Section 34 of the Judiciary Act and review by the Supreme Court caused tension between the federal district and circuit courts' decision making, especially in the bulk of cases involving state law. As Benjamin Porter suggested, however, the sources of state law were sufficiently uncertain that federal judges could exercise considerable discretion regarding the appropriate procedure or rule of decision.[65] Moreover, when a clash between state and federal law or a constitutional provision arose, the issues were so significant that discretion was again inevitable. These indigenous processes and procedures interacted with jurisprudential assumptions that permitted judges to imbue constitutional provisions and state or federal laws with extratextual meaning. The resulting flexibility created broad boundaries within which local factors generally exerted greater influence.

The Relation Between Federal District and Circuit Courts and the Working Legal Culture

The jurisdictional basis on which most private interests brought federal suits was diversity of citizenship. Either as a plaintiff or a defendant, one of the parties was usually an Alabama resident. Various institutional linkages existed between the federal courts and the lawyers appearing in them. Although the state's federal district courts increased from one to three by 1846, the same judge presided in all three. Because of the Supreme Court justice's circuit riding, the same district judge also often exercised circuit jurisdiction.[66] In addition, a relatively small group of lawyers practiced before this judge, so that regardless of whether the case was in district or circuit court in any part of the state, both the bench and the bar were generally well known to each other. This institutional familiarity represented what we have referred to as the courtroom work group or working legal culture. The connection between these natural informal imperatives and the litigant's interests resulted in a wide exercise of judicial discretion.[67]

In Alabama, as elsewhere, the federal courts handled a circumscribed yet important business. Mobile lawyer Josiah Bond observed in 1842 that the federal district and circuit tribunals were the "courts in which non-residents are chiefly interested." There were few other states, he said, "in proportion to their population, more intimately or extensively connected in their business relations with other and distant parts of the Union than Alabama." Selling the "great staple" cotton, "in the culture of which she is almost exclusively engaged—and relying upon her neighbors for many of the necessaries, which otherwise she might herself produce, her laws of debtor and creditor must consequently affect the interest of many, who by their situation are incapacitated from readily ascertaining what those laws are."[68] Insofar as the "nonresidents" involved in national or international business confronted this uncertainty, then, they turned to the federal courts and the relatively small number of lawyers, like Bond, who practiced there.

Congress established Alabama's first federal district court in April 1820, four months after the state joined the Union. The new court's jurisdiction included the entire state. During April and May of 1820, Congress commissioned a district judge, Charles Tait; a United States attorney; a clerk; and a federal marshal. Each year the court held four terms alternating between Cahaba and Mobile. From the beginning, however, settlers in north Alabama complained that distance and poor transportation limited their access to federal justice. Four years later the agitation brought some improvement. Congress divided the state into Southern and Northern districts. Eventually each district had its own annual terms and an attorney, a clerk, and a marshal. Yet in both districts—headquartered in Huntsville in the north and Mobile in the south—the same judge presided. Shortly after the state capital was moved from Cahaba to Tuscaloosa in 1826, the court ceased sitting in Cahaba. Congress established a Middle District in 1839. Soon after Montgomery became the new state capital in 1846, the place of holding court moved there. But still only one judge was responsible for all three districts.[69]

Further complicating the authority of the federal district courts was the circuit court's jurisdiction. After 1831, Congress expanded the federal district judge's powers in northern Alabama to include those of the circuit court. For practical purposes this meant that when sitting in Huntsville, the district judge exercised both district and circuit court jurisdiction, whereas in Mobile his

Old Southern District Courthouse in Cahaba. *Alabama Department of Archives and History*

authority was that of a district judge only. The situation arose in large part because the Supreme Court justice assigned to the circuit that included Alabama traveled farther than any other justice. Accordingly, his travel was somewhat curtailed by extending the jurisdiction of the district judge in the Northern District. The Supreme Court justice's circuit riding was again altered when Congress shifted Alabama from the Ninth to the Fifth Circuit in 1842, reducing the number of states traveled from four to two. Nevertheless, Congress made no change in the circuit jurisdiction of the federal judge sitting in the Northern District. Initially, Congress gave the justice holding the circuit court in Mobile the authority to hear appeals from the Huntsville court. Before long, however, Congress established direct review by the Supreme Court. A similar system evolved governing the relation between circuit and district jurisdiction when Congress created the Federal Middle District based in Montgomery.[70]

Thus the function and authority of the federal district and circuit courts were interconnected. According to the *Democratic Review*, "in each one of the districts into which the United States are divided, there is a District Judge, who presides singly in the District Court, and who is also associated with one of the Supreme Court Judges in holding within his district the term of the Circuit Court, which is a court of higher grade than the District Court." Even so, the journal noted, the circuit-riding justice is "often . . . unable to hold the required terms, in which case the District Judge holds the Circuit term by himself, precisely as he holds his District term." Formally, the "two are distinct courts with different calendars, jury panels, etc." Yet it "very commonly happens that the same District Judge presides singly in both, and often within five minutes is sitting, now in the one capacity and now in the other, adjourning the District and opening the Circuit Court, or vice versa according to convenience."[71]

The system defined the limits of each court's discretion and dependence. First it attempted to parcel out jurisdiction between the two federal courts within Alabama, leaving final appeal to the U.S. Supreme Court. In terms of formal authority, the district judge may have been technically subordinate. As a practical matter, however, the problems associated with riding circuit granted both the federal district and circuit court significant independence. Moreover, the same district judge—whether Tait, Crawford, Gayle, or Jones—presided over all three districts and often in the circuit courts as well; so there was a strong likelihood that discretion would be necessary in order to establish consistent patterns of substantive law and procedure.[72]

The proportion of the state's bar practicing in the federal courts was a measure of its significance. By 1845, the total number of lawyers practicing in Alabama was approximately 664; the number living in the counties included

U.S. Courthouse for the Middle District in Montgomery. *Alabama Department of Archives and History*

within the federal tribunal for the Middle District was about 447. Throughout the period 1839–60, the number of attorneys registered in the federal court for the Middle District was 128, and of these approximately 107 were admitted before 1855. Thus the proportion of Alabama attorneys registering in the Middle District was 20 percent. In the Northern District, the number registering between 1824 and 1860 was just fifty-six.[73] Notwithstanding this disparity between districts, Joseph Baldwin correctly concluded that compared to the state courts, the "United States Courts were equally well patronized in proportion—indeed, rather more so" during the boom and bust years from 1833 to 1845.[74]

A case involving charges of misconduct suggested the nature of the federal judge's discretionary authority. Before the Civil War, Congress considered only one such case from Alabama, concerning the state's first federal district judge, Charles Tait. In 1822, eighty-four captured slaves were the center of a dispute among their owners and two different captors. Pending trial in federal court, one of the parties demanded that the state "interpos[e] ... her right to the possession of the slaves," in the name of Alabama law. Tait refused to consider the challenge, and the case continued in federal court. Undaunted, Edwin Lewis brought charges of official misconduct against Tait before the Judiciary Committee of the United States House of Representatives.[75]

Lewis's charges and the Judiciary Committee's response had implications beyond the legal issues raised in the slave suit. The first basis for the charge of misconduct was that Tait had refused to allow Lewis to practice law in the federal court. The second charge was that Tait used "insulting language and gestures" toward Lewis when he attempted to qualify. The committee conceded that construing these actions as misconduct was "novel" and as such "may not again occur." After an inquiry into the particular facts pertaining to Lewis's claims, the committee noted that normally the grounds for defining misconduct were "corruption, misfeasance, and mal-practice." Finding no clear evidence of any of these, the committee exonerated Tait.[76]

Even so, the committee's reasoning reflected contemporary attitudes toward judicial independence. "Admission to the bar," the committee report stated, was "not a natural right, but a right to be acquired, under the rules and the usages of the courts." The applicant was bound to demonstrate "legal and moral qualifications to the satisfaction of the court." It was the "duty of the judge to exercise his best judgment, conscientiously but freely. The dignity of the tribunals, the purity of the bar, the rights of the people, and the transaction of business, require this to be done firmly and fearlessly—responsible only to the country for the integrity of his mind, not the errors of his judgment."[77]

28

Charles Tait (1768–1835), first Federal District Judge of Alabama, served from 1820 to 1826; Jeffersonian Democrat. *Alabama Department of Archives and History*

Still, the judge operated within certain limits imposed by public opinion. He "expose[d] himself to the wicked aspersion and bitter persecution of every disappointed and unworthy candidate. The fear of denunciation and the dread of public opinion (of which this case furnishe[d] an example) [were] no small inducements to relax the rules and shrink from the danger." In addition, the power of rejection was "dangerous to the liberty of the citizen," and admittedly "a pretence might be seized on by an artful and wicked judge, for the purpose of oppression." The judge, however, performed this duty before lawyers lacking neither "independence nor professional sympathy" and amid "the people who frown[ed] indignantly upon an act of injustice or oppression." There were, too, the "presumptions arising from professional character, official dignity, and religious sanctions." Finally, instances of abuse were rare indeed. Accordingly, the committee concluded that the "right to admit, implie[d] the right to reject" and was "indispensable to preserve the purity of the bar." Thus it was appropriate that this "important right" and "lucrative profession should be left" to the federal judge's "will or discretion."[78]

The permanent offices associated with the federal judiciary were the clerk of the court, the marshal, and the United States attorney. Other officials appointed on an ad hoc basis included special magistrates such as trustees in insolvency and bankruptcy proceedings. The depression of 1839–43 resulted in legislation establishing temporary federal bankruptcy courts in Alabama and the other states, which briefly increased the need for such trustees. As a formal matter, both the permanent and temporary offices were judicial appointments. Even so, getting the job was frequently enmeshed in the vagaries of local party politics. Once in office, however, particularly in the case of the permanent appointments, individuals served for a long period. In the Northern District of Alabama, over nearly forty years, only two different individuals were clerks of the court, while three held the office of marshal. The story was little different in the Southern and Middle districts.[79]

The small yet enduring character of this institutional establishment indirectly strengthened the federal judiciary. Since the bulk of the federal courts' work involved nonresidents, the preparation and trial of cases often required the gathering of evidence from distant places.[80] The lawyers for each party in the suit, of course, primarily performed this task. The combination of the limited jurisdiction and the reliance on these lawyers encouraged the development of a comparatively small and specialized bar closely attuned to the values of a single district judge and the visiting Supreme Court justice. Over the long term, too, many of these same lawyers developed a personal working relationship with the court's other officials. Thus the interplay between the bar and the little-changing federal judicial establishment strengthened the confidence in, reliance on, and the need for discretion in the decisions of Alabama's federal judges.

FACTORS SHAPING CONSTITUTIONAL DECISIONS

Jurisprudentially and politically, constitutional cases occupied a special place in the federal judicial process. Unlike routine litigation, which usually required making choices only between state laws or general commercial principles, constitutional cases usually involved a conflict between national and state authority. Such cases were comparatively few, but they often touched larger political struggles and raised fundamental issues concerning the federal courts' independence and exercise of discretion. The most controversial categories of constitutional litigation arising in Alabama's federal courts were admiralty and slave-trade suits. In both types of cases, establishing the boundary between state and federal power was a major challenge. Even so, in each instance explicit political pressures interacted with local formal and informal institutional factors to shape the decisions.[81]

Admiralty Decisions

Admiralty cases were a comparatively small but significant part of the Alabama federal courts' workload. Article III of the Constitution and federal statutes required federal judges to determine the appropriate sphere of state and federal power. Yet prevailing jurisprudential assumptions permitted wide discretion to determine the boundary. A decision whether to exercise discretion involved the degree to which the outcome of a case might disrupt the wider web of local private interests, particularly in south Alabama. The federal judges' immersion in the legal culture made them profoundly sensitive to local pressures. Ultimately, it was necessary for the Supreme Court to establish a more extensive federal jurisdiction over the opposition of these lower federal courts.[82]

Alabama's federal judges tested the constitutional limits and economic implications of their power in admiralty litigation. Trade on lakes and streams and along the coast was vital to antebellum America's economy. Much of this trade came within the admiralty jurisdiction that the Constitution's framers had given to the federal courts. Throughout the nation's early years, however, the scope of admiralty jurisdiction was much debated because traditionally in England it operated only within the tide's ebb and flow. The rule made sense in an island nation, but in America it created two spheres of regulation. In the federal sphere rules were uniform, while in the state sphere diversity prevailed.

At the same time, the existence of the two spheres raised difficult issues concerning the proper choice of law. Although federal courts had begun to retreat from the English rule during the 1840s, state sovereignty limited their discretion and fostered persistent ambiguity and contentiousness.[83]

The interest groups associated with the federal admiralty sphere were concerned with national and international trade. The interests identified with the second sphere were more local. To be sure, the two spheres overlapped. The constitutional distinction was nonetheless important, because federal admiralty cases, generally, were tried before judges without juries. The state courts, however, did have jury trials. The state trials not only provided local interests greater protection but also obstructed forces that would have enlarged the reach of the national market. Congress dealt marginally with the issue in 1845, requiring federal inspection of boilers on steamships operating along the coasts and throughout the navigable streams and lakes of the nation. The Court, however, was much bolder. In *Propeller Genesee Chief v. Fitzhugh* (1851), it both upheld the statute's constitutionality and extended admiralty jurisdiction to include all large inland bodies of water directly accessible to the sea.[84]

Two cases from Alabama suggest the significance of the new doctrine. *Steamer Oregon* (1855) demonstrated the implications of federal judges' exercising discretion in the choice of law. The steamer and the sailing schooner *William Ozman* collided in the waters of Mobile Bay. Since the bay was directly accessible to the sea, the case unquestionably came within federal admiralty jurisdiction even under the English doctrine. The Circuit Court for the Southern District nonetheless confronted a difficult legal issue. Conflicting testimony failed to establish which vessel was at fault. Admiralty practice normally required both sides to bear the cost. The circuit court, however, held that where one vessel was a steamship and the other was a sailing ship, it was the duty of the steamship to avoid a collision. Other things being equal, the court reasoned, a steamship could be controlled more easily and therefore carried a higher duty of care. Accordingly, the court ordered the *Oregon*'s owners to pay damages. The steamship owners appealed, but the U.S. Supreme Court affirmed the circuit court.[85]

Steamer Oregon suggested how discretion and dependence governed the lower federal courts' admiralty jurisdiction. Since the Constitution's framing, these courts had enlarged their jurisdiction by formulating new rules with relatively little regard for state law. During the 1840s and 1850s, however, the choice-of-law issues became entangled with questions involving state sovereignty. *Genesee Chief* transformed, without settling, the respective limits of state and federal power over admiralty cases.[86]

In a second case, the clash between federal and state authority reached a climax. The steamboat *Wetumpka*, a coasting vessel employed in commerce between New Orleans and Montgomery, collided head-on with the steamer *Magnolia*, which carried trade from Mobile to Montgomery. The collision occurred on the Alabama River. The location was significant because although the river was indirectly accessible to the sea through connecting waterways, it flowed entirely within the state, far removed from the coastal tidewater. The Great Lakes, on which the *Genesee Chief* case had arisen, were not only inland seas but also connected directly to the Atlantic through other waterways. Thus it was difficult to resist the logic of the Court's decision in favor of federal jurisdiction. *Jackson v. the Steamboat Magnolia* (1857), however, raised the important question of whether this jurisdiction extended to the innumerable navigable rivers and streams having only a remote contact with the open sea.[87] Was the navigability of waterways, independent of the tide's ebb and flow, sufficient to bring the case within the federal court's admiralty power?

Alabama's federal district court and the Supreme Court reached opposite opinions in *Steamboat Magnolia*. The *Wetumpka*'s owners sued in the federal court of the Middle District, which dismissed the action for lack of jurisdiction. On appeal, the Supreme Court reversed, holding that the federal judiciary's admiralty power extended to cases of collision on "navigable waters" even when the collision occurred within a county or a state "above the flux and reflux of the tide." The decision prompted strong dissents from Justice Peter V. Daniel and Alabama's own John A. Campbell. Daniel objected to restricting state sovereignty in the name of replacing diverse economic regulations with national equality. "Equality it may be," he said, "but it is equality of subjection to an unknown and unlimited discretion, in lieu of allegiance to defined and legitimate authority."[88]

Campbell's dissent also vigorously defended state sovereignty. After a careful examination, he concluded that the majority's decision went beyond the limits established by the intent of the Constitution's framers. *Genesee Chief* was consistent with this intent because the Great Lakes were more accessible to the sea. In the case of the *Magnolia*, however, the Alabama River was not directly open to such navigation. Indeed, he said, the river traffic involved primarily state products carried for sale to Mobile; this trade was confined within the state and was, therefore, properly subject only to state jurisdiction. Finally, Campbell noted how the decision threatened trial by jury. Alabama law "preserved inviolate" this right as an "essential principle" of "liberty and free government." But in the federal court of admiralty the "people ha[d] no place as jurors." Campbell perceived, moreover, an attempt to place the local cases under the

33

"domination of a foreign code, *whether they arise among citizens or others.*" The states had lost the "power to mould their own laws in respect of persons and things within their limits . . . subject to their sovereignty. The right of the people to self-government [was] thus abridged."[89]

Campbell's defense of the federal district court's decision reflected the state's dominant political and economic values. The claim that the trade carried on the Alabama River was predominantly local was not altogether plausible. Montgomery was a primary exchange center for the black belt's cotton plantations, which sent cotton down the interconnected waterways to Mobile for shipment abroad. Yet Campbell conceived of these market relations in legal and political rather than economic terms. The political presumption underlying the legal principle was that the states exercised greater control over trade than did the federal government. In antebellum America this view was consistent with reality. Admittedly, the Court's enlarged admiralty jurisdiction also represented just as real if lesser federal involvement in the nation's economy. Nevertheless, in Alabama both the Democratic and Whig parties, despite disagreements on many economic issues, had opposed the sort of expanded federal power the *Steamboat Magnolia* decision represented. Thus the opinion of both the Democrat Campbell and the Whig-appointed federal district judge Gayle embodied Alabama's local values.[90]

Prevailing jurisprudential opinion facilitated the Alabama federal judges' rejection of expanded admiralty power. The *Oregon* case showed that the state's federal courts readily exercised discretion in order to establish new rules of decision. The judge arrived at these rules after consciously or unconsciously searching the unwritten sources of law for "scientific principles." Adherence to universal principle left the judge free to ignore stare decisis while also remaining within the precepts of "republican" accountability. In *Steamboat Magnolia*, however, this chain of reasoning clashed with state sovereignty. The case involved not unwritten law but rather the interpretation of a federal statute and constitutional text. Reflecting the political and economic values that prevailed in Alabama, Campbell and Gayle defended state sovereignty against encroaching federal power. The Supreme Court rejected this principle. Neither interpretation was inconsistent, however, with jurisprudential assumptions that encouraged judicial discretion over strict regard for precedent.[91]

These cases suggested too that political and legal factors interacted with the court's informal working culture. Before their appointment to the federal bench, both Campbell and Gayle included extensive admiralty work in their law practices and were familiar with the practical realities of trying admiralty litigation in the separate federal and state courts. Each sphere, moreover, possessed its own informal personal connections between individual attorneys and the officials of either the state or federal courts. Intimately involved in both settings, Campbell and Gayle could not help but be acutely aware of how much the Supreme Court's *Magnolia* decision expanded federal judicial authority. It was not a matter of lawyers losing business, since they would simply spend more time in federal court. It was the more fundamental issue of federal power growing at the expense of state power.

The difference between the *Oregon* and *Magnolia* cases indicated the causal chain among these interacting factors. In the first case, Alabama's federal judges drew on flexible legal assumptions to establish a new doctrine. In the second case, these same judges rejected discretion in favor of stare decisis, particularly the ebb-tide rule. What distinguished the two cases and the lower federal courts' response was the degree to which the linkages between external and internal institutional factors were disrupted. The *Oregon* decision enlarged the choice of doctrines federal judges might apply, yet it did not significantly alter the balance between state and federal jurisdictional authority. The *Magnolia* case, however, did just that. And the extent to which it did so was unavoidable given judges immersed in both state and federal power and public and private interests of south Alabama.

The separation between strictly legal and political or economic factors thus became blurred. The long-established balance between state and federal jurisdiction remained relatively undisturbed in the *Oregon* case; Alabama's federal judges maintained independence and freely exercised discretion. Yet when the resort to discretion threatened the web of local private interests and corresponding institutional arrangements, these same judges balked. In either case, federal courts were carrying out their constitutional duty to provide private parties a judicial forum more removed from local tensions. The *Magnolia* case, however, forced these same federal judges to decide how far to go in their defense of independence. They drew the line at a diminution of state power that would have turned over the defense of many local private interests to the federal courts. Alabama's federal judges denied extending their own power in order to protect the existing state authority. Although ultimately the Supreme Court forced these judges to repudiate their choice and accept a greater independence, the scope of that independence remained unsettled.

Finally, the *Oregon* and *Magnolia* cases suggested the social-class influences on Alabama federal judges' decisions. Admiralty cases involved some of the era's leading commercial interests, including the planter and mercantile groups whose goods were shipped, the vessels carrying the goods, and the credit intermediaries financing the resulting transactions. Broadly, both Gayle and

Campbell belonged to these social-economic groups. Yet the outcome of the two cases indicate how complex were the connections between judicial decision making and class interests. The *Oregon* decision, shifting liability from equal sharing to the steamboat, increased the cost of using the new technology. Indirectly, this may have distributed the costs—albeit unevenly—to all the commercial interests throughout the credit network, but the decision was not explicitly protective of any single group. The district court's dismissal and Campbell's dissent in *Magnolia*, however, were protective. The chief economic beneficiaries of the two opinions were south Alabama planters and traders, who very likely enjoyed the sympathies of juries in the local state courts. Thus, by rejecting federal jurisdiction in *Magnolia*, the two Alabama federal judges supported the local economic elite against outsiders. Ultimately, the Supreme Court reoriented this preference toward nonresident commercial groups.

Slave-Trade Cases

An even more explosive area of federal decision making involved the international slave trade. Initially, the lower federal courts' resolution of controversial slave-trade cases paralleled the record in admiralty. As long as the cases merely required using discretion to decide whether to enlarge the choice of legal doctrines, the lower federal judges' decisions were not successfully challenged. By the late 1850s, however, the nationwide sectional struggle over slavery engulfed the slave-trade issue. As had occurred in the admiralty cases, there was a division of opinion within the federal judiciary itself. But this time Alabama's lower federal courts themselves were at odds, Campbell defending a more expansive federal power. Although the federal district judge sought to protect the economic interests of south Alabama merchants, ironically his opinion was consistent with a defense of greater freedom maintained by the North's personal liberty laws. The explanation for this reversal of roles lay in the tensions between the local legal milieu and the national sectional conflict.[92]

Article I, Section 9, of the Constitution permitted the abolition of the slave trade after 1808. In 1794, 1800, and 1818, Congress enacted statutes governing the prohibition. The federal government vigorously prosecuted American nationals and foreigners who violated the laws. Aggressive prosecution, however, did not prevent repeated transgressions, especially as the number of slave states increased throughout the old Southwest. In such cases, Congress gave original jurisdiction to the federal district courts, and periodically during the antebellum period Alabama's federal judges heard the contentious cases. Following the lead of the Supreme Court, these judges rejected theories of natural justice to invalidate the slave trade. Alabama's federal courts nonetheless struggled to define the limits of federal authority.[93]

Shortly after Alabama joined the Union, several slave-trade suits came before Judge Charles Tait. During the diplomatic and military maneuvering that resulted in the Adams-Onis Treaty of 1819, a U.S. naval vessel in Pensacola Harbor seized the *Merino* and other ships engaged in the slave trade. Although Pensacola was still technically under Spanish rule, it was occupied by United States forces commanded by Andrew Jackson. The Navy took the slave traders to Mobile, where the owners challenged the seizure in federal district court. The owners conceded that the vessels' ultimate destinations were American ports. But they contended that their intent was to unload the slaves in what was still Spanish Pensacola before sailing to those ports. At the same time they denied that the federal court had jurisdiction. The federal government responded that notwithstanding the purported intent, the seized vessels were involved in a trade prohibited by federal laws. Cases prosecuted under those and other federal laws, moreover, were within the federal district courts' jurisdiction.[94]

Tait upheld the government on both counts. Upon appeal, the Supreme Court modified the holding concerning the merits but sustained Tait's ruling in principle, ordering it to be applied in new trials. Throughout the proceedings no serious consideration was given to the proposition that the slaves themselves possessed any rights. The federal judiciary considered only the property rights of the whites and whether federal law could alter those rights under certain conditions.[95] Jurisprudentially this approach varied from that employed in the admiralty cases, in which federal judges invoked universal principles to interpret written and unwritten law. In the early slave-trade cases, by contrast, the federal courts applied restraint and deferred to the will of Congress.[96]

The next time Alabama's federal judges confronted slave-trade cases, major political conflicts were involved. By the 1850s, the struggles over fugitive slaves, the personal liberty laws, and the status of slavery in the territories threatened the Union. These issues touched Alabamians vicariously through controversies involving the slave trade. As noted, President James Buchanan's choice of William Giles Jones as federal district judge was significantly influenced by the controversy surrounding those and related cases. In 1859, south Alabama businessmen purchased slaves that had been brought into the state in violation of the federal anti-slave-trade laws. No evidence established unequivocally that the businessmen had knowingly purchased the illegally imported slaves. Still, in the northern United States the Buchanan administration vigorously prosecuted abolitionists and antislavery proponents who in the name of personal liberty aided and abetted those violating the federal Fugitive Slave Act of 1850. The federal government moved against the south Alabama businessmen in order to maintain the appearance of equal treatment.[97]

During the presidential campaign of 1860, Judge Jones heard the first of these cases, *U.S. v. Gould*. Before taking the bench, Jones had represented another south Alabama businessman in a similar case scheduled for trial later in the year before Justice Campbell's circuit court. The logic of Judge Jones's opinion apparently followed closely the argument he had developed for his former client. The charge, he said, was "simply" that the defendant, "without any participation in the illegal importation, did . . . hold, sell, or otherwise dispose of, as a slave, a negro who had been previously unlawfully imported by some other person." Did this act violate the anti-slave-trade laws? Jones did not question that the full force of federal law restricted the importers and their agents. Congress clearly had the power to regulate the slave trade as a part of foreign commerce. Applying the dominant interpretation of the commerce power—which nonetheless had never been upheld in any sort of slave case—Jones also stated, however, that once these slaves mingled within the local market and population they came under state law. The slave women in this case had already passed from the importer's control into the defendant's hands; both therefore were subject to state, not federal, authority. Accordingly, the federal government lost.[98]

Jones gave his defense of state sovereignty a surprising twist. He considered at length the legal status of illegally imported blacks under the laws of Alabama. Once the "unlawfully imported negro" passed from the importer's control, and therefore the federal government's jurisdiction, and became "mingled with the mass of the population of the state," Jones observed, "he is a free negro alien" subject to state law. Alabama, moreover, had "not neglected her duty in this respect. Her laws most amply provide for the protection of his freedom. If any person, knowing him to be free, should buy or sell him as a slave, such person would be subject to ten years imprisonment." Finally, Jones stated the broad principle in terms that many proponents of personal liberty laws would have applauded. The framers of the Constitution never intended that the "several states should surrender to the general government this power to fix the status, prescribe the rights and provide for the protection of free negroes, or any other inhabitant of a state."[99]

Jones's opinion, including the support of free blacks, reflected the conflict between legal assumptions and politics. Unlike Tait's *Merino* decision, which involved the often litigated legal status of slave importers, the *Gould* case was one of first impression. Thus unlike Tait, who could readily rely on judicial self-restraint, Jones had no choice but to exercise some discretion. Even so, the broad reach of his reasoning was more consistent with the Supreme Court's expansion of admiralty jurisdiction in *Steamboat Magnolia*. Jones took commerce clause precedents, some of which explicitly denied having application to slave controversies, and used them to limit the reach of federal slave-trade laws.[100]

He not only upheld state sovereignty but did so at least in part to defend the rights of free blacks under Alabama statutes. Admittedly, the number of free blacks in the state was small. Even in Mobile, where almost half of the free blacks lived, their ratio to the total population was declining steadily. Yet for this very reason it was likely that Jones was more concerned about the national, rather than the state, implications of his decision. And although his personal motive remains obscure, he could not have been unaware that the attention given free blacks was consistent with the North's personal liberty laws. Thus whether intended or not, Jones's broad exercise of judicial discretion indirectly aided the cause of freedom.[101]

Some months later, Campbell delivered a circuit opinion rejecting the logic and implications of Jones's opinion. In *U.S. v. Haun*, the defendant was a client Jones had represented before taking the bench. For this reason Jones did not join Campbell to form the circuit court. Since the facts in *Haun* were little different from those in *Gould*, the federal prosecutor asked the court whether a dismissal was in order. Denying the plea, Campbell gave a contrary interpretation of the principles Jones had relied on. He surveyed the intent of the framers of both Article I, Section 9, and the federal enforcement statutes, finding that their aim was to reach all "accomplices in the guilt" associated with the slave trade. Indicating correctly that the commerce power had never been directly applied in cases involving slaves, Campbell refuted Jones's use of the clause to defend state sovereignty. He then eloquently endorsed a federal power capable of enforcing a "complete preventive of the holding, selling or disposing of Africans within the limits of the United States." Only such a broad exercise of federal authority "would remove the stain which has fallen upon our country by the abuse of its flag" and thereby suppress a trade civilized nations had "declared to be contrary to humanity and justice."[102]

The two decisions present a striking contrast. Both judges had exercised discretion to come to opposite conclusions. Jones applied prevailing jurisprudential assumptions to construe narrowly the commerce power and to uphold state sovereignty. Campbell used those same assumptions to endorse a broad commerce power and limited states' rights in the name of "humanity and justice."[103] Ironically, Campbell's ringing declaration obscured the degree to which the cause of freedom received more aid and comfort from Jones. At the time, few seriously defended the slave trade in principle. Thus Campbell was merely affirming a national consensus, which the Buchanan administration played upon in an effort to weaken growing northern resistance to the enforcement of the Fugitive Slave Act. By defending the state's right to protect free blacks, however, Jones supported the interests of those who used the Personal Liberty Laws to circumvent the Fugitive Slave Act. The particular factors motivating Jones remain obscure; yet it is apparent that each judge's exercise of judicial discretion had significantly broader political ramifications.

During the antebellum era, the impact of external factors on the federal court's working legal culture changed. Unlike admiralty and other categories of suits comprising a fairly continuous source of federal litigation, slave-trade cases were episodic. In Alabama, the two significant periods were around the time the state joined and left the Union. During the early 1820s, Tait's *Marino* decision indicated general popular support for the federal court's independence. International tensions involving Spain's cession of West Florida to the United States aroused statewide and national defense of federal authority, including Tait's strict adherence to the laws suppressing the slave trade. As the state's first federal judge, Tait was at the center of the new informal personal and institutional relations developing around the court. Even so, the patriotic environment and the emergent character of the court minimized controversy arising from Tait's use of discretion on the jurisdictional issue while deferring to Congress in the law's enforcement.[104]

By 1860, the nation's sectional struggle had politicized the federal courts. The Buchanan administration attempted to preserve impartiality by calling on federal judges to enforce strictly the Fugitive Slave Act in the North and the anti-slave-trade laws in the South. The comparative independence of federal judges, as well as ambiguities in constitutional validity and enforcement of the northern states' personal liberty laws, undermined Buchanan's stance. In Alabama, Jones defended a south Alabama merchant's rights over the slave-trade laws. Campbell, however, followed Tait's earlier practice by ignoring precedent and enforcing the law in the name of judicial restraint.[105]

That Jones and Campbell disagreed can perhaps be explained by the strength of political pressures on the local legal culture. Both were Democrats who had supported Buchanan and his platform favoring equal treatment of North and South in cases touching sectionalism and slavery. Before becoming federal judges, both Jones and Campbell had represented Alabama merchants whom the federal government sued in *Haun* and *Gould*. Both judges were fully aware, then, that the extension of the slave-trade laws beyond ship captains, importers, and other traditional malefactors would affect innocent third-party merchants. Still, Campbell probably felt freer to uphold the law because he was closer to national policy concerns as a Supreme Court justice. He stated publicly that back in Alabama most local juries opposed his stance. Campbell's vigorous support for Buchanan's policy was nonetheless consistent with his position as a southern moderate within the Democratic Party.[106]

Although Jones had supported Buchanan, previously he had been a longtime Whig. States' rights advocates always contended that the Whigs' loose-construction constitutional arguments ultimately favored the antislavery cause. Certainly Jones protected Haun's interests through an elaborate defense of the Alabama law concerning free blacks. He likely resorted to this rationale, however, not out of sympathy for the personal liberty laws but because of the more prosaic desire to preserve the rights of his former clients. Called on to choose between the court's informal working legal culture and the enforcement of a controversial national policy, Jones sided with the local private interests.

Although infrequent, constitutional cases tested to the limit the lower federal court's independence. In the admiralty litigation, the results were uneven. As long as the state's federal judges worked within the old ebb-tide principle, the local legal culture did not inhibit the formation of new doctrines. The *Steamship Magnolia* case, however, raised an explicit clash between decision-making imperatives rooted in the local courtroom and national pressures, and Alabama's federal judges remained faithful to the local culture, requiring the Supreme Court's intervention. The slave-trade cases raised a similar state-federal controversy. This time, however, Jones as district judge and Campbell as circuit-riding justice split. Jones's decision showed a deference to local institutions and interests, whereas Campbell's rejection of that opinion reflected his deep and long-term involvement in the national sectional struggle. Thus, the flexibility inherent in the prevailing jurisprudential opinion facilitated diverse results.

ROUTINE LITIGATION AND LOCAL LEGAL CULTURE

Generally, the litigation coming to Alabama's federal courts raised comparatively routine issues. The single largest category involved commercial credit transactions on which depended the entire antebellum economy. An intricate web of contractual rights and obligations bound together local and nonresident commercial interests, making them at once debtors and creditors engaged in interstate business.[107] Alabama's property titles provided another significant source of litigation tied to complex local interests.[108] In each category the relatively routine character of the issues, procedures, and processes encouraged federal courts to assert their independence and exercise discretion. Despite periodic review by the Supreme Court, formal and informal linkages between the state's federal judges and the local establishment interacted with the prevailing jurisprudential climate to shape decision making. A few famous commercial and property cases presented larger problems, but ultimately their outcome did not undermine the dominant influence of the federal court's institutional autonomy.[109]

Bank Cases and Alabama's Federal Courts

Probably the most famous case arising in antebellum Alabama involved banks. The American federal system allowed the states to charter and control nearly all corporations, including banks. During the 1830s, Alabama led other states in enacting laws that protected local banks and debtors from competition with nonresident banks. In important and widely applauded decisions, the Supreme Court attempted to circumvent the state law and to uphold the rights of the nonresident banks. The Court acted, however, over the opposition of Justice John McKinley.[110] Seven years later, a similar case arose in which a bank chartered in Mississippi ran afoul of Alabama law. Again the federal judge, this time William Crawford, upheld the local debtor in the name of his state's law, and again the Supreme Court intervened.[111] Political party affiliation did not adequately explain McKinley's and Crawford's stance. Other formal and informal institutional factors shaped the two judges' defense of local control.

Alabama sought to exclude foreign corporations from the state. Attempting to protect in-state corporate interests from out-of-state competition, the Alabama legislature cut off the rights of the nonresidents to enforce contracts in the state. Banks chartered in Georgia, Louisiana, and Pennsylvania sued in Federal Circuit Court for the Southern District of Alabama to recover on contracts made between themselves and residents of the state. Justice John McKinley upheld the Alabama law and denied the right of foreign corporations to make contracts that were against state policy. The opinion imposed severe restrictions on economic growth. It generated fear and anger among those whose business involved interstate trade, threatening directly the nation's system of capital and credit. The banks appealed to the Supreme Court in three different suits collectively known as the *Alabama Bank Cases*.

In *Bank of Augusta v. Earle* (1839), the Supreme Court reversed the circuit opinion, McKinley in lone dissent. The Court upheld the right of corporations to sue in federal court as citizens; it refused at the same time to sanction without reservation Alabama's efforts to exclude the three banks from interstate business. "We think it well settled," said Chief Justice Roger B. Taney, "that by the law of comity among nations, a corporation created by one sovereignty is permitted to make contracts in another, and to sue in its courts; and that the same law of comity prevails among the several sovereignties of this Union."[112]

Yet the comity principle assumed voluntary compliance among the several states, and Alabama led the way in reaffirming the protectionist policy. Seven years after *Earle*, Judge William Crawford in the new federal Middle District court upheld the right of an Alabama debtor against a corporate creditor chartered in Mississippi. Crawford accepted the argument that the corporation should not be allowed to practice banking within Alabama since it was chartered in another state. On appeal, the Supreme Court reversed citing as precedent the *Earle* decision.[113]

McKinley's circuit court opinion upholding the state law protecting local corporations and debtors favored local interests. It was consistent with his grassroots political involvement as an elected representative and his wide-ranging personal contacts among lawyers representing corporate and debtor clients. Similar external and informal relationships undoubtedly influenced Crawford's decision favoring an Alabama debtor. Accordingly, in both cases the Supreme Court intervened to enforce the comity principle.

Political party affiliation did not explain the divergence between the lower federal tribunals and the Supreme Court. McKinley was a Jacksonian Democrat and Crawford a Jeffersonian Republican who had opposed Jackson. What both men shared beyond a similar experience in grassroots politics, however, was extensive personal connections within the small community that was the federal bar. Both McKinley's and Crawford's defense of local control suggested that this culture was influential.

Informal institutional imperatives were probably more important than explicit social-class interests. Crawford's local social status was somewhat higher than that of McKinley before the latter achieved his noteworthy succession of state and federal electoral victories. Once both became federal judges, however, their social standing was about the same as the many corporate and debtor interests that benefited from Alabama's protectionist policy. To that extent, the judges and the interests shared social bonds that could have been reflected in the Alabama and Mississippi bank cases. Yet as many other commercial and property cases suggested, neither judge hesitated to decide against these same local commercial and corporate groups. Generally, all commercial and property cases involved intraclass conflict, so the judge's decision was between two similar private interests. In the Alabama and Mississippi bank cases, accordingly, McKinley and Crawford defended local interests less because of social-class affinities than because of wider linkages between those interests and the working legal culture.[114]

Finally, the bank cases suggested the interplay between jurisprudential assumptions and local factors. Given the state's control of corporations, the best the Supreme Court could do in seeking to defend nonresident banks from the Alabama law was to rely on the principle of comity. Under comity, each state voluntarily decided whether banks chartered in another state possessed legal rights of doing business in that state. The state's protectionist law embodied a policy denying such rights.[115] Nevertheless, both the comity principle and the state's law reflected the flexibility inherent in prevailing legal views. Inquiry into first principles allowed courts to ignore precedent and to rely on extratextual readings. McKinley and Crawford applied these readings to favor the state's protectionist policy, whereas the Supreme Court used them to enforce comity.

Commercial Litigation and Judicial Discretion

The largest category of cases tried in federal court involved commercial bills and notes. Unlike the few but politically explosive admiralty, slave-trade, or bank cases, commercial litigation was numerous, routine, and characterized by legal technicality.[116] Also, local parties to commercial contracts were usually both debtors and creditors to residents in other states. Accordingly, it was difficult to distinguish a strictly local interest from one that was interstate in nature. Doctrinal intricacy, the variety of suits, and the prevailing belief in a general commercial jurisprudence transcending state and national boundaries diffused narrow political exigencies. It was more likely that the legal milieu determined the federal judge's decisions.[117]

Because trade depended on credit, the law governing commercial contracts was vital to the economy. Long-distance credit transactions generally were made through the medium of bills of exchange and promissory notes. A significant difference between them was that a bill involved three parties whereas a note was a transaction between two individuals or firms. So important were these commercial instruments that a specialized body of rules governing their use gradually developed as part of the commercial law. The law recognized that notes were negotiable and transferable like money; this was a quality denied ordinary contracts between two or more parties.[118]

Several requirements had to be met before a commercial instrument was considered negotiable, that is, before its holder acquired a bona fide right of recovery. First, it was necessary that the bill or note be transferred in the normal course of business; it could not be a special accommodation, which

William H. Crawford (1784–1849), Federal District judge from 1826 to 1849; Jeffersonian Democrat. *Alabama Department of Archives and History*

might involve fraud. Next, the instrument had to be given for a "valuable consideration" in a regular business transaction. Finally, the holder of the instrument must be innocent of any knowledge of wrongdoing in the original drawing of the bill or note. In any dispute arising over the rights of a commercial contract, if the holder could prove that he satisfied these requirements, his contract was negotiable, and the law guaranteed recovery. Even though the principle of negotiability was crucial to sound credit, state law governing the principle was uncertain. This resulted from the inability of American state courts to formulate exact standards governing the requirements for negotiability.[119]

The federal judiciary offered escape from this uncertainty. The federal courts, of course, exercised little direct influence over the states' local laws, but they could formulate a fairly uniform standard within their own jurisdiction. Because nonresidents preferred to sue in federal court, and because many of these suits involved interstate commercial disputes, the lower federal tribunals had ample opportunity to develop a uniform commercial law. This potential for uniformity rested on the relative independence of the federal judges and on such procedural forms as jury instructions, equity, and the right of appeal. Through use of these devices, the district and circuit courts—in conjunction with the Supreme Court—exercised a unifying and nationalizing influence over the commercial law administered throughout the whole federal judicial system. Accordingly, from the 1790s on the Supreme Court gradually evolved a general commercial jurisprudence culminating in the famous decision of *Swift v. Tyson* (1842).[120]

The *Swift* case involved the issue of whether state court decisions bound federal judges under Section 34 of the Judiciary Act of 1789. In the *Swift* opinion, the Court formally affirmed the principle it had followed for years, that federal judges were free to ignore state court precedents. Alabama's federal judges followed the same course of action. On certain points, the Alabama rules governing local commercial disputes were unsettled and often against the interests of nonresidents.[121] Accordingly, as long as no state statute was directly at issue, the federal courts exercised discretion regarding state judicial opinions and drew freely on general commercial principles. Alabama's federal judges, like their counterparts elsewhere, were sufficiently effective in evolving doctrinal uniformity that the Supreme Court rarely overruled their decisions.[122]

A typical case involving commercial common law was *Brander v. Phillips* (1842). New Orleans commission merchants Brander and McKenna represented the Mobile firm of Phillips & Co. By August 1834, Phillips owed its agents $1,316. At that time the agents agreed to advance Phillips $8,000 on a bill of exchange drawn by them and any two of six people named. Phillips shipped Brander cotton valued at $22,460 but also drew other bills, some with joint signers and some not, amounting to $29,796. Brander applied the cotton proceeds to the liquidation of the Phillips & Co. bills, to the exclusion of those drawn jointly. These later bills exceeded the proceeds from the cotton sales, and so Brander sued for $3,000. The trial occurred in federal court of the Southern District of Alabama. The judge instructed the jury that a creditor (Brander) was bound to apply proceeds to pay the most urgent bills of the debtor (Phillips), unless specifically directed otherwise, and regardless of the possible wishes of cosigners whom the creditor knew to be mere sureties. Brander challenged the instruction, and the issue was appealed to the Supreme Court, which upheld the trial judge.[123]

Two different cases suggested the complexities surrounding commercial issues involving state statutes. *Ellis v. Taylor's Administrator* (1843) arose on a bill drawn by Ellis and three others to pay Taylor $5,000. After the bill was due, Taylor died, and Jones, the administrator of the estate, sued the four men. Although each of the four made different pleas, to settle the issues the federal trial court looked to an Alabama statute of 1821. The central issue was whether the debtors might evoke the state law to preclude recovery where they had signed a bill specifically stating that they were jointly and severally responsible for payment. The trial judge construed the statute in favor of Taylor's estate. The debtors appealed to the Supreme Court, where the issue was sufficiently complex that the justices were unable to reach a decision, whereupon the trial court's judgment stood.[124]

In *Withers v. Greene* (1850), Robert A. Withers executed a bill for $3,000 to A. B. Newsom of Tennessee. Before it became due, Newsom assigned the bill to a third party who died. Meanwhile, the Depression of 1839 descended on the nation. William B. Greene, a citizen of Alabama, was the administrator of the deceased man's estate. At the trial, Greene argued that the bill was given by Newsom in partial payment of a pair of fillies, which Newsom had alleged were healthy. But the fillies died before Greene rescinded the contract, and he contended that the original note was void for Newsom's misrepresentation. Withers demurred, and the circuit court sustained the demurrer, whereupon Greene appealed to the Supreme Court.[125]

The Alabama federal judge and the Supreme Court confronted a difficult legal question. Technically, the issue was whether the obligor of a sealed bill may plead the misrepresentation as a reason why the bill ought to have been void. Yet the pleading issue involved the broader problem of negotiability. Had

Greene assigned the bill to an innocent third party he would have had to pay even though the bill originated in fraud. Thus the federal judiciary was deciding at what point the law should recognize fraud as the ground for limiting the transferability of the note. Leaving Newsom altogether free of accountability would have ultimately restricted negotiability because it would have cut off the rights of innocent parties such as Greene.

At the time, the point was unsettled in the common law of many American states and England.[126] Even so, the weight of authority, the court observed, held that the "old common-law notion," which allowed fraud to be used as a defense to prevent recovery even by one in Greene's position, was "exploded."[127] An Alabama statute applied to the technical point of pleading. The federal court had to decide, however, whether the old or new common law rule should govern the interpretation of the statute. The federal judge in Alabama applied the old rule; on appeal the Supreme Court reversed, upholding the new principle. "This interpretation of the law," the Court held, was "accordant, not only with the language and the rational meaning of the statute, but . . . [was] sustained by the decisions of the courts" of Alabama and "by decisions in other States on statutes containing provisions similar to those in the statute of Alabama."[128]

The three cases suggested the boundaries within which Alabama's federal judges exercised discretion. In cases such as *Brander v. Phillips*, which involved no state statute, the federal courts liberally followed the principle of the *Swift* doctrine, applying their own view of commercial law. The Supreme Court's repeated affirmation of these decisions not only facilitated uniform commercial principles in federal diversity cases but also left federal judges considerable independence and discretionary authority. Consistent commercial doctrines strengthened national and international business, which relied on negotiability and the sound credit the principle represented.

The presence of a state statute restricted but did not preclude the exercise of judicial discretion. The Court conceded that the "legal principles and inquiries involved in" *Withers v. Greene* were "to a great extent local in their character and operation." At the same time, the case "embrace[d] rules, both with respect to pleading and to the interpretation of contracts, extending . . . beyond the influence of merely local jurisprudence."[129] Construing the Alabama law according to the newer common law rules, the Court rejected the opinion of Alabama's federal judge in favor of greater national and international commercial certainty. The Court thus imposed a check on the federal district judge's judicial discretion. In *Ellis v. Taylor*, by contrast, the issue was no less complex, yet the federal court felt free to interpret the statute in favor of the local creditor. This time, however, the judge's exercise of discretion in interpreting state law raised such intricate questions that the Supreme Court was unable to agree, and the lower court prevailed.

The lower federal courts were scarcely reflecting party preferences in cases involving bills and notes. By the 1840s, especially after the disruption caused by the Depression, both the Whig and Democratic parties agreed on the need to establish uniform principles of commercial law. Of course, the question of how best to do this in a particular case often was disputed. Accordingly, the factors shaping the outcome in the lower federal courts reflected local institutional or personal relations and general legal assumptions rather than partisan political preferences.[130]

Furthermore, unlike other types of federal litigation, commercial cases did not necessarily tie the legal community to particular local interests. The web of commercial contracts extensively crossed and recrossed state borders, with most instate debtors at the same time being also nonresident creditors, so that establishing a strict line separating the two was difficult. Many state courts nonetheless attempted to protect local interests. As the courts primarily responsible for adjudicating the rights of nonresidents, however, federal judges were more attuned to the truly interstate quality of commercial transactions.

Undoubtedly the same was true of the lawyers who generally tried these cases in federal court. In commercial suits, most of the lawyers' work involved routine matters of gathering evidence from nonresidents. The time and distances concerned, the diverse range of situations, and the fairly consistent doctrines of commercial jurisprudence for settling these cases discouraged rigid identification of particular results with specific local interests. In one case, a local interest might want a result favoring interstate credit, and in another case, the opposite might be true. Thus the federal bar's overriding need was for doctrinal predictability that transcended narrowly local exigencies.

The three cases suggested that Alabama's federal judges and the bar shared similar goals. Deciding *Phillips* required choosing a doctrine from among the principles of general commercial jurisprudence. The Supreme Court's endorsement of the lower court's choice indicated that the decision was consistent with predictable credit transactions among interstate rather than local business interests. The *Greene* and *Ellis* cases, by contrast, turned on the federal judges' interpretation of Alabama statutes that had codified certain commercial doctrines. In each suit the lower court construed the statute, and the Supreme Court either overturned or at least questioned the result. But again, neither the lower tribunal nor the Supreme Court doubted that an appropriate construction of the Alabama law should follow general commercial principles.

Again the overriding issue was what commercial doctrine to choose, not whether the choice disrupted interstate commercial credit.

In these cases, prevailing jurisprudential assumptions reenforced the federal judges' exercise of discretion. Legal commentators generally agreed that in the scientific search for first principles, commercial law was unique.[131] Throughout the period during which Alabama's federal courts decided commercial litigation, the dominant view was that federal judges were free to consult the "general law received by all the commercial world."[132] The diversity and inconsistency of state law created "discrepancies . . . among us in respect to our commercial law," which was "likely to increase rather than diminish."[133] Federal courts could not impose their will on the states, but they did offer an alternative forum in which greater uniformity and predictability were possible. As the Supreme Court's affirmation of decisions in which state statutes were not at issue suggested, the federal courts in Alabama maintained their independence and freely upheld general commercial principles.

Commercial suits raised other complex issues. Since courts purportedly did no more than declare or discover law, federal judges followed accepted legal opinion when they interpreted state statutes. State judges and the U.S. Supreme Court, however, construed these same statutes differently. The laws pertaining to technical points of pleading were as diverse as the view of the facts to which they were applied. Furthermore, jurisprudential assumptions encouraged judges to endow legal texts with extratextual meaning. The corpus of the general commercial law provided any judge a wide range of rules from which to choose, depending on the facts of a case. At any given time throughout the period, no more than two judges and a comparatively few lawyers tried the great bulk of commercial suits arising in Alabama's federal courts. The small and cohesive character of this working legal culture established a basis for uniform and predictable decisions.

Considering which litigants prevailed in each case suggests the significance of social class interests. In *Phillips*, a Mobile mercantile firm prevailed over their New Orleans agent. Nothing in the commercial doctrine that both the lower tribunal and the Supreme Court accepted, however, indicated that it was expressly oriented toward protecting the Alabama interest. Indeed, agreement of the two courts' decisions conveyed the marked impression that even if the status of the parties had been reversed the result would have been the same. A review of similar cases supports this conclusion.

Generally, then, the federal judges' decisions in nonstatutory commercial cases involved litigants from the same class whose interests were distinguished primarily by place of residence. Even so, the federal courts' commercial opinions reflected a greater concern for the interstate character of credit transactions than a willingness to protect a particular local group whose interests, after all, cut across state lines. In such cases, moreover, uniformity and predictability of decision were of first importance.[134]

Cases involving state statutes were more complex. In *Withers v. Greene*, neither the lower nor higher federal court questioned the need to apply the state statute. It was true that the Alabama federal judge had construed the law in favor of the Alabama business resident. By reversing the judgment, however, the Supreme Court did not necessarily negate this outcome; the Court merely ordered a new trial, holding that its own interpretation of the state statute should be followed. The lower court's decision in *Ellis* interpreted the Alabama law in favor of a North Carolina resident who had become the administrator of an Alabamian's estate. The Supreme Court's inability to agree on a decision suggested how intricate, if not outright murky, were the technical issues. Yet taken together both cases were consistent with the creation of a federal uniform commercial law that would aid the credit transactions of interstate business.[135]

Property Cases and the Limits of Discretion

Property litigation included politically sensitive as well as routine and relatively uncontroversial cases. In addition, no other category of suits raised quite so many technical legal issues. Commercial law, too, was intricate, but its identification with a general jurisprudence transcending state and national boundaries meant there was comparatively less room for doctrinal difference. Property law was dominated by local variation. Not only did every state have its own distinctive customs, but within states there were often two or more different doctrines that might govern an issue. There were few if any property suits to which both the state's common law and statutes were not applicable. Also, in property litigation the results differed depending on whether the case was tried in equity or at law. Finally, technical distinctions between procedure and substance might determine whether federal law governed, which ironically often limited the federal judges' discretion by requiring them to follow state law.[136]

Alabama's property titles were entangled in the Indian land cessions and the treaties between Spain and the United States involving West Florida, including Mobile. Initially, the federal government's authority over both territorial issues led Alabama to assert a superior claim in the name of states' rights. In the case of the Cherokees, President Andrew Jackson ultimately vindicated Alabama, and at the same time he preferred Georgia's interests in a clash with Chief Justice John Marshall over *Worcester v. Georgia* (1832). The

Supreme Court also settled in Alabama's favor a lengthy litigation concerning the Spanish cessions.[137]

Despite these states' rights victories, the most common cases involved the conflicting claims of private litigants. *Smith v. Whitaker* was tried before William Crawford and a jury in the federal district court of northern Alabama in 1829. John Smith claimed land in that part of the state held by William H. Whitaker and two others. The issue was whether title originally belonging to the Chickasaw Nation before 1800 had passed to the state of Georgia upon a grant by that state to Alabama purchasers and thence to either or both of the parties to the suit. The jury found against Smith's claim and gave a verdict for the defendants.[138] In 1827, Crawford tried a property claim in the Southern District court concerning the Spanish cession. Based on a questionable Spanish survey, the plaintiff sought to eject the individual who now held possession. After Crawford ruled against him, the plaintiff appealed to the Supreme Court but again lost.[139]

Property titles arising from the Indian and Spanish cessions involved major questions of national and state sovereignty. In each instance the status of land titles aroused patriotic sentiments and demands for local control among Alabama residents and those in other states sharing similar interests. The issues were sufficiently controversial that the cession process itself generated political conflict. Neither the lower federal tribunals nor the Supreme Court escaped entanglement, and ultimately the national government and the Court decided these controversies favorably to Alabama.[140] After these settlements, however, more mundane suits between individuals arose, which lacked clearly defined political exigencies. *Smith v. Whitaker* and the Spanish-survey ejectment case tried by Crawford were the sort of routine suits that Joseph Baldwin described in *Flush Times* as accounting for so much business in federal court. As Baldwin suggested, such cases fit easily into the cohesive legal community revolving around the state's two federal judges. As was true of commercial litigation, the lawyers, their clients, and the federal judges themselves were more concerned about establishing predictable and secure property rights than favoring a particular local interest.[141]

Suits requiring federal judges to prefer the law of one state over another further suggested the primary influence of nonpolitical factors. One such case was *Townsend v. Jemison* (1850). Thomas Townsend of Mississippi sued Robert Jemison of Alabama in the Federal Middle District Court of Alabama to recover damages for nonperformance of a contract dating from 1839. At trial Jemison contended that the Mississippi statute of limitations had run out. Townsend demurred, noting that the Alabama statute of limitations should apply. Federal district Judge John Gayle sustained Townsend, whereupon Jemison appealed. The Supreme Court upheld Gayle's judgment that the law of the forum in which the case was tried governed procedure. In this case the federal district court was asked to decide a procedural rather than a substantive legal point. The rule of the federal courts "in respect to pleas of the statutes of limitations has always been that they affect the remedy, and not the merits," the Court declared.[142]

The *Townsend* case involved applying conflicting local laws, which required the exercise of judicial discretion. The federal judiciary acknowledged that it was bound by local law in property cases where substantive issues were at stake. In *Wayman v. Southard* (1825), the Supreme Court decided, however, that federal judges were comparatively free to determine the appropriate procedure. In *Townsend*, the federal courts chose the Alabama over the Mississippi statute of limitations after an elaborate consideration of the "admitted maxims of international jurisprudence." In the absence of a "positive rule, affirming, denying, or restraining the operation of foreign laws," the Court declared as it examined these maxims that "courts establish a comity for such as are not repugnant to the policy or in conflict with the laws of the state from which they derive their organization." The precedent establishing the "foundation of comity, the manner of its exercise, and the extent to which courts can allowably carry it" was *Bank of Augusta v. Earle*.[143]

Factors associated with the local legal culture more than other interests thus influenced the *Townsend* decision. District Judge Gayle and the Supreme Court both applied the Alabama statute in favor of a Mississippian and against the local resident. Neither federal court, therefore, sided with the local propertyholder, though by upholding the Alabama law the judiciary facilitated more secure and predictable property titles within the state. Still, the decision itself involved a technical procedural point on which the choice of state law turned. In such cases, the Court held, federal judges could on the basis of comity exercise discretion. As a practical matter, the link between discretion and procedure meant that federal judges fashioned the procedure prevailing in their own district. Since the settlement of property titles depended on these procedural rules, procedure constituted special local knowledge, the possession of which gave an advantage to lawyers who routinely practiced before the state's federal judges. This special knowledge combined with the lawyer's informal contacts and familiarity with the federal court shaped decision making more than did explicit political exigencies.

Still, this procedural discretion operated within certain limitations. Equity practice was especially vital to the settlement of many property cases. Yet while most states had their own equity statutes, equity procedure in federal court was regulated by federal law. In cases at law, however, federal courts seriously considered state law and its construction by the state supreme court. In *Sears v. Eastburn* (1850),[144] the federal court for the Southern District did not follow an Alabama statute that abolished fictitious proceedings in ejectment, requiring instead that plaintiffs bring such actions in trespass. On appeal, the Supreme Court reversed, holding that a federal law required certain federal court proceedings to conform to the practices of the state's highest court. Since the Alabama law applied to the procedure of the state's supreme court, that law controlled the federal courts in Alabama.

The issues in *Sears* were technical, involving choice of law and equity. Since both parties to the suit were Alabama residents, the controversy touched only local property interests and the rules governing their rights in the state's federal court. Indeed, Chief Justice Roger B. Taney noted that the "point in this case" was "a narrow one" concerning "only the practice" in the federal circuit court of the Southern District of Alabama.[145] Alabama's federal judges exercised discretion and ignored state law in deciding the case. The local practice undoubtedly was familiar to those few lawyers who belonged to the local courtroom culture and regularly brought property-title suits before the federal judge. The judges' preference for their own rather than the state practice probably was due to the extraordinarily complicated status of titles inherited from the Spanish cession. As the court that handled the bulk of such cases year after year, the federal judges had consistently adhered to their own process and thereby permitted greater predictability than if they had relied on changing state court opinions. The Supreme Court's reversal of this local federal practice in accordance with a federal statute thus required repeated searching of state law, which, because that law was often unsettled, ironically called for more rather than less discretion.

In property litigation, the discretion federal judges exercised was circumscribed but still significant. The basic principle was that federal courts applied state law, which was consistent with the general affirmation of states' rights prevailing in the Indian Nations and Spanish cession disputes. When federal judges confronted the great bulk of ordinary cases between private claimants, however, states' rights doctrines provided little guidance. Every state, of course, possessed an elaborate code of laws governing property titles. In addition, even before *Swift v. Tyson*, federal judges had interpreted Section 34 of the Judiciary Act of 1789 to mean that local law bound them in property cases. Since such cases often came to federal court on diversity of citizenship jurisdiction, however, federal judges repeatedly confronted conflicting laws either within or between states. Where the state law was unsettled, the federal court supposedly applied the same sort of reasoning a state judge would have used to determine the rule of decision. But often this was easier said than done.[146]

The limits of judicial discretion were most ambiguous in property cases involving conflicts of laws. Where federal judges were called on to choose between the laws of Alabama and Mississippi in *Townsend*, they looked for guidance to the international "maxim" of comity. The court exercised discretion as to the procedural, not the substantive law, of the case, yet the procedure still significantly influenced who won. In other cases, federal statutes and the Supreme Court restricted this procedural flexibility. Overall, however, the rules governing equity and law merely determined the broad outlines within which federal judges retained considerable freedom over litigious outcomes.

As in the commercial cases, the diversity of local property titles was too complex to permit a clear-cut preference for a particular social-class interest. Even so, Alabama's smaller, more cohesive federal judicial establishment was, Baldwin and other commentators suggest, better able to establish predictable and secure property rights than the state courts. The Supreme Court imposed some limits on the federal judges' discretion, but even the Court's periodic intervention did not significantly diminish the lower federal judges' comparative independence. This institutional independence encouraged the fashioning of specific procedural practices and processes that strengthened the autonomy of the federal court's legal culture. The limits established by the routine decision of cases within this context, as much as the Supreme Court's review, thus influenced the federal judges' "packing" of state or federal statutes with interpretations and meanings borrowed from international law and elsewhere. The Supreme Court's sanctioning of comity in many such cases, moreover, fostered the independence and discretionary judgment on which the federal court's institutional culture depended.

CONCLUSION

Alexis de Tocqueville noted long ago the significant yet ambiguous place the federal courts occupied in American democracy. Federal judges in Alabama and elsewhere provided individuals, particularly the residents of different states, a forum relatively independent of local interests. Their role was ambiguous, however, because they were not only subordinate to the Supreme Court but often also were technically bound by state law itself. Indeed, during the federal court's formative development in antebellum Alabama, federal judges sanctioned certain state protectionist policies until overruled by the Supreme Court. Nevertheless, despite the institutional and political pressures for dependency, federal courts exercised considerable discretion in decision making, thereby preserving their independence. Ironically, local more than national considerations facilitated the triumph of discretion over dependency.

Although state power predominated, federal judges maintained their influence through indirection. As Tocqueville indicated, the states' protectionist policies invariably affected private interests that were subject to federal jurisdiction. In Alabama, federal judges usually did not challenge the constitutional principle on which state protectionism rested. Instead, they considered the state policy and the particular facts of a case within local and external institutional constraints, employing discretionary judgment to reach a result. The salient outside influences were the nation's sectional struggle involving slavery and the political and economic tensions between north and south Alabama. Yet formal and informal internal institutional arrangements associated with the federal judicial establishment itself were of more immediate significance. The circuit system in conjunction with Section 34 of the Judiciary Act, local federal procedures controlling process and jurisdiction, and prevailing jurisprudential assumptions significantly influenced decision making. These elements became focused, however, through the local legal culture emanating from the lawyers and judges working in each federal court, diffusing the impact of more remote conflicts.

The decisions of Alabama's federal judges supported the priority given the local courtroom culture. The judicial selection process indicated that generally the informal social and political connections rooted particularly in south Alabama influenced the district judges' and justices' views of both constitutional and routine litigation. Notwithstanding exceptions involving the appointment of Justices McKinley and Campbell, federal district judges and the circuit-riding justices usually considered cases in terms of their local implications. The split between Jones and Campbell in the slave-trade suits was the conspicuous exception. Jones's stance, however, was best explained by local concerns. And even though Campbell's position in the slave-trade cases reflected national sectional pressures, his admiralty and other opinions followed the established pattern.

Similar factors shaped the results in routine litigation. In commercial law and property suits, establishing and maintaining predictability and stability in the contractual obligations of Alabama and nonresident debtors and creditors were consistent with the primacy of local influences. Outcomes in both statute and nonstatute commercial cases, as well as certain admiralty and property opinions, demonstrated further that local orientation and interstate commercial stability were compatible. Such outcomes were reconcilable, moreover, with the sanction of protectionism in the *Alabama Bank* cases and even Campbell's slave-trade decision. All resulted primarily from the interplay between Alabama federal judges' local institutional establishment and their discretionary judgment.

II

The New Parameters of
Federal Judicial Authority, 1865–1940

INTRODUCTION

Between the Civil War and the Great Depression, the factors influencing federal judicial decision making changed. Reconstruction transformed the paradoxical nature of federal judicial power in which the judge's discretionary authority was both constrained by and independent of state sovereignty. Although the struggle to defend the freedman's equality before the law ended in defeat, it nonetheless established the constitutional subordination of state to federal power. From Reconstruction on, Congress responded to national economic and social tensions with new laws and an expansion of the federal court's jurisdiction.[1] Before the Civil War, Tocqueville had observed that federal courts exerted power indirectly by protecting private interests. Beginning with Reconstruction and reaching a climax during the New Deal, the progressive enlargement of federal jurisdiction created a new market for legal services in which federal questions either superseded or at least steadily reduced the importance of state law. Whereas before, the interplay between the federal court's discretion and dependence had generally required interpreting state law, increasingly the parameters governing that interaction involved federal issues.[2]

Expanded jurisdiction gradually altered the factors influencing judicial appointments. Alabama's economic and population growth entered a long, relative decline after the Civil War. The number of federal district judges serving the state nonetheless increased from one to three, while throughout most of the seventy-five-year period one of the judges sitting on the Fifth Circuit was also an Alabamian. When Reconstruction formally ended with the Compromise of 1877, moreover, conservative Democrats were in power. Nevertheless, party affiliation provided an insufficient guide to a judge's decision making, especially concerning two of the era's most prominent judges, Thomas Goode Jones and William I. Grubb, both of them active Democrats appointed by Republican presidents. As had been true before the Civil War, personal connections and substate sectionalism circumscribed the influence of national partisan politics, even in the case of two out of three Reconstruction appointees.

Thus, generally, a judge's membership in either party was of secondary value in explaining his opinions.[3]

National pressures shaping expanded federal power and partisan party conflict interacted with formal and informal institutional relationships. The strength and clarity of federal appellate or state court precedents, whether the issues were routine or new (particularly constitutional questions), and the local context in which a case arose established the limits within which federal judges exercised discretion. The more routine a suit, the less likelihood that external political or social considerations overcame the established institutional imperatives in governing discretion versus dependence. Where institutional constraints facilitated conflicting tensions, however, the influence of other more informal factors increased.

This multiplicity of influences included a small but significant group of lawyers. As had been the case before the Civil War, comparatively few lawyers were admitted to practice before the federal courts. In the Northern District, where by 1900 a majority of Alabama's population lived, only nine lawyers were admitted to the federal bar as late as 1920. The new demands for legal services fostered by the Great Depression resulted in the number growing from just 88 in 1930 to 155 in 1940. Even so, this bar remained small enough that it and the federal court itself formed a distinctive and independent courthouse culture. This culture embodied a set of values growing out of the expanding yet specialized federal jurisdiction, which in turn served as a model for the reform policies advocated by the Alabama State Bar Association. The interaction between the values and formal institutional arrangements constituting this culture on the one hand, and the federal laws and national pressures on the other shaped the court's decisions.[4]

Even so, the strongest factor affecting the federal judge was the local bar's adversarial function. It was through the litigants represented by the small federal bar that the local courthouse culture influenced the decision-making process. Ongoing contacts between the lawyers and the judge of each of Alabama's three districts created perceptions and assumptions regarding the court's approach to routine or new issues, including constitutional questions. These informal considerations were so entwined with objective institutional factors that interaction was unavoidable. The local courtroom culture was so influential that more distant pressures shaped the exercise of judicial discretion only in the exceptional case.[5]

Occasionally, an Alabama federal judge was embroiled in controversy testing the limits of discretion and dependence. Richard Busteed, one of three judges appointed during Reconstruction, ran afoul of the local legal culture to the point that he faced impeachment proceedings and eventually resigned. Oscar R. Hundley became embroiled in a confrontation with the Birmingham bar that interfered with his confirmation and led to his resignation. The charges against these men alleged abuse of discretion. A closer look at the local context in which the allegations arose, however, reveals that both judges failed to conform to the local legal culture. Disregarding this relationship transgressed a significant bond of dependency.[6]

From Reconstruction to the Great Depression, the federal judiciary's organizational structure changed, strengthening independence. During Reconstruction, Congress expanded the limits of jurisdiction to the maximum permitted by Article III of the Constitution. In addition, a major extension of the right to remove cases from state to federal court occurred. This removal power, combined with the federal common law based on the *Swift* doctrine, facilitated the federal court's independence, at least until 1938 when the Court overruled *Swift* in *Erie R.R. v. Tompkins*. The most conspicuous institutional change, however, was the creation of the circuit court of appeals in 1891, which ended the circuit-riding duties of members of the Supreme Court. Alabama maintained a noteworthy influence on the new Fifth Circuit. The state's federal district judges regularly served on the circuit's three-judge panels, often with the circuit judge who was also from Alabama. As the federal courts acquired greater self-governance through the new Judicial Conference, moreover, Grubb was a leader in its administrative operation.[7]

This greater institutional autonomy strengthened the appellate court's authority over the district courts. Yet the active role of Alabama's district judges in the circuit system facilitated deference toward the lower court's exercise of discretionary judgment. Appeals from Alabama's district courts were the exception.[8] Accordingly, although organizational systemization theoretically increased the district court's dependence, its limits generally were defined more by local relationships than by national exigencies. Reinforcing the influence of this local legal culture was a practical conservative-activist jurisprudence that was consistent with the values of the Alabama State Bar Association.

Between 1865 and 1940, federal judicial power in Alabama was transformed. Once the Civil War and Reconstruction destroyed state sovereignty, federal law increasingly superseded state law as the primary source of litigation.[9] The new circuit court of appeals potentially heightened the district court's dependence within the federal judicial system. Routine and constitutional litigation still arose, however, in a particular community, served by a small, specialized bar. This bar, in turn, linked the federal courtroom to the national or local interests at odds in each case. The formal and informal institutions and values embodied in the local legal culture operated within the appellate court structure. Organizational realities and the influence of Alabama's judges within this structure nonetheless more often than not gave precedence to local over national factors in shaping decisions. Thus the federal courthouse culture established limits on the state's federal judges' independence.

External Imperatives and Local Institutional Culture

Party affiliation was a weak predictor of decision making among Alabama's federal judges. Democrats and Republicans both owed their appointment more to local than national factors. And as was the case before the Civil War, these local factors still helped to shape decisions in particular categories of litigation. Institutional development was consistent with the policy agenda of the Alabama State Bar Association. This agenda, and the distinctive legal culture that it reflected, provided a better guide to the role of discretion and dependence in the state's federal judicial process than partisan affiliations.

The Vicissitudes of Judicial Appointment

Despite relative economic decline, Alabama experienced sufficient growth to justify increased federal judgeships. Throughout Reconstruction, Alabama followed the antebellum practice of having one district judge presiding over the state's three districts, sharing trial and appellate duties with a Fifth Circuit judge who generally was also from Alabama. During the mid-1880s, however, Congress added a second district judgeship. One served the southern section, sitting principally in Mobile; the other district judge presided over the Northern and Middle districts, the latter centered in Montgomery. Reflecting the rise of Birmingham and the increasingly more populous north, Congress divided the Northern District into northern and southern divisions, located in Huntsville and Birmingham respectively. In 1907, Congress added another judgeship solely for this district.[10] In addition, Congress created the federal circuit courts of appeal in 1891, which transformed the trial and appellate work the district and circuit judges had shared for so long.

Party politics played an equivocal part in the appointment of Alabama's federal judges. During the Reconstruction era, both the district and circuit judges appointed from Alabama initially supported the Republicans' commitment to defending the freedman's rights, even after the Democrats had regained control of the state in 1876. Irish-born Richard Busteed, a former New York City Democratic politician and Union Army veteran appointed by Abraham Lincoln, served from 1864 to 1874. Suggesting the stereotype of carpetbagger,

Busteed confronted impeachment proceedings before resigning and returning to New York. His successor, John Bruce from Iowa, was also a Union Army veteran; Ulysses S. Grant appointed him in 1875. Bruce was, however, quite a different sort of carpetbagger from Busteed, making Alabama his permanent residence in 1872 and representing Wilcox County in the state legislature from 1872 to 1876. Bruce was a district judge until he died in 1901. William B. Woods was the same sort of carpetbagger. A Union Army veteran from Ohio, he moved to Mobile in 1866 and served as a local chancery judge until appointed to the Fifth Circuit by Grant in 1870, remaining on that court until 1880 when he became an associate justice of the United States Supreme Court. Unlike Busteed, Bruce and Woods were socially accepted and professionally respected as effective judges by Alabama's bar, despite their Republican and Reconstruction origins.[11]

Even so, the weakness of partisan party influences was apparent in other federal judicial appointments. Thomas Goode Jones, whose father had served as a federal district judge before the Civil War, belonged to south Alabama's conservative Democratic Party establishment. A much decorated Confederate Army veteran, he represented Montgomery in the state legislature during the 1880s, becoming speaker of the House, and then was elected governor in 1890. He was a prominent railroad lawyer as well as one of the architects of the Constitution of 1901, which established the ongoing political influence of south Alabama and established Jim Crow segregation as the law of the land. Partially because of the influence of Booker T. Washington, however, Jones was chosen as Bruce's successor by Progressive Republican Theodore Roosevelt. Also, when Roosevelt's appointment of Huntsville lawyer and Republican Oscar R. Hundley failed to be confirmed, Republican William H. Taft won confirmation of his appointment of Birmingham Democrat William I. Grubb in 1909. Before World War I, the only person whose selection was consistent with the Alabama Democratic Party's dominance was Harry T. Toulmin from Mobile, who served in the Southern District from 1887 to 1914. Also a Confederate Army veteran, he was appointed by Democrat Grover Cleveland.[12]

North Alabama's party politics were less clearcut than those of the southern section. Hundley was a Democrat-turned-Republican who had been elected to local office in Huntsville. Similarly, Huntsville lawyer David D. Shelby was from a prominent north Alabama family. A longtime Republican who nonetheless had served briefly in the Confederate cavalry, he was elected to various local offices before Republican William McKinley appointed him in 1899 to the Fifth Circuit Court of Appeals. He died holding that position in 1914.[13]

John Bruce (1832–1901), judge of the Northern District from 1875 to 1901; Republican. *Alabama Department of Archives and History*

Not until 1914 was there a clear congruence between Democratic presidents and their federal judicial appointees. Woodrow Wilson appointed the well-known Democratic United States congressman Henry D. Clayton from southeast Alabama to the Northern and Middle District in 1914. He served until he died in 1929. The other Wilson appointee was Mobile lawyer Robert T. Ervin to the Southern District in 1917. The grandson of Alabama's first federal judge Charles Tait, Ervin retired in 1935. Prior to 1940, no president appointed more federal district judges in Alabama than Franklin D. Roosevelt. He appointed Birmingham attorney David J. Davis to the Northern District in 1935 amid concern that Grubb had decided consistently against the New Deal. When Davis died three years later, Roosevelt appointed another Birmingham lawyer, Thomas A. Murphree. To the Southern District Roosevelt also appointed Democratic U.S. congressman John McDuffie as Ervin's successor in 1935. During this period of Democratic dominance, the only Republican to become a federal district judge was Charles B. Kennamer. Several times an unsuccessful Republican candidate for Congress and a federal prosecuting attorney from north Alabama, Kennamer was appointed by Herbert Hoover in 1931 to the Northern/Middle District. In 1936, Congress made the Middle District independent, and Kennamer remained there.[14]

Democratic Party affiliation also only partially characterized the Alabama judges appointed to the Fifth Circuit Court of Appeals. Before 1914, Alabama's representatives on the federal appellate court were Republican, first Woods and then Shelby. Wilson, by contrast, appointed Huntsville attorney and former Democratic state legislator Richard W. Walker as Shelby's successor. Walker retired in 1930. Eight years later an Alabamian again sat on the appellate bench, when Roosevelt appointed Leon C. McCord. He had practiced law in Scottsboro and Montgomery and served as a state railroad commissioner before being elected to various state judgeships.[15]

Establishing a direct connection between party affiliation and Alabama's federal judicial appointees is complicated. Clearly, Republican and Democratic presidents usually appointed members of their own party as federal judges. Theodore Roosevelt's selection of Jones and Taft's selection of Grubb suggest, however, that more complex factors were at work. Even among the Reconstruction carpetbagger appointees—Busteed, Bruce, and Woods—the differences in their reception by Alabama lawyers indicated a more complex picture. The broader question arises: Why did Alabama, where Democrats established dominance after Reconstruction and preserved it for so long thereafter, continue to have Republicans appointed as federal judges, including Shelby, Hundley, and Kennamer?

Part of the answer was the influence of substate political sectionalism. Prior to the Civil War five out of six of Alabama's federal judges came from politically dominant south Alabama, the part of the state experiencing the greatest population growth. After the Civil War, Alabama's population center shifted to the north, especially around Birmingham. With the Constitution of 1901, however, the pervasive force of race in state politics fostered a conservative coalition of business and planter interests, which meant that southern Alabama retained a disproportionate degree of political clout. As a result, until the addition of the federal district judgeship in north Alabama in 1907, each of the state's district judges came from south Alabama after Busteed's resignation. The Republican Bruce and the Democrats Toulmin and Jones were from Prairie Bluff, Mobile, and Montgomery respectively in the southern part of the state. After 1907, with rare exception, district judges were nominated from the districts in which they lived, confirming the primacy of local, as opposed to national, political considerations in their selection. The exception was Kennamer from north Alabama, who nonetheless remained in the Middle District in Montgomery after 1936, when Congress separated the Middle from the Northern District.[16]

State sectional party politics had a less direct influence on the appointment of appellate judges. Prior to the Civil War, national political considerations determined the selection of Alabamians to the Supreme Court, first John McKinley and then John A. Campbell, whose circuit included their home state. After the Civil War, the pattern continued. Woods was a respected lawyer and state judge from south Alabama. The fact that he came from the politically dominant section was less important than his wider connections in the national Republican Party. Similarly, Shelby was a Republican from Huntsville, appointed before the 1901 constitution effectually fostered a one-party Democratic state. Shelby had been elected as a Republican to local offices and the state senate. Nevertheless, it is unlikely that he would have been appointed to the Fifth Circuit by McKinley had his political involvement not also satisfied national party leaders. Once the Democrats established control, state sectional differences also were of secondary importance: Walker and McCord were from northern and southern parts of the state respectively.[17]

Ironically, the removal of Busteed suggested the degree to which partisan political considerations were not sufficient in and of themselves to justify judicial appointments. Lincoln appointed the New York City Democrat during the Civil War, so national political interests explained his selection. Throughout his service, moreover, the attacks on Busteed were consistent with the wider battle Alabama Democrats fought to regain control from the radical Republicans and their black freedman and white allies. Accordingly, the

Robert T. Ervin (1863–1949), Southern District judge from 1917 to 1935; Democrat. *Robin Holeb-Ableman, U.S. District Court, Southern District of Alabama*

Democrats charged that in the administration of his office Busteed was politically biased. Not surprisingly, a Congress controlled by Republicans was unsympathetic to such charges. Those same Republicans ultimately considered impeaching Busteed, however, on the charge that except when court was in session he did not reside in Alabama. On this point, moderate congressional Republicans, concerned with the protection of property, as well as civil, rights, understood that the federal court was part of a wider local legal culture to which it must remain responsive. Thus Busteed's successor was Bruce, a respected south Alabama lawyer.

The significance of local factors was seen in Theodore Roosevelt's appointment of powerful south Alabama conservative Democrat and former governor, Thomas Jones. By 1900, Republicans such as Shelby and Hundley continued to be electable locally, yet Roosevelt nominated Jones. Part of the explanation was that Jones was one of the foremost members of Alabama's bar. He authored the state's code of legal ethics that the American Bar Association adopted as its own provision. In addition, although he helped to draft the 1901 constitution that established racial segregation, he urged that the law otherwise be administered as fairly as possible toward African Americans. This proviso was enough to win the support of Tuskegee's Booker T. Washington, who wrote Roosevelt a letter favoring Jones's nomination. Also, to Alabama's legal profession the appointment of Jones as Bruce's successor became a symbol of post-Reconstruction reconciliation. Roosevelt's appointment thus reflected the primacy of wider local interests over narrow party partisanship.

The Hundley and Grubb appointments further suggested the ascendancy of local imperatives. When Congress increased the number of federal district judges in the Northern District in 1907, the appointment of a north Alabamian was expected. Unlike the rest of the state, Republicans continued to be a force in grassroots politics in some north Alabama counties even after Democratic control triumphed. Nevertheless, the leading population and political center of the northern section was Birmingham, which voted solidly Democratic. Hundley was a Democrat-turned-Republican from Huntsville, a noted lawyer active in state bar affairs. Grubb was a successful lawyer from Bradley, Arant, one of Birmingham's most important corporate-defense firms, and a Democrat. Roosevelt chose Hundley, but because of the active opposition of prominent members of the Birmingham bar he was never confirmed; the city's bar wanted as judge one of their own.

Taft then had the opportunity to appoint Grubb. Like Taft, Grubb was from Cincinnati, and the two had been classmates at Yale University. Personal considerations were thus undoubtedly present in Taft's choice. Also Taft,

Leon C. McCord (1878–1952), judge of the Fifth Circuit Court of Appeals from 1938 to 1951; Democrat. *Alabama Department of Archives and History*

perhaps more than any other president, selected judicial candidates from outside his own party. Even so, partisan party politics clearly did not explain Grubb's appointment, which lent credence to the disavowal of political motives on the part of the Birmingham lawyers in their opposition to Hundley. A published report claimed that a judicial nominee's politics were "of as little concern as his religion." The members of the bar of the Northern District were "utterly indifferent to the party affiliations of appointees on the Federal bench." Moreover, "never in the history of the South" was there "more independence in political thought than there [was] in Alabama today." Indeed, "life-long Democrats in Alabama" had voted in the "thousands" for Taft in the election of 1908. The potential for hyperbole notwithstanding, the statement suggested the importance of looking beyond partisan politics to explain Grubb's selection. Finally, the report admitted candidly that the bar opposed Hundley in part because the bankruptcy magistrates he appointed were not from Birmingham. A judge chosen from the city's bar very likely would have looked to his local peers to fill such lucrative posts.[18] The vicissitudes of federal judicial appointment in Alabama from the Civil War to the Great Depression indicated the extent to which Grubb's experience was not unique.

The Alabama State Bar Association's Policy Agenda and a Federal Courtroom Culture

Alabama's federal judges were the center of a distinctive courtroom culture. The suits involved a specialized, if growing, body of law that was different from that arising in state tribunals. Also, as was true before the Civil War, a much smaller proportion of the bar had a federal practice. A Birmingham lawyer summed up the federal court's comparative insularity: "conduct of business by a United States judge is hardly known outside the lawyers practicing before him." State judges, by contrast, generally were at the center of a more extensive network of political and social influences, which, according to the Alabama State Bar Association, weakened the independence and professionalization of judicial administration. Jones put the issue in the most neutral terms: "In short, the diligent lawyer cannot always get his case ready for trial and have it tried [in state court], without running counter to deep rooted professional customs and traditions which the lawyer . . . will hesitate long before violating."[19]

An indicator of the legal culture influencing federal judges was the Alabama State Bar Association. The association began in 1878, fewer than two years after Reconstruction ended. From the start, future federal judges occupied prominent positions: Clayton and Toulmin were vice presidents, and Jones was chairman of the executive committee. Clayton and Jones were just twenty-five

Oscar R. Hundley (1854–1921), Northern District judge from 1907 to 1909; Democrat, then Republican. *Alabama Department of Archives and History*

and twenty-eight respectively when they occupied these positions, while Toulmin was forty-four. At this point Bruce and Woods were Republican carpetbaggers holding the state's district and circuit federal judgeships. In 1884 Toulmin was the first "native" Alabamian to become a federal district judge after Reconstruction; Jones became the second in 1901; Clayton, the third in 1914. From Toulmin on, most of Alabama's federal judges were members of the association, during a period when two out of three of the state's lawyers declined to join.[20]

Thus Alabama's federal judges belonged to a professional organization that was generally less representative of the state's bar. Even so, the number of lawyers admitted to practice before the Northern District's federal court, which embraced the state's most populous section, remained comparatively small: 9 in 1920, 88 in 1930, and 155 in 1940. In 1882, Alabama had fewer than 1,000 lawyers and only 142 were Bar Association members. Nearly two-thirds of these were from Mobile or Montgomery, while the number from Huntsville was just four. In time, Birmingham's and north Alabama's proportion of membership grew steadily. A key point nonetheless was that the Bar Association as a whole and its members who became federal judges in particular broadly represented the state's larger urban areas. Yet at no time before 1940 did the state's urban population reach 35 percent. Accordingly, the Bar Association's programs very likely reflected interests different from those of most of the state's attorneys who practiced in rural areas.[21]

This more urban orientation indirectly influenced those who became federal judges. In rural areas, most lawyers had a general practice. In urban centers with enough business to support specialization, however, there was a rough but pronounced split: trial lawyers who represented individual plaintiffs or criminal defendants before juries and law firms retained on a more or less permanent basis by corporations. Unlike plaintiffs' or criminal defense lawyers, who served many different clients one case at a time, corporate lawyers became expert in areas of law relating to large, incorporated enterprises. A common area of litigation involved personal injury in which a plaintiff sued a corporation for damages, arguing that the harm occurred because of the company's negligence. The jury decided whether the facts warranted recovery and, if so, what amount. These realities of practice meant that plaintiff and corporate lawyers generally occupied distinct professional roles and one rarely represented the clients of the other. Alabama's federal judges came from either law practice. Jones and Grubb were prominent corporate lawyers; Clayton was a leading prosecuting attorney.[22]

The jury and contingency-fee system contributed most to the success of a plaintiffs' lawyer's practice. In accident cases, a lawyer won by tapping community values, and success resulted in a contingency fee, a percentage of the amount a jury awarded the plaintiff. In Birmingham, as elsewhere, the law restricted those eligible for jury service to taxpaying, property-holding male citizens. Women, blacks, and the poor usually were excluded. The litigants, however, came from all walks of life. Consequently, a trial lawyer had to know just what emotions to touch amid the tangle of hopes, fears, prejudices, sympathies, and interests jurors shared regarding ethnic, racial, religious, worker, and business groups.[23]

Throughout Alabama, the close association between a community's lawyers and the local courts often resulted in extensive social and political connections between the state's bench and bar. In 1882, Jones described a problem that continued to be an object of the association's criticism and reform efforts up to the 1930s. There were state judges "inclined to favoritism" and lawyers "boasting of 'personal influence' " with a judge. One consequence was that often the jury box was filled with "professional jurors," many of whom had personal ties not only with the judge but also the lawyers appearing before the court. "Bad, ignorant or timid juries, in any community, may overthrow the entire code as to that locality," Jones warned, "leaving no means of enforcing any law, and thus force the preservation of order by the lawless and irregular methods of mob violence, which is as bad as the evils it seeks to remedy."[24]

Personal influence was a particular problem in state criminal trials. The "great complaint" involved the "delays in the administration of the criminal law," said Jones. Many courts allowed continuances without any showing of cause. "As a general rule, two or three continuances in a criminal case are almost tantamount to an acquittal" because in the "meantime a just public resentment may calm down, or witnesses may die or remove out of the jurisdiction." At the same time, "by importunities, and the efforts of friends, and the aid of false sympathy" the defendant "procures a dismissal . . . or submits to the smallest punishment, when this could not have been affected if public attention had been directed to the case, watching with jealous eyes the proper enforcement of the law."[25]

Two particularly pernicious results of this weakened state judicial independence were the interconnected fee and convict-lease systems. Local judges frequently fined and imposed lengthy sentences on the poor whites and African Americans passing through their courts. Various law enforcement officials benefited from the fees. Once incarcerated, the prisoners became a source of cheap labor for local businesses under a lease system. A variation of this system degenerated into peonage. Courts, law enforcement authorities, and businesses cooperated to entrap small debtors in a web of obligations they could never pay while they were required to work for court-assigned employers as long as the debts remained. Federal judge Jones attacked peonage, and Birmingham lawyer Hugo Black led a campaign against the fee and convict-lease systems, but despite such efforts the practices in various forms persisted.[26]

An indirect outcome of the state judiciary's openness to such influences was the "commercialization" of the legal profession. The Bar Association repeatedly condemned the extent to which lawyers pushed clients to the point that, according to a "scurrilous jibe," they might even "tell the truth if necessary to win the case." Accordingly, the "spirit of commercialism, corporate greed, and the unlawful designs of monopolies" too often resulted in a "delay of justice."[27] On the other side, plaintiffs' lawyers pursued business so aggressively that they earned the epithet "ambulance chasers." It was "an indisputable fact, that, whenever a person is injured, or killed, on a railroad or street railway," particularly in cities, "there will be at the home of the injured, or killed, within the next twenty-four hours following the accident a representative from a number of prominent law firms; who go on foot, on motorcycles, on street cars, in buggies and automobiles; and for no other purpose than that of soliciting business."[28]

The remedy for such evils was the legal profession's professionalization and the state judiciary's increased independence. Again as early as 1882, Jones set out much of the Bar Association's reform agenda. Increased salaries would attract to the state judiciary more "competent and able men" with the character to resist personal influence. Similarly, reform of the jury system required the end of numerous provisions that exempted the "best men" from jury service. A reform of the code of procedure simplifying the pleading system would improve judicial administration and efficiency, while diminishing the use of technicalities to thwart justice. Specific changes in the pleading and practice of criminal trials would attain the same benefits. In addition, a code of ethics would end not only explicit corrupt practices but also indirect forms of abuse associated with the "commercialization" of the bar. The code would facilitate such results by providing a focus of public disapproval turning the profit motive in support of higher rather than lower professional standards. A further reform the Bar Association advocated was improved legal education at the University of Alabama School of Law.[29]

Alabama's federal courts were central to the Bar Association's efforts to achieve its reform agenda. Commonly, the association's spokesmen defended change by comparing state courts to their federal counterparts. Usually, federal courts adopted remedies to problems sooner than did state courts. The Bar Association thus pointed toward the federal judiciary's willingness to change as well as the substantive changes themselves to support its reforms. Concerning

Thomas Goode Jones (1844–1914), judge of the Northern and Middle districts from 1901 to 1914; Democrat. *Alabama Department of Archives and History*

the criminal and civil procedure reforms, for instance, the bar solicited Grubb's opinion as "deserving of the highest respect by reason of his learning, and his experience with the new practice." In criminal trials especially, said Jones, the federal court's reputation for certainty stood in marked contrast to state practices "remarkable only for vagueness and uncertainty, and which, in effect, converts a trial into a jumble of pleas, replications and evidence, submitted at once to a confused jury."[30] Federal courts overcame the jury problem, moreover, by drawing on a larger pool of jurors, creating fewer exemptions and reducing the likelihood of bias.[31] The federal judge's constitutional independence ameliorated potential favoritism and also facilitated the imposition of higher standards of lawyerly conduct and practice. To achieve these goals, however, the federal judge's exercise of discretion was inevitable.

The Changing Social and Economic Environment

Judicial appointments and the Bar Association's policy agenda were part of a changing social and economic environment. Unlike the rest of the nation outside the South, Alabama remained predominantly rural and possessed of small-town values regarding self-respect, government, politics, religion, and race. Nevertheless, the federal judiciary's local institutional culture was more directly involved in the state's growing urban areas, particularly Birmingham, Montgomery, and Mobile. In addition, although Alabama was poor compared to the rest of the nation, it partook of the same general pattern of economic development associated with the railroads and industrialization that climaxed in the Great Depression. The defeat of Reconstruction meant that the conservative Democrats established dominance not only over blacks but over the state's broader economic policy making as well. The distinctive institutional culture to which the federal courts belonged, however, ensured greater independence from these wider tensions while at the same time fostering the need for discretionary judgment.

Alabama, like the entire South, reflected the nation's experience, albeit distinctively. Between the Civil War and the Great Depression, the South became America's poorest region. Its increasing poverty amid an overall trend of national growth nonetheless signified only relative decline. During the forty years from statehood to secession, the state's overall population grew by 70 percent, with the lowest percentage increase in 1860 of 25 percent. In the two forty-year periods following 1860, however, Alabama's population grew by just 17.7 percent and 11.8 percent respectively, with lows of 3.4 percent in 1870 and 7.1 percent in 1940, and an overall growth throughout the period of 15 percent. The relation of urban to rural population centers—with cities designated as places with 10,000 people or more—represented another contrast with the national trend. Before 1860, the state's urban places rose from one to five. From 1870 to 1900, the number of such places increased from seven to twenty-seven; and between 1910 and 1940 the increase was from twenty-eight to fifty-nine. The proportion of urban to rural, however, was marked: 94.9 rural in 1860, declining to 69.8 rural in 1940.[32]

These quantitative patterns suggest several qualitative comparisons, contrasts, and differences with national trends. Although Alabama's and the South's growth continued over the long period following secession, relative to their own antebellum past and to the nation as a whole that growth had slowed significantly. In addition, the state and the region shared with the rest of the nation urban expansion. To a significantly greater extent, however, Alabama and the South remained predominantly rural even after 1920, when most Americans had come to live in cities. More particularly, this meant that Alabamians and other southerners continued to share common small-town experiences and values to a greater extent over a longer period than most other Americans. Accordingly, the region and state underwent the national historical transformations associated with the Civil War and Reconstruction, urbanization and immigration, a revolution in transportation and industrialization, World War I and the 1920s, and cycles of growth and bust climaxing in the greatest economic depression Americans had ever known with the corresponding triumph of liberal big government during the 1930s. Yet these changes remained regionally distinctive.[33]

Alabama's relative economic decline altered the state's sectional makeup. Before the Civil War, the southern section centered in Mobile was dominant. By the turn of the century, the sectional balance had shifted in population and growth to the north around the new urban community of Birmingham. Just six years after Appomattox, its founders had begun building on the rich coal, iron, and limestone deposits a steel-producing city destined to rival its namesake in the English Midlands. In fewer than forty years, Birmingham's mills and mines attracted nearly 133,000 residents, creating Alabama's largest urban center.[34]

The northern and southern sections differed in several ways. The north was, of course, more industrial and economically diversified. Correspondingly, it was more ethnically diverse. Throughout the state, the majority of whites were of English or Scotch Irish descent. But in the south the proportion of blacks was much larger; African Americans outnumbered whites in certain counties. In and around Birmingham, moreover, the next largest white ethnic group was German American, and there were also a fair number of Jews and Italians and a few Chinese and Syrians. Corresponding to ethnic differences were pronounced religious cleavages, particularly evangelical Protestants versus Jews and Catholics.[35]

The differing racial composition of each section's population directly influenced Alabama's politics. A conservative coalition including a business group known as Big Mules (because of their "pull") centered in urban areas, and black-belt plantation owners dominated local affairs throughout the state. Yet from the end of Reconstruction to the New Deal, various groups periodically challenged the conservative Democrats, aggravating racial and sectional tensions. Although many north Alabamians assumed that racial separation was appropriate on the basis of social custom, they nonetheless supported civil rights for African Americans as a matter of law.[36]

Black-belt whites, however, pushed a campaign to establish legally enforced racial segregation. Whenever conservative Democrats felt threatened by a coalition of whites and blacks, they fought for segregation imposed by law. The struggle was central to the end of Reconstruction and the Populist revolt of the 1890s. In 1901, the conservatives triumphed when Alabamians ratified a constitution incorporating racial segregation as a fundamental principle. This victory destroyed equal rights before the law, reducing African Americans to second-class citizenship. It also undercut the political participation of poorer whites by as much as 25 percent, which weakened the northern section's population advantage and thereby enabled the south to remain politically powerful. Nevertheless, the conflict persisted, first with the challenge of the Progressives before World War I and then during the 1920s and 1930s as a few Alabama Progressives such as Hugo Black contributed to the emergence of liberalism.[37]

The all-white primary epitomized the way Alabama's southern section retained political clout. After the collapse of Reconstruction, Alabama, like the rest of the South, increasingly became a one-party state. Although Republican presidents periodically made patronage appointments—including federal judgeships—Democrats generally controlled the state after 1876. Candidates chosen out of group struggles within the Democratic Party left the victor in the primary virtually always the winner in the general election. Although blacks could no longer vote after passage of the 1901 constitution, they nonetheless counted as population in determining the number of each district's elected officials, giving the black belt proportionately more representatives than the north in statewide primary elections. The discriminatory political and constitutional measures reduced the political clout of Alabama's entire northern section.[38]

Once the white primary created essentially a one-party system in Alabama, any attempt to achieve political goals through rival party organizations became futile. In addition, the 1901 constitution empowered local officials to determine voter qualifications by literacy tests, poll taxes, and "good character." Black-belt bosses triumphed over north Alabama in the 1901 constitutional convention because they effectively manipulated popular faith in white supremacy. Once Jim Crow segregation triumphed, the more intense racial beliefs of the black belt acquired a primacy that public figures in north Alabama and elsewhere could little afford to challenge. Yet the sectional roots of the state's political struggles also meant that at times Alabama's federal judges could become embroiled in conflicts in which conservative values and interests were defeated.[39]

Cutting across sectional political conflicts were certain basic values. Religion exercised a strong influence. Outside a few major urban centers such as Birmingham and Mobile where Catholics and Jews were visible minorities, most Alabama churches were of some Protestant denomination—Methodist, Episcopalian, and Congregationalist, with the evangelical Baptist church by far the largest. Although fragmented into numerous sects, Baptist congregations reflected and shaped the community's hopes and fears. The church was often a significant factor in elections, with ministers encouraging their congregations to vote for particular candidates and politicians using biblical language and stories to arouse the people's concern. Many evangelical Protestant sects urged state and local governments to prohibit the manufacture and sale of alcoholic beverages, injecting government into the community's private life.[40]

Also, in cities, small towns, and rural areas most Alabamians, like southerners generally, cherished respectability. It was vital to social stability, responsible individual behavior, personal independence, and moral accountability. Ideally, the unity of the community and the rights of the individual reinforced each other. Respectability was integral to this balance because it liberated individuals from material or social dependence. Such independence was profoundly significant in a society intimately familiar with slavery and racial segregation.[41]

This mix of values and interests influenced Alabamians' paradoxical support of activist big government. From Reconstruction to the New Deal, major political factions and economic groups within Alabama struggled to overcome resistance to greater state and federal government intervention. Each national movement toward larger government had its counterpart within Alabama, and each victory had its local opposition. The state's federal judges could be found sometimes on one side, sometimes on the other. In 1887, Congress created the Interstate Commerce Commission to regulate the railroads and in 1890, passed the Sherman Antitrust Act to protect farmers and small businesses from large corporations. During the 1890s, the Populists failed in their efforts to win stronger antitrust laws, more favorable credit policies, and stricter railroad regulation, but after the turn of the century the Progressives began enacting such measures at the state and federal level. The New Deal pushed such intervention to levels previously known only in wartime. As lawmakers intervened directly in social and economic affairs by imposing racial segregation, they also considered statewide prohibition of the manufacture and distribution of alcohol as well as increased economic regulation. The primary legal basis for increased government intervention was the police power, a principle that traditionally sanctioned state responsibility for preserving community health, morals, and welfare, values embraced in the attachment to respectability.[42]

From the Civil War to the Great Depression, conflicting external factors thus influenced Alabama's federal judicial process. The national economic transformation that began with the railroads and reached a climax during the Depression followed a parallel if somewhat distinctive course in Alabama. The state's federal judges were called on to decide between local and national exigencies. Social tensions associated with the collapse of Reconstruction and the rise of Democratic Party dominance generated further uncertainties reflected in the appointment of federal judges. The local institutional culture, affiliated more with an urban than rural market for legal services, however, provided a particular perspective from which to view these tensions. In either case, the constitutional separation of the federal courts combined with the degree of conflict facilitated independence and the exercise of discretion.

THE PARAMETERS OF LOCAL FEDERAL LEGAL CULTURE

External pressures were filtered through a local institutional culture centered on the federal courthouse. From Reconstruction to the New Deal, the federal courts increasingly applied national law. These laws created more cases to which the federal government was a party, a significant growth in criminal litigation, new conflicts over state and federal jurisdiction, and litigants who now included more women, members of the working class, and the poor. The continuing expansion of national law thus tested anew the limits of the federal court's independence. As a result, federal judges applied a practical conservative-activist jurisprudence.

The Growth of National Law and Alabama's Federal Courts

Alabama's federal judges applied the national law in stages. Banking legislation enacted during the Civil War established national standards, ameliorating the protectionism characteristic of the state's bank laws since the *Alabama Bank* cases of 1839. Passage of the Thirteenth, Fourteenth, and Fifteenth amendments and implementation of civil rights legislation shaped Alabama's experience with Reconstruction. Briefly it seemed that this constitutional revolution might at least make possible attainment of legal and political equality for the state's African Americans. But political exigencies involving the national political parties, the Supreme Court's reactionary treatment of civil rights, and the rise of such groups as the Ku Klux Klan killed such hopes, as the move to impeach Busteed symbolized. But the death of one promise opened up the possibility of fulfilling another. After 1875, the state's federal courts, although treating civil rights equivocally, used enlarged federal jurisdiction to balance the state's police power against a steady centralization of federal regulatory and criminal justice authority in the Interstate Commerce Act of 1887, the Sherman Antitrust Act of 1890, the Bankruptcy Act of 1898, the Progressives' legislative program, Prohibition, and the New Deal.

Expanded federal jurisdiction gave the state's federal judges more authority than ever. In 1867, because of Reconstruction and the struggle over the freedmen's rights, Congress extended diversity jurisdiction to cases where local prejudice reduced the chances of a fair trial. These cases were removable to federal court, where Busteed and Wood presided. In 1875, Congress enlarged the right of removability and the scope of diversity jurisdiction to the limits permitted by the general terms of the Constitution's Article III. The Supreme Court in 1877 construed this new law to include corporations, which opened the district courts of Bruce and Toulmin to considerable corporate litigation. At the same time, the Supreme Court began significantly extending the *Swift* doctrine into a more uniform federal common law. This growing "general law," combined with the removal process, favored corporations engaged in national business over state regulatory efforts. Periodically, Jones and his colleagues confronted the state's regulatory authorities.[43]

In 1891, Congress further transformed the judicial system. The Circuit Court of Appeals Act of 1891 ended the Supreme Court's circuit-riding duties that Woods and his antebellum predecessors John McKinley and John A. Campbell had endured. The law created a new intermediate appellate system—the circuit courts of appeals. It also altered the basis for appeal to the Supreme Court by increasing the Court's control of its own docket through an enlarged writ of certiorari. Under the new system, Alabama remained within the Fifth Circuit, to which Shelby and later McCord were appointed. Throughout the period, moreover, Bruce, Toulmin, and Grubb regularly did duty on the circuit as well.[44]

District and circuit judges continued to serve with each other under the Three-Judge Court Act of 1910. States disliked the ease with which lone federal judges in Alabama and elsewhere issued injunctions restraining state regulatory agencies. Supporters believed that corporations would have more difficulty convincing three judges of the need for an injunction. The law strained the federal court's limited resources, requiring circuit and district judges to make up each panel, over which the Supreme Court exercised direct review.[45]

The federal judiciary's enlarged authority extended the opportunity for "forum shopping." Since 1820, the state's federal courts provided nonresidents a forum more removed from local tensions. The removal legislation expanded this power to the constitutional limit, opening federal tribunals to corporations, the main form of national business. The new circuit court of appeals system strengthened the federal judiciary's regional character, which through Shelby, McCord, and the district judges Bruce, Toulmin, and Grubb enhanced the relative autonomy of the federal courts within Alabama. An especially important dimension of this autonomy was the power to remove suits from state to federal court. The Act of 1875 empowered either party to initiate a removal in diversity suits, even if one of the parties was not a resident of Alabama. The act sanctioned removal of any case posing an issue of federal law. These institutional factors encouraged forum shopping, whereby litigants, particularly corporations, could choose the state or federal forum, depending on which was most favorable to their interests.[46]

By the turn of the century, a second expansive phase occurred under the Progressives. Congress extended federal control over food, drugs, merchant seamen's working conditions, labor-management relations and rates in the railroad industry, farm credit, antitrust in the Clayton Act of 1914, and, perhaps most significantly, currency and credit through the new Federal Reserve System. Other important manifestations of congressional authority were Prohibition, the income tax, and child labor laws. To carry out these new responsibilities there was a concomitant expansion of federal executive power exercised through a growing bureaucracy and a corresponding increase of judicial responsibility. No one knew better the impact of all this on Alabama than the Northern District's judge, Henry D. Clayton. A member of Congress throughout the Progressive Era and chairman of the House Judiciary Committee that shaped the Clayton Antitrust Act, Clayton as a judge exercised jurisdiction over many of the laws he had voted on or helped to write.[47]

By 1900, moreover, federal judges had taken an increasingly activist stance. Through the due-process clause of the Fourteenth Amendment and other principles, tighter judicially imposed standards governed state authority.

82

Henry D. Clayton (1857–1929), judge of the Middle and Northern districts from 1914 to 1929; Democrat. *Alabama Department of Archives and History*

Jones fought a particularly protracted battle with Alabama's railroad commission. Yet the state's federal courts followed the Supreme Court's commerce clause and other decisions that generally upheld the bigger federal government the Progressives established. During the same period, Judge Jones supported the Justice Department's campaign against debt peonage, though in most other ways neither Alabama's federal judges nor the national government as a whole significantly challenged the triumph of the South's Jim Crow segregation system.[48]

During the 1920s, economic concerns remained dominant. After federal centralization ended following World War I, neither Progressive policies nor the Supreme Court significantly circumscribed the state's regulatory power, and parochialism persisted. The federal government's and the Supreme Court's continuing respect for federalism encouraged decentralization by sanctioning extensive (although by no means complete) state control over such vital areas as public utilities, bus and truck transportation, and pricing in retail stores. Whether the federal government or the Alabama Power Company should develop the power resources of Muscle Shoals was an ongoing controversy in Alabama politics and the United States Congress, where Senator Hugo Black fought for greater public control. During the same period, Prohibition and a campaign against the convict-lease and fee systems intertwined federal and state law enforcement. In other ways, too, federal criminal justice authority steadily increased. Meanwhile, defeat of the federal antilynch law meant that racial segregation remained seemingly impregnable.

In Alabama as elsewhere, the Great Depression transformed popular attitudes toward big government. Despite opposition from conservative Democrats, Alabamians overwhelmingly supported Roosevelt's New Deal liberalism. Aided by the state's influential Senators Black and John H. Bankhead, Jr., the production and prices of primary agricultural crops came under federal control with the Agricultural Adjustment Act. First through the National Recovery Administration (NRA), then by other means, industry and labor also were subject to greater centralized direction. With the Wagner Act of 1935 and the initiation of minimum wage and maximum hours standards in the Fair Labor Standards Act three years later, the federal government established a leading role in labor-management relations. Also beginning in 1935, Congress enacted the Social Security and Unemployment Compensation System, with both state and federal governments sharing responsibility for its administration. Of particular importance for north Alabama, the federal government promoted public utility regulation and conservation and reclamation activities with the Tennessee Valley Authority (TVA).[49]

Alabama's federal courts tested the constitutionality of TVA, the Social Security Act, and the NRA. Following the constitutional "revolution" of 1936–37, however, the Supreme Court increasingly deferred to the will of Congress regarding the New Deal's legitimacy. In a dramatic series of cases, the Court, including newly appointed Hugo Black, sustained a broad-ranging congressional authority over agriculture, labor-management relations, social welfare, and business. Thus Black helped to overturn the old constitutional principles his fellow Alabamians in the lower federal courts had tested. Even so, Black's role as the Fifth Circuit's presiding Supreme Court justice generally facilitated harmony throughout Alabama's federal courts.[50]

The decision of *Erie Railroad Co. v. Tompkins* (1938) ironically reflected greater federal influence. The Court held that in all cases but those presenting a federal or constitutional question, state law must govern federal judges, reversing the nearly century-old *Swift* doctrine. Yet the new rules of federal procedure, in conjunction with the federalization of so many areas formerly under state jurisdiction, broadly enlarged the lower federal court's power over state law. Forum shopping did not end; the procedural environment in which it existed merely became more complex, requiring Alabama's lawyers to increase their understanding of federal authority. Ultimately, the State Bar Association's respect for the leadership of such federal judges as Grubb was enhanced. The legal process and practice of Alabama's three federal district courts, said the association's spokesman, "take rank among the first in the United States." The state judiciary led by the Alabama Supreme Court, by contrast, was "not measuring up to its high estate." Even in cases involving racial injustice where federal judges did not fundamentally threaten the status quo, they at least showed greater respect for protecting individual rights than did their state counterparts.[51]

For more than twenty-five years, moreover, the Fifth Circuit relied extensively on the services of Alabama's William I. Grubb. The controversy facilitating Hundley's resignation resulted in Grubb's appointment in 1909 to the new north Alabama federal judgeship. Following the formation of the Circuit Court of Appeals in 1891, the Fifth Circuit lobbied periodically for additional judges, with infrequent success. Exacerbating the problem were poor health and other difficulties that at times prevented certain circuit judges from performing their duties. Thus, the circuit often called on district judge Grubb to serve in the appellate role. Indeed, one commentator observed that during Grubb's twenty-six-year tenure he "would continue to sit with the Court frequently enough that it is safe to venture the observation that he participated in more Court of Appeals decisions than some judges who were members of the Court."[52]

Grubb's service indicated larger issues involving the federal court's changing structure and function. As federal judges in Alabama and elsewhere increasingly became responsible for the enforcement of national legislation, their role as alternative forums to state courts gradually diminished. This did not mean that federal district judges lost touch with the state law, which before the Civil War was their main source of litigation. However, the institutional orientation of the district courts more than ever before raised questions involving federal procedure and administration. On the national level, such pressures fostered a move toward strengthened judicial self-government by removing the judiciary from the budget of the attorney general's office. At the same time, the financial and organizational administration of the federal judiciary slowly came under the Judicial Conference. Beginning in 1922, Chief Justice William Howard Taft had pushed for a more active conference. Grubb was one of the most influential district judges involved in this process. He was a member of a special committee charged with investigating the need for at-large federal judges to remedy onerous backlogs in certain federal courts. The effort was an important step in the development of the judiciary's self-government.[53]

Civil Rights issues associated with Reconstruction gave way to questions involving enlarged federal authority over criminal justice and regulation of the economy. At the same time, technical but nonetheless formidable institutional elements such as jurisdiction, forum shopping, and the administrative relationship between federal district and circuit courts and the federal and state judiciaries increased the autonomy of Alabama's federal judges. Thus the extension of national standards governing the subordinate status of the lower federal courts in the judicial system strengthened their use of discretion and independent judgment.

The Changing Patterns of Federal Litigation

Between 1876 and the 1930s, the growth of national law changed the state's federal market for legal services. The business of Alabama's federal district courts in 1876 reflected the course of future developments. The civil suits to which the federal government was a party included customs, tax (primarily excises on alcohol), post office, and miscellaneous. The numbers of these suits pending in the Southern, Middle, and Northern districts respectively were seven, thirteen, and eighteen. Yet the fines the government won in these districts were $16,213, $1,005, and $800. The differences in money settlements were due to the fact that the bulk of the cases in the Northern and Middle districts involved primarily poorer moonshiners and small post office offenses, whereas those in the Southern District concerned more financially significant customs. The civil suits to which the United States was *not* a party followed a different pattern, with forty cases commenced in the Southern District (of which fifteen were admiralty), fifty-nine in the Middle District, and only four in the Northern District. In criminal suits, the mix of cases commenced disproportionately favored the Northern District at 169, with the Middle and Southern districts having just 51 and 16 respectively.[54]

The outcomes in the civil and criminal cases to which the government was not a party suggested further differences among the three districts. In the criminal suits the amount of fines, forfeitures, and penalties were closer at $2,246; $1,950; and $2,800 in the Southern, Middle, and Northern districts. In the civil suits, however, the amount of judgments disproportionately favored plaintiffs in the Southern and Middle districts at $57,132 and $151,093 respectively, with the Northern District receiving just $2,371.[55]

The general patterns of 1876 indicated gradual change compared to the antebellum period. Before the Civil War, criminal cases took up an insignificant part of the federal court's docket; civil suits involving diversity jurisdiction constituted the bulk of the court's business. Also, suits to which the federal government was a party were few but financially significant. In 1876, by contrast, the number of criminal cases was significant, primarily because of the enforcement of Internal Revenue Service laws against north Alabama's moonshiners. Diversity civil suits continued to make up the bulk of Alabama's federal judicial business, and in such cases the Northern District had the least activity. The main change was that the Middle District had begun to rival the Southern District in the amount of litigation commenced. Accompanying this gradual growth of business was a moderate expansion in the size of Alabama's federal judicial establishment. The number of clerks, federal attorneys, and marshals remained the same between 1865 and 1876. The increase occurred in the special assistants and commissioners employed to aid in the enforcement of federal criminal and bankruptcy legislation. Prior to the Civil War, the court hired special assistants on an ad hoc basis. By 1876, there were seven special assistants employed in all three districts more or less continuously. Their work involved primarily the enforcement of criminal statutes, including the prosecution of counterfeiters. By 1885, there were ten, eight, and ten special assistants in the Southern, Middle, and Northern districts, respectively. In addition, for all three of the federal district courts there was a permanent registrar in bankruptcy to handle that ever-growing administrative load. Finally, the full cost for the operation of the districts was a comparatively moderate $81,000: Southern, about $14,000; Middle, $30,000; and Northern, $37,000.[56]

The dramatic increase in the number of criminal cases also altered the social composition of federal litigants. Prior to the Civil War, the great bulk of federal cases were civil suits arising under diversity jurisdiction out of some sort of business dispute between white males with at least some property. In 1876, by contrast, the growing criminal docket included laborers as the largest single group. In the entire nationwide federal judicial system, those arrested totaled 14,144; of these, 4,457 were laborers. The trades and callings of those in the next closest categories were servants, housekeepers, prostitutes, and "thieves" at 754, 644, 633, and 563 respectively. Thus, more than ever before, federal jurisdiction touched the lives of women, the working class, and society's underdogs.[57]

Persistence and change characterized the business of Alabama's federal courts by the 1930s. The mix of criminal and civil cases was reversed, with the latter overtaking the former in number; the overall numbers in each category also grew significantly. In 1938, the number of criminal cases pending in all three districts totaled 568. The Northern District led with 401, compared to 13 and 154 in the Middle and Southern districts respectively. During the preceding year the total number filed was 1,086, with the Northern District leading by nearly two to one. The total terminated cases was 964, resulting in 434 convictions.[58]

Compared to 1876, the proportion of civil cases declined, while the proportion of government to nongovernment cases also was reversed. In 1938, there were 331 pending government and 171 nongovernment civil cases. In each category the Northern District again handled by far the most litigation, with 274 filed and 206 terminated of government and 117 filed and 93 terminated of nongovernment litigation, compared to 99 filed and 74 terminated government cases and 73 filed and 88 terminated nongovernment cases for the Middle and Southern districts combined.[59]

The criminal cases resulted in high conviction rates. The disposition of defendants in criminal cases for all three districts totaled 1,759. Of these, 1,371 defendants were found guilty as charged, 147 were guilty in part, and 145 were not guilty or acquitted, while 43 cases were discontinued and 38 were quashed or dismissed. The result was unknown in 25. In each category the Northern District led, except in cases quashed or dismissed. In both the Middle and Southern districts there were 33 such cases, compared to the Northern District's 5. Yet in the Northern District, there were 98 not guilty outcomes and acquittals, compared to 37 in both other districts. Similarly, 117 partial guilty results occurred in the Northern District, but only 30 in the two others.[60]

Corresponding to the high conviction rates was growth of federal supervision of convicted defendants. Throughout most of the nineteenth century, few of Alabama's federal defendants received probation, reflecting the paucity of federal criminal cases. By 1938, however, the administrative function associated with more flexible sentencing standards significantly expanded the supervisory role of Alabama's federal courts. The number of convicted defendants receiving sentences in all three of the state's federal courts was 1,518. Of those, 402 were placed on probation, 133 received a fine, and in another 154 cases probation followed a term of imprisonment.[61]

Most defendants went to jail and served out their full sentence. The federal prison population continued to grow; the population of the federal prison camp in Montgomery increased by about 6 percent from 1937 to 1938 alone. Even so, the percentages of sentenced offenders receiving probation were 45.5, 51, and 34 percent in the Northern, Middle, and Southern districts respectively. Gender was a factor in some of these cases; 45 of those on probation in Alabama were women.[62]

The civil case load had changed notably, too. Although the proportion of government to nongovernment cases had reversed since 1876, with government litigation constituting the bulk, diversity cases continued to be common in the nongovernment category. Yet perhaps the most significant change involved the conspicuous growth in bankruptcy proceedings. To be sure, the year 1938 was near the end of the nation's worst depression. But the mid-1870s were depression years as well, so the disrupted market was not the only factor causing the increase. The 1867, 1898, and 1938 bankruptcy legislation established a national system under the jurisdiction of the federal judiciary. Until that system was in place, federal bankruptcy business continued to be more or less ad hoc. The Great Depression was perhaps the ultimate test of federal bankruptcy jurisdiction, and the system worked well enough to justify enlarged administrative functions requiring increased federal authority. In all three districts, the total number of bankruptcy cases concluded after a granting of petition was 1,907. Of these, the Northern District was most active by far, handing 1,633.[63]

The comparative cost of Alabama's judicial establishment was another measure of change. In 1876 the total was about $81,000; sixty-two years later it had risen to $339,056. Expenses for jurors and witnesses and salaries of court officials including clerks, marshals, commissioners, and district attorneys were common to both eras. The most obvious additional cost involved criminal justice administration, particularly the support of prisoners and the probation system, amounting to $23,546. The criminal docket also generated expenses for

89

the greater numbers of jurors required and the costs associated with arrest and prosecution.[64]

A comparison of the patterns of federal litigation in 1876 and 1938 suggests the changing market for legal services. Civil litigation increasingly involved the enforcement of national standards governing economic regulation over diversity cases requiring a determination of state law. Perhaps the most conspicuous change, however, was the growth of federal criminal justice litigation, which in turn brought women, workers, and the poor into federal court on a larger scale than ever before. The scope of these changes inevitably expanded the boundaries of judicial independence and discretion.

Conservative-Activist Jurisprudence and Judicial Discretion

This changing market for legal services called for a practical, working jurisprudence. Between the Civil War and the Great Depression, legal thought became increasingly refined. The flexible principles by which Alabama's federal judges had enlarged their discretionary power before 1860 gave way to a strict formalism characterized by the respect for technicality over substance. Formalism masked the degree to which judges "made law," such as antebellum courts working within natural law assumptions to establish new interpretations of statutes and the common law. By the turn of the century, Oliver Wendell Holmes, Jr., pioneered a jurisprudence that expressly recognized the lawmaking function of courts. Holmes's famous aphorism that the life of the law had been not logic but experience fostered the full-blown philosophies of sociological jurisprudence and legal realism. The former stated that judges should expressly accept social measures favorable to labor and other groups, deferring to the legislature. The legal realists went farther, assuming that virtually all judges decided cases in accord with their personal predilections.[65]

Alabama's federal judges reflected Holmes's basic insight. The state's mainstream legal culture adhered to the dominant formalism. Federal judges such as Jones and Clayton shared with fellow members of the State Bar Association a fundamental conservatism consistent with formalistic legal thought. At the same time, however, both the Bar Association and its members who were federal judges advocated certain limited reforms consistent with sociological jurisprudence and legal realism.[66]

In the annual Bar Association address of 1924, Clayton summed up what might be called conservative activism. Lawyers "cannot," he said, "consider the law as a fully developed science," but they must be "cognizant" that "it must grow and expand according to the needs of our civilization with its problems current and those yet to come." Yet in virtually the same breath

Clayton affirmed that the legal profession's "conservatism, [its] hesitancy to do or advocate radical or rash things constitute[d] a shining virtue." Nevertheless, this virtue could "lose some of its wholesomeness, as salt can lose its savor," when lawyers and courts so far practiced it "as to ignore needful changes demanded by new developments in the progress of our civilization so fraught with complex problems."[67]

Conservative activism was a commonsense jurisprudence reflecting the special place of Alabama's federal courts. As federal legislation increasingly competed with state law as a primary source of legal disputes, a more diverse market for legal services emerged. The transforming impact was such that a rigid attachment to formalism was difficult, especially in the context of Alabama's intricate pleading system. Clayton captured the difficulties when federal judges blindly bound themselves to formalism's dictates. Pleadings of "unnecessary length" were "drawn out, redundancies indulged, meticulous refinements set forth . . . at lengths . . . inexcusable and intended to create confusion, or to delay or prevent the consideration of the real merits of the case, traps [were] set for the lawyer not highly skilled in technicalities, and the busy judge . . . [did not] always discover the Senegambian hidden in the monstrous verbal woodpile."[68]

Clayton suggested that courts employ a trial process that enabled the fullest and fairest test of the issues raised by the parties to the suit. The adversarial process worked best when not obfuscated by intricate formalism. Accordingly, federal judges such as Clayton supported the State Bar Association's campaign to reform criminal and civil procedure. Congress and the state legislature had a role here, for the "application of common law principles" to "our growing society and our industrial life" was "sometimes best had by way of legislative enactments." Still, judges and the bar itself unavoidably had a leading role because the "people" were "not acquainted" with the procedural core of the legal process. Thus it was "incumbent" on the legal profession to ensure that the law "keeps pace with modern development so that court house business may be dispatched as speedily and as economically as possible."[69]

This mild reform depended significantly on the quality of lawyers. Again, Clayton adopted the agenda of the State Bar as the surest means of attaining the broader purpose of necessary but circumscribed change. Codes of legal ethics, which the Bar Association had advocated since its inception, had "tended greatly" to diminish "bad practices." As a result, the public had less reason than ever to complain that lawyers "stir up strife, originate litigation for selfish purposes, or are eager to prevent the amicable settlement of justiciable controversies." According to Clayton, the ambulance chaser was no longer conspicuous. Just as significant a threat to the quality of the profession, however, was that the "increasing number of lawyers will cause the law practice to become more or less competitive." The greater the competition, the harder it was to maintain adequate fees, which in turn encouraged some lawyers to undercut fixed rates and thereby foster perpetual instability. Such a competitive environment, moreover, facilitated sharp practices to the point of hindering effective legal process through formalism or, worse, corruption.[70]

The national government and the federal courts in particular served a special constitutional function. According to Clayton, the intent of the Constitution's framers was to "guarantee . . . individual liberty through the medium of constitutional limitation; limitations imposed on the majority." The system of checks and balances limited not only the three branches of the federal government but also the power of the states. In order for "justice" to "be attained and secured for the federated society and its components under our legal system," Congress enacted and the executive enforced "adequate laws to meet the exigencies constantly arising." Federal law and its implementation thus "harmonized" the nation's law, facilitating inevitable yet orderly change. The Supreme Court and the federal judiciary, moreover, further moderated this process of change as the "great stabilizing influence or force in government." Generally Clayton supported for federal judges a degree of discretionary authority commensurate with the power of the federal and state governments so that the former would always exercise sufficient check on the latter.[71]

This commonsense jurisprudence conceived of judicial discretion as working along a conservative-activist continuum. One end represented a resistance to change consistent with formalism. Amid the depths of the Great Depression, the federal circuit judge from Alabama, Leon McCord, articulated this sanguine faith in the status quo. Americans generally had "grown to believe that conditions which were ill could and would be changed by laws," he said. "The idea of right living, correct conduct, work and thrift have been driven from the stage while . . . [reform-minded] clowns played before the foot-lights and promised relief on the morrow which no law could ever bring to a harried and sorely tried people." As citizens forgot or ignored their duty to "obey the laws," crime "skirted our end and . . . headed for a touchdown." McCord relied on the deterrent effect of strictly enforced law, trusting that "right down at the bedrock" Alabamians and Americans generally were "sound," needing only sufficient education to ensure that the courts and other public officials preserved order. Faced with the "reformer" and "clap-trap politicians" with their "half-baked theories," the "only place left where we try to think through things" was the courthouse.[72]

Clayton's views favoring limited reform facilitating a more effective adversarial process represented the limits of activism. The people of Alabama and the nation "all demand that our substantive law keep up with the demands of this progressive age," he said.[73] It was essential, therefore, that the law "always" be "progressive, and . . . [the legal] profession should do its full part to seeing to it that the law in its practical application means justice." Even so, procedure was the "flower" and justice was the "fruit of jurisprudence." The public at large no less than the "avowed anarchist, with the red emblem pinned to his lapel" thus required the "benefit of a capable lawyer to defend" them. Reform reached its limit with the legal profession's "endeavors to bring about betterment in the administration of justice." As such efforts succeeded, the "laity" would attain "a just appreciation" of the "indispensable usefulness of lawyers." In this course of orderly change, moreover, the federal judiciary occupied a special place, exercising wise discretion over whether supporting or checking change was constitutionally proper.[74]

Finally, the legal education of Alabama's federal judges reinforced this practical jurisprudence. Prior to about 1900, most lawyers in Alabama and the nation as a whole learned law through self-study and apprenticeship. Formal instruction in law school was exceptional. By these standards, the state's earlier federal judges received quite good legal training. Busteed had no college education, relying entirely on individual study. Bruce, however, graduated from Franklin College in Ohio before following the traditional route to law practice in Iowa. Woods was a college graduate, receiving formal legal training at Western Reserve and Yale. Toulmin attended college and took a few law courses at the University of Virginia and Louisiana State University. Shelby studied law at Cumberland Law School in Lebanon, Tennessee. Ironically, Jones, who wrote the state's legal code of ethics provision that was later adopted by the American Bar Association, had no formal academic legal education.[75]

Each of Alabama's federal judges appointed after 1901 received a formal legal education. Hundley graduated from Marrietta College, Ohio, and then attended the law course at Vanderbilt University. Grubb graduated from Yale and took the law course of the University of Cincinnati. Clayton and Ervin combined self-study and practice before graduating from the law department of the University of Alabama. Murphree, too, was a graduate of the University of Alabama School of Law. Kennamer studied law at Georgetown. Walker received his undergraduate education at Washington and Lee and Princeton before attending Columbia University Law School. McCord graduated from Vanderbilt Law School. Davis earned his LL.B. at Yale University.[76]

The extent of formal legal education among Alabama's federal judges reflected opportunities resulting from social class rather than the profound influence of any particular jurisprudential theory. Each of these men came from a solid middle-class background, and some were quite prominent. For such people a college education and academic legal study were the norm. Even so, little if any evidence suggests that these men acquired a deep attachment to a particular school of jurisprudence. Instead, through academic legal study they mastered the basic legal institutions and modes of doctrinal theory, which they sharpened through professional practice in court and, as was true of most, work as public officials. Lifetime experiences combined with the realities of lawyering within a comparatively specialized courtroom culture shaped their practical, conservative-activist jurisprudence. Within broad limits this jurisprudence facilitated the federal courts' exercise of judicial discretion and reinforced their institutional autonomy.

RECONSTRUCTION AND NEW PATTERNS OF ROUTINE LITIGATION

Reconstruction influenced the course of routine litigation long after the Republicans retreated in 1877. In persistent confrontations over voting rights, Woods, Busteed, and Bruce initially tried to ensure that blacks possessed equal rights. But by 1883, in a decision written, ironically, by Associate Justice Woods, the Supreme Court undercut such efforts. Nevertheless, Alabama's federal courts continued to use discretion over procedure and statutory or constitutional interpretation to protect individual rights in cases involving other minorities and women. The nature of routine litigation changed in other ways. Before the Civil War, routine suits generally required federal judges to apply state law in property or commercial contract cases arising under diversity jurisdiction. From Reconstruction on, the proportion of these cases declined as the number of suits involving the application of federal criminal and civil statutory provisions rose. Meanwhile, Busteed's failure to meet the demands of the local legal culture resulted in his resignation. Notwithstanding periodic conflicts with local officials, Alabama's other federal judges handled the new pattern of routine litigation effectively enough to maintain the support of the small but influential legal community they served.

Reconstruction and Busteed's Resignation

Alabama's federal judges worked within narrow limits to decide issues involving the voting rights of blacks. During Reconstruction, blacks took a conciliatory position toward whites who adamantly opposed equal rights. "I have no desire to take away any of the rights of the white man," said a black delegate to the state's constitutional convention of 1867. "All I want is equal rights in the courthouse and equal rights when I go to vote."[77] The white Democratic establishment, however, was unyielding. It "must be understood that, politically and socially, ours is a white man's government," exclaimed Alabama's Robert M. Patton. "In the future, as in the past, the state affairs of Alabama must be guided and controlled by the superior intelligence of the white man."[78]

During and after Reconstruction, the response of federal authorities was equivocal. Republicans framed the Fifteenth Amendment not expressly to grant the right to vote but merely to forbid its deprivation for reasons of race. Southerners proved themselves adept at disfranchising black voters without express proof that race was the cause. The Supreme Court supported this narrow construction in *U.S. v. Reese* (1876), declaring unconstitutional provisions of the Enforcement Act of 1870 that provided penalties for interfering with any person voting in state elections.[79] The next year, U.S. Attorney General Charles Devens told Alabama's Senator John T. Morgan that federal attorneys were being "instructed to prosecute only important cases, where guilt is clear and the evidence overwhelming, and in such prosecutions to act without bias in favor of or against any political party."[80] As a result, the Court established enforcement standards in federal elections that did not require unqualified proof of racial discrimination.[81]

Within these limits, federal judges from Alabama defended their own judicial power in voting rights cases. In connection with a federal suit during the congressional election of 1878 in the Middle District of Selma, public officials indicted and imprisoned the district's federal attorney and marshal for seizing "ballot-boxes, poll-lists, ballots, inspectors' certificates, inspectors' returns, tally-sheets, statements, and all other papers pertaining" to the election. The two federal agents petitioned the federal court for a writ of habeas corpus. Presiding on the federal circuit court, Woods had to decide whether to grant the writ. After demonstrating that the two federal officials had acted formally as the agents of the federal court, Woods declared that it was "unwarranted in law, and grossly disrespectful to the [federal] circuit court, to invoke the interposition of the state court." The action was of "vital importance," touching the "very foundation of the powers and jurisdiction of the federal courts." Woods granted the petition ordering the discharge of the two men.[82]

In a jury charge involving another voting rights case, Bruce also maintained the court's power. During the congressional election of 1880 in Madison County of north Alabama, Democrat Joseph Wheeler received 142 votes to Republican William M. Lowe's 54. Enough irregularities existed,

Justice Department authorities believed, to bring criminal charges against poll officials for failure to prevent ballot boxes from being stuffed. More than a year elapsed before the trial took place, leaving an ambiguous trail of evidence. In his charge to the jury, Bruce was scrupulously balanced. *Negligence, intent, obligations, false certification, duty* were the terms of the law's criminal sanctions requiring interpretation, and Bruce was rigorously neutral in explaining to the jury the meaning of each one. "An official is bound to use that care and diligence in the discharge of his duties that a conscientious and prudent man, acting under a just sense of his obligation, would exercise under the circumstances of a particular case," Bruce concluded. "Gentlemen of the jury, judge the conduct of these officers by that rule and by it, as you find the facts, acquit or convict them of fraudulently making a false certificate of the result of the election in question."[83]

Even so, the new criminal authority the Congress conferred raised difficult issues of interpretation. Until the Fourteenth Amendment became law, matters pertaining to citizenship—including most criminal violations—were left to the states. In principle, the federal citizenship established by the Fourteenth Amendment superseded the authority associated with state citizenship. How far the amendment created a conflict between state and federal power to determine criminal conduct, however, was unclear. Particularly difficult were issues involving the action of individuals who banded together to prevent others from carrying out their rights of citizenship. The fundamental question was: Did the Fourteenth Amendment protect rights of citizenship from vigilante groups such as the Ku Klux Klan?

Woods revealed that the answers to this question could not escape a certain formalism. In 1871, the Justice Department prosecuted under the Voting Rights Enforcement Act John Hall, William Pettigrew, and others for interfering with the "freedom of speech" of Charles Hays and William Miller. The confrontation grew out of South Alabama Democrats' struggle to dispute the voting rights of the freedmen and their Republican allies. But unlike the cases involving Woods's granting of the habeas writ or Bruce's jury charge, the defendants in the *Hall* case were not state agents. Thus Woods and Busteed sitting as a circuit court were called on to determine whether the Fourteenth Amendment protected the free speech of Hays and Miller from private intimidation as opposed to the action of state officials. The court conceded that the First Amendment's guarantee of freedom of speech applied only to Congress, not the states. The Court declared, however, that free speech and indeed all of the first eight of the Bill of Rights were nonetheless fundamental rights of citizenship protected under the privileges and immunities clause of the Fourteenth Amendment. Congress, therefore, could enact laws punishing the private action of Hall and his cohorts and the court would enforce them.[84]

The Supreme Court, however, gradually gutted the Fourteenth Amendment's civil rights protection and Woods eventually followed precedent in *U.S. v. Harris*. Beginning in the *Slaughterhouse* cases of 1873, the Court provided a narrow interpretation of the rights protected from state action.[85] The next year, Justice Joseph P. Bradley, sitting on circuit in a Louisiana case whose facts were similar to those in *Hall*, nonetheless rejected Woods's application of the privileges and immunities clause to private action.[86] In 1877, Congress ended Reconstruction and in *Reese* and other cases the Court established constitutional interpretations that made civil rights guarantees hollow. Woods was on the Supreme Court when it decided *Harris* in 1883. The specific issue was whether the equal protection clause prevented vigilante-like private action, and Woods's decision stated that no provision of the Fourteenth Amendment did so. Thus he broadly repudiated the opposite principle Alabama's federal courts had upheld twelve years earlier.[87]

Busteed's most important constitutional decision favored Alabama's lawyers. The Federal Test Oath Act of 1865 required lawyers seeking to practice in federal court to swear that they had "never borne arms against the United States or furnished aid or encouragement to their enemies." With this law the Republicans hoped to restrict the opportunity of former Confederates and their sympathizers. The law also benefited pro-Unionists working in the same trades or professions as those stigmatized as disloyal.[88] If Busteed was as dedicated a carpetbagger as his opponents claimed, he should have upheld the Test Oath Act during December 1865, when a number of attorneys sought admittance to practice at the federal bar without taking the oath. Busteed, however, declared the law unconstitutional.[89]

His decision was wide-ranging, drawing on various legal, philosophical, and historical sources. The basic constitutional grounds were that the oath violated the due process of law and prohibitions against bills of attainder and ex post facto laws. Busteed's reasons anticipated those of the Supreme Court's decisions striking down the oath two years later. Still, Busteed suggested the influence of personal motivation in his opinion. He pointed out that a British subject who had taken the oath of naturalization to become a citizen of the United States would nonetheless technically be subject to the test oath. Prior to naturalization, the British subject would have been giving "aid and comfort" to a former enemy of the United States. Busteed noted particularly that the law was not "confined to any period," but "cover[ed] the lifetime" of a naturalized citizen. The judge himself, of course, was born in Ireland and was therefore a former British subject. Busteed thus had a personal interest in striking down the law, which explains why he decided in favor of those who attacked him as a carpetbagger.[90]

Busteed's decisions in other fields did not justify impeachment. His admiralty opinions followed the same accepted principles as the decisions of Alabama's other federal judges, including the Democrat Toulmin.[91] In bankruptcy cases, the largest single category of cases, he upheld enlarged federal power, but Alabama's debtors and creditors alike generally favored such power because of the dislocation caused by the Civil War. Busteed's bankruptcy opinions, moreover, were indistinguishable from those of Woods decided during the same time and from the decisions of Busteed's successor, Bruce.[92] Also, in the cases involving black civil rights Busteed generally decided the same way as Woods.[93] Yet lawyers practicing in federal court did not resist Woods and Bruce as they did Busteed.[94] Finally, critics attacked Busteed's railroad finance decision, which favored the interests of another political faction *within* the state.[95]

These considerations suggested why the attack on Busteed at first failed. The criticism directed against the judge followed the lines of the struggle for control of Alabama between Republicans and Democrats during Reconstruction. Yet the state's general repudiation of carpetbaggers in and of itself was not enough to explain Busteed's case, since neither Woods nor Bruce was subject to the same abuse. Similarly, Busteed's civil rights decisions followed the same principles as those of his Republican contemporary and successor, neither of whom suffered the opposition Busteed did, while his decisions in the field of economic rights benefited significant groups within Alabama's business order. Finally, the judge's test oath decision actually benefited lawyers, the very group that eventually undermined his position to the point that he resigned.

The lawyers succeeded because of what Busteed failed to do. An attack directed at Busteed's decisions was unlikely to succeed because he was a competent judge. The decisions themselves, moreover, benefited not only the Republicans but also influential groups of Alabamians. Busteed's problem was that he neglected the courtroom culture that reinforced the federal court's authority within the state. The decisions favored many of the clients of the small but generally prominent bar that argued before the court. Busteed's long absences from the state, however, undercut the institutional linkages between the federal court and this wider legal culture. Busteed's repudiation of these formal and informal institutional realities provided a basis for objection that even congressional Republicans, concerned as they were about secure property rights and due process, could readily accept, creating the grounds for the judge's resignation.

Other Minorities and Women

The federal courts' strict solicitude for procedure nonetheless also favored individual rights after Reconstruction. In *U.S. v. Long Hop* (1892), the government sought under Chinese exclusion laws to expel a Chinese national who had resided in New Orleans and Mobile for some years. The procedure governing the government's authority was not well defined, leaving much to the discretion of the local federal magistrate. In Long Hop's case, a New Orleans federal magistrate attempted to exercise jurisdiction in Mobile. The jurisdictional conflict unsettled Alabama's judge Toulmin, who construed the exclusion laws "liberally" to undercut the validity of the magistrate's action. Following precedents established in other lower federal courts, Toulmin declared that the evidence did not support the magistrate. He ordered Long Hop's release from federal custody and sanctioned his continued residence in the United States.[96]

Toulmin showed how far this procedural formalism extended in *U.S. v. Zes Cloya* (1888). Zes Cloya was an Apache Indian captured with Geronimo. Imprisoned on a U.S. military reservation in Mobile County, he escaped, taking with him an eleven-year-old Indian girl. The federal troops who recaptured the Indian found that he had "cruelly treated" the child and "forcibly had sexual intercourse with her." No federal law applied directly to the facts, so the federal government prosecuted Zes Cloya under a law forbidding abduction for purposes of prostitution or concubinage. Toulmin charged the members of the jury that it must apply the law, "discard[ing] . . . any feeling of indignation, prejudice, or passion which his conduct or acts towards the unfortunate girl might excite in [their] bosoms." The jury should try the case, Toulmin concluded, as "that of any other man, and give him the same consideration regardless of his race, color, or condition in life." Notwithstanding the brutality of the defendant's actions, they clearly were to "gratify" his own "lawless lust" and therefore were not within the statute's meaning. Following Toulmin's instructions, the jury acquitted.[97]

Where the facts were less dramatic, Toulmin continued to resist a loose interpretation of federal criminal statutes. In 1892, Congress passed a law generally making it a misdemeanor for anyone employed in the "public works of the United States" to labor for more than eight hours a day. The U.S. Corps of Engineers hired a private Mobile firm to construct certain barges. The work was subject to federal inspection but was not otherwise under government control. The firm's employees labored for nine hours or more a day, whereupon the government sued, charging violation of the eight-hour law. The issue was whether federal funding of a project built by a private firm was a "public work" within the meaning of the statute. Toulmin decided that the eight-hour law did not "apply to the case of a man who, entirely at his own risk and cost, although under government inspection, builds barges which United States engineers agreed to purchase."[98]

Admiralty

Admiralty law involved two broad categories of issues. The first was whether the court should exercise the jurisdiction at all, leaving the matter instead to state juries; the second general question was, once jurisdiction was established, how far the court should go in applying or developing substantive rules. Prior to the Civil War, Alabama's federal judges were reluctant to expand the jurisdiction to include cases arising on inland waterways, as opposed to those within the tide's ebb and flow. On this point the Supreme Court reversed them in significant decisions. In cases involving the second category, however, the state's federal judges not only claimed but succeeded in exercising greater discretionary authority.

This pattern continued after the Civil War within the context of expanded admiralty power imposed by Congress. In *U.S. v. King* (1885), the federal government sued an agent of a steamboat that plied the predominantly inland waters of the Mobile and Alabama rivers between Mobile and Montgomery. The government charged that the agent's recruitment of steamboat deckhands violated the Dingley Act of 1884, which regulated the negotiation of wages between a vessel's agent and the crewmen. The issue was whether the statute applied to steamboats navigating primarily inland waterways. Judge Bruce noted that the statute's language was "broad and sweeping," permitting a liberal construction favorable to the government. Following contrary authorities, he nonetheless applied a narrow construction to decide against the government.[99]

Where substantive rather than jurisdictional issues arose, however, Alabama's federal courts exercised discretion, extending their authority. An injured seaman employed on a tugboat working within the tide's ebb and flow sought damages, charging negligence. Toulmin acknowledged that the precedents governing the case were mixed, whereupon he denied an award of damages. Nevertheless, he declared that admiralty could require the seaman "to be healed at the expense of the ship, even after the voyage has terminated, and the seaman is discharged."[100]

Harry Toulmin (1838–1916), Southern District judge from 1886 to 1916; Democrat.
Robin Holeb-Ableman, U.S. District Court, Southern District of Alabama

Busteed displayed the same willingness to apply discretionary judgment in a more unusual case involving a riverboat gambler. The gambler and a confederate employed a scam to relieve an eighteen-year-old boy of $750. The youth's mother sued the boat's captain in admiralty, arguing that because his agent was aware of the gambler's reputation, the captain was liable for the loss to her. Whether the admiralty court had jurisdiction was a question that Busteed answered in the affirmative. The judge's treatment of the merits revealed clearly the motives governing his use of discretionary authority. A basic principle of maritime law was that a vessel's captain owed women and minors "as a matter of right" the fullest protection. Did that right extend, however, to a youth who lost his money because of a gambler's scam? More specifically, should the admiralty court make the captain liable for the $750 because he allowed the gambler to ply his trade with a minor? "The enlightened judgment of mankind ... stigmatize[d] gambling as a most pernicious vice," Busteed declared. "Every Christian code denounces it as a crime, and punishes it as such. A common gambler is a common nuisance. Insensible to honor, deaf to pity, and bent on plunder, he is a human cormorant, more detestable than the bird of prey itself." Busteed affirmed the captain's negligence and obligation to pay, therefore, because it was the "clear duty of the managers ... of public conveyances to save the traveling community from contact with them."[101]

Tax

Increased prosecutions under the continuously expanding federal tax code also tested the federal court's discretionary authority. Recalling the protectionist policy the Supreme Court had confronted in the *Alabama Bank* cases of 1839, Alabama's bankers challenged the constitutionality of a 10 percent tax Congress imposed in the National Banking Act. The Federal Circuit Court for the Southern District held that the "constitutional right" to pass such a tax "scarcely admit[ted] of question at this day." Congress, therefore, had "a right to protect ... [the nation's] currency, and by so doing, protect the people from a vicious and unsound currency."[102] A more routine, though in terms of income no less significant, issue involved taxing the production, sale, and distribution of liquor. The famous Whiskey Rebellion of the 1790s dramatized congressional power to enact taxes on and license requirements for the production and sale of "distilled spirits" and tobacco. Even so, after 1800 Congress again passed such measures only temporarily during the War of 1812 and then the Civil War. After Appomattox, however, Congress kept the laws in force; between 1870 and 1893 they accounted for over one-third of the federal revenue.[103]

In Alabama, those seeking to avoid criminal penalties under the liquor law raised various procedural issues. One such case required Toulmin to consider a motion to set aside the jury's conviction of a retail dealer selling "malt liquors" without a license because the law referred generally to distilled spirits but not particularly to malt liquors. Consistent with formalistic jurisprudential principles, Toulmin said that initially he was prepared to decide in favor of the retailer. After the government presented elaborate evidence showing how the production of malts involved the distillation process, however, he changed his mind and denied the motion.[104]

In another case, Woods reviewed the provisions of the tax laws applying to tobacco sales. The issue was whether the law's provisions controlling the presentation of evidence to sustain an indictment permitted a certain exemption. Woods decided against the defendant. Where the evidence otherwise proved that a tobacco retailer had not paid the tax, Woods said, the law raised the "presumption of guilty intent." Interpreting the exemption provision to overthrow this presumption would be to "exculpate" the accused on the basis of his "unsworn declarations made in his own favor after the offense was committed."[105]

The stakes rose considerably in cases involving moonshiners. Although the illegal production and sale of alcoholic beverages occurred throughout the state, counties in poverty-stricken north Alabama were the most active. Fruit products and corn were bulky and difficult to transport in the mountainous region; especially during a glutted market it was easier to convert this produce "into a compact and imperishable product by the distillers art."[106] It was more profitable, too. A wagon loaded with corn might bring $10, whereas the same wagon loaded with moonshine (which took twice as much corn to make) could net $150 or more. A glut would destroy the market for produce, but according to a U.S. attorney, there was "always a market for moonshine."[107] The poverty and isolation of the area combined with the pervasive demand engendered for moonshiners widespread community support, which often included local law enforcement officials.

These factors fostered resistance to federal prosecution. The federal court of the Northern District sitting in Birmingham and Huntsville heard far more of these cases than its counterpart in the Middle and Southern districts. In addition, jurors in the federal court came from a wider area than those in state courts, which made it easier to avoid counties where popular sympathies supported the moonshiners. Even so, successful prosecution depended on various evidentiary issues over which the federal judges had considerable discretion. The high conviction rates indicated how readily the Northern District's federal judges used this discretion to uphold federal law. Usually the facts of the cases were routine. Federal prosecutions, moreover, usually sought indictments on grounds involving retailing because proof was less difficult.[108]

Although federal prosecutors usually faced considerable danger in moonshine cases, there was rarely unified resistance. In 1893, in the northeast Alabama counties of Cleburne and Cherokee, however, opposition briefly coalesced in the form of vigilante attacks. Organized groups of moonshiners beat and seriously injured members of families in each county who had served as informers for federal agents. In neither county were any criminal actions brought in state court so federal officials hit on a novel strategy to prosecute in federal court. Unlike the routine tax evasion litigation, these cases involved assault and battery, issues ordinarily within state jurisdiction. To get the cases before the federal court in Birmingham, therefore, U.S. Attorney (and future governor) Emmet O'Neal decided to charge the vigilantes with conspiracy to violate the rights of individuals testifying in federal trials. The cases received press coverage throughout Alabama and drew the attention of Governor Thomas G. Jones.

The two cases had different results. In the Cleburne trial, the defense counsel for the vigilantes were prominent Birmingham lawyers, including former governor William H. Smith. Seeking to undermine federal jurisdiction, they argued that the violence was not the result of a conspiracy. U.S. Attorney O'Neal played on the jury's sympathies for a female victim who hobbled to the witness stand because the assault had resulted in amputation of her leg. On the basis of the conspiracy theory, the jury took only twenty minutes to find a guilty verdict. The court sentenced six men to serve six years in the federal prison at Stillwater, Minnesota, and levied fines of $500. O'Neal's task was more difficult in the Cherokee County moonshiner case because local law enforcement officials attempted to undermine the conspiracy argument by providing evidence favorable to the defendants. Nevertheless, the jury declared a guilty verdict. The court imposed four year prison terms and $500 fines on thirteen men. The defendants avoided the sentences, however, when the U.S. Supreme Court overturned the verdicts on a technical point that did not pertain directly to the conspiracy theory.[109]

State Law

Although the proportion of cases involving the application of state law was declining, such suits nonetheless remained important. Prior to the Civil War, Alabama's federal courts followed the principle established in *Swift v. Tyson* to decide the interpretation of state statues or whether state decisions bound federal judges at all.[110] Following Appomattox, in commercial contract litigation the federal courts exercised considerable discretion to create a general commercial law. In property cases these same courts usually followed state law, while asserting an independent judgment as to the appropriate construction of a statute governing property rights. Finally, in a family law case the court refused to intervene in state process favoring an estranged wife.

After the Civil War, Alabama's federal judges continued to apply the *Swift* doctrine, especially in corporate litigation. A corporation charged a Mobile resident with embezzlement. When a grand jury found no evidence supporting the charge, the resident sued the corporation in Bruce's district court, alleging malicious prosecution. The corporation raised the defense that it was not liable because a corporation as an artificial entity was "incapable of malice." There were certain Alabama court opinions supporting this principle, though others could be read to deny it. Bruce conceded that there was "some conflict of authority, but the tendency of judicial opinion" was "clearly marked" favoring corporate liability. The question involved, moreover, "no state statute or constitutional provision," but was "a general principle of law, in the solution of which" federal courts were "not bound by the decisions" of the state's supreme court. Finally, "really and practically" a corporation's "mind" was its management, who "controll[ed] . . . these great engines of power in society and government" and were capable of "sometimes us[ing] their power for improper or even malicious purposes." The corporation, therefore, lost.[111]

Meanwhile, the federal courts followed the Alabama Supreme Court's decisions in private property suits. The issue arose whether under Alabama's married woman's property act a wife's separate estate could be mortgaged to cover her husband's debt. Although the state supreme court's precedents were conflicting, Woods followed the most recent decision, holding that the mortgage was invalid. The U.S. Supreme Court affirmed the decision.[112] Similarly, in another case the state legislature changed the equity rules governing fraudulent property conveyances. Bruce held that when a state statute established a right that did not "conflict" with federal law or the constitution, federal courts "sitting in such states, can and must enforce such right in cases in which such courts have jurisdiction."[113]

Federal courts exercised greater discretion in cases involving local governments' finance of railroads. Before the Civil War, the Alabama legislature, responding to community enthusiasm for development and pressure from real estate promoters, passed laws giving municipal governments the authority to float bonds in order to attract railroads. By Reconstruction, however, many of these schemes had collapsed, forcing the municipalities either to default or raise taxes. Many of the creditors had in fact purchased the bonds as speculative investments, while others had been involved in fraud. These considerations nonetheless did not prevent numerous suits demanding tax levies by local governments to pay the bondholders. During the 1870s and 1880s, state officials and courts followed the dominant public opinion opposing such taxation. Predictably, the creditors turned to the federal courts.[114]

Generally, Alabama's federal judges exercised their discretionary authority in favor of the creditors. A creditor sued in the federal court for the Middle District and won a $13,722 judgment against Lee County. Local officials refused to levy the taxes required to pay the judgment and got from the state court an injunction blocking the creditor's recovery. The creditor then asked Woods for a writ of mandamus to compel collection of the tax. Woods issued the writ, rejecting an interpretation of the U.S. Supreme Court's precedents that would have favored the county.[115] A more complicated case arose in Mobile, where the city won from the legislature measures that permitted the use of tax revenues for purposes other than payment of the bondholders, even though their debts existed prior to the obligations the city wanted to pay. Again, however, Woods upheld the bondholders and compelled compliance with a writ of mandamus.[116] In 1882, a bondholder sought a mandamus to compel Selma's levy of a tax. The city attempted to use another change in the law to prevent compliance, but the court once more decided in the creditor's favor.[117]

An unusual case arose in Montgomery, and this time the city won. The legislature granted the town council the power to hold an election to decide whether to extend a debt bond for ten years. The law included a novel proviso requiring a majority of the city's real estate owners to vote in favor of the extension. The real estate owners voted against the extension 105 to 57. The city council nonetheless passed a resolution asserting the principle that the "just and honorable" course was to make "some provision . . . for . . . payment." Notwithstanding the realtors' vote, a creditor sued seeking an order to enforce the council's resolution. The federal court reluctantly decided that the specific provisions of the law that gave a majority of the realtors their power defeated the creditor's claim.[118]

Toulmin's formalistic regard for process had an ambivalent outcome in *Ex parte Murray*. John Murray was a U.S. customs officer found guilty by a state court of abandoning his wife. The state chancery judge ordered Murray to pay alimony. Murray absconded but was arrested and jailed under the appropriate state laws. Murray petitioned the federal court for a writ of habeas corpus.

He argued a novel interpretation of a federal law that subjected to fine and imprisonment anyone who interfered with customs officials carrying out their duty. Murray contended that the state authorities' implementation of state law violated the federal statute. Toulmin rejected the claim, holding that the federal law applied only to those interfering with custom officials who were carrying out their official duties. "Such is not the case with the sheriff here," declared Toulmin. "He was acting under [the state's] legal process,—at least process which issued from a court, and regular on its face." Thus Toulmin's regard for state process kept John Murray in jail until he paid what was due his estranged wife.[119]

Further Changes and Interpretation

Until the Court's dramatic reversal of nearly a century of precedent in *Erie RR v. Tompkins* (1938), the removal of diversity cases from state to federal courts was so routine that forum shopping, especially by corporations, was regarded as virtually inevitable.[120] Prohibition raised further difficult questions.[121] In addition, the federal court's jurisdiction over bankruptcy grew steadily following Reconstruction, and the Northern District located in Birmingham was rated as among the nation's leaders, especially during the Great Depression.[122]

In 1925, the Supreme Court addressed the issues involving bankruptcy. Henry Lewis, an illiterate, indigent convict working under the lease system, was seriously injured in a mining accident because of the company's negligence. A jury in the state court awarded Lewis $4,000 damages, but before paying the company filed for bankruptcy. In order to win recovery, Hugo Black removed the case to federal court, arguing for Lewis's claim against the company's estate under federal bankruptcy law. The federal court in Birmingham decided against Lewis because he was an indigent. Black appealed to the Supreme Court, which unanimously reversed the lower tribunal.[123]

Prohibition transformed the federal court's criminal enforcement role. Poorer moonshiners and large-city brewers had traditionally run afoul of the federal criminal code for failure to pay taxes. Under Prohibition, federal cases saw a wealthier and more socially prominent class of litigants. For example, Mobile, the state's leading port and a city with a large Catholic population and strong Latin traditions, was an illegal liquor center. In 1923, federal authorities indicted 117 leading Mobilians for violation of national Prohibition laws, including the chief of police, a county commissioner, and a wealthy businessman who eventually represented the city in the U.S. Congress. Republican U.S. Attorney General Harlan Fiske Stone appointed Hugo Black special prosecutor in the case. After months of proceedings—reported daily as front page news across the state—the police chief and several others were convicted.[124]

Reconstruction shaped the course of routine litigation. The expansion of the federal criminal and civil code, which began for purposes of defending the freedman, accelerated despite the government's and the Supreme Court's retreat from that original purpose. Similarly, the extension of diversity jurisdiction, the right of removal, the writ of habeas corpus, and the writ of mandamus strengthened the federal judiciary's autonomy. The gradual yet steady growth in the proportion of federal as compared to state legal issues reflected the growing specialization in urban law practices, especially the division between defense and plaintiffs' bar. The nature of litigants changed, too. More than ever before, the parties to suits included corporations, workers, women, the poor, and the dispossessed. Thus new federal laws potentially enlarged the opportunities for the Supreme Court's review of the decisions of Alabama's federal courts. But the greater scope of appellate review had less impact than the exercise of discretion arising from those same laws.

This dependence and discretion operated within limits. In voting rights and to a lesser extent the municipal bond litigation, Woods, Bruce, and Busteed decided cases in ways that arguably were consistent with the Republican's original Reconstruction purposes. Once Congress and the Court embraced the Compromise of 1877, however, Alabama's federal judges had little choice but to follow suit. Similarly, in the bond cases they adhered to the Court's procreditor policy. Sooner or later in the cases arising directly out of Reconstruction, dependence prevailed over discretion.

In cases involving women and minorities, the issues did not have national political implications, and the lower federal courts, left more to themselves, exercised discretion to restrict the government in favor of individual rights. In business cases involving the application of the *Swift* doctrine or state law, the use of discretion again was the norm. The federal courts also employed a liberal discretionary judgment to vigorously enforce the liquor taxes and Prohibition. Finally, in admiralty and bankruptcy suits, they followed the traditional pattern of Alabama federal cases.

The disparity in outcomes was a result of the interaction between external and local factors. Voting rights and municipal bonds were issues of direct significance to the national policy of Reconstruction, issues, in other words, that touched the ideological exigencies central to the Republican Party. Thus it was possible to establish a causal connection between the decisions of Woods, Bruce, and Busteed in these areas and Reconstruction. Move from the exceptional realm of Reconstruction to routine litigation, however, and this causal connection weakens. The Democrat Toulmin no less than Woods and Bruce displayed a willingness to limit the government's criminal authority in favor of minorities or women. Regarding bankruptcy, Prohibition, moonshiners, state law and *Swift*, and admiralty, the pattern of Toulmin's decisions was like that of the Republicans. Significantly, this was especially true of the much maligned Busteed. Busteed was forced to resign not so much because of his pro-Reconstruction decisions but because he failed to serve effectively the local bar that brought routine litigation before him.

The closest and most persistent influence on routine litigation was the local legal culture. As federal gradually supplanted state legal issues from Reconstruction to the New Deal, the actual form in which disputes arose in federal court was a lawsuit involving local parties. The lawyers representing these clients, including the federal attorneys, were members of the local bar. Except for Busteed, moreover, each of Alabama's federal judges had been an active and respected member of that same bar before occupying the bench. In addition, the specialization of federal practice meant that this legal community was small. As late as 1930, only eighty-eight attorneys were admitted to practice in the federal court's Northern District, the state's most populous region that included Birmingham.[125] The backgrounds of the practicing federal lawyers, like the judges themselves, were also generally urban, in an environment that remained predominantly rural up to 1940. A further element facilitating cultural coherence was that most of these lawyers, again like the judges, shared in varying degree the professional values of the Alabama State Bar Association.

The State Bar Association's policy agenda suggested the values that gave further coherence to the federal courtroom culture. Except for the three appointees having direct connection to Reconstruction, most of Alabama's federal judges were Bar Association members, including especially Toulmin, Jones, Grubb, and Clayton. Between these four and the Bar Association, moreover, there were sufficient interchanges to indicate a coincidence of values. The association, for instance, lauded Grubb's innovative uses of equity procedure.

Jones and Clayton elaborated on the content and scope of these and other policies. Overall the association's agenda supported a degree of judicial independence and discretionary judgment that was basically conservative-activist. Taken as a whole, these values were consistent with the more specialized market for legal services represented by the federal courts. Indeed, in the association's championing of greater professionalization of judges, juries, and the bar, the federal courts represented the preferred comparative standard.

The values that the small federal bench and bar shared influenced the court's decision making. These values demanded a high level of professionalism, technical expertise, and doctrinal clarity, which in turn required greater judicial independence and more informed discretionary judgment than were true of Alabama's state courts. To a certain extent this meant that federal courts approached the local issues involving both national and state law from a jurisprudential perspective that transcended mere formalism. For the federal adversarial process to represent fairly the growing categories of routine litigation, some activism was necessary. At the same time, this activism was unlikely to transcend the essentially conservative legal experience of the predominantly urban bar that made up both the State Bar Association and the federal bench. Thus, conservative activism supported sufficient judicial independence and discretion to enable federal courts to provide the clients of a specialized urban bar fair and adequate representation.

This narrowly procedural definition of justice nonetheless permitted results that strained the status quo. Without regard to social class, federal courts sustained the prosecution of poorer rural moonshiners, city brewers, and socially prominent violators of Prohibition. In admiralty, the federal courts limited the application of prolabor federal wage legislation, which favored local firms. Yet they required local business interests to pay for the medical care of seaman and to protect minors from gamblers. Decisions limiting federal criminal enforcement authority in favor of minorities and women were clearly contrary to dominant social interests. The federal court was establishing consistent and predictable standards having implications for the trial of the rich and powerful, as the Prohibition prosecutions showed. Similarly in bankruptcy and state law litigation, the only consistent winner was the federal court and its ultimate authority over the outcome.

Thus, starting with Reconstruction, the social impact of federal decisions was mixed. Busteed's decision in the test oath case suggested the difficulty of defining unequivocally the winners and losers, with the exception of the African Americans who were forced into a status of second-class citizenship. The test oath decision benefited the same local bar that urged Busteed's impeachment. Overall this ambiguity characterized the diverse outcomes in most routine litigation. The values that prevailed consistently were those favoring a reasonable degree of procedural fairness sufficient for an effectively functioning adversarial process. Given the changing market for legal services, this narrowly defined principle of justice was the primary interest the federal bench and bar shared.

CONSTITUTIONAL ISSUES: RAILROAD REGULATION, PEONAGE,
AND THE NEW DEAL

Some of the nation's most important constitutional questions arose in Alabama. These cases engendered distinct tensions between local and external factors influencing the role of discretion and dependence in the federal courts' decisions. The Supreme Court's restriction of the Interstate Commerce Commission's power over rates prior to 1900 partially followed opinions decided by Alabama's federal judges. These decisions reflected sectional and interest-group conflicts, culminating in a protracted struggle involving Judge Jones, the railroads, and state authorities. Jones also challenged corrupt local officials in a campaign against peonage. Ultimately, he allied himself secretly with Booker T. Washington, a few Montgomery lawyers, and a local judge to support a successful test case before the United States Supreme Court. Suits challenging the constitutionality of three of the New Deal's most important programs—the National Recovery Administration, the Tennessee Valley Authority, and Social Security—also arose in Alabama. Grubb was central to this story.

Railroad Regulation

Alabama's federal courts narrowly construed the Interstate Commerce Commission's power. During the decade following passage of the law establishing the ICC in 1887, Supreme Court decisions effectively denied the commission authority to fix railroad rates. Since the law did not specifically grant the rate-fixing authority, the Court would have had to apply a liberal interpretation to establish that power. This the Court refused to do.[126] Alabama cases raised the question of whether the ICC could indirectly establish a rate through its power to compel compliance with findings of fact arising from a community's claim that the railroad's rates were discriminatory. A particularly ambiguous provision of the 1887 law enabled the commission to address rate differentials justified in terms of "substantially similar circumstances and conditions." In 1893, Toulmin had decided against an interpretation of the law favoring the ICC.[127]

In the *Alabama Midland RR* case, the ICC ordered the railroad to cease maintaining a rate differential that favored Montgomery over Troy, a nearby small town. The railroad refused to follow the order, and the ICC and Troy sued the railroad in federal court. Bruce dismissed the case. He narrowly construed the ambiguous "substantially similar circumstances" provision, declaring that using it as basis to enforce the order would indirectly allow the ICC a rate-fixing power the law did not specifically grant.[128] The ICC appealed to the Fifth

Circuit, which affirmed Bruce's opinion.[129] The commission took the case to the Supreme Court and again lost by an eight to one majority that substantially followed Bruce's reasoning. The lone dissenter, Justice John Marshall Harlan, declared that the restrictive interpretation of the ICC's powers "goes far to make the commission a useless body for all practical purposes." As a result, railroads could impose discriminatory rates and thereby "build up favored centers of population at the expense of the business of the country at large."[130]

The clash with the ICC preceded a protracted struggle between Jones and Braxton Bragg Comer. Comer was a businessman, planter, and leader among Birmingham mercantile interests who fought for a strengthened state railroad commission, eventually winning election as governor on the issue in 1906. Opposing Comer was Milton H. Smith of the Louisville and Nashville Railroad Company (L&N).[131] Smith persistently resisted state or federal regulation of rates, stating that "people having a democratic government, with a majority rule, create commissions . . . with power to confiscate—to . . . destroy the value of the property to the owner." Once the "people have gotten a taste of blood," the railroad had little choice but "to enter politics—become parties to the dirty work . . . [in order] to protect their property from injurious, destructive, and confiscatory legislation."[132] Before becoming a judge, Jones had been counsel for the L&N; as a member of the state railroad commission, as House leader in the legislature, and as governor he had continued to be responsive to the railroad's interests.[133]

The struggle among Jones, Comer, and Smith involved the political and economic split between northern and southern Alabama. During Reconstruction, financial interests associated with the Democrats and centered in the southern section had supported the L&N, while many Republicans in the north were close to another railroad. After Reconstruction collapsed, Alabama Democrats in the legislature assisted the bankrupt L&N to attain financial revitalization and prosperity under Smith. Meanwhile, by the end of the century, Birmingham's prominence created a mercantile constituency led by Comer, whose business favored low local freight rates benefiting from the available water transport on the Tennessee River. The rate structure that dominated the state, however, favored south Alabama and the L&N.[134] Bruce's opinion, which the Supreme Court sustained in the *Alabama Midland* case, favored Montgomery, and Toulmin's earlier decision did the same for Mobile, while both decisions aided the interests of the L&N.[135]

As the struggle among Comer and Smith and Jones continued, Grubb from Birmingham and Shelby from Huntsville became involved at important stages of the litigation. Grubb was a lawyer in one of the city's major corporate defense firms, representing some of the business clients who undoubtedly were aligned with Comer's mercantile group.[136] Shelby was a member of the Alabama legislature serving on the judiciary committee during 1884-85, when the state—facing considerable L&N opposition—attempted to strengthen its railroad commission. The judiciary committee considered the measures that went to the Senate for a vote. Shelby favored stronger railroad regulation in eighteen out of nineteen votes, his one dissent being on the Sunday freight train bill. Taken as a whole, the votes for stricter regulation were votes against the L&N and south Alabama, but ultimately the measures did not pass, and Shelby's section lost.[137]

The legal and constitutional issues presented in Jones's court emerged before the confrontation. Comer wanted and eventually won passage of measures giving the state's commission greater power over rates.[138] Nevertheless, the ICC faced the consequences of *Smyth v. Ames* (1896), in which the Supreme Court declared that under the Fourteenth Amendment's due process clause the standard governing the legitimacy of a state commission's rate regulation was whether the railroad received a "fair return" on its investment. The assessment of what amounted to a fair return fostered considerable litigation, which left federal judges little choice but to employ discretion.[139] Bruce's and Toulmin's decisions against the ICC's readjustment of the short- and long-haul rates preceded *Smyth v. Ames*, but the result of both cases was favorable to the L&N and other railroads. By 1906, following the *Ames* precedent, the core rate-making policy that the federal judiciary had accepted was effectively that the railroads knew best.[140]

Comer's success in strengthening the Alabama commission's rate-making authority coincided with the emergence of a stronger ICC. In 1910, Congress weakened the effect of the fair return standard by giving the ICC the authority to set rates. Meanwhile, in Alabama, Comer, first as chairman of the state commission and then as governor, attempted to alter the state's rate structure. Although some railroads surrendered, the L&N sought numerous injunctions from federal court, which Jones granted, employing the fair return standard.[141] At the same time, Jones became embroiled with local officials who refused to comply with one of the injunctions. A Dale County solicitor threatened to arrest the U.S. marshal ordered to enforce the injunction. The confrontation subsided, but the clash of Jones, Comer, and Smith became increasingly personal.[142]

In 1909, the federal circuit court reviewed Jones's decisions in the first Alabama rate case. Jones had issued injunctions enjoining the state commission from enforcing new rates; at the same time the L&N challenged the constitutionality of the law strengthening the commission. A Fifth Circuit Court of

Appeals three-judge panel, including Shelby, A. P. McCormick, and Don A. Pardee, unanimously upheld the state's expansion of the commission's power. Regarding the injunctions, the vote was two to one declaring that Jones had "improvidently issued" them. Shelby's majority opinion therefore ordered the injunctions dissolved but left open the question of whether the fair return standard was appropriate. Overriding the L&N's contention that property rights deserved the protection guaranteed by applying the fair value standard, Shelby held that "passengers and shippers . . . [had] a pecuniary interest in the enforcement of the rate laws. So there are rights on both sides deserving careful thought. And the public has an interest in the enforcement of every law until it is repealed or judicially annulled."[143]

Neither the L&N nor Jones gave up, however. The Supreme Court declined to review Shelby's circuit opinion, so Comer's rates went into effect. Jones then appointed two special masters in chancery to determine the legitimacy of the rates under the fair return standard. Meanwhile the ICC began altering the nation's rate structure, while the Supreme Court reviewed the *Minnesota Rate* case that directly challenged the fair return standard. But the Court did not settle that case before Jones decided against Comer on the basis of the special masters' findings that the commission's rates did not permit the railroad a fair return on investment. This time Jones issued a permanent injunction against the state.[144]

The political confrontation between Comer and Smith continued until early 1914. The railroad charged the commission with contempt, and this time it was Grubb who heard the case. He decided for the state. The railroad nonetheless raised further procedural issues before a Fifth Circuit three-judge panel, but before there was a decision the Supreme Court in June 1913 decided the *Minnesota Rate* case. The Court held that the financial tests the railroads had used to measure fair return were invalid. Although the Court did not mention *Smyth v. Ames* by name, it destroyed the methods by which the railroads had been able to argue that state rates were confiscatory. The legal basis for Jones's injunctions thus was swept away. When the Fifth Circuit panel decided the L&N's appeal—this time before Shelby, Pardee, and Grubb—the court by a two to one vote applied the *Minnesota Rate* precedent to uphold Alabama's commission. Shelby and Grubb composed the majority. The Supreme Court declined review, so the L&N lost. In February 1914, the commission and the railroad negotiated a compromise rate structure, and the long struggle at last ended.[145]

The conflict between Alabama's regulatory agents and the railroads tested the federal courts' discretionary authority. In the early ICC rate cases, Bruce and

Toulmin narrowly interpreted the ICC's rate-making power, establishing a course the Supreme Court itself followed. Jones liberally applied the flexible fair-return standard against the state and in favor of the L&N. Finally, Shelby and Grubb construed that standard and the new one formulated in the *Minnesota Rate* case to uphold Alabama's rate regulation. The result of each judge's decision making benefited particular urban centers over others. The Bruce and Toulmin decisions restricted the ICC's authority, leaving the railroads free to establish a long-haul rate favorable to the urban areas of Montgomery and Mobile. The effect of Jones's repeated decisions against the state's rate-making power on behalf of the L&N sustained a rate structure that was generally consistent with Montgomery's market interests. Shelby's and Grubb's opinions, however, aided a rate structure that was in the interests of north Alabama, particularly the two leading urban centers, Birmingham and Huntsville.

Other factors suggested that these patterns were not coincidental. As state public officials, practicing lawyers, and finally as federal judges, Bruce and Toulmin, despite different party affiliation, were part of a local legal culture and market for legal services rooted in south Alabama. These institutional ties were especially consistent with the predominantly urban orientation of the State Bar Association in which the Democrat Toulmin was active. The Republican Bruce was not a Bar Association member; he had, however, represented the area near Mobile as a state legislator for several years before being appointed to the federal bench. He served on the bench for more than twenty-five years, and though after 1886 Toulmin had primary responsibility for the southern area around Mobile, Bruce continued to live and hold court in Montgomery. Thus he maintained the tradition that had characterized five out of six of antebellum Alabama's federal judges of being oriented primarily toward the southern section. It was understandable that both judges should consider the ICC's rate structure in terms that took into account the interests of the two urban centers with which each was most familiar.

The localistic orientation of Jones, Shelby, and Grubb was no less pronounced. Jones's connection with the L&N was long-standing and intimate, particularly given his service as that railroad's counsel for some twenty years. More significantly, perhaps, the L&N's long-haul rate structure tended to favor south Alabama and especially Montgomery over the northern section whose market ties with the Tennessee River fostered a preference for lower local rates. This divergence in rate structures influenced the entire business order in the urban areas of each section, including the interests that had been potential clients of Jones, Shelby, and Grubb before they became federal judges. These different local clients and their lawyers were leading litigants in the district courts of Jones and Grubb. On the Fifth Circuit's three-judge panels, Shelby and Grubb had the opportunity to try cases involving litigants from each section's legal culture and business community, as did Jones, who sat in both Birmingham and Montgomery (though more often in the latter). In addition, as legislators, Shelby's and Jones's votes on railroad regulations reflected a preference for the interests of each one's own section. Thus Shelby's and Grubb's rejection of Jones's decisions, like those decisions themselves, were consistent with conflicting sectional interests rooted in the different local markets and legal culture.

Initially, external institutional factors circumscribed discretion and enforced dependence to a limited degree. In the ICC rate cases, Toulmin and Bruce had to choose whether to uphold or restrict the federal commission's rate-making power. The law establishing the ICC did not specifically grant the power to set rates, requiring only that they be "reasonable." Also, when the Alabama cases arose there were no precedents directly on point from the Supreme Court. The Interstate Commerce Act itself represented a new form of federal power. Unrestrained by precedent, the exercise of discretion was inevitable. The result was consistent with a practical conservative-activist jurisprudence that reinforced the primary influence of the local legal culture and market. Neither judge questioned Congress's power to create the ICC, but without express guidance as to the scope of its power each judge employed his discretion on behalf of the local interests he best understood. In *Alabama Midland* the Supreme Court affirmed and in *Smyth v. Ames* it extended this broad discretionary authority over rates.

The confrontation centering on Jones's use of this same discretion indicated the limits of discretion. Jones enjoined the state from regulating the L&N's rates on the basis of the fair value standard. Even after Shelby and Grubb reversed him on this point, Jones attempted to favor the L&N over the state. Only after the Supreme Court did away with the fair value standard and Grubb and Shelby on the Fifth Circuit again reversed Jones did the confrontation end. Still, until the Court curbed the lower federal judge's authority over rates, discretion was broad enough to permit the contrary results reached by Jones on the one hand and Shelby and Grubb on the other. Similarly, partisan political factors had little discernible bearing on these divergent results since all three judges were appointed by Republican presidents, and two of them were prominent Democrats. Again within the broad limits of dependence established by the Supreme Court, a conservative-activist jurisprudence facilitated the dominance of local over national institutions and interests in Alabama's federal courts.

116

Peonage

Alabama's federal district courts and other federal authorities fought peonage. Like other southern states, Alabama enacted laws that gave white local officials and employers the power to control black labor. One such law established a surety system whereby white plantation, railroad, and mine owners in rural areas cooperated with local justices of the peace and sheriffs to entrap blacks and sometimes foreign whites as well in a web of debt-labor contracts that were virtually inescapable. The federal Peonage Statute of 1867 outlawed forms of involuntary servitude that linked debt and coercion. Where debt resulted from and was perpetuated by coercion, peonage existed and was illegal under the federal law. Beginning with the Black Codes of the Reconstruction era, strengthened with lien laws once Reconstruction collapsed and continuing with various contract labor laws passed by the turn of the century, this legislation nonetheless replaced free labor with a kind of slavery.[146]

In Alabama peonage existed principally in the turpentine and railroad construction business. During the early twentieth century, federal prosecutions were most extensive in several south Alabama counties; yet in 1910, the Southern District's federal attorney, Warren Reese, Jr., exclaimed, "I had imagined that the vigorous prosecutions of these cases in the District for the last ten years had virtually stamped it out, but I find that though this is to some extent true in the Northern portion of the District, in the southeastern portion of the District . . . this practice is quite extensively carried on."[147]

Peonage was intransigent partially because of the interdependence of local law enforcement, courts, and employers. As noted, many of Alabama's justices of the peace and sheriffs benefited from the corruption associated with the fee and contract-labor systems, which one federal grand jury described as a "disgrace to civilization." Even so, another U.S. attorney in the Southern District, William H. Armbrecht, found that the "members of the Grand Jury in that section of Alabama are not disposed to find true bills in cases of peonage." Another Justice Department official was still more candid: It was "generally understood in this section that no white jury will convict a white man for anything he might do to a Negro."[148] In addition, the employers who benefited from peonage were often prominent members of a community's business establishment.

Given such an environment, successful federal prosecutions usually depended on local interests being divided. Although some employers benefited from close association with local law enforcement officials, others lacked such advantage. The latter group could favor limited federal prosecution, as long as there was no fundamental threat to white dominance. Accordingly, a special federal agent investigating peonage in Monroe County reported that "certain citizens" there were "willing that the Government should make a test case, provided that if the defendant is convicted a fine only [would] be imposed." If the government won, the planters agreed to "abandon the custom." On other occasions, however, the complexity of local circumstances was such that federal authorities concluded "that it would not be wise for the Government to pursue . . . [a] prosecution any further."[149]

Prosecuting peonage in Alabama's federal courts thus aroused conflicting interests. Most white Alabamians assumed that the poor blacks entrapped in the debt-labor system were shiftless, unwilling to work except under coercion. Evidence demonstrating that African Americans yearned to enjoy the fruits of their own labor was easily ignored. The abuse inherent in the system, however, undermined respect for law and order, which respectable whites—particularly in the cities—counted on to preserve peace within the black community. In addition, some white employers resisted the system because it created unfair competition with free wages and labor contracts. Failure to hold local public officials and their private employer associates accountable for clear violations of the law, moreover, encouraged community instability associated with race and class conflict.[150]

These were the conditions in which federal district judge Jones attempted to end peonage in Alabama. Confederate war hero and ex-governor, Jones belonged to the state's conservative political establishment. Still, like some of his associates in the State Bar Association, Jones viewed the status of blacks in terms of preserving social order and respectability. In the 1901 constitutional convention he supported the disfranchisement of the state's African Americans. He urged, however, that a black deserved from whites "all the civil rights that will fit him to be a decent and self-respecting, law-abiding, and intelligent citizen."[151] Because of these sentiments, Jones maintained a close association with Booker T. Washington, whose support had influenced the Republican Roosevelt to offer the judgeship to so prominent a Democrat.[152]

Jones became involved with the peonage cases in early 1903. Erastus J. Parsons, a young lawyer whose grandfather had been governor of the state, sought the release of a black laborer from local custody in Coosa County under habeas corpus proceedings. Local officials evaded the writ, and Parsons soon realized that the law enforcement system was corrupt. He appealed to U.S. District Attorney Warren S. Reese, Jr., who discovered that Parsons's client was caught in a wider peonage system common to Coosa, Tallapoosa, and other counties. Reese contacted Jones, who in turn urged U.S. Attorney General

Philander C. Knox to begin an investigation by sending a federal agent to the area. Reese had told Jones that local officials and employers cooperated in a "plan . . . to accuse the Negro of some petty offense, and then require him, in order to escape conviction, to enter into an agreement to pay his accusers so much money, and sign a contract, under the terms of which his bondmen can hire him out until he pays a certain sum." Immediately on signing the contract, however, the laborer was "treated" as a "convict."[153]

Jones was the presiding judge of the district court in Birmingham and Montgomery. The U.S. attorney in each city sought grand jury indictments that resulted in peonage prosecutions against nine individuals. By June, President Theodore Roosevelt himself had expressed interest in the cases. The nation's leading progressive newspapers gave extensive coverage. Booker T. Washington worked quietly behind the scenes to further the campaign. Reese took the lead in popularizing the workings of a system in which justices of the peace in the pay of local planters placed blacks in "a condition of involuntary servitude . . . [where they were] locked up at nights in a cell, worked under guards during the day from 3 o'clock in the morning until 7 or 8 o'clock at night, whipped in a most cruel manner . . . [and] insufficiently fed and poorly clad." The condition, moreover, could easily become endless. "When the time of a good working Negro is nearing an end," Reese said, "he is rearrested on some trumped up charge and carried before some bribed justice and resentenced to an additional time." If the "helpless peons" tried to "run away the dogs are placed on their track and they are invariably retaken and subjected to more cruel treatment."[154]

Throughout proceedings lasting for months, Jones methodically explained to grand and petit jurors why peonage was illegal. He not only emphasized legal principles but also appealed to values of self-respect and distrust of special privilege. "One of the most valuable liberties of man" is "to work where he pleases, and to quit one employment and go to another," Jones said. The Alabama contract law that fostered the Coosa and Tallapoosa peonage system was "a vicious species of class legislation designed solely in the interest of the employer or landlord."[155] Eventually, the efforts of Jones and the federal authorities resulted in ninety-nine indictments. The local officials and planters received from Jones severe reprimands for "prostituting the authority of God" and Alabama in the "administration of justice." At another point he in effect charged the jury to return a guilty verdict. "The question between us and God and our consciences is, can we rise above our prejudices, if we have them, so for that we as white men are able and willing to do a Negro justice."[156]

Ultimately, the results of Jones's efforts were disappointing. One prominent case ended in a hung jury. Even though the government won convictions in most of the other suits, Jones meted out small fines and modest jail terms. In major cases he condoned presidential pardons of those who were imprisoned. At times he suspended sentences and reduced fines. Jones undoubtedly believed that his declaration that the Alabama laws that supported peonage were unconstitutional bespoke successful prosecution and the demise of the evil.[157] Another federal official was more critical, finding that the "sentencing [had] the same outward appearance as the sentencing of a moonshiner." In the end, Jones's actions added up to four individuals serving a total of just five months in jail; the others paid fines amounting to only $500."[158]

The publicity surrounding the cases in Jones's court, however, encouraged further action. During the litigation in 1903, the Alabama legislature changed a provision in the state's contract-labor code that had favored workers. Known as a "false pretense" law, it involved workers who signed a contract, received a money advance, and then departed without repaying the money. The original law enacted in 1885 placed the worker in the condition of having undertaken the employment solely to procure the advance before absconding. Nevertheless, conviction was difficult because it required the prosecution to prove intent. The Alabama Supreme Court upheld the difficult standard in the 1890s, and in a number of cases workers won. But in 1903 the legislature reversed the presumption of evidence standard.[159] A worker's mere taking of money without either repaying it or working it off became "prima facie evidence of the intent to injure or defraud his employer." Four years later, the legislature amended the statute to permit a fine to be "double the damage suffered by the injured party," up to $300.[160]

The revised law engendered opposition from Booker T. Washington and some white Alabamians. The statute, Washington said, meant "that any white man, who cares to charge that a Colored man has promised to work for him and has not done so, or who has gotten money from him and not paid it back, can have the Colored man sent to the chain gang."[161] Erastus J. Parsons, the lawyer whose habeas writ had indirectly set in motion the 1903 peonage cases and who had since then become U.S. attorney in Montgomery, agreed. Like so many measures enacted since Reconstruction, the law intended "uniformly, to weave about the ignorant laborer, and especially the blacks, a system of laws intended to keep him absolutely dependent on the will of the employer and the land owner."[162]

Perhaps the most persistent white critic was William H. Thomas. Appointed by the state Senate as a Montgomery circuit judge in 1901, Thomas instructed a jury in 1905 that the false pretense law was unconstitutional. Upon appeal, the Alabama Supreme Court overruled Thomas's position. Determined to prevail, however, by 1907 he had contacted Booker T. Washington, urging a cooperative effort to fund an appeal to the United States Supreme Court. Meanwhile Thomas continued looking for a test case. A Democrat whose former law partner had been governor of Alabama, Thomas had strong connections with the state's political establishment, including the progressive faction to which Hugo L. Black eventually belonged. He had written numerous articles, several of which embraced the New South vision conservatives such as Jones shared with progressives like Black. Thomas was also active in numerous civic causes ranging from education reform to abolition of child labor to the universal congress of lawyers and jurists and state and national bar associations.[163]

During April 1908, Alonzo Bailey brought to court the case Thomas sought. Bailey, a black agricultural laborer, filed a habeas petition claiming that the false pretense law was unconstitutional. The previous December Bailey had contracted to work for a year as a farm laborer with the Riverside Company in Montgomery. He received a $15.00 advance from which $1.25 was to be deducted from his $12.00 monthly salary. Bailey worked only about a month before quitting. Alleging violation of the false pretense statute, the company got Bailey jailed. His wife went to a young Montgomery lawyer named Edward S. Watts, who took the case before Thomas. Bound by the state supreme court's earlier rulings, Thomas denied the habeas petition.[164]

Watts appealed the denial to the Alabama Supreme Court, setting in motion larger proceedings. A group led by Booker T. Washington, which included a few white citizens of Montgomery, began a secret collaboration to raise money to take the case to the United States Supreme Court. Washington sent a representative to Judge Thomas in order to determine the cost of making an appeal. Thomas was cooperative but urged that the role of both Washington and the judge himself be "kept secret."[165] Meanwhile, Washington got one of Judge Jones's former law partners, Fred Ball, to join Watts in Bailey's defense. Jones himself also became directly involved, again under the presumption that secrecy would be maintained. As expected, the Alabama Supreme Court decided against Bailey. Everything was in place for an appeal to the U.S. Supreme Court. The Justice Department joined the suit, and President Roosevelt notified Washington of his support.[166]

Initially, the results were disappointing. In December 1909, a decision for the Court's majority written by Justice Oliver Wendell Holmes decided against Bailey, declaring that a constitutional challenge to the law was premature without a showing of whether a jury would have found evidence proving fraud. Dissents from Justices John Marshall Harlan and William R. Day nonetheless encouraged a further appeal. The secret group again raised money, while Jones helped Watts and Ball to prepare the briefs. Meanwhile, Thomas grew concerned that U.S. Attorney Parsons, whom the group had not consulted, was indirectly assisting state officials by informing them of the federal government's progress. At about the same time, Bailey disappeared. After further delays, Thomas was not reappointed to his judgeship in 1910, though he continued to support the case. Finally, in October 1910, amid extensive news coverage from the press, the Supreme Court heard a final appeal.[167]

Announced on January 3, 1911, the Court's decision emphasized the issue of fraud. Alabama officials had argued that the purpose of the statute was to "punish fraud, not the mere failure to pay a debt." Bailey's lawyers had responded that placing so heavy a burden of proof on the defendant in effect denied the right of trial by jury because the intent test prevented a rebuttal to the "prima facie evidence" of guilt. Accordingly, the unfair test enabled the "employer to keep the employee in involuntary servitude by the overhanging menace of prosecution."[168]

The majority opinion written by Justice Charles Evans Hughes accepted the defendant's argument. There was "not a particle of evidence . . . indicating that he made the contract or received the money with any intent to injure or defraud his employer." The statute "stripped" Bailey of the "presumption of innocence, and exposed" him before the jury "to conviction for fraud on evidence only of breach of contract and failure to pay." The law thus violated the 1867 peonage statute because it "compel[led] one man to labor for another in payment of a debt, by punishing him as a criminal if he does not perform the service or pay the debt." The "most likely victims" of this "instrument of compulsion," moreover, were the "poor and ignorant." Holmes and Horace H. Lurton dissented, favoring a broad police power on the state's part to pass such laws.[169]

The impact of the Court's decision was mixed. The legal foundation for much of the contract-labor system was shattered, inviting further court challenges to what remained. Three years later, the Justice Department initiated litigation testing the constitutionality of the surety system. In *U.S. v. Reynolds*, the government won.[170] Just as significant, perhaps, through secret interracial cooperation Washington, Thomas, and the others had succeeded with vigorous prosecution where Jones's earlier experiment in leniency had failed. To be sure, Thomas lost his city judgeship and faced a heavy debt for supporting the litigation. Nevertheless, four years later the people of Alabama elected him to the state's Supreme Court and he won reelection repeatedly thereafter.[171] Ultimately, however, peonage based on customary practice persisted into the 1930s though on a smaller scale than before.[172]

The peonage cases suggest how Alabama's federal courts balanced discretion and dependence. Constitutional separation removed the federal judicial establishment from direct local political and social pressures. In and of itself, this institutional independence only begins to explain the causes and consequences of the federal court's role in the campaign against peonage. In the *Reynolds* case, for example, the Justice Department exercised more consistent leadership than local federal officials in attacking the surety system. Yet the government's victory merely built on a decade of struggle in which Alabama's federal officials and their local allies had taken the initiative and, within limits, prevailed.[173]

Given the extent of the grassroots political and economic interests on which peonage depended, how could Alabama's federal judicial establishment achieve even the modest successes that it did? Part of the answer involved the conflicted interests of local employers. After the *Bailey* decision in 1911, the influential *Mobile Register* reported that the "majority of the farmers in Monroe County" were "anxious" that the labor contract system "be discontinued, as it has a demoralizing effect on labor." In certain instances a worker was "afraid to even leave the place without the permission of the farmer fearing that he will be arrested before he can get back for violating the contract."[174] A south Alabama farmer who said he "handle[d] lots of Negroes" revealed another dimension. Admitting participation in the "worst form" of peonage, he nonetheless complained that " if a "poor man . . . renting any land" was convicted on some minor charge, his "wife and children . . . see me at once and demand I pay him out. If I do not pay this fine his wife and children will get another to pay it and move off my place and leave the cotton to rot in the field."[175]

This view put a humane face on the brutalities inherent in the peonage system. It hinted, however, at underlying competitive tensions threatening the market relations of dominant whites. Individuals felt unable to abandon the system unless their neighbors did the same. Yet many of these neighbors had close relations with the local law enforcement authorities, an advantage that perpetuated peonage.[176]

Even so, the link between corrupt legal institutions and peonage encouraged local support for reform. As the State Bar Association emphasized repeatedly, corrupt local law enforcement was a problem throughout the state. Representatives of the conservative and progressive factions of the Democratic political establishment such as Jones and Thomas agreed that corrupt legal institutions undermined their vision of a good society. Also, many of those who shared this vision resided in the cities. Accordingly, a common interest favoring change emerged between urban opponents of corrupt legal institutions and white farmers who perceived disadvantages in maintaining peonage.

This linkage helped to explain why the *Mobile Register* changed its view. In 1903 it criticized Judge Jones's campaign; eight years later the paper supported the *Bailey* and *Reynolds* cases. "With the foregoing facts [revealed in the litigation] to base an opinion on, the vast majority of the public must feel a satisfaction that the protecting arm of the federal law is extended in such cases," editorialized the paper in 1911. Mobile's U.S. Attorney Armbrecht noted privately how unusual was the paper's new editorial stance. Southerners generally and Alabamians in particular were "very jealous of state rights, and . . . any interference by the Federal Government with customs established by usage, or laws passed by the state legislature, whether such customs and laws be right or wrong, usually meets with fierce opposition."[177] It was particularly noteworthy, Armbrecht concluded, that the cases against peonage had won the support of one of Alabama's leading Democratic newspapers. Jones' policy of leniency and the limited reach of the Supreme Court's decisions left intact the fundamental racial status quo. Alabama's Democratic establishment thus supported federal intervention only after it became clear that attacking peonage would not threaten Jim Crow segregation itself.

The peonage cases further suggested the factors influencing Jones. He had links with both the local conservative Democratic establishment and Washington, whose toleration of segregation served conservative interests. Moreover, Jones's leniency toward those convicted in the peonage cases was consistent with the local agricultural and urban media interests that had begun questioning peonage partially because of the pernicious consequences resulting from the competition with free labor. In addition, Jones's own concern about protecting the respectability of blacks involved preserving a stable social order. These values helped to explain why a few members of the local bar secretly joined Jones, Washington, and Thomas to win the appeal of the *Bailey* case. The lawyers took a publicly contentious position that under other circumstances might have threatened their standing in the community. That the case had the reverse effect indicated the extent to which important segments of the local community that were otherwise the clients for those same lawyers had come to accept Jones's values.

Ultimately, the fight against peonage suggested the limits of the federal courts' independence and discretion. Federal judges were sufficiently removed from local interests to challenge one of the basic institutions of Jim Crow segregation. They were able, however, to get ahead of the dominant social and political interests only moderately. This moderate action served as a catalyst for powerful groups to change, but the change neither prevented the perpetuation of peonage on the basis of private custom nor significantly challenged the system of racial segregation itself.

The New Deal

Alabama's federal courts' stance toward the New Deal had national ramifications. From 1934 to 1937, the cases testing the constitutionality of several of Roosevelt's key New Deal measures arose in the state's Northern District. The Justice Department prosecuted an Alabama producer for violating the National Recovery Administration's code governing the lumber industry, though the attempt to use the suit to establish the NRA's constitutionality before the Supreme Court failed. The constitutional test of the TVA, however, not only arose from Alabama but became the Supreme Court's leading decision in the field. The same was true of the case challenging the Social Security Act of 1935. In the NRA and TVA suits, Grubb's role was central, whereas in the Social Security case, Davis presided. The two judges did not agree concerning the result of the fundamental constitutional issues, suggesting how much over the three-year-period the institutional realities influencing the exercise of judicial discretion had changed.

The first case pitted William Belcher against the NRA. Lumbering was one of the ten major industries the NRA targeted for code-making governing prices, worker's wages and hours, production, and other factors aimed at limiting competition. The lumber industry's national giants convinced the NRA's lawyers that the government could remedy the problems arising from cutthroat competition and overproduction only by enforcing a code having unusually specific price and production controls. William Belcher and his family owned and operated several sawmills in central Alabama's soft-pine region. The national code went into effect during August 1933. A few months later, Belcher publicly opposed instituting the wage and hour provision for his workers. Belcher claimed that his employees readily accepted working longer hours for less pay than the code provided. Several workers told NRA investigators, however, that Belcher had fired employees who urged compliance with the code. Local ministers confirmed this testimony.[178]

After some vacillation, the Justice Department decided that Belcher's actions were appropriate for a test case. National newspapers had expressed suspicions that the NRA was dragging its feet, especially after a federal judge in Florida had declared the citrus industry's code unconstitutional. The press thus hailed the Justice Department's announcement that it would use the Belcher case to settle the issue. The government's lawyers had gone to some lengths to secure the cooperation of the U.S. attorney in Birmingham and Judge Grubb himself. Privately, however, the lawyers doubted whether the case was in fact the best for their purposes. Especially troubling was the rigidity of the code's price and production controls.[179]

Nevertheless, Grubb's cooperation encouraged pushing the prosecution. U.S. Attorney Jim Smith initiated a grand jury investigation once Belcher's continued recalcitrance was clear. In addition, the NRA and Justice Department lawyers learned that Grubb believed that the code was unconstitutional. Accordingly, the government arranged with Belcher's counsel and Grubb to use the Criminal Appeals Act of 1907, which allowed direct review by the Supreme Court of a district court order sustaining a demurrer to a criminal indictment where the district judge found the statute at issue was unconstitutional. The strategy avoided a jury trial while assuming that Grubb would declare the code unconstitutional.[180]

The grand jury indicted Belcher in August 1934. At the end of October, his lawyer filed a demurrer to the indictment, alleging three grounds that challenged the code's constitutionality. First, the wage and hour provisions were not within the commerce power. Next, the code violated the Fifth Amendment's guarantee of due process of law since Belcher had not signed it. Finally, the power Congress delegated to the president and the bureaucracy (the NRA) was unlawful. Grubb had prepared his order in advance, so on the day of the filing he sustained the demurrer and dismissed the indictment, deciding against the NRA on each point. He then sanctioned a direct appeal to the Supreme Court. But by April 1935, the original doubts concerning the appropriateness of the case as a test resurfaced among the Justice Department's lawyers after the Supreme Court decided against the government in cases testing the constitutionality of other New Deal programs. After some deliberation, they decided to drop the *Belcher* appeal. This decision paved the way for review of the well-known *Schechter* case in which the Court unanimously declared unconstitutional the power Congress had delegated to the executive under the NRA. By the time the Court decided the case in 1935, Grubb had died; his opinion regarding the NRA's unconstitutionality seemed, however, vindicated.[181]

Grubb's court was also the source of the case challenging the constitutionality of the TVA. During World War I, the federal government had developed electrical power for nitrate production at Muscle Shoals, Alabama. Since then, progressive U.S. senators, including Hugo Black and Nebraska's George Norris, had called for a larger program in which the Tennessee Valley would become the center of electrical power production that the federal government could use as a "yard stick" to regulate the prices, quality, and production of the nation's public utilities. The program also included improvement of the area's environment and navigable waterways. TVA was one of the major projects Congress enacted during Roosevelt's first 100 days of 1933. Questions concerning TVA's constitutionality had impeded its enactment earlier, however, and they remained alive. The law's drafters relied on the federal power over defense and navigable streams. But the main purpose of TVA was electrical power production and distribution, authority Congress had rarely, if ever, exercised in peacetime.[182]

Different Alabama business interests challenged the TVA and its various programs. A group of coal and ice producers, many of whom operated in Birmingham and north Alabama, alleged that TVA's production and distribution of electrical power caused "irreparable injury to or annihilation of their . . . business and industry through competitive capture of an important and indispensable part of the existing market for" energy. The general constitutional argument was that the powers involving national defense and navigable waters on which Congress based the law were "in fact, from the outset . . . secondary to certain social and economic functions and purposes having no reasonable relation to the war or commerce power." These "functions . . . moreover . . . [were] beyond the lawful power of Congress to authorize . . . to undertake or execute." The firms alleged too that Alabama Power Company's purchase of power from TVA was unlawful because it threatened the same destructive results to their business.[183]

Some of Alabama Power Company's own stockholders also challenged the purchase of electricity from TVA. The suit by George Ashwander and others alleged that the purchase contract between the two corporations was the result of duress; the APC could, therefore, void the contract. A broader claim nevertheless denied the constitutionality of TVA on grounds similar to those argued in the coal/ice producers' suit. Ultimately, *Ashwander* was the case that went to the Supreme Court testing TVA's legality, and like *Belcher* it began with adverse decisions by Grubb.[184]

In November 1934 and February 1935, Grubb rendered judgments in the complex litigation. He dismissed the allegations of duress and declined to consider directly whether the law creating TVA was constitutional. These holdings were significant because they narrowed the issues reviewable on appeal. The key question, said Grubb, was one of degree. Without question Congress could, as it had in World War I, in the name of national defense and the commerce power charter a public corporation having the power to sell and distribute electricity. The exercise of this power, however, must be subsidiary to the main purposes involving military necessity and navigable waterways. The

127

facts proved at trial, Grubb held, showed that TVA was engaged in "producing and selling electric power in Alabama" on a scale so "elaborate" that it had "no substantial relation to . . . any constitutional power." The federal corporation was performing functions normally reserved to the states under the Tenth Amendment. He issued an injunction enjoining TVA from entering into contracts like the one with Alabama Power, which furthered "a proprietary adventure."[185]

The course of the *Ashwander* appeal coincided with significant changes.[186] In July 1935, the Fifth Circuit Court of Appeals unanimously reversed Grubb, holding that neither the production nor sale of electricity by TVA, nor the projects pursued to further those purposes, was inconsistent with congressional authority. Alabama Power Company's stockholders appealed to the Supreme Court but lost again. Not long after the Supreme Court decided that case, Roosevelt won a massive reelection triumph in 1936, after which he proposed the controversial court-packing plan aimed at increasing the Court's member-ship with appointees favorable to the New Deal. Early in 1937, the Court began handing down decisions upholding the constitutionality of New Deal programs. Unbeknownst to the general public, however, Justice Owen Roberts had decided to switch his vote to support the New Deal. The switch occurred because of Roosevelt's landslide victory, not the court-packing plan, which in any case was defeated. Before long a Court majority, including new liberal appointees such as Hugo Black, began affirming the constitutionality of the New Deal programs.[187]

Roosevelt's appointment of David J. Davis as Grubb's successor oc-curred shortly before the *Social Security* case arose. The Social Security Act of 1935 established a payroll deduction tax on workers' wages, which the federal government and the states would share in order to fund and administer unemployment compensation, senior citizens' pensions, and aid to dependent children, the blind, and the crippled. The Charles C. Steward Machine Co. of Birmingham sued the IRS to recover a tax of $46.14 collected from it as the employer of eight persons during 1936. The firm charged that the tax unlawfully coerced private employers in violation of powers reserved to the people and the states under the Ninth and Tenth amendments. Judge Davis dismissed the suit. The company appealed to the Fifth Circuit, which affirmed Davis. The firm went finally to the Supreme Court, which again upheld the lower courts.[188]

The New Deal raised constitutional issues on a scale unprecedented in peacetime. The divergent results reached in the courts of Grubb and Davis suggested how national could supplant local imperatives as the primary factors influencing decision making. Little is known about Roosevelt's choice of Davis to succeed Grubb (except that Davis had been , years before, Hugo Black's law partner), and Davis's illness and untimely death in 1938 prevented him from establishing a record of judicial opinions. The *Social Security* case resulted in virtually his only significant decision.[189] Nevertheless, Roosevelt appointed Davis after Grubb had established unequivocal opposition to the first New Deal programs. In addition, his appointment and the *Social Security* suit itself coincided with the political and constitutional transformation that culminated in the Supreme Court's dramatic switch from opposing to supporting Roosevelt's New Deal liberalism.[190] The Social Security Act, too, represented a new and profound exertion of national policy over local governmental control and market relations. Whatever else may have influenced Davis's dismissal of the constitutional challenge to the act, his acceptance of the dominance of national authority over local interests was apparent.

Grubb's opposition to the New Deal further suggested how profoundly national policies disrupted local interests. The scale of bureaucratic incursion represented by the NRA and TVA went far beyond that of either the state or federal railroad commissions. The direct federal assertion of control over labor-management relations and prices transformed local market imperatives more fundamentally than did the attack on peonage. These changes in turn fostered new markets for legal services, which potentially threatened the institutions and values sustaining the federal courtroom culture. An indication of the significance of change was that the number of lawyers admitted to practice in the federal courts' Northern District rose from 88 in 1930 to 155 in 1940.[191] These lawyers brought suits involving new social and economic issues governed by national standards. Yet the established federal courtroom culture represented the dominance of local urban interests and values supported by the State Bar Association.

Grubb did not oppose government regulation per se. In the Alabama railroad rate litigation, he had supported greater state commission control over rates than had Jones. In *Ashwander*, moreover, he declined to decide directly whether TVA was constitutional, addressing its exercise of power as a matter of degree. He did declare the NRA unconstitutional, but on grounds that tracked the Supreme Court's unanimous *Schechter* decision as well as the concerns that had led the government's own lawyers to drop *Belcher* as a test case in the first place. Finally, Grubb's decisions carefully denied that the Alabama Power Company had liability in either case. As a result, his decisions effectively benefited the various small, owner-operated lumber and coal/ice energy producers while at the same time protecting the interests of the state's leading corporate utility.[192] These considerations suggested that Grubb favored a degree of regulation consistent with the conservative-activist jurisprudence that had prevailed up to the Great Depression. This jurisprudence accepted an expanding federal incursion into state affairs, though not on the scale the New Deal represented.

The New Deal's experience in Alabama's federal courts indicated the tensions shaping discretion and dependence. Consistent with dependence, Grubb's decisions followed the Supreme Court's precedents, yet at the same time they asserted considerable discretion by confronting to a greater or lesser degree the constitutional issues. Davis, however, apparently felt unconstrained by Supreme Court precedent and dismissed the constitutional challenges to the Social Security Act. Grubb decided in accord with the past, whereas Davis looked to the future.

Even so, Grubb affirmed a level of federal intervention that had been contentious since Reconstruction. As long as the system of Jim Crow segregation was not threatened, this degree of intervention was favored by the specialized urban legal culture represented by the State Bar Association. Grubb and his court fostered a special market for legal services served by a segment of this culture, the small bar on whom local business interests depended. Grubb's decisions in the constitutional cases would have perpetuated the interdependence of the federal courts and local business and legal interests. Roosevelt's appointment of Davis, however, injected national political and institutional pressures capable of transforming the established order. Thus, more than any time since Reconstruction, federal courts would be called on to exercise discretion to enforce national over local interests.

CONCLUSION

For Alabama's federal courts, the period from 1865 to 1940 began and ended with major constitutional crises. During Reconstruction, Congress enlarged federal jurisdiction in order to defend the principle of equality before the law in the South. Woods, Busteed, and Bruce attempted to support this principle even though Congress and the Supreme Court retreated from it. Insofar as the freedmen were concerned, exercising discretion to enforce individual liberty gave way to the national government's policy of denial. Still, the federal court's power did not disappear with the freedman's liberty; Reconstruction paved the way for new patterns of routine litigation in which federal law, federal litigants, and federal issues were more important than ever. State law as a source of litigation remained significant, but as a proportion of the whole it was declining. Federal jurisdiction thus created a new market for legal services involving government regulation, criminal liability, and new classes of litigants. The New Deal transformed this market to an even greater extent, as the dramatic increase in lawyers admitted to federal practice between 1930 and 1940 suggested.

The outcome of constitutional cases indicated the equivocal relation between dependence and discretion. Busteed's test oath decision notwithstanding, during the Reconstruction era Woods, Busteed, and Bruce generally interpreted constitutional provisions and federal law in favor of individual rights until the Supreme Court established contrary precedents. Even so, the dependence engendered by the federal government's and the Supreme Court's retreat from Reconstruction did not prevent the exercise of judicial discretion in the protracted struggle over railroad rates, the peonage cases, and the suits testing the New Deal. Indeed, the conservative Democrat Jones pressed his discretion significantly to fight peonage and protect railroads. Similarly, the Democrat Grubb upheld stronger state regulation of rates than did Jones but opposed the unparalleled expansion of peacetime federal government established by the New Deal.

The interaction between national and local institutional and cultural relationships helped to explain these constitutional decisions. Congress expanded federal jurisdiction in response to national political and economic pressures; the working content of this federal power nonetheless found expression in suits involving local conflicts. A federal judge considered these suits not only as a manifestation of federal authority but also in terms of adversarial process and the lawyers' presentation of the issues. Constitutionally, the federal courts were removed from local pressures. But as the interrelation between railroad rates and substate sectionalism or the intricate web of conflicts in the peonage and New Deal suits suggested, formal and informal institutional ties nonetheless linked the federal courts to local urban communities and the state as a whole. Unlike state courts of the era, and with the exception of Busteed and Hundley, favoritism or corruption was not an issue involving Alabama's federal judges. Moreover, because of the mixed partisan political background of judicial appointments, after Reconstruction at least the party affiliation of Alabama's federal judges had a discernible influence on constitutional decision making only rarely, most notably in Davis's Social Security decision.

In routine litigation, local factors were no less significant. Criminal and admiralty decisions generally affirmed federal authority. The outcome in particular cases, however, often upheld the individual's or the state's interest over that of the federal government. The enforcement of railroad bondholder's rights, Prohibition, and the tax cases involving moonshiners or local metropolitan brewers revealed that local interests were divided. Even so, major segments of the state's residents objected to alcohol consumption on religious or moral grounds, which created local support for federal prosecution. Similarly, the bondholder cases pitted local as well as foreign creditors against local taxpayers. The bankruptcy litigation and the cases in which the application of state law was an issue also usually required the federal courts to decide among competing local interests. The only clear pattern in these outcomes was that the federal courts affirmed their own independence and discretionary judgment. The fragmentation of interests helped to explain too why federal judges periodically decided in favor of women, the poor, and other underdogs. Finally, in most categories of routine suits the Reconstruction judges, including the controversial Busteed, decided no differently from conservative Democrats such as Toulmin.

Even so, in most constitutional and routine litigation, federal decision making was consistent with particular values. With the exception of the freedmen cases and the Social Security decision, the values the federal courts enforced reflected the interests of those in or with close connection to Alabama's urban centers. These urban interests relied on a small, specialized bar who shared the same interests. Except for Busteed, moreover, each of Alabama's federal judges came from or was otherwise intimately connected with this predominantly urban market and institutional culture. This local urban orientation was at odds with the rural, small-town political and economic interests that dominated the state's legislature and judiciary. The organization whose official agenda best defined urban-rural conflict was the State Bar Association. Its agenda emphasized judicial independence maintained through flexible and uniform procedure as the cure for favoritism and corruption. The Bar Association presented the federal courts as a model. The degree of independence and discretion the federal courts applied in decision making reflected a practical, conservative-activist jurisprudence that was also attuned to the values the Bar Association advocated.

The dominant values the federal courts enforced thus suggested the relation between discretion and dependence. These values favored effective judicial procedure and process over particular substantive results. This did not mean that federal judges were unconcerned about or absolutely neutral toward given groups and interests. In specific suits the application of federal or state law or constitutional provisions brought into clear focus the connection between the federal courts' independence and a given decisional outcome. Even so, local interests were fragmented. In addition, the circumscribed character of the federal court's institutional subordination to Congress and the Supreme Court was such that usually the exercise of discretion was not only permitted, it was required. Nevertheless, the degree of discretion was defined not by direct

132

national institutional or political pressures but within the parameters of a local formal and informal legal culture. And the fundamental value shared by the bench and bar constituting this culture was that diverse and conflicting interests should be governed by consistent, if flexible, procedures. Activism was necessary but confined within conservative limits.

III
The Ascendency of National Judicial Institutions Since 1940

INTRODUCTION

During the half century following World War II, Alabama's federal courts entered a new era of change. Before the Civil War, litigation involving private business interests and the interpretation of state law reflected a paradox in which state sovereignty prescribed the boundaries of federal judicial discretion and dependence. The Civil War and Reconstruction subordinated the states to the federal government, and federal judges gained greater independence and discretionary authority. But despite this transformation, a small, local courtroom culture continued to shape the decision making of the state's federal judges. The Great Depression and the triumph of big government identified with the New Deal did not significantly diminish the interrelation between the federal judges' independence and local institutional autonomy. From the Second World War on, however, continuing federalization of litigation and national centralization of the federal judicial establishment collided with state leaders' political interests. The persistence of struggle, combined with a new market for legal services characterized by increased specialization, fostered the ascendency of national judicial institutions over the traditional federal courthouse culture.[1]

 The politics of Alabama's federal judicial appointments also changed. From the end of Reconstruction until the civil rights struggle and the rise of George Wallace, black-belt planters, urban business groups, and state courthouse bosses formed a conservative Democratic coalition that generally controlled state politics. Periodically, however, more progressive individuals such as Hugo Black used a populist campaign style to challenge the conservatives, laying the basis for the emergence during the 1930s of Alabama's National Democrats, a faction associated with Franklin D. Roosevelt's New Deal liberalism. For more than three decades, this more progressive faction dominated the federal judicial selection process. Meanwhile, during the 1950s a different brand of conservative Alabama Democrat eventually identified with George Wallace triumphed. Nevertheless, the National Democrats' role in the appointment of Alabama's federal judges was often decisive—even in the selection of Republican candidates. The stability that had characterized this judicial selection process gave way during the 1970s to a new era of confrontation represented by the growing political success of the Republican Party. Yet during the following twenty years, Democratic Senator Howell Heflin exercised a strong personal influence over judicial appointments distinct from both the Republicans and conservatives within his own party.[2]

Alabama's fragmented political culture encouraged federal judges to reconcile judicial dependence and discretion. Since before the Civil War, federal judges working within an institutional culture used jurisprudential reasoning to insulate the decision making process from direct political pressure. Following the Second World War, the new priority given individual rights by the Supreme Court, combined with the popularization of theoretical assumptions identified with legal realism, increased federal judges' willingness to explain their process of decision making. Confronted with recurring attacks from political leaders, federal judges resisted being categorized according to political labels. Conceding that one's social, professional, and political backgrounds created a precondition for deciding cases, they nonetheless asserted that national judicial institutions emerging since about 1940 exercised the controlling influence. The state's federal judges disagreed concerning the extent to which federal centralization increased dependence and circumscribed discretion. But the decline of the local federal courthouse order was clear.

The balance federal judges struck between discretion and dependence was evident in routine and constitutional litigation. At the end of the 1930s, the Supreme Court's overruling of the federal common law and adoption of the Federal Rules, combined with the New Deal's expansion of national authority, fostered an ongoing federalization of routine litigation. Accordingly, throughout the rest of the twentieth century, diversity suits involving matters of private law declined in number and importance on federal dockets, superseded by a steady increase in cases raising federal or constitutional questions. State officials' recurring lack of cooperation or outright resistance encouraged federal courts to make decisions within national institutional constraints, though Alabama's federal judges disagreed as to the scope of these limitations.[3]

THE CHANGING POLITICS OF JUDICIAL APPOINTMENTS

From World War II to the 1990s, the social background of Alabama's federal judges was fairly consistent. Generally, they came from solid middle-class or upper-middle-class families. Many, too, had military experience, including wartime service. Before becoming a judge, each had considerable experience as a general practitioner or as a plaintiff's or defense lawyer. Some sort of public service either as an elected state or federal official, administrator, or party operative was also the norm. Continuity did not, however, characterize the political dynamics of the appointment process. During Franklin Roosevelt's administration, the state's New Deal supporters formed a faction that generally determined the appointment of federal judges over the next three decades. By the early 1970s, the state's Republican Party gained increased clout under President Richard Nixon, bringing to a close an era of stability. Yet the next twenty years witnessed a persistence of Democratic influence over Alabama's judicial appointments because of Senator Howell Heflin, who adapted quite successfully to the new period of controversy. The tension between these national and local political pressures suggested that party affiliation was an inadequate measure of judicial decision making.[4]

The Era of Stability

For the first thirty years after 1940, Alabama's National Democrats controlled the state's federal judicial appointments. The National Democrats were politically connected to several long-serving U.S. senators who supported Roosevelt's New Deal liberalism. Initially identified with the politically prominent Bankhead family and then for many years tied to Senators Lister Hill and John Sparkman, the group was at odds with the state's powerful Democratic Party conservatives, including George Wallace. Despite ongoing factional struggle, the National Democrats determined the appointment of every judge chosen from the Democratic Party's ranks. During the 1950s, Alabama's small Republican Party selected Eisenhower appointees Frank M. Johnson, Jr., and Harlan H. Grooms. Both of these men nonetheless had indirect links with the National Democrats. By the early 1970s, the state's Republican organization attained greater unity and influence under Nixon, who appointed more federal judges in Alabama than even Roosevelt. Despite the Republicans' newfound strength, the National Democrats led now primarily by Sparkman continued to exercise influence, setting the stage for a new era of confrontation.

During the 1940s and 1950s the Southern and Middle districts each had one judge. From 1935 to 1950, Roosevelt appointee John McDuffie was the judge of the Southern District; Truman appointed as McDuffie's successor in 1951 Daniel H. Thomas. Both judges were Democrats. In the Middle District, Republican Charles B. Kennamer, appointed by Herbert Hoover, died in 1955; to replace him Eisenhower appointed fellow Republican Frank M. Johnson, Jr. There were two judges in the Northern District. Thomas A. Murphree,

U.S. Courthouse, Northern District, Birmingham, 1917–87. During the 20th century, Birmingham became the state's leading population center; the economic and social issues accompanying that transformation came to this courthouse. *Alabama Department of Archives and History*

Hugo Black Courthouse, Northern District, Birmingham, 1987–present. Social and economic issues of Alabama in the 21st century will come to this new courthouse in Birmingham. *Virginia Hare, Library, U.S. District Court, Northern District of Alabama*

appointed by Roosevelt in 1938, served until he died in 1945. Truman appointed Seybourn H. Lynne to replace Murphree in 1946. Roosevelt also appointed Clarence Mullins in 1943. Both of these men also were Democrats. When Mullins retired in 1953, Eisenhower appointed as his replacement Republican Harlan H. Grooms. In 1951, Truman appointed Richard T. Rives, a Democrat, to the Fifth Circuit Court of Appeals to succeed Leon McCord.

These appointments grew out of stable political factions within the Democratic and Republican parties. Murphree, Mullins, and Lynne were National Democrats, and their appointments resulted from this group's close, informal connections. In the case of Lynne, the choice occurred while he was still on duty in the Pacific at the end of World War II. Thomas was not as directly involved with the National Democrats; he was appointed because of the influence of his law partner and friend, Joseph Lyons of Mobile, who was associated with the group through Senator Lister Hill. Also a confidant of Hill, Rives was an important figure in the state's National Democratic organization. By the 1950s, Alabama's Republican Party divided its loyalty between Eisenhower and Ohio's Senator Robert A. Taft. The Eisenhower faction was more moderate, seeking to build a new southern Republican Party from the ground up. The Taft group by contrast wanted to win over disaffected conservative Democrats. Both Johnson and Grooms were Eisenhower Republicans.[5]

McDuffie had been a state prosecuting attorney, state legislator, and U.S. congressman. Murphree and Mullins had successful law practices in Birmingham, while Rives and Thomas belonged to major law firms in Montgomery and Mobile, respectively. Both Rives and Thomas had significant wartime military experience. Thomas also served as a city solicitor. After practicing for some years in north Alabama, Lynne was elected there as a state judge, a position he held for eight years before serving in the Judge Advocate General Department during the Second World War. Grooms came from Kentucky to Birmingham, where he established an active law practice; he was also an unsuccessful Republican candidate for the U.S. Congress. Johnson was a noted north Alabama lawyer from legendary Winston County, a strong Republican area ever since the Civil War, when many of its sons fought on the Union side. Johnson had been a supervisor in the Works Progress Administration during the Great Depression, and for two years before his nomination as a federal judge, he had served as U.S. attorney for north Alabama.

During the 1960s, these patterns continued as Congress added federal judgeships in Alabama. Following John F. Kennedy's election, a district judge was added to the Northern District; Alabama was also allotted a second position on the Fifth Circuit Court of Appeals. Appointed to fill these positions were

John C. Godbold (b. 1920), U.S. Court of Appeals judge from 1966 to the present; Democrat. *Montgomery Advertiser*

Clarence Allgood for the district court and Walter P. Gewin as circuit judge. Both of these men were very active in the informal National Democratic group surrounding Senators Hill and Sparkman. In addition, Allgood was a nationally recognized expert on federal bankruptcy, and Gewin was one of the state's foremost trial lawyers.

In 1966, Rives moved to senior status on the Fifth Circuit Court. President Lyndon Johnson appointed John C. Godbold to replace him. Rives had helped Godbold establish a successful law practice, facilitating his membership in Rives's old politically influential Montgomery firm that was identified with Hill and the National Democrats. Congress allocated a new judgeship to the Southern District in 1966, with Lyndon Johnson appointing former FBI agent Virgil Thomas Pittman, then serving as a state circuit judge in northern Alabama. Pittman had worked hard for Kennedy's presidential campaign. He also was involved in both the Hill and Sparkman races, remaining always a National Democratic loyalist in confrontations with Wallace over control of the state Democratic committee. Both Godbold and Pittman also had served in the military during World War II.

From the 1940s to the 1960s, the politics of federal judicial appointments were complex. Among the Democrats, affiliation with the state's two powerful U.S. senators was a prerequisite. Even so, all successful candidates had established themselves as National Democratic loyalists through local partisan activity in support of those senators. Grooms and Johnson, of course, lacked such involvement; formally, at least, they owed their nomination to the Eisenhower wing of the state's Republican organization. However, it was conceded publicly that during the period no Republican nominee received confirmation without the approval of the two Democratic senators. Thus Grooms was formally endorsed by both Democrats, and Sparkman spoke on his behalf at the confirmation hearing. Johnson received no less support. In addition, all the Democratic federal judicial appointees embraced to a greater or lesser extent Roosevelt's New Deal liberalism, which Bankhead, Hill, and Sparkman had defended against shifting groups of Alabama conservatives. Significantly, the Eisenhower Republicans supported at least in principle this same economic liberalism. Thus, Johnson had been a supervisor in the WPA during the Depression.[6]

Neither the Democratic nor Republican advocates of New Deal liberalism in Alabama directly challenged racial segregation. Godbold described this economic liberalism aptly. Liberals were "interested in rural electrification and social security and Tennessee Valley Authority and rivers and

142

roads. They were . . . lifting the level of life in the South through economic measures." These same individuals acquiesced to limiting individual liberties. They were not, Godbold concluded, "able to exercise too much force in . . . civil rights. They were pretty well silenced on that and the chang[e] to viewing liberal persons as primarily interested in individual rights came with another generation."[7]

This bipartisan consensus favoring economic liberalism encouraged a non-confrontational confirmation process. During the 1940s the associates of the National Democratic inner circle so dominated nomination and confirmation proceedings that Lynne was chosen as a federal judge while still on duty in the Pacific. During the 1950s and 1960s, brief hearings were held in which FBI and ABA reports were submitted supporting the qualifications of Rives, Thomas, Grooms, Johnson, Allgood, Gewin, Pittman, and Godbold. In every case only a few senators were present to acknowledge that Hill and Sparkman favored or at least did not oppose confirmation. After a few routine questions, confirmation was automatic.

The experience of Grooms was typical. Hill and Sparkman sent blue slips, stating no objection to the appointment. The ABA, Alabama State Bar, and Birmingham Bar "endorsed and urged appointment." There was no objection on file. The chair of the hearing asked Grooms if there was "anything" in his record that "would be apt to cause someone to blackmail" him. Grooms said, "I know of nothing." The chair observed that "very rarely do we get such a fine F.B.I. record as we have here. I want to congratulate you." The Democrat Sparkman then said regarding the Republican Grooms, "Mr. Chairman, I will not delay your proceedings. I just wanted to put in a good word for Judge Grooms. He will make a very good official." The chair then recommended confirmation.[8]

Godbold described how routine was the confirmation process during the mid-1960s. "The hearings before the [judiciary] committee were nominal . . . and the questioning was minimal," he said. "Of course if there had been someone whose qualifications were really invalid or serious questions had been raised it would have been different but . . . all those that appeared [before the committee] . . . were people about whom there were no problems and no reason to go deeply into it." Finally, what questions there were purposely avoided consideration of the nominee's views concerning particular legal or constitutional issues. It was "an approach" whereby "appointees who were questioned were not questioned about their views on any sort of issue that might come before them" once they became judges.[9]

This noncontentious appointment and confirmation process during years of civil rights struggle persisted until the end of the 1960s. By then, Democrat James B. Allen had succeeded Hill in the Senate, serving alongside Sparkman, the symbol of continuity. Yet Nixon's election presaged a change in national politics in which Republicans would dominate the presidency for most of the next quarter century. In Alabama, Republicans gained new influence with the election of Congressman John Buchanan of Birmingham and Richard Nixon's appointment of Montgomery businessman Winton M. Blount to be U.S. postmaster general. At this point the factions within the Republican Party had as much reason as the National Democrats to resist George Wallace, who had run for the presidency in 1968. Even so, when Grooms sought senior status in 1969, Blount and Buchanan nominated to succeed him Birmingham lawyer and Republican loyalist Frank McFadden. A partner in one of the state's most prestigious law firms (to which Alabama's well-known federal judge during the 1930s, William I. Grubb, had also belonged), McFadden had effectively represented Blount's enterprises. Consistent with established tradition, McFadden was confirmed without opposition, including no objection from either Sparkman or Allen.[10]

External political struggles nonetheless gradually politicized Alabama's federal judicial appointments. During the 1970s, the rising influence of the Republicans within the state and the nation put the National Democratic establishment on the defensive. By 1973, retirements and the creation of new district judgeships resulted in a seven-to-one ratio of Republicans to Democrats. No one, including Franklin Roosevelt, appointed more federal judges in Alabama than Nixon. Retirees such as Lynne and Allgood remained active, serving on senior status. Nevertheless, Sparkman, who for more than thirty years had been used to an appointment process dominated by National Democrats, felt the pressure of change. "The next time there is a federal judgeship vacancy in Alabama," Sparkman announced in 1973, "I am going to do whatever I can to see to it that a Democrat is nominated." Allen disagreed, favoring the more radical administrative move of splitting in two the Fifth Circuit leaving Alabama within a smaller circuit, thereby purportedly reducing the need for new judgeships. Accordingly, the only Democrat appointed during the period was Robert S. Vance, who joined the Fifth Circuit Court of Appeals in 1978.[11]

The growing political contentiousness surrounding Alabama's judicial appointment process coincided with the Republicans' increased advantage. During the 1970s, George Wallace continued to exploit the federal courts as

144

scapegoats in order to perpetuate his hold on the governorship. Amid the racial conflict engendered by Wallace's assault on the federal judiciary's civil rights decisions, Republicans worked to reconcile internal factional conflicts dating back to the split between Taft and Eisenhower supporters. The party's patronage committee, which selected candidates, was the object of considerable political maneuvering. Made up of the state's U.S. congressmen and various other party activists, the committee balanced not only ideological and patronage concerns but also sectional interests involving the demands of south and north Alabama. The resulting competition among the party faithful was such, observed one aspirant for judicial office, that "it appears that one must campaign for selection as judge somewhat similarly to campaigning for elective office."[12]

During the early 1970s, Nixon made five judicial appointments (he had already appointed McFadden in 1969). In the Northern District, Congress created in 1970 a new district judgeship, which Birmingham attorney Sam C. Pointer, Jr., filled. At the time of confirmation, Pointer, the former vice chairman and general counsel for the state Republican Party, was the nation's youngest federal judge. The next year, Lynne and Allgood retired in the Northern District, as did Thomas in the Southern District, and Congress added a new judgeship in the Middle District. With the retiring judges moving to senior status, the Republican patronage committee selected north Alabama attorney J. Foy Guin, Jr., Birmingham lawyer James H. Hancock, and William Brevard Hand, a member of a prestigious Mobile law firm. Guin and Hand were active Republican Party leaders on the county level, while Hancock was general counsel for the Republican Party of Alabama. Robert E. Varner, a prominent lawyer and longtime Republican from the black belt, was the patronage committee's selection to fill the new Middle District judgeship. Varner's grandfather was an Alabama Supreme Court judge; his family was one of the oldest in the southern part of the state.[13]

The Senate confirmed these appointees without opposition, but soon thereafter some encountered criticism. Like McFadden before them, Nixon's five nominees received no negative reports in the Senate hearings. The only problem associated with the nomination process was that initially the patronage committee had considered filling one of the seats in the Northern District with an individual who resided outside the district. Expressions of concern from the Birmingham and north Alabama bar defeated this move. Amid other controversy Wallace and U.S. Senator Allen denounced Pointer for a school desegregation decision he handed down in 1971. Described as a "frocked dictator" and "irresponsible," Pointer joined the company of Judge Frank

J. Foy Guin, Jr. (b. 1924), Northern District judge from 1973 to the present; Republican. *Judge Guin's Chambers*

Johnson as the object of such attacks. Thus even as the era of stability came to a close, there was continuity with the past.[14]

A New Era of Confrontation

By the late 1970s, the political party process controlling judicial appointments was fragmenting. The solidarity of the National Democrats was enhanced by Sparkman's survival until 1979; it was perpetuated by the skill of his political associate Robert S. Vance, chairman of the State Democratic Executive Committee. Nevertheless, Heflin's election in 1978 on the platform of "Alabama values" indicated how race had sufficiently divided even the National Democrats. A racially neutral, state oriented campaign slogan was necessary to ensure victory. Similarly, the successful struggle within the state GOP to defeat the reelection of moderate Republican congressman John Buchanan of Birmingham in 1980 was part of a realignment of factions in which conservatives prevailed. Alabama's Republican conservatives gravitated toward the party's rising star, Ronald Reagan. More so than the old Eisenhower moderates, the Reagan Republicans sought to woo conservative Democrats to the Grand Old Party.[15]

As the 1970s ended, the political stakes of judicial appointments increased because Congress again added new judgeships. Led by Heflin and new Democratic Senator Donald Stewart, Congress allotted Alabama a new position on the enlarged U.S. Fifth Circuit Court of Appeals, three new judges in the Northern District, and one additional slot in the Middle District. The growth anticipated the division of the Fifth Circuit, creating the new Eleventh Circuit Court of Appeals in 1981. Further complicating the judicial appointment process was a merit policy endorsed by President Jimmy Carter, aimed at ensuring the selection of women and minorities. In Alabama and the South generally, this meant that the nomination of qualified African Americans was necessary. Although the purpose of the merit system was also to appoint women, in Alabama it was conceded that such a nomination was "unlikely" despite the availability of such eminently qualified individuals as Camille Cook, a dean of the University of Alabama School of Law, and state supreme court justice Janie Shores.[16]

The appointments reflected a fragmented political process. When Gewin retired from the Fifth Circuit in 1976, his successor was the Democratic Party stalwart Robert S. Vance of Birmingham. Vance's leadership of the state's Democratic Committee was so effective that all factions supported his confirmation, including National Democrats, blacks, independents, and even George Wallace. Similarly, Truman Hobbs, National Democrat and member of

Rives's old law firm in Montgomery, received unopposed and speedy Senate approval for one of the two Middle District positions. Hobbs filled the new seat Congress created. Nevertheless, Heflin and Stewart each recommended a candidate for the opening, leaving the decision to the Carter administration, which picked Hobbs, Heflin's choice. The appointment of Frank Johnson to the new Fifth Circuit position, by contrast, did not involve Alabama's Democratic Party organization at all. Attorney General Griffin Bell had invited the well-known Johnson to apply for the post, and he was confirmed expeditiously.[17]

Party unity was also not conspicuous in the appointment of Robert Propst and Bert Haltom to two of the Northern District positions. From the north Alabama towns of Anniston and Florence respectively, Propst and Haltom received high approval ratings from professional legal organizations. Within the party, by contrast, the support was more focused. Haltom had often been associated with the Wallace faction, and Propst described himself as an independent. Even so, Propst once had been Stewart's law partner, and Haltom had supported Heflin's campaign, thus providing a more personal basis for confirmation.[18]

Implementation of the Carter administration's merit policy further indicated how conflicted was the appointment process. To increase support for the merit policy among the state party factions, the administration had assigned an additional district judgeship to Alabama. The nomination of an African American to the Middle District nonetheless divided Heflin and Stewart, though both ultimately agreed on Hobbs as the white nominee. Meanwhile, Stewart's nomination of Fred Gray, a prominent black civil rights lawyer from Tuskegee, to fill the place vacated by Johnson became controversial, and Gray finally withdrew his name from consideration. Heflin then nominated a little-known young black lawyer from Dothan, Myron Thompson. Only thirty-three years old, a Yale Law School graduate, and former assistant in the state attorney general's office, Thompson was a respected member of the local south Alabama bar. His appointment nonetheless encountered sufficient opposition that Heflin initially estimated the odds of Thompson winning confirmation to be just 50-50.[19]

The appointment of an African American to the remaining Northern District post engendered further controversy. Among several candidates, the choice finally was between J. Mason Davis, favored by a faction associated with the old National Democrats, and Heflin's former political ally, U. W. Clemon. A graduate of Columbia Law School and a state senator representing Birmingham, Clemon was a prominent civil rights activist. In the state senate he had

148

Robert S. Vance (1931–1989), U.S. Court of Appeals judge from 1978 to 1989; Democrat. *Birmingham Public Library Archives*

given valuable support to Heflin's campaign (while Heflin was chief justice of the state's supreme court) to reform and modernize Alabama's antiquated judicial system. Clemon was also associated with future Birmingham mayor Richard Arrington. Nevertheless, allegations involving tax liens jeopardized Clemon's nomination, arousing a heated response from Heflin in Clemon's defense.[20]

The confrontations involving Gray, Thompson, and Clemon suggested how politicized the judicial appointment process had become. The Carter administration's merit policy required bringing into the state Democratic Party's selection process groups that previously had been excluded. Unsettled by this new competition, white lawyers demanded and received an additional judicial position to mitigate adoption of the policy. As each of the three candidates was considered, questions were raised concerning qualifications. Without explanation, the American Bar Association gave Gray and Clemon an "unqualified" rating, whereas Thompson's rating was "qualified." The basis for the ratings was unclear. Between Gray and Clemon, moreover, the charges were quite different in substance. There were no allegations raised against Thompson; only the length of his professional experience was questioned, though he was only two years younger than Pointer had been when he was nominated.

Indeed, the difficulty of ascertaining what was the standard against which the African-American nominees were being measured was apparent in the Birmingham Bar Association's resolution opposing Clemon's confirmation. It was the "unanimous opinion" of the association's Executive Committee that Clemon was "a competent and skillful lawyer who rightly enjoys a professional reputation of discharging his obligations to clients in a highly professional manner." Against the committee's "unanimous opinion" were its "serious reservations about the appointment to the Federal bench of any person who has a record of handling personal income taxes in the indifferent manner in which Mr. Clemon has handled his own."[21]

Ultimately, Heflin's role suggested how politically fragmented the nomination and confirmation process had become. Within the state Democratic Party, the selection of the five candidates, including Thompson and Clemon, left "old political allies . . . estranged," "stunned and bitterly disappointed." As a result, the "contest for state party leadership and the presidency" was conflicted. More particularly, Heflin was caught between the "black wing" of the state party and the "mostly white Alabama legal establishment, which played a role in the negative ABA report on the black judgeship nominees."

150

Bert Haltom, Jr. (b. 1922), Northern District judge from 1980 to the present; Democrat. *Judge Haltom's Chambers*

Typically, Heflin tried to satisfy both groups by withdrawing his endorsement of Gray while vigorously supporting Clemon and Thompson. At the same time, Heflin maneuvered skillfully on the U.S. Senate's Judiciary Committee to mollify Republicans who had delayed the confirmation of Democratic appointees in other states, hoping for a GOP presidential victory in 1980. Regarding the Alabama appointments, however, Republicans complied with Heflin's wishes. There were full hearings accompanied by lengthy questioning of Clemon and, to a lesser extent, Thompson. But when this process ended with Heflin's strong endorsement, Republicans and Democrats alike overwhelmingly approved both nominees.[22]

The politics of federal judicial appointments had changed. Allgood described the old system employed by Senators Bankhead, Hill, and Sparkman. When a judicial vacancy opened up, said Allgood, the "senators would gather their close political family around them . . . and they'd go over the possibilities." The two basic qualifications were, first, a solid enough legal and ethical record so as not to be an "embarrassment," and second, "he's got to be a friend and supporter and a good Democrat, not necessarily in that order."

Under the new Carter policy, reliance on the merit commission to filter candidates and promote minorities and women had two consequences. First, the commission increased the immediate involvement of the president and the attorney general in the selection process, from the grassroots state party level to the confirmation stage in the Senate. Second, the merit policy increased the importance of nominees having personal associations with an influential senator. The commission's presence lifted from the senator much of the political onus for supporting a controversial nominee. Ironically, the commission's implementation of a merit policy disrupted the local party, thereby heightening the value of personal connections. Thus, despite the rift it caused in the state party, Heflin supported the first black candidates in the state's history. Similarly, Hobbs belonged to the old National Democrat wing, Haltom had been closer to Wallace during the struggle over the executive committee's leadership, and Propst was an independent though his former law partner was Senator Stewart. Yet Heflin's organization was fluid enough to include all these groups.

Regarding the triumph of Thompson and Clemon especially, Heflin's more ecumenical influence was important. Those associated with the old National Democrats favored J. Mason Davis of Birmingham as one of the minority candidates. Nevertheless, Heflin never wavered in his support for Clemon, whose aid had been instrumental in bringing about the overhaul of the state's judicial system when Heflin was chief justice. As a senator, moreover,

Heflin benefited from the endorsement of future Birmingham mayor Arrington, one of the most powerful black defenders of Clemon. Thus Heflin deferred to a mix of personal and political associations over the expectations of the traditional Democratic party establishment. Heflin's contribution to Thompson's appointment was more complicated but no less important. Senator Stewart had vigorously pushed Gray's nomination. When Gray withdrew, the number of available black candidates in the state, let alone in south Alabama where Gray was from, was quite small. The Democrats' black leadership urged one seasoned civil rights lawyer from the southern section, but he turned them down. Only then did the leadership turn to Thompson, whom Heflin quickly endorsed. Heflin's advocacy in the Senate, moreover, brought speedy confirmation.

During the 1980s, the number of Republicans appointed to federal judgeships in Alabama increased. The traditional process involved the state executive committee and affiliated individuals, including the growing number of congressmen, selecting candidates. The congressmen passed the name along to the president, who formally made the nomination. Since the late nineteenth century, Alabama's senators were Democrats, but they officially deferred to the local GOP's candidates when a Republican was in the White House. Over the four decades after 1952, Republicans controlled the presidency for twenty-eight years, while Democrats held the Senate for most of that same period.

During the Nixon administration, a seven-to-one majority of Republican district judges was achieved. The addition of five Democratic judges under Carter diminished but did not erase this dominance. Even when Frank Johnson, whose stature transcended party affiliation, was taken into account, Nixon and Reagan appointees held the edge in the district courts. Regarding the Alabama seats on the circuit court, Republicans did not occupy a majority until 1987, and again one of these was Johnson.[23]

During the 1980s and 1990s this Republican dominance increased. In the election of 1980, Reagan's coattails carried into the U.S. Senate a Republican majority, including Jeremiah Denton. A true hero of the Vietnam War, Denton was the first Republican elected to the U.S. Senate from Alabama in over a century. Until 1994 Denton was also the only Republican, because in 1986 he was defeated for reelection by Democrat Richard Shelby (Shelby switched to the Republican Party in 1994). Still, the combination of a Republican in the White House and, for much of the period, a Republican Senate provided Alabama Republicans with new opportunities to increase their numbers on the state's federal bench. In 1982, McFadden, a Republican, resigned in the Northern District to be succeeded by Republican Party loyalist William M. Acker, Jr., of

Birmingham. The same year, Pittman, a Democrat in the Southern District, took senior status, leaving a vacancy filled by Mobile GOP member Emmett R. Cox. When Godbold retired in 1986, Cox replaced him on the circuit court, opening up the district court seat taken by Mobile Republican Alex T. Howard. In 1984, Varner moved to senior status, and Montgomery federal magistrate and local Republican leader Joel F. Dubina filled that vacancy. By 1994, in all three districts and on the circuit court, there were only three active judges appointed by a Democratic president: Clemon, Thompson, and Propst, and Propst described himself as an independent.[24]

Ironically, the appointment process producing this Republican majority was conflicted. Despite Republican control of the Senate and Denton's membership there during most of the 1980s, more controversy than ever arose involving Republican judicial appointments. Denton's impressive credentials as a war hero did not prepare him for the dynamics of patronage politics. Following each of the vacancies, there were delays while the Republican leadership and Denton sorted through candidates. When Pittman moved to senior status, Denton expressed surprise. Of the several candidates who emerged for the post, Cox was the least prominent Republican, though one of his law partners was a Denton confidant. Ultimately, Denton sent several names to the White House, and Cox was the choice. The length of time it took to sort out candidates irritated Acker, who then looked more to Heflin for leadership in the confirmation process than to Denton. Similarly, Dubina's nomination resulted more from local support in Montgomery than from Denton's. In the confirmation process, Heflin, for whose election campaign Dubina had worked in 1978, again was more conspicuous.

Howard's experience indicated how uncertain was Denton's contribution to the selection and confirmation process. Godbold's retirement and Cox's succession to the circuit court left the Southern District vacancy, which the Republicans sought to fill with Mobile U.S. Attorney Jeff Sessions. Denton supported the nomination. Civil rights groups, however, charged that Sessions was not friendly to their cause. After considerable conflict, Heflin stated that there was sufficient substance to the allegations that he declined to support the nomination, and Sessions was defeated. The Republican committee and Denton then turned to Howard, whose pro–civil rights reputation was strong enough that he received the formal endorsement of the NAACP. After Heflin as well as Denton strongly supported Howard, the Senate Judiciary Committee gave him a unanimous vote. That same committee had not long before rejected Sessions. Thus Heflin's role influenced the defeat of the one and the victory of the other.[25]

Between 1988 and 1994 there was some turnover among Alabama's federal judges. In the Southern District, Hand took senior status and Congress added a third judgeship: To the first, Reagan appointed Charles R. Butler, Jr., and Bush chose Richard W. Vollmer, Jr., to fill the second. Hobbs took senior status in 1989, shortly after the death of Robert S. Vance, and Dubina was elevated to the Eleventh Circuit Court of Appeals from the Middle District; to fill these district court positions Bush appointed W. Harold Albritton and Ira DeMent. In the Northern District, Guin and Haltom took senior status; Bush appointed to replace them Edwin L. Nelson and Sharon Lovelace Blackburn (the first woman appointed as a federal judge in Alabama). When Johnson retired, Bush appointed Edward E. Carnes to the Eleventh Circuit in 1992. The constant in these changeovers was Heflin's influence.

The social and professional background of Alabama's federal judges remained consistent even as the politics of appointment changed. Notwithstanding tensions associated with race and regardless of political party affiliation, each judge came from a middle- or upper-middle-class family. Many, too, served in the military during wartime. Each judicial appointee also had some sort of public service in elected or appointed office, as well as professional experience in a general or specialized legal practice. George Wallace and others (both Democrats and Republicans) attacked federal judges throughout much of this time. But that confrontation was less significant than the changing mix of local and national pressures identified with the shifting influence of the National Democratic or Republican operatives. This culminated in the political fragmentation represented by the influence of Senator Howell Heflin beginning in the late 1970s. Despite certain important exceptions, during each phase of change local personal connections within national party membership determined federal judicial appointments, making party affiliation alone an inadequate indicator of judicial decision making.

LOCAL POLITICAL CULTURE AND JURISPRUDENCE

The shifting influence of National Democrats, Republicans, and Senator Howell Heflin reflected Alabama's changing political culture. During the postwar period, when the National Democrats determined federal judicial appointments, a commitment to New Deal liberal economic policies diluted Alabamians' otherwise tenacious attachment to conservative values of weak political democracy, limited government, and racial segregation. But initially the National Democrats vigorously supported neither the civil rights crusade

W. Harold Albritton, *left*, being welcomed to the federal bench by Myron H. Thompson. Albritton (b. 1936) was appointed Middle District judge in 1991; Republican. *Montgomery Advertiser*

Ira DeMent (b. 1931), Middle District judge from 1992 to the present; Republican. *Montgomery Advertiser*

Edwin L. Nelson (b. 1940), judge of the Northern District from 1990 to the present; Republican. *U.S. District Court, Northern District*

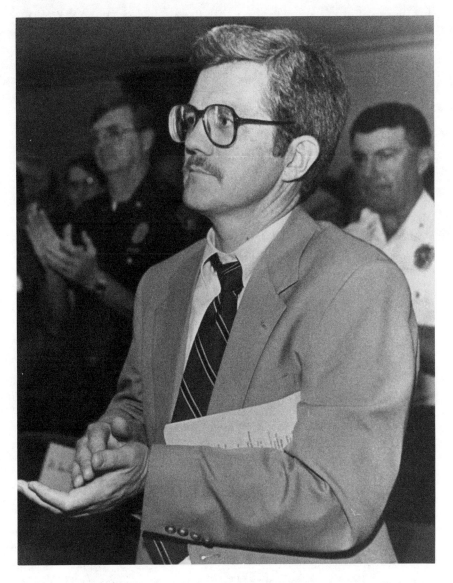

Edward E. Carnes (b. 1950), judge of the Eleventh Circuit Court of Appeals from 1992 to the present; Republican. *Montgomery Advertiser*

nor individual rights generally. Not until the 1970s were southern defenders of more active government generally identified with favoring civil rights and liberties. George Wallace and others advocated a political ideology that equated racial justice with liberalism and federal court intervention. As a result, the state's political culture became increasingly fragmented, reflected by Heflin's ambiguous platform of "Alabama values." Meanwhile, the state's federal judges espoused a jurisprudence consistent with the precepts of legal realism, addressing the relative balance between judicial activism and self-restraint, government or private authority and individual rights. The tenets of this jurisprudence—indicated by interviews with Alabama's federal judges and suggested further by their legal education—ran along a continuum, which nonetheless reflected the local political culture's weak influence on decision making.[26]

Local Political Culture and Individual Rights

By World War II, the local political culture shaping the appointment of Alabama's federal judges was changing. After the Civil War, a small group of conservative, wealthy white men in the Democratic Party, who represented the black belt, courthouses beyond the black belt, and industrial corporate interests located in Birmingham and a few other cities, defeated Reconstruction and instituted Jim Crow segregation. These conservatives maintained control through a policy based on low voter participation, minimal government, and white supremacy. As the rise of Hugo Black and others during the 1920s indicated, however, coalitions of less powerful interests could defeat the conservatives under certain circumstances. During the administration of Franklin Roosevelt from 1933 to 1945, an opposition coalition emerged built around the national programs instituted to combat the Depression and to fight the Second World War. Between 1940 and 1969, most of the federal judges coming from Alabama directly or indirectly owed their appointment to Alabama's National Democrats.

Several powerful U.S. senators from Alabama identified as National Democrats were chiefly responsible for these appointments. Reenforcing the group's solidarity were informal but significant social, professional, and political connections. An important factor, particularly for Sparkman, was membership in the Pi Kappa Alpha fraternity, active chapters of which were located at the University of Alabama and Auburn University. The "Pike" connection influenced not only the appointment of Democrats such as Allgood and Lynne but also that of Republican Frank M. Johnson, Jr. Membership in certain law firms also overlapped with these political and social connections, particularly the firm founded by National Democrat Richard Rives in Montgomery. Rives's two law partners were close relatives of Lister Hill; as congressman and senator, Hill relied on Rives to mobilize support for the loyal National Democratic organization in the conservative black belt. Because of Rives's success, Hill supported his appointment to the Fifth Circuit Court of Appeals in 1951. Two other Alabama federal judges who had been politically active National Democrats and also members of Rives's law firm were John C. Godbold and Truman Hobbs.[27]

The National Democrats' position within the state's larger Democratic Party changed. In 1948, many of the conservative Democrats bolted the party to form the Dixiecrat States' Rights opposition. Calling themselves Loyalists, the National Democrats seized control of Alabama's Democratic Executive Committee in 1950. Throughout the 1960s and 1970s, George Wallace displaced the old conservative Democrats with his own coalition, which nonetheless relied on black-belt whites and the courthouse leadership outside the black belt. Yet even during the Wallace period, the Loyalists retained control of the executive committee machinery. As a result, the influence of the National Democrats in the appointment of federal judges persisted until the 1970s.[28]

From the 1940s to the 1970s, Alabama's Republican Party also influenced judicial appointments. Since the turn of the century, the Republicans had remained active on the local level in Alabama despite the Democrats' statewide dominance. Between 1940 and 1980, there was no Republican U.S. senator and only a few Republican congressmen. But the Republicans held the presidency for sixteen years, and during those years there were more Republicans than Democrats appointed as federal judges in Alabama. Although the Republicans were divided between moderates and conservatives, the division was not pronounced enough to prevent unified control of the state party's executive committee. This committee and various other affiliated individuals made the initial selection of judicial nominees, though throughout much of the period the final choice had to be acceptable to Hill and Sparkman.

During the 1970s and 1980s Alabama's political party structure became more fragmented. George Wallace and the civil rights movement brought an end to the old conservative elite. As a result, new leadership made up of Republicans and Democrats emerged. During the twelve years of national Republican rule beginning in 1981, Alabama became very much a two-party state, symbolized by the election in 1980 of the first Republican U.S. senator since Reconstruction, Jeremiah Denton. Democrat Richard Shelby defeated Denton for reelection in 1986, but the Republicans' statewide power remained strong. Throughout the same period, however, African Americans, poor whites, and women exercised increasing influence through the faction of the Democratic Party that evolved out of the Loyalists.

No public figure reflected the state's new political order better than Democratic Senator Howell Heflin. Voters from all factions elected Heflin in 1978, supporting his platform of "Alabama values." He became a powerful member of the Senate's Judiciary Committee, and neither Republican nor Democratic nominees for Alabama's federal judgeships were appointed without his support. Heflin's influence rested primarily on personal connections that cut across all factions, including Republicans and Democrats, liberals and conservatives. When Congress increased the number of Alabama's federal judgeships just prior to the division of the Fifth Circuit in two and the creation of the new Eleventh Circuit Court of Appeals, three out of five of the Democrats appointed to the new district courts possessed political ties to Heflin. Similarly, during the twelve years the Republicans controlled the presidency beginning in 1981, some of Alabama's Republican judicial appointees supported Heflin.[29]

The shifting political influences shaping judicial appointments also reflected changing values. Long after the last of the Reconstruction Republicans left the state's federal bench early in the twentieth century, the values of minimal government, low political participation, and racism dominated Alabama's political culture. The Democratic judicial appointees identified with the National Democrats. Their acceptance of the basic New Deal policies weakened, but did not altogether displace, the belief in minimal government. Even as more Republicans came to the bench, the general trend of Alabama judges' decision making regarding economic regulation and social welfare was one of moderation. If anything, this rejection of either an extreme liberal or conservative stance became more pronounced during the political fragmentation prevailing during the 1980s and 1990s.[30]

The Alabama federal judiciary's role in the struggle for the rights of dispossessed groups was more complex. Beginning with Rosa Parks's refusal to give up her seat on a bus to a white, which set off the Montgomery boycott led by Martin Luther King, Jr., in 1955, a few of Alabama's federal judges acquired a reputation as defenders of individual rights, primarily Johnson in the Middle District and Rives on the Fifth Circuit. Lynne, Thomas, Grooms, Allgood, and Gewin approached such issues cautiously, sustaining segregation until the Fifth Circuit and the Supreme Court established unequivocal precedent. Ironically, when George Wallace, Eugene "Bull" Connor, and others sought political advantage by defying the authority of Johnson and Rives, they encouraged stronger federal intervention, which in turn compelled the state's other federal judges to defend individual rights more vigorously.[31]

Formal political party affiliation inadequately explained the federal judiciary's uneven decisions in the field of individual rights. Johnson and Grooms were Republicans; Rives, Gewin, Thomas, and Lynne were Democrats. The divergence between Rives and the other Democrats was especially pronounced, since each of them was affiliated directly or indirectly with the National Democratic organization of Senators Hill and Sparkman. Meanwhile, beginning in the mid-1960s, Democratic Loyalists Pittman and Godbold gained reputations as moderates. The distinction between the Republicans was only a little less explicit. Grooms and Johnson were nationally active Republicans from what at the time was a small state party, though Johnson benefited from knowing and being chosen by the Eisenhower administration's attorney general, Herbert Brownell. Although both men were appointed by the same Republican administration only two years apart, Grooms took the more moderate stance toward individual rights. To most Alabamians and many other Americans, by contrast, Johnson was the quintessential liberal judge defending civil rights and liberties.

Amid the growing dominance of Republican judicial appointments during the 1970s, the inconsistency involving individual rights persisted. Professional legal organizations labeled Nixon appointee Fred Pointer a moderate, as well as one the nation's most effective district judges. Wallace and others nonetheless attacked Pointer as a liberal because of his desegregation decisions. Nixon appointees James Hancock, Robert E. Varner, William B. Hand, and J. Foy Guin, Jr., were regarded as conservatives. Rarely if ever did Wallace assault these judges because of their civil rights decisions. Appointed by President Jimmy Carter to the Fifth Circuit in 1978, Loyalist Robert S. Vance was the only Alabama Democrat who became a federal judge during the 1970s. He was considered a moderate on individual rights.

The triumph of Reagan Republicanism in 1980 further complicated individual rights in Alabama. The allocation of the state's new federal district judgeships, coinciding with the creation of the Eleventh Circuit Court of Appeals in 1981, provided Democrats an opportunity to make appointments before the Republicans took over the presidency and the Senate. In the selection process, Heflin's influence was marked. Receiving two of the appointments were Propst and Haltom; Haltom was especially active in Heflin's 1978 senatorial campaign. Both lawyers described themselves as moderates on issues involving individual rights.[32]

U. W. Clemon was the first African American appointed to the state's federal court. He was also a prominent civil rights activist. As a state senator on the legislature's judicial committee, Clemon's support had been vital to Heflin

Left to right: Walter P. Gewin, Richard Rives, U.S. Supreme Court Justice Arthur Goldberg, John Godbold. Gewin (b.1908), a Democrat, was appointed to the Fifth Circuit Court of Appeals in 1961. Rives (b. 1895), also a Democrat, served as a judge on the Fifth Circuit Court of Appeals from 1951 to 1966. *University of Alabama, School of Law, Special Collections*

when as chief justice of Alabama's Supreme Court he fought to modernize the state's judicial system. Only Myron Thompson, the state's other African-American federal judicial appointee (but the fourth judge selected), had no direct Heflin connection. He was, however, favorably disposed toward civil rights. The fifth appointee was Truman Hobbs, a National Democrat and Heflin supporter. A member of Rives's old law firm and former law clerk of Justice Hugo L. Black, Hobbs was also considered a liberal on individual rights issues.

During the 1980s, these five Democrats were joined on the bench by Reagan Republicans. Yet the Republicans proved no better than the Democrats at selecting judges whose decisions were ideologically uniform concerning individual rights. Dubina was a careful judicial craftsman adhering consistently to moderation in cases involving civil rights and liberties. Howard described himself as a believer in the same values as conservative Democrats, except on individual rights issues where he said he was more moderate. The most complex individual was William H. Acker, Jr. A one-time Democrat, he fervently espoused the Reagan conservative credo, and many of his decisions reflected this faith. Nevertheless, lawyers generally considered Acker an iconoclast and, especially in the field of individual rights, unpredictable.[33]

Again, the relationship with Heflin provided a reference point for the Republicans' uneven decision making. The formal nomination of all three men came from Denton. Dubina's political values were sufficiently ecumenical, however, that prior to becoming a judge he had worked in Heflin's election campaign while he voted Republican in presidential elections. Acker also voted for Republican presidents but asserted that the U.S. senator whom he felt represented him personally was Heflin. Howard enthusiastically supported both Denton and Republican presidential candidates.[34]

This mixed judicial stance toward individual rights reflected the complex position of race in the postwar South. During the first two decades following the Second World War, the civil rights movement first challenged and then won abolition of the legal basis of Jim Crow segregation. During the next twenty-five years, however, racial tensions persisted. The enfranchisement and increased officeholding of African Americans perpetuated racially polarized voting. Indeed, race was central to the voting patterns of both the Democratic and Republican parties. By the 1980s, many Southerners, like a majority of Americans, denied believing in racism and white supremacy. Yet the political culture perpetuated coded beliefs and modes of thought that reduced many problems to racial causation.[35]

Alabamians shared with other Southerners and Americans generally this tendency to think in racial code. Within the state and across the nation, the struggle over individual rights centered on equality. To the leaders of the civil rights movement such as Martin Luther King, Jr., equality meant an end to racial discrimination imposed by law so that African Americans could achieve economic independence, opportunity, and dignity. For whites, however, the defeat of legally sanctioned discrimination was enough. Equal treatment before the law and equality of opportunity were the same thing, and the only job of both the government and the courts was to enforce a simple principle of nondiscrimination. Nevertheless, critics pointed out that doing away with Jim Crow segregation did not remedy the harm and inequality of economic opportunity African Americans had suffered because of the long history of racial subordination. Accordingly, what was needed was a definition of equality that took race into account until the heritage of exploitation was destroyed.[36]

In Alabama, the contentiousness involving the changing meaning of equality unevenly influenced judicial appointments. From the 1940s to the 1980s, the federal judges appointed through the National Democrat and Republican state selection processes did not possess uniform attitudes regarding racial equality. This diversity suggested that local political considerations and relationships dominated the nomination process. Primarily, personal connections and loyalties within the controlling factions of either party determined who received nomination as a federal district or circuit judge. Thus the National Democrats from Bankhead to Hill and Sparkman nominated a Rives or a Lynne as a reward for service in battles against the old conservatives, the Dixiecrats, or Wallace. Bonds of loyalty transcended and obscured possible views toward race, so Rives's judicial liberalism was not predictable. Although he was the personal choice of Attorney General Brownell, the same was true of the Republican's selection of Frank M. Johnson, Jr., whose father had been for years the only Republican in the state legislature. During the 1970s and 1980s both parties attempted to impose more accountability in order to take race into account. But as the mixed appointments resulting from Heflin's clout suggested, diversity prevailed.[37]

The Jurisprudence of Alabama's Federal Judges

Although local political considerations and personal connections determined judicial appointments, political pressures generally did not control a federal judge's jurisprudence. The Supreme Court's constitutional revolution of 1936–37 paved the way for a recurring struggle in which more than at any time since Reconstruction, local politicians in Alabama and elsewhere attacked the federal

166

Truman M. Hobbs (b. 1921), Middle District judge from 1980 to the present; Democrat. *Montgomery Advertiser*

courts as lawmakers. The politicalization of the federal judiciary reflected a popularization of legal realism. The claims of George Wallace and others that the judges were applying their own will rather than following the law was consistent with certain teachings of the legal realists. Thus, because of the political controversy, Alabamians instinctively absorbed a basic jurisprudential insight.[38] Judges admitted that their personal backgrounds influenced their decision making, but they recognized the greater importance of the law.[39]

The public's perception of the factors motivating judicial decisions was shaken during the 1930s. As a result of the constitutional revolution of 1936–37, the Supreme Court abruptly changed to a policy upholding Roosevelt's New Deal. In *Palko v. Connecticut* (1937) and *U.S. v. Carolene Products Co.* (1938), the Court also began a new course of decisions defending individual rights. This simultaneous reversal of precedent meant that the Court would approach economic issues with cautious self-restraint, whereas in the field of individual rights it would employ stricter scrutiny and greater activism. Despite the scale of change, most laypeople and lawyers were slow to grasp the significance of the 1936-37 transformation. The Court's initial rejection of the New Deal and Roosevelt's ill-fated court-packing attempt stirred the public's awareness that judges did more than merely find the correct law and apply it. Yet for most Americans, the limits within which judges exercised discretion were more obscure than ever. The legal realists' contention that a judge's background influenced decision making more than precedent or other judicial canons was little known outside the legal profession's elite.[40]

The uncertainties accompanying this constitutional revolution had tangible ramifications for Alabamians. During the 1930s, several cases involving the constitutionality of New Deal programs arose in the state. In the 1940s, Jehovah's Witnesses and organized labor also brought suits that resulted in pioneering Supreme Court opinions reversing precedent and applying the guarantees of the First Amendment to the state through the due process clause of the Fourteenth Amendment.[41] The Court's activism had a still wider impact on public opinion in cases involving racial justice. The *Brown v. Board of Education* decision in 1954 overturned half a century of precedents favoring racial segregation. After *Brown*, racially separate but supposedly equal public facilities were declared inherently unequal under the equal protection clause of the Fourteenth Amendment.[42]

The massive resistance of white Alabamians to the *Brown* principle began with Rosa Parks and the Montgomery bus boycott. A confrontation of enormous proportions developed. Central to the conflict was George Wallace's repeated criticism of the federal judiciary's civil rights decisions, which insisted that federal judges decided civil rights cases according to personal whim rather than formal judicial canons. Wallace's contention received support from Richard Nixon's 1968 presidential campaign. Urban racial violence and the painful and divisive struggle over the Vietnam War weakened public sympathy for the civil rights movement. To many Americans, including no doubt most Alabamians, Nixon's assertion that the Supreme Court's vigorous defense of individual rights was a primary cause of unrest rang true. His promise to appoint only judges who believed in judicial self-restraint seemed compelling. A writer for *The New Yorker* observed that "Mr. Nixon's attacks on the Court undoubtedly helped him win." Nixon followed a campaign strategy Wallace had exploited for years in Alabama.[43]

Thus, Alabamians instinctively embraced the legal realist's jurisprudential insight, even without knowing the formal term. Faced with the repeated assertions of Wallace and others, white Alabamians could readily believe that such cherished ideals as racial segregation were no longer considered valid merely because federal judges were now interpreting the Constitution and laws according to their own liberal philosophy. Many of Alabama's federal judges conceded that this was the popular view. Said Judge Guin, the "public incorrectly thinks that judges decide cases the way they personally believe they should be decided. Judges are in reality bound by the law. The press aggravates this problem. It should be made clear that judges are guided by the law, not their personal opinions."[44]

The federal judges' own perceptions of the factors shaping their decisions existed along a continuum. At one end were those who said that basically they found and declared the law. Judge Propst even denied being influenced by "*any* personal ideology." He applied the "law if it can be determined," and it was not his "responsibility to be 'progressive,' 'reactionary,' or 'activist' but only to seek and apply law." The discretion that inevitably existed operated in large part on the level of procedure. As a result, the judge employed his judgment to "move cases as rapidly as reasonably possible. Try to resolve cases at this [the trial] level but do not *force* settlements. Quickly address legal issues." Otherwise, he concluded, "I have no preconceived notions that I am aware of. I am a stickler for the facts. Judges are not privileged to have personal leanings or philosophies."[45]

Essentially, this perception assumed that judges were able to be strictly neutral. Beyond the flexibility required in resolving procedural concerns, decision making involved adapting innumerable facts and situations to changing statutes or court opinions. "You have to realize that the largest percentage of today's cases have theories that were unknown twenty years ago," Judge Propst

Robert B. Propst (b. 1931), Northern District judge from 1980 to the present; Democrat.

said, "either because of changes in statutes or because of case law development." He well knew that a judge possessed considerable leeway in such cases, because as a lawyer in personal injury suits he had a well-deserved reputation for employing precedents to develop new theories that often won. In one of his best-known victories he overcame the established doctrine that the federal government was immune to private suit, creating a new precedent that required that on military bases the federal government was bound to operate maintenance equipment safely even if the functions were not performed by on-duty personnel. In another case he used this same theoretical acumen to win the "largest personal injury judgment against an individual in Calhoun County."[46]

Near the other end of the continuum were judges who acknowledged exercising discretion to the point of being unpredictable. Acker described himself as "chimerical and difficult to get a handle on. Many ha[d] tried to determine my direction, but failed . . . I could not predict it myself." He was sure that "facts do not solve a case" and that decisional outcomes were shaped by the judge's "background." Still, if someone were "to read all his opinions to abstract a direction they would probably be wrong." Although this unpredictability had caused the bar and the appellate bench to consider him "an activist," he denied that he was. Ironically, he observed that to "regain the constitutional moorings that legal realists have discarded requires activism, game playing, risk taking, and malice aforethought."[47]

Judge Clemon was just as forthright. He started with an "orientation" that was "libertarian." His background was such to "leav[e] me very little to be conservative about," and as it was with "all judges," one's background was reflected in any given "unique judgment." Yet his orientation often made "no difference." In certain cases his criminal decisions were "more severe," and in "some civil rights cases plaintiffs [were] completely wrong." Like his colleagues he was "bound by the rule of law" and "follow[ed] the decrees of both the Supreme Court and the Circuit Court of Appeals."[48]

Closer to the middle of the continuum were judges who explained their basis for making exceptions. No judge denied the obligation to seek the law and apply it. In situations where just exactly what was the law was in doubt, Judge Guin applied what he called "traditional values." He emphasized that this did not make him "a radical." Judges who attempted "to legislate violated their oath." Nevertheless, there were "certain traditional American values which had developed out of the common law." His "undergraduate training in history" made the identification of these values "easier." Similarly, "human experience gave rise to law." In most cases the applicable law could be determined, but the search could involve "a great deal of struggle." Even so, the judge's oath

U. W. Clemon (b. 1943), Northern District judge from 1980 to the present; Democrat. *Montgomery Advertiser*

"required" that he "find the specific law or precedent and apply it. The Supreme Court has the ability to change a law, but this is not a district judge's job. If a situation arises where there is no clear precedent," then he applied "traditional moral standards."[49]

Judges employed other rationales to settle cases in which the applicable law was not readily apparent. Judge Haltom described himself as a "pragmatist" who relied on the "commonsense approach." Judge Pittman conceded that each of his colleagues followed "a certain approach." Still, especially with regard to the trial court, the district judge was bound by the Eleventh Circuit and the Supreme Court. Within these limitations, he "looked to the spirit of the law" inherent in statutes or decisional precedents. He "would never intentionally establish a principle of law," maintaining wherever possible doctrinal "uniformity."[50]

At the center of the continuum were those who distinguished interpreting from making law. The application of legal rules required employing more discretionary judgment than the mere finding of law. The exercise of discretion was sufficiently circumscribed by the circuit court and the Supreme Court, however, that it did not entail originating a principle as would the legislature when it enacted a statute. If a judge was unable to "follow these basic rules he should resign," said Judge Dubina. This conception of interpretation nonetheless conceded a degree of discretion that could lead to "the politicizing of the court." Accordingly, he tried to "keep personal opinions out of decisions." He "like[d] to be seen as flexible and not stereotyped into one view or behavior." The "best judges" were those who were "right down the middle."[51]

Most judges acknowledged that the issue of discretion had unique meaning when determining whether a statute violated the Constitution. Exercise of this power was an unavoidable judicial function. Most of Alabama's federal judges described themselves as conservative on the issue, with the district judges especially conscious that their resort to judicial review was exceptional. Virtually all the judges agreed that, as a practical matter, the Supreme Court possessed far greater authority to invalidate statutes or overrule established precedent than either district or circuit courts.[52]

The discrete elements involved in judicial review were intent, interpretation, and clarity of meaning. All judges acknowledged that the first consideration was whether the intent of the Constitution's framers or a law's maker was discernable. At the same time, only rarely was the question of intent altogether free of ambiguity. Accordingly, intent inevitably required interpretation, so the question usually came down to a judgment as to how little or how much interpretation to employ. Here a valuable guide was the *Federalist Papers*. Still, for self-described conservatives especially, resort to the Constitution's framers to ascertain intent was justified primarily only in cases of first impression. And even in such cases, most of Alabama's district judges avoided depending solely on the framers' intent, preferring to rely to a greater extent on analogous Supreme Court or appellate court decisions. Sometimes district judges might consider deciding a constitutional question by anticipating the Supreme Court's decision. But of those few judges who indicated this as a hypothetical alternative, only two admitted ever having actually followed such a course. A few judges also conceded that in arriving at an interpretation they took into account traditional values identified with history.[53]

Another approach blended constitutional and procedural functions. Even though in constitutional cases original intent was a valuable guide, especially as set forth in the *Federalist Papers*, it was the Supreme Court's judgment concerning intent that explicitly bound the lower federal courts. In the realm of ordinary litigation, law arose from the facts. In either case, the judge should strive to convince all those involved in a suit that "evenhanded justice [was] being administered." Generally, the content of this justice was confined to procedural fairness. Frank Johnson and some other Alabama judges acknowledged that fairness included giving weak and underrepresented groups wide-ranging access to federal judicial power. Most other federal judges defined the judicial function in narrower terms, emphasizing primarily the need for treating all parties to the suit with strict procedural neutrality.[54]

A few judges described their general view of judicial functions in legal realist terms. Judge Acker, who suggested that he employed the realist approach in order to overcome the errors resulting from realism, was unique in his frankness. Judges Thompson and Godbold, perhaps unconsciously, articulated views embracing legal realist assumptions without formally designating them as such. Godbold observed that "all of us developed interests, special sensitivities, special perceptions to differing things in the institutions around us." A businessman "on the street may have perceptions about social issues, political issues, constitutional issues, but he doesn't operate in an environment in which his differing views have consequences." But for a judge, those "differing perceptions come pretty sharply to bear in a world in which our job is deciding disputes between people or groups, or principles." The judge, moreover, "operates in an area where the reason people are gathered together in a courtroom is their differences of view about some principle or perception. He is called on to be a decider." Accordingly, "one's perceptions that might have very little consequence in other areas ... get revealed and accentuated and sometimes embroiled

Joel F. Dubina (b. 1947), Middle District judge from 1986 to 1990; judge of Eleventh Circuit Court of Appeals from 1990 to the present; Republican.
Judge Dubina's Chambers

by others because within our evolving society somebody had to decide and he is called on to decide. The focus comes upon him."[55]

Judge Thompson, although an African American, did not consider himself "solely African American" but was "a composite of a lot of things. Shaped by my own history. That history includes growing up in Tuskegee in a segregated society, includes going to Yale and going to law school, includes practicing law. All of that." He did not see himself as catering to the African-American community: "I'm a judge to everyone. All my experiences are clearly unique to me. I am not a judge for blacks. When someone walks into my court I am going to judge that person." When a judge enters the courtroom, he said, "you are open, before you hear any evidence. You are not proplaintiff or prodefendant. All you are is prowhichever the way the evidence persuades you. I am definitely not proplaintiff or prodefendant. In fact, the plaintiff has the burden of proof. I just call them like I see them."[56]

Thompson, like Frank Johnson, believed that the Constitution gave federal courts a special duty toward individual rights. Following the principles established in *Palko* and *Carolene Products*, he said that the "function" of the federal judiciary was "to make sure that the democratic process works ... to make sure individual rights [were] not trampled on by the majority." Whether the issues involved the First or Fourteenth Amendment, his duty was "to insure that those clauses [were] enforced and to make sure that even through the democratic process these rights are not violated." That, he believed, was "one of the principal functions of the federal judge and I think that is why we are not elected. Because we don't have to answer to the whim of the majority."[57]

He also distrusted relying on formalistic principles to guide decision making. He found that whether a judge was labeled "a strict interpreter of the constitution" often depended on who was being "done in." He explained, "people who claim to be strict interpreters will not do so when it's to their advantage not to be soft." Those who say they seek only to find the literal meaning of a law or the Constitution "don't always do so in practice. When confronted with an instance where the literal application ... doesn't always jibe with their view of what the law ought to be they seem to have no problem with varying from it." He believed that the dispute over such formalism was "a bogus issue" involving a principle that was "not workable. Words are ambiguous. To say that you apply the literal language in the law, whether it's the Constitution or a statute, begs [the] question. And if you mean by strict construction what they [the framers] . . . believed back at the time it was adopted, [it] still begs a question." Thus, ultimately it was the evidence in the case filtered through the lens of the judge's individual experience that determined the court's decision.[58]

Finally, the different institutional character of the trial and appellate court influenced the decisional process. The trial judge, in discussion with the attorneys, was primarily responsible for identifying and shaping the issues, including the overall direction the case would take. Even so, the federal district judge exercised this influence over the trial by himself. A collegial relationship with fellow district judges was important for preserving general institutional cohesion. But in each individual case the judge operated alone. On the circuit court level including the three-judge panels, by contrast, the interplay of judges made the collegial relationship itself a significant influence on the outcome of a given case. Because of multiple personalities and the resulting diverse views toward the issues, disagreement was inevitable. In order to exercise influence beyond the mere casting of a vote, the appellate judge had to learn how to disagree discreetly enough so as not to damage collegiality.[59]

Legal education further suggested jurisprudential thinking. Of the thirty-four judges serving between 1940 and 1994 who, unlike Judge Rives, graduated from law school, twenty-one received their law degrees from the University of Alabama School of Law. Four others graduated from Yale Law School, while those remaining earned their law degree from either Vanderbilt (1), Harvard (2), Columbia (1), Cumberland (3), or the University of Kentucky (1). One judge attended a night law school in Birmingham and then passed the state bar examination.[60] Most of the judges attended law school during the first half of the twentieth century, when legal realism emerged as a major force in American legal education. Only Acker and Godbold, however, indicated any direct awareness of it during their time of study. Although nearly all of the judges interviewed had fond or vivid memories of particular professors and courses, all approached their legal education as essentially an accreditation process.

Individual judges became the object of professional and public scrutiny periodically when handling controversial cases. But the quality of their judicial work suggested little relationship between formal legal training and jurisprudential reasoning. Perhaps the best example was Allgood. His preparation at night law school enabled him to pass the state bar exam. Yet in the field of bankruptcy, Allgood was recognized as one of the nation's foremost experts and innovators. Long before attending law school, he acquired this expertise as a businessman in Birmingham during the Depression; because of his political contacts, moreover, he significantly influenced passage of major national bankruptcy legislation.[61]

Still, a possible causal linkage between educational content and decision making could be inferred. As a group, Alabama's federal judges serving between 1940 and 1990 attended one of eight law schools. Only three of those

Myron H. Thompson, *left*, being sworn in by Frank M. Johnson, Jr. Thompson (b. 1947), a Democrat, was appointed to the Middle District in 1980. Johnson (b. 1918), a Republican, was a Middle District judge from 1955 to 1979, then served on the Fifth Circuit Court of Appeals, and on the Eleventh Circuit Court of Appeals. *Montgomery Advertiser*

institutions—Yale, Columbia, and to a lesser extent, Harvard—figured prominently in the legal realist movement. Between 1908 and 1958, when the judges acquired their education at one of the five other law schools, moreover, the curriculum was considered primarily applied rather than theoretical. At the three institutions influenced most directly by legal realism, viewing law strictly in terms of self-contained legal forms, doctrines, and procedures was discouraged. At the other law schools, the pedagogical focus was on understanding the discrete elements of law as structurally autonomous and separate from a wider social or institutional context.

Most of the judges who attended one of the five institutions possessing a primarily applied pedagogical focus made a distinction between finding and making law. The seven judges who received their legal education from Yale, Columbia, or Harvard, by contrast, described the judicial function in terms suggesting the least formalistic institutional autonomy. One admitted employing a legal realist rationale to overcome the impact of realism on American law. Two others explained their function as a "decider" whose total experience shaped his perception of which side made the best case. A fourth judge frankly categorized the starting point for his analysis as "libertarian."[62]

Employing the distinction between judicial roles to suggest causal connections was also not without difficulties. While the great majority of judges articulated the formal dichotomy between law finder and lawmaker, only one asserted categorically that his only function was to discover and declare the law. All the others conceded to varying degrees that, where explicit precedent or legislative intent was unclear, their decision was influenced by extrainstitutional factors, such as historically defined "traditional" values, "pragmatism," personal background, or the "spirit" of the law. A variation of this was the emphasis placed on "being fair," which went beyond merely declaring what the legislature had enacted or a higher court had handed down. They also recognized that collegiality influenced decision making.[63]

Finally, nearly all judges said that constitutional issues were special. The Constitution granted federal judges the unique power of judicial review, which theoretically at least depended primarily on the exercise of individual discretion. All the judges espousing the declaratory theory agreed that the exercise of discretion went beyond a strict reliance on what the Constitution's framers may have intended. Usually this meant giving primary deference to Supreme Court precedents, whether or not these seemed consistent with the framers' original purpose. In the case of Frank Johnson and one or two others, moreover, the federal judge's constitutional independence sanctioned a broad authority to provide institutional access for traditionally excluded or exploited groups. A judge's oath to uphold the Constitution compelled such action, even where no or contrary precedent existed.[64]

During the second half of the twentieth century, George Wallace and others increasingly attacked Alabama's federal courts. Not since Reconstruction had such a divergence existed between the local political culture and the federal judge's jurisprudence. The struggle between the National Democrats and shifting conservative groups left a heritage in which both Republican and Democratic federal judges generally approached federal regulation of the economy with restraint. During the same period, however, individual rights linked to federal judicial enforcement became steadily more contentious. The resulting politicization of the federal courts was identified by many Alabamians as the clash between Wallace and Judge Frank Johnson. The tenaciousness of this struggle obscured the degree to which federal judges relied more on national judicial institutional pressures than on the local political culture. Interviews with the judges, as well as their legal education, confirmed the importance of these institutional constraints.

A DISTINCT NATIONAL JUDICIAL SYSTEM EMERGES

From the 1940s on, a distinct national judicial system increasingly arose. The federalization of litigation and increased administrative centralization established a new judicial order possessing national cohesion. As a result, the local courtroom culture lost much of its influence.[65]

Federalization of Litigation and Administrative Centralization

Congress steadily enlarged the federal court's jurisdiction over federal issues. Since the nineteenth century, diversity suits had taken up significantly more of the docket than litigation based on federal or constitutional subject matter. Although the proportion of federal subject matter litigation continually increased between the Civil War and the Great Depression, it did not dominate the docket until after the Second World War. By the 1980s, Alabama's federal district judges estimated that the proportion of diversity suits on their dockets had dropped to about 20 percent. The postwar rise in federal or constitutional issues was complex. Congress expanded the New Deal policies of active government to include civil rights, environmental protection, occupational health and safety, and consumer welfare. Federal crimes significantly increased. Federal courts in Alabama also led the way in developing important institutional innovations such as structural litigation, fee enhancements for public interest law suits, and complex tort management techniques. There was a corresponding increase in federal judicial self-governance and administrative systematization accompanying greater cooperation between federal and state court systems.[66]

From the 1940s on, federal litigation involving diversity jurisdiction and removal from state court declined steadily. Ever since Reconstruction, corporate defendants had used the right of removal to avoid state courts, placing plaintiffs at a disadvantage because of procedural technicalities such as the declaratory judgment or the substantive rules of the federal common law built up around the *Swift* doctrine. In 1929–30, for example, suits removed from state to federal court exceeded federal cases initiated on original jurisdiction. The Federal Rules of Civil Procedure promulgated in 1938 and the Supreme Court's reversal of the *Swift* doctrine in *Erie R.R. v. Tompkins* during the same year, however, undercut these advantages. In the 1940s alone, removals dropped from half of the total diversity docket to under one-third. The business in Alabama's federal courts reflected this same general trend.[67]

Cases involving federal authority and individual rights rose significantly. The rise of federal issues associated with the plethora of regulatory agencies spawned by the New Deal is well known. Less familiar, but from the perspective of federal litigation just as important, was the change involving claims under such laws as the Federal Employers' Liability Act (FELA). Before 1941, injured plaintiffs brought on average fewer than 150 cases annually in federal courts. The number of FELA actions increased steadily, from 321 in 1944 to more than 1,000 in 1948. By 1951, the average number of actions was seven times the number in the late 1930s. In cases from Alabama and elsewhere, the Supreme Court enlarged the rights plaintiffs claimed under FELA, until the justices divided over whether the time necessary to consider appeals was appropriate. Justices Hugo Black, William O. Douglas, Frank Murphy, and Wiley B. Rutledge usually favored review of FELA decisions from the lower courts, whereas Felix Frankfurter and others opposed such action. Nevertheless, in Alabama and the rest of the nation the trend of decisions favoring federal plaintiffs was clear.[68]

From 1948 to 1958, Congress affirmed this change. With little controversy, the Revised Judicial Code of 1948 repealed the local prejudice provision of Reconstruction era legislation that had enlarged the federal judiciary's removal authority. Since the 1870s, corporate defendants had used the claim of local prejudice to justify removing cases to federal courts. The American public's embrace of the consumer economy identified with giant corporations following World War II and the Court's coincident increased defense of federal plaintiffs fostered the noncontentious repeal of the local prejudice provision. Within a decade, however, a coalition of self-described conservative southern

Democrats (including those from Alabama) and Republicans proposed measures aimed at further limiting federal jurisdiction. The Warren Court's decisions mandating racial desegregation, its opinions that revealed diminished concern for communist subversion, and other decisions that used federal doctrines to preempt state right-to-work laws culminated in an omnibus bill restricting federal jurisdiction, sponsored by William E. Jenner of Indiana. After protracted struggle, the Senate tabled Jenner's proposal in August 1958 by an eight-vote margin. Congressman William M. Tuck of Virginia proposed similar bills aimed especially at diversity jurisdiction; these measures also were defeated.[69]

Between the 1960s and the 1990s, Congress steadily expanded the federal court's jurisdiction in other fields. After a decade of massive white resistance in Alabama and the South generally, the Civil Rights Act of 1964 and the Voting Rights Act of 1965 finally gave effective national protection to minorities and women. Throughout the next quarter century, Congress periodically amended these laws, generally enlarging the rights that could be litigated in federal as well as state courts. Similarly, Congress increased the reach of the federal bureaucracy into such new fields as environmental protection, occupational health and safety, and consumer welfare. Growing social dislocation resulting from drug-related violence and weak firearms control led to a steady expansion of federal crimes, culminating in the Violent Crime Control Act of 1991. Numerous other measures extended federal authority over organized crime. Each increase in federal authority usually required a commensurate extension of federal court jurisdiction.[70]

Another dimension of increased federal jurisdiction involved the allocation of attorneys' fees in public-interest litigation. In 1972, Alabama's federal district judge Frank M. Johnson, Jr., awarded attorney fees in an employment discrimination case "as part of the effective remedy a court should fashion to encourage public-minded suits and to carry out congressional policy." A lawyer "representing black plaintiffs in . . . any civil rights litigation, is likely to suffer social, political and community ostracism," Johnson said. "Even more damaging to an attorney involved in such litigation is the probability that he will be estranged from other members of his profession who are unwilling to participate in, or even lend moral support to, suits seeking to vindicate the public good." Thus, because of "these factors and the paucity of damage awards in civil rights suits," and to "encourage *pro bono publico* litigation and to carry out congressional policy, an award of attorneys' fees is essential."[71]

In several enactments, Congress gave statutory sanction to the policy Johnson and others supported. Three provisions—42 U.S.C. § 1988 and 28

U.S.C. § 2432 (known as the Equal Access to Justice Act) and the class action provisions of the Federal Rules of Civil Procedure Rule 23—provided monetary incentives for lawyers to litigate under Title VII of the 1964 Civil Rights Act and other measures providing for the enforcement of rights and entitlements. Through such provisions, Congress and the courts adapted the proplaintiff policy the Supreme Court developed in diversity FELA cases during the 1940s to the field of public-interest litigation. Essentially, this new policy permitted the federal judges to shift the fees to support what Johnson called "increased victims' access to the mechanisms of redress." This new market for legal services in turn encouraged a modest increase in the number of public-interest lawyers.[72]

The judicial and congressional sanction of individual rights encouraged procedural innovations having significant social and political impact. No innovation was more important than the development of structural litigation involving groups rather than individuals and creative procedures for implementing and monitoring compliance. Traditional lawsuits dealt with an individual's claim of wrongdoing. In the structural suits, the focus was on a social condition affecting such groups as minority schoolchildren, patients in mental-health facilities, or prison inmates. The judiciary's interpretation of constitutional provisions and congressional measures that gave them national bureaucratic sanction broadened the reach of constitutional values and the need for their enforcement. Accordingly, Frank Johnson and other federal judges pioneered new uses of the injunction that not only applied to disaffected groups claiming protection but also maintained an ongoing supervision of state and local officials, often lasting for years, to ensure compliance. In these cases the scale of constitutional violation was so massive that a commensurate remedy was essential.[73]

Structural litigation developed largely because state authorities had no political incentive to correct many social evils. In the South, segregated public schools and other forms of discrimination were supported by the white majority. Yet inhuman conditions affecting mental patients and prisoners were endemic to large, publicly funded institutions throughout the nation. Like southern blacks, these groups lacked political influence. To correct such massive evils, increased funding was necessary, something few politicians would advocate. As a result, federal courts in Alabama and elsewhere fashioned remedies of injunctive relief aimed at correcting constitutional violations in the future through ongoing judicial supervision. Politicians in turn were able to blame federal judges for the increased state funding these remedies required.[74]

By the 1990s, these procedural innovations encouraged new cooperation between state and federal courts. Judges in both jurisdictions applied the lessons learned from employing the structural injunction in class-action and large institutional suits to new areas of complex tort litigation including asbestos and breast implants. The federal-state cooperation this litigation demanded fostered pioneering administrative mechanisms permitting fair determination of the parties' rights and efficient implementation of remedies. Special masters and other management experts were put to new uses suggested by several judges' reliance on the expertise of Professor Francis McGovern of the University of Alabama School of Law, a leading innovator in the field of mass tort and complex litigation. These advances also facilitated continuing reform efforts in other fields. According to Chief Justice William H. Rehnquist, the widespread resort to habeas corpus appeals in capital punishment cases "cried out for reform." Capital habeas, Rehnquist remarked at the National Conference on State-Federal Judicial Relationships in April 1992, "presents essentially a question of federalism—striking the proper balance between the lawful authority of the states and the role of the federal courts in protecting the capital defendant."[75]

The pressures on states both to follow and cooperate with federal courts facilitated reforms in state court systems. Beginning in the 1880s, the Alabama Bar Association challenged the system of justice dominated by political and social ties linking local lawyers, judges, and juries. The opportunities for abuse inherent in such a system became particularly apparent during the civil rights struggle. Yet these problems were symptomatic of wider institutional tensions that many state bars had struggled to remedy through various programs fostering increased professionalization.[76]

In Alabama, the State Bar eventually achieved success, despite the state's record of brutal and defiant opposition to the civil rights movement. The bar's efforts culminated during the 1970s in the wholesale restructuring of the state's judicial system under the leadership of Chief Justice Howell Heflin. The continuing willingness of Alabama's public officials to shift to the federal courts the responsibility for addressing intractable and politically difficult problems indirectly supported this reform, building a professional constituency Heflin and others mobilized to transform the state's judicial system. Heflin's successor as chief justice of the Alabama Supreme Court explained the need for states to take control of their court system. All those "involved with the state courts of this nation need to be more active and purposeful in shaping their future," Chief Justice C. C. "Bo" Torbert, Jr., said. "We are the ones who best understand the problems of our justice system; we have given the most thought to solving them; and we are the best equipped, by our experience, our insights, and our positions of leadership, to make lasting improvements to the system." By 1990, when Torbert spoke as chairman of the board of directors of the State Justice Institute,

Alabama's system of judicial administration was recognized as one of the nation's best.[77]

These procedural and institutional changes coincided with the growth of the federal judiciary's own independent structure of self-governance. Before Congress passed the Administrative Office Act of 1939, the Justice Department administered the budget appropriated for operating the federal courts. The act turned over the department's administrative role to the judiciary itself, creating an Administrative Office of the United States Courts. The chief justice of the Supreme Court had a titular role in the appointment and supervision of the office. Yet it was the Judicial Conference, composed initially of representatives from the circuit courts of appeal, that prescribed the director's duties and exercised actual control. In practical terms, a committee of federal judges supervised the office's operation, including the financial and business functions previously under the Justice Department's authority and "the preparation of statistical data and reports of the business transactions of the courts." The purpose of the act was thus to bring about "a greater coordination of the judicial machinery, a better method of assembling data and continuous oversight by the judiciary itself of its functions and efficiency."[78]

The system's organization was both centralized and decentralized. It exercised supervisory and policy-making functions through a decentralized structure of councils operating within each circuit, which served "as vehicles for socializing district judges and for facilitating communications within the circuits and between the circuits and both the Judicial Conference and Attorney General in Washington." District judges acquired a growing role within this system. In addition, a specialized committee structure evolved to facilitate the administrative functions. Reenforcing a trend toward uniformity in judicial administration was the establishment of a Federal Judicial Center in 1967; during the late 1980s, it was under the direction of Judge John C. Godbold. "Research into the administrative problems of the Federal courts and development of recommended solutions are the primary functions of the Center," said a congressional sponsor. "Management experts, systems analysts, data interpreters, personnel experts, as well as judges, academicians, and practicing attorneys" would "bring the skill and experience of their disciplines to the Center" in order to "collect data, conduct research, depict the contours of each problem," and then "formulate recommendations for solution."[79]

These organizational units served the circuit councils, which encouraged uniform process and procedure throughout the system. Provided for in the Act of 1939, the councils generally relied on "a diplomatic handling" of situations where "cooperation of the district judge [was] necessary" rather than "coercion under authority of law." Simply "turning the light of day on the judges, probably in most instances" was enough to foster conformity. Even so, as Congress expanded the judiciary's responsibilities and jurisdiction over federal bankruptcy, Social Security, and other magistrates, as well as established rules governing such vital areas as criminal justice administration and jury selection, a plethora of complex procedural issues arose. The circuit councils exercised formal authority as arbiters when lower federal courts disagreed over administrative policies. Seybourn Lynne, Frank Johnson, John Godbold, Richard Rives, and other Alabama federal judges rendered important service on the committees of the conference system and to the administrative and research functions of the Judicial Center.[80]

The federalization of litigation and increased administrative centralization strengthened the external institutional factors influencing federal courts' decision making in Alabama. The displacement of diversity suits by federal issues on the federal docket indicated a marked change in the federal market for legal services. The *Swift* doctrine governing diversity cases required expansive exercise of judicial discretion not only with regard to the rejection of state law but also in order to determine the appropriate federal role of decision. After *Erie*, state law generally governed diversity suits; federal courts employed discretion in such cases, therefore, primarily to ascertain and apply that law. Meanwhile, new federal statutes and the Supreme Court's growing doctrines involving individual rights became the federal court's principal sources of law. Federal laws and constitutional principles, of course, also required interpretation. The scope of discretionary judgment such interpretation demanded was necessarily less, however, than that existing under the *Swift* regime. The Judicial Conference system and improved information transfers facilitated by greater administrative centralization tended to circumscribe further the boundaries of judicial discretion. As the federal judiciary's institutional structure and decisional process became more systematized, cooperation with Alabama state courts, which by the 1970s underwent significant reform, was more common despite continuing attacks from state and national authorities.

The Decline of the Local Federal Courtroom Culture

As federal sources of law and administrative centralization increasingly dominated, the local federal courtroom culture declined. For more than a century after Congress established Alabama's first federal courts, the interaction between a few lawyers practicing before even fewer judges constituted an indigenous institutional culture. In conjunction with the Alabama State Bar's reform agenda, which around the turn of the century used the federal courts as a model, the federal judicial establishment became still more insulated from state political pressures. Not until after the Second World War, however, did the national judicial structure begin significantly to displace the traditional local federal order. Facilitating this change was a decline in the region's distinctiveness, associated with changing population distribution and urbanization. Demographic changes fostered an expanding market for specialized legal services, accompanied by a pronounced increase in the number of lawyers. As a result, the proportion of federal practitioners to federal judges grew sufficiently that local institutional autonomy eroded.

The growth and distribution of Alabama's population encouraged an increase in the number of federal judges. In 1940, the state's population was 2,832,961, nearly 70 percent of which lived in rural areas or small towns. There were only four cities with populations exceeding 25,000: Gadsden in northeastern Alabama; Mobile; Montgomery; and Birmingham, by far the leading urban center. Half a century later, in 1990, the state's population had grown to 4,041,000, with 60 percent living in urban areas. The greater Birmingham area continued to be the largest population center, followed by Mobile and Montgomery. In addition, Tuscaloosa, Huntsville, and Gadsden (all in northern Alabama) had urban populations approximating 100,000 each.[81]

The number of Alabama's federal judges increased at a greater rate than did the state's population. In 1940, there were two federal district courts located in northern Alabama, one in Birmingham, the other in Huntsville. Mobile and Montgomery had one district court each. On the Fifth Circuit Court of Appeals there was one seat for Alabama. Fifty years later, the Southern District centered in Mobile had three positions, as did the Middle District based in Montgomery. Reflecting the population advantage of north Alabama, the number of district courts making up the Northern District had increased to seven. In conjunction with these active district court positions, several judges on senior status continued to handle cases in all three districts. Finally, by the 1980s, there were three judgeships allotted to Alabama on the circuit court of appeals.

Comparing the growth of population to that of the federal judicial establishment is illuminating. The state's population increased by 43 percent from 1940 to 1990. During the same period, however, the number of Alabama's active district judge positions more than tripled, increasing from four to thirteen. Senior judges shared the workload in each district. In addition, the number of circuit court judges assigned to Alabama tripled. The judiciary's expansion took place, moreover, in conjunction with the growth of magistrates or administrative law judges charged with handling routine bankruptcy, social security, employment practices, and workmen's compensation matters. The courts retained jurisdiction over these administrative law actions, but their role was generally supervisory. This expansion of the federal judicial establishment meant that proportionally more people than ever before could be served by the federal courts. Thus, federal judges' periodic requests to Congress for additional positions because of continued increases in case loads were understandable, but that should not obscure the degree to which, by contrast with population growth, the increases in federal bench and bar were magnified.[82]

As Alabama's federal judicial establishment grew apace, the state's population distribution also changed. In 1940, most Alabamians lived in rural areas and small towns. Fifty years later, more than half of the state's population lived in urban and suburban areas. As a result, Alabama, like much of the South, increasingly was part of a national culture. The state and the region gradually lost much of their traditional distinctiveness. This, combined with the changing market for legal services, diffused the local institutional factors and external pressures from the political culture that previously influenced the federal judges' decision making.

Accompanying Alabama's changing market for legal services was a precipitous growth in the number of lawyers. During the 1920s, the Alabama State Bar established the integrated bar, which made the practice of law contingent on membership in that organization. Throughout the first half of the twentieth century, the State Bar's membership nonetheless grew at a modest rate. In 1960, the total number of lawyers was 2,070, of which 1,821 were listed as "active." By 1970, the total had risen to 3,380, with 2,974 active. By 1980, the bar's membership nearly doubled, reaching 6,578, with 5,788 active. The total in 1990 had grown to 10,595, with 9,333 active. Thus, while Alabama's population did not quite double between 1940 and 1990, the State Bar's membership increased five times. This pronounced growth paralleled, moreover, the increase in the number of federal judges serving the state.[83]

The coincidental expansion of Alabama's bar and federal judicial establishment also reflected increased specialization. Throughout the first half of the twentieth century, most of the state's lawyers were general practitioners. The greater specialization identified with the split between the plaintiffs' and defense bar was characteristic of the state's few major urban centers. By the 1970s, with the state's population primarily urban and suburban, the market for legal services became even more specialized. Yet the increase involved not only defense and plaintiffs' lawyers; it was also part of a significant growth in the number of lawyers practicing before federal courts, magistrates, and administrative law judges. In 1940, 155 attorneys were admitted to practice in the Northern District of Alabama, the state's largest. A decade later, the number more than doubled, reaching 398. During the next two decades, the growth, like that of the State Bar's membership generally, was noteworthy: 601 in 1960; 1,610 in 1970. By 1980, the number admitted to federal practice more than doubled, reaching 2,298. But unlike the State Bar membership, the number of new lawyers admitted to the federal bar in the Northern District declined in 1990 to 572.[84]

The growth in the federal bar suggested marked changes in the courtroom culture. The comparatively small federal bar of the 1940s was indicative of a distinctive institutional culture that had emerged in Alabama's three urban centers during the late nineteenth century. Rooted in the expanding yet still specialized federal jurisdiction that had reached new limits with the New Deal, the culture's values reflected the moderate reform policies advocated by the Alabama State Bar. The smaller, autonomous federal judicial establishment pioneered procedural innovations that the State Bar adopted as a model in its campaign to reform a state judicial system dominated by local connections among judges, law firms, and prosecutors. The federal courts' indigenous courtroom culture thus was insulated from the uncertainties and potential abuses found in the state's politics and judicial system. That very autonomy, however, strengthened the influence of the lawyers practicing before Alabama's three federal judges. Ongoing interaction facilitated informal perceptions and assumptions regarding the court's approach to routine or new issues to such an extent that more distant pressures shaped decision making only in exceptional cases.

During the second half of the twentieth century, local external factors increasingly transformed the federal courtroom culture's autonomy. The overall growth in the state's lawyer population relative to the population of Alabama's three federal court districts ensured that proportionally more and more developed some sort of federal practice. Steady growth in the number of lawyers admitted to the federal bar nonetheless diluted the informal influences gained from ongoing interaction with a given judge. In 1940, a possible 155 lawyers practiced before two active federal judges in the Northern District. Forty years later, there were six active judges in the Northern District, but the number of attorneys admitted to practice before them had risen to 2,298. Accordingly, in 1940 the ratio was 1 active federal judge to 77.5 lawyers; in 1980 that ratio was 1 to 383! In addition, as the number of federal judges increased, the clerk of the court reworked the docketing process to ensure that as much as possible the case load assignments were random. In 1940, such a change would have had minimal impact on the working courtroom culture; forty years later it reflected a real alteration of traditional institutional bonds.[85]

A federal judge's increased reliance on law clerks further insulated the court from external pressures. In Alabama and elsewhere before the 1950s, top law school graduates did not routinely clerk for federal judges. The federal district judge in Alabama who began the clerkship tradition was Daniel H. Thomas after his appointment in 1951. The first Alabama federal judge to employ an African-American or female clerk was Sam C. Pointer, Jr. By the 1990s, judges received funding to hire on average two clerks. Judges taking senior status, depending on their workload, could select one or two clerks. Prior to the emergence of the clerkship tradition, federal judges depended on their own work and the arguments presented by counsel to determine the law of a given case. Employment of young law graduates not only increased the research and writing capability of the judge's chambers but also created a bond between clerk and judge, which heightened the institutional autonomy of the courtroom. As computerized technology expanded access to legal materials, moreover, the judges and their clerks achieved still greater independence in the decisional process.[86]

Expanding federal jurisdiction and a mounting number of cases appealed to the circuit court further circumscribed the local courtroom's autonomy. From the Civil War on, Congress enacted legislation requiring a commensurate enlargement of the federal court's authority. As late as the 1960s, however, the strength of the federal courtroom culture was such that in many cases indigenous more than external institutional pressures shaped the local enforcement of national law. The federal courts' response to the civil rights struggle paved the way for new institutional influences. More often than not, federal district courts in Alabama and other southern states met the white majority's massive resistance with moderation and gradualism. The creative support federal district judge Frank Johnson and circuit judge Rives gave individual rights was exceptional. As a result, appellate courts, especially the Fifth Circuit, increasingly were called on to provide leadership in the implementation of the Supreme Court's pathbreaking civil rights decisions and the civil rights legislation of the 1960s. A pronounced growth in the number of cases appealed from Alabama's federal district courts to the circuit court suggested the degree of change. During the 1940s, the average number of cases appealed was 25; during the 1980s, it was 628. In 1940 there were 28 cases appealed, whereas in 1990 the number was 872—an increase of 3,114 percent.

But such statistics are only one indication of the external institutional constraints circumscribing courtroom autonomy. As the appellate case load grew, the conference system exercised increased administrative control, leading to a corresponding demand for more representation of district judges on the system's policy-making committees. In the past, Alabama's district judges had exercised significant influence in this administrative structure. Even though the state's judges continued to be well represented from the 1950s on, the system nonetheless became steadily more centralized, benefiting from the research resources of the Federal Judicial Center. Improved systemization of information gathering and distribution reinforced the centralizing pressures associated with appellate court review.[87]

During the 1940s, Alabama's federal district judge John McDuffie suggested the course of change. The growing influence of the judicial conference system was, he said, just the start of "a subtle design on the part of those who believe in bureaucracy or statism which with a deadly grasp is gradually strangling and destroying the ideals of our American form of government . . . [and] the independence, as well as the judicial functions of the District Courts, which are destined to become administrative offices." McDuffie initially resisted a measure prepared by one of the Judicial Conference's committees and subsequently adopted by the circuit courts, entitled *Handbook for Petit Jurors*. Not only "was it written, in part at least, by one who has limited experience with courts and juries," he said, but it was yet another example "of a tendency toward too much reformation, standardization, and . . . centralization of control over duties and functions which are and should be solely the responsibility of the judges of the District Courts." Nevertheless, McDuffie ultimately conceded that "my experience on the bench," compared with that of most of the judges constituting the committee's membership, was "so limited . . . [that] I do not seek now an argument with you about the *Handbook*."[88]

McDuffie was prophetic. Congress enacted more and more federal statutes while the Supreme Court increased the constitutional protection of individual rights. Meanwhile, the conjunction of a decline in regional distinctiveness associated with urbanization, the resulting specialized market for legal services sustained by the pronounced growth in the number of lawyers, and the greater organizational unity and centralization of the national judicial system dissolved the local institutional autonomy of Alabama's federal courts. The state's federal judges owed their appointment to local political interests, and they fulfilled their duties under mounting local political pressures. But from World War II on, the federal judiciary's national organizational structure and life exercised greater influence on Alabama's federal judges than did local political or institutional exigencies.

ROUTINE FEDERAL LITIGATION AND CONSTITUTIONAL QUESTIONS

In routine federal litigation and constitutional questions, Alabama's federal judges sought to balance discretion and dependence. By the 1940s, the Federal Rules, the Supreme Court's *Erie* decision, and the federal government's dominance resulting from New Deal liberalism established a fuzzy borderline between state and federal jurisdiction in many suits involving social and economic policy or individual rights. Routine issues arising under diversity jurisdiction, such as summary judgment, could present simultaneously hard questions of federal procedure and the interpretation of state law. Similarly, the growth of constitutional questions fostered by the *Palko* and *Carolene Products* doctrines presented procedural and substantive law issues requiring the adjustment of state and federal authority. Still, in both types of litigation the national judicial establishment more than external political tensions or local institutional imperatives shaped decision making in Alabama's federal courts.

Discretion and Dependence in Routine Litigation

From the late 1930s on, increased federalization of routine litigation coincided with persistent political criticism. As a result, the national judicial system steadily circumscribed the federal district court's local autonomy. The proliferation of cases appealed from the district to the circuit courts, which coincided with a pronounced increase in the number of lawyers practicing, suggested the strength of the institutional constraints within which Alabama's federal judges employed discretion.

The Federal Rules of Procedure adopted in 1938 established rule 56, increasing the federal judiciary's discretion over granting summary judgment. The purpose of rule 56 was to allow federal judges to clear their dockets of superfluous cases in accordance with the streamlining of pleading established by the Federal Rules. This increased discretion, however, fostered variation among federal courts within Alabama and other states. In 1986, the Supreme Court handed down three cases regarding the filing of motions for summary judgment, which held parties who objected to removing cases to a higher standard of proof and generally increased judges' discretion over such issues. Meanwhile, from 1938 on, a principal result of this enlarged discretion was increased grounds for appellate court review of the district court's granting of summary judgment.[89]

Thus, after rule 56, courts subordinated achieving particular outcomes to broader concerns involving the exercise of their independent authority. Two suits involving the Alabama workmen's compensation law were cases in point. The issue in *Sanders* was whether in a wrongful death action the state's descent and distribution law or workmen's compensation statute governed F. W.

John McDuffie (1883–1950), Southern District judge from 1935 to 1950; Democrat.
Robin Holeb-Ableman, U.S. District Court, Southern District of Alabama

Woolworth's payment of compensation to the decedent's heirs. Neither side contested the facts. Judge Virgil Pittman granted the heirs' motion for summary judgment, holding in favor of the descent and distribution statute. Woolworth appealed, and the Fifth Circuit held that *both* laws applied. The case went back to Pittman, who decided accordingly.[90]

The Alabama workmen's compensation law raised a similar issue in *Phillips v. Unijax.* The decedent's wife filed a wrongful death action, presenting the question whether the workmen's compensation statute would provide the exclusive remedy for the widow. As in *Sanders*, the facts were not disputed. The widow, however, received workmen's compensation benefits before bringing the wrongful death case. Pittman granted Unijax's motion for summary judgment, reasoning that once the widow accepted benefits under the workmen's compensation act, she could not recover additional benefits from Unijax under a theory of wrongful death. On appeal, the Fifth Circuit reversed, holding that the issue was a matter of substantive state law, which the federal court lacked jurisdiction to decide. The case was remanded to the Alabama Circuit Court for settlement.[91]

The two cases presented similar issues, which Pittman and the circuit court nonetheless approached with independence. In both cases, Pittman granted a summary judgment after a thorough review of the state law and federal rules. That he had no overriding concern about whether the outcome favored a particular side was suggested by the fact that, despite very similar facts, the plaintiff won in the first case and the defendant won in the second. Consistent in both of these decisions, however, was Pittman's use of discretion to maintain an independent judgment. The Fifth Circuit, in turn, employed its own independent judgment to establish parameters for the trial court's exercise of discretion. Arguably, in both cases the circuit court evidenced a more explicit concern for preserving the interests of plaintiffs by broadening the range of benefits potentially receivable under state law. Yet a broader conclusion to be drawn from comparing the course and outcome of the two suits is that the local legal culture influenced the result less than institutional imperatives within the federal judiciary itself.

Comparisons of Pittman's and the appellate court's treatment of motions for summary judgment involving the Internal Revenue Service or insurance companies as defendants support the conclusion that concerns regarding institutional autonomy within the circuit dominated. In each case Pittman displayed neutrality toward the result, except that he adhered to an overriding concern for fairness.[92] In suits involving motions for summary judgment where Social Security disability claims were at issue, Pittman consistently

Virgil Pittman (b. 1916), judge on the Alabama Circuit Court
from 1951 to 1966 and Middle and Southern District judge from
1966 to the present; Democrat. *Judge Pittman's Chambers*

tended to uphold the government's denial of benefits to plaintiff claimants.[93] Yet in civil rights cases he generally granted the plaintiff's motion for summary judgment.[94] Finally, his decisions on motions for summary judgment in criminal litigation generally favored government prosecutors over criminal defendants.[95]

In considering petitions for habeas corpus relief, Judge Pittman employed a similar discretion favorable to criminal prosecution. The basic policy concerns involving the granting of habeas petitions and summary judgment are different. The intent of the latter is to clear court dockets of superfluous cases and therefore to limit access. Habeas petitions, however, open the courts to a convicted criminal's claim, thereby increasing access. Yet despite these policy differences there are similarities in the analysis used in both types of cases. To determine whether to grant either motion, the judge must decide whether a jury would likely disagree with the result of the case. The judge should grant the summary judgment if a jury would probably agree on the outcome. In the habeas petition, the judge decides whether the evidence presented to the jury was such to create a reasonable doubt. If so, the judge should grant the petition. Thus the analytical concerns are similar in either type of motion. In five out of six habeas petitions, Pittman denied the motion, further suggesting a willingness to employ discretion on behalf of the government.[96]

Taken together, Pittman's decisions suggest influences shaping decision making. The overall outcomes were too inconsistent to demonstrate causal connections to social-class background. A more direct link may be identified between the consistent pattern of progovernment habeas judgments and Pittman's experience as an FBI agent and state judge.[97] In civil rights cases, by contrast, he usually granted the plaintiff's motion for summary judgment. In the wrongful death and workmen's compensation suits, and in the IRS or insurance company cases, the pattern indicated an adherence to basic standards of procedural fairness. And yet Pittman usually upheld the government in Social Security claims.

Apparent causal linkages are discernible. Broadly, the diverse outcomes in the IRS, insurance, and Social Security cases were compatible with the policy preferences and trust in big government that were institutionalized as a result of the triumph of Roosevelt's new liberalism that defined Alabama's National Democrats. A commitment to civil rights did not become part of the liberal consensus in Alabama until the 1970s. Even so, Pittman was a Loyalist National Democrat; he decided the civil rights decisions, moreover, during the 1970s. Pittman's habeas judgments, however, harkened back to the old National Democratic faith in government. Meanwhile, Pittman's wrongful death and workmen's compensation cases evidenced an overriding concern for fairness and neutrality.

Pittman's jurisprudence clarified these apparent inconsistencies. He explained the diversity of results in his opinions by reference to his search for the "spirit" of the law. As a popularly elected state judge, he had learned that a respect for fairness inherent in the adversarial system of justice was consistent with that "spirit." The federal judicial system, including appellate court review, preserved the same value. Pittman supported the National Democrats' liberalism. Its direct influence on decision making was obscured, however, by the fact that by the 1970s many Alabama federal judges possessing either a National Democratic or Republican affiliation shared the same values, while other judges, both Democratic and Republican, accepted some of these values but not others. This pervasive yet uneven attachment reflected the moderation prevailing in Alabama regarding the social and economic policies inherited from the New Deal. At the same time, Pittman and most other federal judges affirmed that, although their backgrounds undoubtedly had some bearing on decision making, the values and institutions of the national judicial system exercised the dominant influence.[98]

Regarding civil rights, the record was even clearer. During the 1950s and 1960s the Democrat Rives and the Republican Johnson were identified as liberals. The rest of the state's federal judges, both Republicans and Democrats, described themselves as moderate or conservative on civil rights issues. Judges appointed during the 1970s and 1980s revealed a similar split: A few said they were liberal or independent on civil rights issues; the rest, regardless of party affiliation, affirmed they were moderate or conservative. Most nevertheless conceded that although their backgrounds were certainly an influence, national judicial institutions and values primarily shaped decision making.[99]

Additional parameters governing discretion are suggested by comparing two district judges' experience in the appellate court. The rate at which the Eleventh Circuit reversed Thompson and Acker was similar: 33 percent for Thompson and 38 percent for Acker. The reversal rate itself, however, was only a partial indicator. Over a twelve-year period, the Eleventh Circuit heard 60 appeals from Thompson's court, while during a ten-year period it heard 110 appeals from Acker's. Thus the annual number of appeals Thompson generated was five compared to eleven generated by Acker. The comparatively greater number of appeals from the latter's court is suggestive. Given the cost of appeals, lawyers usually seek review when they believe the circuit court will find serious error. This is particularly the case for contingency-fee suits. Furthermore, even as the circuit court reviews a growing percentage of cases from the district courts, it strives to discourage all but the most significant cases. The standard governing findings of fact is that those findings must be "clearly erroneous." Because district court judges are skillful at fashioning facts, this is not an easy standard for lawyers to meet. Even so, Acker was far more likely to run the risk of appellate review than was Thompson.[100]

Consideration of "death-knell" devices indicates how actively each judge invited the possibility of appellate review. A number of federal rules of procedure allow the district judge considerable discretion over whether a jury will hear a plaintiff's case. The authority to grant the defendant a summary judgment is termed a "death-knell" device because it prevents a jury trial. Over a ten-year period, Acker granted summary judgment twenty-one times and was reversed nine times. Employing another death-knell device that allowed a defendant to move for a dismissal (Rule 41[b]), the circuit court reversed Acker four out of eight times. During a twelve-year period, Thompson, by contrast, granted twenty-four motions for summary judgment, of which the circuit reversed one. He dismissed one case in which there was no appeal and granted one new trial. These figures suggest that Acker was more willing than Thompson to use the death-knell procedures to stop a suit.[101]

Acker's high reversal rate on death-knell procedures suggested a degree of activism evidenced in other areas. Contrary to established Alabama precedent that the Eleventh Circuit had confirmed, Acker used the power of summary judgment to challenge the state's requirement of an identity of issues and parties under collateral estoppel doctrine. Although only a few states adhered to this mutuality requirement in such cases, the rule in Alabama was generally settled. In two cases Acker attempted to align Alabama's doctrine with the majority of states; in both cases, however, the Eleventh Circuit reversed. Had Acker succeeded, the practical result would have been to deter plaintiffs from pursuing further claims.[102]

Further instances of creativity involved civil rights. The first case involved a clash between the Ku Klux Klan and African-American demonstrators. The defendant-Klansman sought to suppress depositions obtained by a private attorney. Holding that the attorney was effectively an agent of the government, Acker suppressed the documents. A series of appeals and reversals followed in which Acker used procedural discretion to keep the documents out of the trial. Finally, Judge Frank Johnson for the Eleventh Circuit ordered the cases to be reassigned to another judge.[103] In the second case, an Asian female chemist sued the TVA, alleging that racial and sexual discrimination were the reasons that she was fired. Her lawyers argued from the Eleventh Circuit's established precedents, which were favorable. Acker conceded that "a good argument can be made that one or more of Dr. Liao's complaints was valid," and he decided the case in her favor. He did so, however, on the basis of a new affirmative-action theory announced by the Supreme Court in *Johnson v. Santa Clara County* (1987). The Eleventh Circuit reversed Acker because he had failed to follow its precedents. Acker admitted that his decision "knocked out the [TVA's] voluntary [affirmative action] program, by game playing."[104]

Acker's most significant resort to activism was his defense of the right to a jury trial. The Constitution's Seventh Amendment guarantees the right of trial by jury in common law suits where the value in controversy exceeds twenty dollars. The Constitution also provides for equity jurisdiction, which of course leaves trials to the judge alone. Throughout the nation's history, Congress passed laws allocating jurisdiction to the court's law or equity side. Meanwhile, the Supreme Court established a two-pronged test for determining whether there was a right to a jury: "First, the statutory action is compared to 18th-century actions brought in the courts of England prior to the merger of the courts [of] law and equity. Second, [courts] examine the remedy sought and determine whether it is legal or equitable in nature." Responding to the repeated bias of white southern juries evidenced during the 1950s and 1960s against black and white civil rights activists, Congress stated that employment discrimination cases could be tried under Title VII of the Civil Rights Act of 1964, on the equity side of the federal court. Although the statute does not directly deny the option of a jury trial, at best the right would have to be inferred.[105] Acker was the first and as of 1994 the only lower federal court judge to specifically hold in a Title VII case involving employment discrimination that a jury trial was permissible. There was evidence that certain members of the Supreme Court supported Acker's position, but at least prior to 1994 a majority of the Court had not so held, leaving Acker in a solitary minority. Finally, Eleventh Circuit precedent expressly adhered to the equitable rule.[106]

In controversial cases, Thompson, too, employed discretion innovatively, but less so than Acker and with different results. Prior to 1988, the Supreme Court had not settled whether the federal trial judge's discretion over the award of attorney fees included the authority to enhance fees. The theory of fee enhancement recognized that larger fees are necessary in order to ensure that lawyers will risk taking contingency cases, especially representing poorer clients in civil rights and other unremunerative types of litigation. By 1988, the Court had held that fee enhancement could be appropriate, but a majority had not agreed on a ruling standard. Justice Sandra Day O'Connor stated in a concurring opinion a restrictive standard according to which a court placed on the fee applicant the burden to prove the extent to which a given market generated adequate contingent fees. In such a market, O'Connor held, the judge could enhance the fee only to the point necessary to ensure all clients competent counsel. Her theory required further that unless it was shown that the litigant "faced substantial difficulties in finding counsel in the relevant market," there should be no enhancement.[107]

Adopting O'Connor's standard, Thompson established the guiding precedent in the Eleventh Circuit. In *Hidle v. Geneva County Board of Education*, the plaintiff won a Title VII claim and sought attorney fees. Thompson found that within the Alabama market, lawyers who once had "handled contingency-fee employment discrimination cases had ceased doing so because the fees are not high enough to justify taking the risk of losing the case, and as a result, there is a severe and critical shortage of civil rights lawyers in this state." To ensure that "alleged victims of employment discrimination" had competent counsel, fee enhancement was "not only appropriate but necessary." Thompson nonetheless enhanced the fee by the bare minimum necessary to "attract competent counsel."[108]

Thompson stated clearly his opinion's policy goals. First, he wanted to further "Alabama's continued full and vigorous commitment" to the nation's "lofty, but as yet unfulfilled, agenda to make the promises of this land available to all citizens, without regard to race or sex or other impermissible characteristic." In order to achieve this basic goal, it was necessary to prevent the "indirect" and "somewhat insidious" denial of equal justice. As "undisputed evidence" demonstrated, an "economic market" existed in which attorneys could not afford to represent "victims of discrimination." Accordingly, the relief was "not an isolated measure, but rather ... a broad recommitment of Alabama's legal resources to the full and vigorous pursuit of civil rights."[109]

Thompson employed similar innovation to remedy hiring discrimination among Alabama's state troopers. In 1968, the U.S. Justice Department began a suit challenging the entrenched racial discrimination that characterized Alabama's state employee system, including the troopers. During more than a decade, Judge Frank Johnson used creative remedies to steadily overcome state resistance until significant desegregation was achieved. In the part of the case involving the state troopers' hiring practices, Johnson found that because the Department of Public Safety had purposefully "frustrated" and "delayed" enforcing his order, he had no alternative but to impose temporary quotas. The Fifth Circuit affirmed Johnson in 1974, holding that "quota relief . . . is a temporary remedy that seeks to spend itself as promptly as it can by creating a climate in which objective, neutral employment criteria can successfully operate to select public employees solely on the basis of job-related merit." The court also stated that the department's use of selection procedures that "dispropor-tionately excluded blacks" overcame any contention that temporary "quota hiring produces unconstitutional 'reverse' discrimination, or a lowering of employment standards, or the appointment of less or, unqualified persons."[110]

In 1981, the Alabama state trooper case entered a new stage before Judge Thompson. Although Johnson's action had ended hiring discrimination, the Department of Public Safety had not developed an adequate promotion policy. As a result, there were "232 state troopers at the rank of corporal or above . . . [but] *still not one black*." The case was reassigned to Thompson following Johnson's appointment to the Eleventh Circuit. The reassignment coincided with the new Reagan Justice Department's decision to use the case to argue that the imposition of a quota constituted reverse discrimination and was therefore unconstitutional. Following a remedial theory similar to Johnson's, Thompson found that the evidence showed that "the discriminatory effects of past discrimi-nation . . . will not wither away of their own accord," making necessary "immediate, affirmative, race-conscious action." When the department failed to develop a nondiscriminatory promotion procedure, Thompson ordered an independent agent to do so. While this was underway, he imposed a temporary promotion quota that applied only to objectively qualified blacks. In addition, the order did not lead to the removal, replacement, or demotion of any whites, or interfere with their promotion. Within six months, Thompson approved a nondiscriminatory promotion procedure, whereupon he terminated the quota. In a five-to-four decision the Supreme Court affirmed Thompson's remedial procedure.[111]

Political party values inadequately explained Thompson's and Acker's decisions. In the affirmative-action cases, the Democrat Thompson upheld a temporary quota, whereas the Reagan Republican Acker resisted a voluntary affirmative action program with ingenuity. The two outcomes seemed consis-tent with the opposing national party platforms. On closer examination, however, the results were less clear. In both cases, the judges applied the precedents of the Supreme Court, a court, after all, dominated by Republican appointees. The circuit court reversed Acker in the *Liao* case because he avoided the Eleventh Circuit's established affirmative-action doctrine. The precedent Acker believed should have governed was the Supreme Court's more recent *Johnson* decision, a case that nonetheless sanctioned voluntary affirmative action programs. Similarly, Thompson's remedial order in the trooper case was con-sistent with Frank Johnson's judgments, which both the circuit court and the Supreme Court had upheld. Put another way, Acker decided in favor of *Liao* at the district court level in order to make the case a vehicle for changing ruling precedent. But the precedent he wanted to apply to control the case still allowed affirmative action programs. Thus on the policy level Thompson and Acker agreed; they differed in their regard for the circuit court's precedent.

External political or social factors also did not explain other decisional outcomes. Applying summary judgments and other procedural rules, Thompson more often than not favored enlarged access, while Acker often supported the opposite position. Any connection between these divergent outcomes and political party agendas was at best uncertain, since both Thompson and Acker appealed to the precedents of a Supreme Court dominated by Republicans. Similarly, the possible influence of social class was diminished by the fact that each judge came from a prosperous upper-middle-class family. A stronger correlation existed between enlarged access and Thompson's heritage as an African American, a background that sensitized him to the evil of unequal rights. And yet, in the fee-enhancement cases, Thompson not only followed a course pioneered by Judge Frank Johnson, but the theory Thompson applied was the comparatively moderate one subsequently upheld by Justice Sandra Day O'Connor. Acker had been a successful trial lawyer, representing whites as well as blacks. In addition, as a judge he stood virtually alone defending the right of jury trial in Title VII cases.

The principal institutional imperative separating Thompson and Acker was respect for circuit court precedent. As the similarity of reversal rates indicated, the circuit court reversed each judge in roughly one-third of the appellate cases. It was in the mix of reversal judgments, however, that Acker was much more willing than Thompson to follow an independent course, exercising discretionary judgment to avoid the circuit court's lead. Ironically, Acker's independence strengthened the circuit court's control. The majority of cases in which he employed discretion to establish new precedent were the very ones in which the clarity of the circuit court's doctrine encouraged lawyers to undertake the cost of appeal, which were the Acker opinions most likely to be reversed. Thompson displayed no such pattern, keeping his resort to discretionary judgment within the circuit court's prescribed boundaries.[112] Thus, diverse outcomes in cases involving routine yet complex procedural and substantive issues suggested that external political tensions influenced the decisional process less than the national judicial system's institutional constraints.

Constitutional Questions

The approach of Alabama's federal judges toward civil rights issues emerged in the Montgomery bus boycott case of 1955–56. Following the confrontation resulting from Rosa Parks's refusal to comply with the city's ordinances segregating seating on buses, local black leaders sued the city in federal district court, charging that the ordinances violated the Fourteenth Amendment's equal protection clause and federal law, including the Civil Rights Act of 1866. Lynne, Rives, and the new judge Frank Johnson heard the case. The panel decided two to one against the city, Lynne dissenting. Instead of flatly accepting the black leader's arguments, which raised complex questions involving contrary precedent, Rives and Johnson based their decision on the recent *Brown* decision overruling the separate but equal doctrine for public education. Rives and Johnson analogized the principle to strike down segregation in the Montgomery bus system. Lynne's dissent rejected the reasoning by analogy, arguing that his colleagues had ignored numerous precedents that permitted segregated buses. Until the Supreme Court specifically overruled the precedents in the field of public transportation, Lynne said, those precedents bound the lower federal courts.[113]

In civil rights suits, Lynne nonetheless freely exercised discretion when it came to fashioning remedies. Following precedent, he imposed an injunction on the Jefferson County School Board when black teachers claimed that the board had discriminated against them in the payment of salaries. After the board failed to end the discrimination, one of the black teachers asked Lynne to find the board in contempt and impose a fine to cover the loss of pay during the period the injunction was in effect. A magistrate's report Lynne had ordered found that despite the injunction an indisputable disparity persisted between the salaries of black and white teachers at the same rank. Lynne held first that the discrimination clearly violated the injunction. Yet he exercised discretionary authority over the remedy by deciding that the imposition of a fine was impermissible because it would be the result of a suit against the agent of the state without its consent, which was contrary to the Eleventh Amendment. In order to reach this outcome, Lynne narrowly construed precedent that may have applied by analogy. Accordingly, despite the admitted violation of the injunction, Lynne did not order the board to pay a fine, and the salary disparity was not remedied without further litigation.[114]

The Fifth Circuit reviewed Lynne's application of discretionary judgment in another desegregation case. While operating in accord with the Alabama Pupil Placement law, Birmingham's Board of Education refused to submit a desegregation plan. Black parents sued, asking Lynne for an injunction to prevent continued operation of the racially segregated school system. The case arose during one of several violent clashes between city authorities led by Eugene "Bull" Connor and Martin Luther King, Jr.'s protesters. Lynne did not issue an injunction. Noting the massive popular opposition to desegregation, he

Seybourn Lynne (b. 1907), Northern District judge from 1946 to the present; Democrat. *Alabama Department of Archives and History*

observed that the pupil assignment law permitted admission of black children to white schools on the basis of individual merit; that the board had found few if any blacks who met this criterion was not the fault of the law. Moreover, in a decision by Judge Rives, a three-judge panel had upheld the law and its application by the Birmingham School Board. In addition, Lynne reasoned, the Supreme Court's *Brown* II decision left local district courts considerable freedom to implement desegregation orders. Finally, other circuit courts had upheld pupil assignment laws.[115]

Despite Lynne's marshaling of precedent, the Fifth Circuit reversed. Judges Elbert P. Tuttle and Walter Gewin joined Rives on the panel that heard the appeal. By a two-to-one vote, Gewin dissenting, the court overruled Lynne's refusal to grant the injunction. Rives pointed out that four days before Lynne decided the Birmingham case, the Fifth Circuit unanimously had overturned the Savannah School Board's use of Georgia's pupil assignment law to prevent meaningful desegregation. Rives held also that, contrary to Lynne's reasoning, the burden of initiating a desegregation plan fell not on the black plaintiffs but on the school board. In addition, the majority expressed disappointment that three years of litigation had resulted in little if any real desegregation. Finally, in accordance with the Savannah precedent, the court ordered the Birmingham School Board to prepare and implement a desegregation order. Gewin's dissent defended Lynne's decision because the facts did not warrant an injunction to be issued; the refusal was therefore consistent with the judge's exercise of discretionary judgment.[116]

Lynne's most important test of judicial discretion involved Title II of the 1964 Civil Rights Act. Congress passed Title II to outlaw discrimination in various privately owned and operated businesses, including hotels, theaters, and restaurants. Unlike other provisions of the Civil Rights Act, Congress referred generally to the commerce clause as the basis of Title II, thereby extending to civil rights the constitutional clause that historically applied almost exclusively to business and labor relations. Congress did not categorically tie Title II to the commerce clause. Those who defended the use of the clause primarily wanted to defeat the claim that discrimination by private businesses was permissible because it was not the sort of state action that the Court found contrary to the Fourteenth Amendments's equal protection clause. Reliance on the commerce clause thus avoided altogether the "state action" controversy. In addition, since 1937 the Supreme Court had decided numerous cases that expanded the peacetime market activities that the commerce clause reached. Civil rights, the supporters of the commerce clause theory argued, represented merely a further incidence of an ongoing trend.[117]

In 1964, Birmingham restaurateur Ollie McClung challenged Title II as an unconstitutional extension of the commerce clause. McClung admitted that he discriminated against blacks seeking service in the dining area of Ollie's Barbecue. He argued, however, that Title II went beyond the power Congress possessed under the commerce clause. Furthermore, enforcement of Title II would take away McClung's property without due process of law. Through procedural devices, the Justice Department refined the commerce clause claim, emphasizing that Ollie's Barbecue was located some distance from interstate highways and sold food prepared principally with locally purchased products.

A three-judge panel composed of Lynne, Gewin, and Harlan H. Grooms heard McClung's case. Lynne wrote the opinion for a unanimous court. He considered the intent of the framers of the commerce clause, the Supreme Court's interpretation of the clause between 1824 and 1937, and Congress's expansion of the power since the New Deal. Under each of these potential sources of constitutional legitimacy Lynne found no basis for extending the clause to include racial discrimination. He held further that McClung's business was too localized to have any impact on interstate trade. If Congress could claim a power that reached such market activity there was no effective limit to congressional authority. This claim violated the constitutional principle that the federal government was a government of delegated powers. Title II of the Civil Right Act was, therefore, unconstitutional.

The Supreme Court reversed, upholding the law. The Court based its decision on more recent commerce clause precedents than Lynne had cited, which had greatly expanded congressional authority to regulate even intrastate trade when it touched interstate commerce. The Justice Department's briefs also cited evidence drawn from congressional hearings, showing that Congress recognized the burden civil rights struggles imposed on trade, though in only one or two instances did the debates state categorically that the commerce clause was the basis of Title II. Thus precedent and policy sanctioned Congress's effort to overcome this burden through Title II.[118]

Lynne's use of precedent in *McClung* was consistent with his exercise of discretion in later decisions. In two employment cases, Lynne followed precedent to broaden the reach of Title VII and the Federal Rules of Civil Procedure to strike down employment practices that discriminated against black union members. In two other cases, Lynne's application of precedent had inconsistent results. The issue in *Moody v. Flowers* was whether the Supreme Court's standard of "one person one vote" employed under the Fourteenth Amendment's equal protection clause to reapportion state legislatures should be extended to include district divisions within counties. At the time, the Supreme Court had not applied the "one person one vote" standard to such political subdivisions. Lynne followed precedent and maintained the status quo. Yet in the other constitutional case, when Birmingham's Elmwood Cemetery refused to sell a burial plot to an African-American woman whose son had died in the Vietnam War, Lynne applied precedent to overturn racial segregation. The Supreme Court had interpreted the Civil Rights Act of 1866 to include any racial discrimination arising from the sale or rental of property. Still, the Court did not address squarely whether the act prohibited racial discrimination in the sale of cemetery plots. Conceding that his decision was clearly innovative, Lynne nonetheless extended the Court's precedent in favor of the mother's rights.[119]

Lynne explained his judicial role in terms of history and the reconciliation of independence and discretion. First, like his friend Justice Hugo Black, he viewed the Constitution as the result of the historical conflicts shaping its creation and development. The American people were, he said "unwilling to surrender the priceless jewel of state sovereignty unless they could be assured that it would not be eroded by a central government. For that reason, the Bill of Rights was adopted and appended to the Constitution before it was ratified." Yet history was secondary to the primary influence of the Supreme Court. Not until the Civil War and the adoption of the Fourteenth Amendment and the due process and equal protection clauses, for example, did the Supreme Court evolve the incorporation doctrine. This development demonstrated, Lynne said, "a truism, that the Constitution ... means what the Supreme Court says it means." And unless the Constitution was "subject to interpretation in the light of social changes and desires, it would never have survived these two hundred years." Compare, he said, the Constitution's few amendments to the constitutions of Alabama and "our sister-states with hundreds of amendments, [and] you can see what would have happened to that great document but for the flexibility of interpretation."[120]

The federal trial and appellate courts were independent of yet subordinate to the Supreme Court. For most of the nation's history, diversity jurisdiction provided most of the district court's business. Since World War II, however, an "explosion of federal statutes" caused the trial dockets to "dramatically expand," Lynne said. During the same period, the Supreme Court's decisions in *Brown v. Board of Education* (1954), *Baker v. Carr* (1962), and *Roe v. Wade* (1973) had a "tremendous impact on the social and political life of . . . Alabama." Emphasizing his dependent status within the judicial system as a trial judge, Lynne said he had "no right to overrule an opinion" of the Supreme Court or of the appeals court above him. "It is my duty to follow those opinions and to implement them to the best of my ability and understanding." The separation of powers was the "genius of the founders of our Constitution," and without the "power of the Supreme Court" America "would not have a republican form of government."[121]

Obedience to precedent set the limits of discretion. The "only way that I, as a trial judge, can decide a case in those areas [whether they are controversial or not] is to read and try to determine what the Supreme Court has said and then to apply it," Lynne said. "We would have chaos if every judge had a right to express in his opinions his own personal views. Nobody is required to agree with everything." The "bottom line" was that he was "bound by what superior courts have said." It was not necessarily the "fear" of reversal that compelled obedience to precedent. Instead, when an appellate court reversed the lower court's opinion it "change[d] the approach" of the lower court: "when the case is remanded for trial . . . we're bound then by what the [higher] Court has said." There were trial judges, Lynne admitted, who when they encountered an opinion they thought was "wrong, will go . . . [their] own personal way and say this case could be distinguished from that case." For Lynne, however, this was "an artificial effort to escape from an opinion which you don't agree with, and I try not to do that."[122]

Lynne explained his own controversial decisions within these limitations. In the Montgomery bus boycott case he dissented because the Supreme Court had not specifically established a precedent that guided the lower courts. The three-judge court should have followed the Supreme Court's traditional acquiescence to segregated transportation facilities rather than play the role of pioneer. According to this logic, Rives's and Johnson's reliance in the majority opinion on the analogy to *Brown*, was the sort of "artificial effort to escape" precedent that Lynne sought to avoid. In the Ollie's Barbecue decision, Lynne presented a contrasting rationale. He justified the three-judge panel's unanimous decision to overturn Title II on the ground that Congress had not explicitly incorporated civil rights into the commerce clause. Lynne and his colleagues reasoned, therefore, that Congress had not placed Title II "squarely on the Commerce Clause. We realized that if they had that power as they did in . . . other laws affecting industry, if they just said that a proscription of the right to go to a public eating place was an obstruction of state commerce, our decision would have been different, but they made no reference to any finding in the passage of that act." According to this logic, Lynne ignored more recent commerce clause–stretching precedents because they had no bearing on the manner in which Congress had drafted Title II.[123]

Lynne resisted being categorized but accepted the label of moderate. He recognized that "laymen label judges." Activist judges exceeded the scope of their power "in trying to promote social change." Strict constructionists wanted to "keep the Constitution within its original bounds." Moderates like himself belonged to neither group, adhering to the framers' purpose of creating the system of checks and balances to protect liberty while serving as a "restraining influence on the proclivities of the people to take extreme positions." Since 1946, when Lynne became a federal judge, the Supreme Court's role in the constitutional system had been "more stringent . . . on the public, than perhaps acts of the Congress or acts of the Executive Department . . . because of the problems which came to the Court."[124]

The federal judiciary did not actively pursue this role. The solution to these problems came to the federal courts rather than the other branches or the states because "lawyers are ingenious and they raise problems that have never been thought of before and we face that every day." In dealing with those problems, Lynne concluded, the Supreme Court had not "exceeded the sphere of its power." He felt at perfect liberty to "philosophically disagree" with some opinions. But he and all Americans were bound by the Supreme Court's decisions because the "Constitution means what the Court says it means." Indeed, Lynne's skillful approach to precedent resulted in his being reversed by the Supreme Court only once, in the Ollie's Barbecue case.[125]

Judge Sam Pointer's approach to discretion presents a useful contrast to Lynne's. Early in 1971, African-American parents went before Pointer seeking to have their children transported for free from Jefferson County to the new, virtually all-white Pleasant Grove school system. Local authorities had created the new system to avoid complying with a busing order governing Jefferson County decided by the Fifth Circuit. To enforce compliance, Pointer held that the Pleasant Grove system was "deemed to have elected to transfer responsibilities for general administration and supervision of public education within the Pleasant Grove zone to the Jefferson County Board of Education." For all practical purposes, Pointer's decision ended the independent existence of the white school system. Governor George Wallace, Senator James Allen, and white parents publicly condemned Pointer as a "dictator" guilty of "premeditated murder." A group of Pointer's fellow Republicans called for his resignation. Pointer's busing decision was creative but nonetheless consistent with established court of appeals precedent and the Supreme Court's pathbreaking affirmation of busing in the Swann case, also decided in 1971. In litigation involving conditions at the Birmingham and Jefferson County jails, Pointer again straightforwardly applied clear precedent requiring improvement of overcrowding, sanitation, and prisoners' rights.[126]

Pointer's treatment of Title VII employment discrimination claims suggested further how he reconciled activism and restraint. Where litigants attempted to bring new claims stretching established statutory constructions, Pointer decided against creating new doctrine. The Equal Employment Opportunity Commission tried to enter a case that an individual had already filed. In addition, the EEOC's action occurred after the 180-day deadline required by statute. Pointer decided against the EEOC first because it failed to comply with a clear statutory deadline. He then held against the commission on the other point, emphasizing that the statute's history showed that Congress intended to prevent duplicate claims. In another case, Pointer rejected white steel workers' assertions that a seniority system favorable to blacks and women constituted reverse discrimination. Pointer refused to disturb a seniority system that was the result of a previous court order. The white plaintiffs sought, he said, to reconsider issues that already had been fully litigated and settled. A third case involved an individual plaintiff's request to be certified as a member of a class in order to allege that he had not been hired for reasons of race at any of the employer's mines. Again following precedent, Pointer held that he would grant class certification only for a suit involving the specific mines at which the plaintiff had sought employment, thus limiting the potential reach of the suit.[127]

Pointer's attitude toward his judicial role thus balanced discretion and dependence. How the public perceived his decisions was of secondary importance. During the desegregation decision, Pointer was willing to explain his opinions to citizens either in informal face-to-face meetings or on the phone. "I wanted people to see that I'm not passing the buck and they could talk with me," he said. "I wanted to assure the public that I had some realistic sense of the way people were feeling and of practical problems." At the same time, merely because "a decision is unpopular, that's not a reason to stay away from it— regardless of who likes it." He conceded that many blacks labeled him "too conservative," while many whites said he was "too liberal." But Pointer was "not overly concerned about labels." Indeed, his "general persuasion" was "fairly conservative," the Nixon appointee said. A court's "principal job" was nonetheless "to do what's right and not to make a decision based on the image you create. Be aware of the image and improve it if there's a way of bettering it, yes, without sacrificing what you feel is right." Given this consideration, "I like to try to call them as I see them."[128]

In addition, Pointer was keenly aware of his "responsibility" within the federal judicial system. His view was that he was responsible to the Supreme Court and the circuit court, and "I don't think I should on my own do

Sam C. Pointer, Jr. (b. 1934), Northern District judge from 1970 to present; Republican. *Virginia Hare, Library, U.S. District Court, Northern District*

something contradictory to what they've said. Within the bounds of those decisions I try to follow and come up with something acceptable to everything laid out by those courts." He gave particular attention to the possibility of being reversed on appeal. A judge should not decide a case "feeling it likely to be reversed. That's not being responsive to the oath, and as a practical matter is a problem when a lot of people are affected." Pointer was "concerned about reversals in the sense that I try to follow the law." The role of the appellate courts to "correct errors" was "one of the good things" about the federal judicial system. "It can give you more cause for reflection." Unsurprisingly, Pointer was seldom overruled. Similarly, he emphasized that the trial court's role was to try cases. Early in a suit he pointed out to the parties that settlement was always an available option. If they did not choose to settle quickly, however, he tried the case without hesitation and expeditiously.[129]

Reinforcing Pointer's successful reconciliation of discretion and dependence was his leading involvement in matters of judicial administration. He was an active member of various judicial conference committees. His handling of his own court's docket was one of the best in the nation; he maintained this high degree of efficiency when as chief judge he monitored the dockets of the courts of the Northern District of Alabama. In 1981, a poll conducted by the *American Lawyer* based on interviews with hundreds of federal appellate judges, courthouse reporters, lawyers, and law professors ranked Pointer the best district judge in the Fifth Circuit and among the top eleven federal district judges in the nation. Within the Northern District itself, members of the bar also regarded Pointer highly. When the Jefferson County Young Republican Club urged Pointer's resignation because of the busing decision, the Birmingham Bar Association responded with a public notice stating that "beyond any question whatsoever" the judge had interpreted and applied correctly the Supreme Court's and Fifth Circuit's precedents.[130]

Sustaining Pointer's blend of activism and restraint were deeply held convictions. He believed in personal responsibility for one's actions. Wrongdoing should be punished. He was also confident that the "system in which we live . . . the judicial and legislative and executive branches" would usually treat all fairly. Pointer was sensitive to social tensions. He was the first federal judge in Alabama to employ an African-American law clerk; among the judges of the Northern District he was also the first to hire a female law clerk. "A court's primary function and goal" was, he said, "doing justice."[131]

Diverse factors influenced the decision of constitutional questions, but political party affiliation was a poor indicator. In the Montgomery bus boycott and

Ollie's Barbecue cases, Lynne participated with Gewin, Rives, Johnson, or Grooms. Each of the three Democrats had been part of the National Democrats' inner circle. Notwithstanding their Republican loyalties, Grooms and to a lesser degree Johnson possessed personal connections with the same group. When it came to deciding the two leading civil rights cases, however, the five men split with little or no regard for party affiliation: Rives and Johnson supported civil rights, while the others took a contrary position. Similarly, Pointer was a Republican and a Nixon appointee. Nevertheless, in the busing case and civil rights suits generally, his decisions went against the views of both Nixon and fellow Alabama Republicans. In addition, except for Johnson, who as a WPA supervisor had worked with blacks on nondiscriminatory terms, little or nothing in the social backgrounds or professional experience of the other men, including Pointer, explained the diversity of holdings regarding civil rights issues.

Lynne and Pointer explained the decisional process in terms of the interplay between institutional dependence and discretion. Individual judges were relatively free to apply an independent judgment in constitutional and routine cases. But both Lynne and Pointer generally declined to follow such a course themselves, and by so doing they exercised discretion with a degree of moderation that characterized most of Alabama's federal judges during the half century following World War II. Nearly every judge conceded that personal background influenced decision making to some indeterminable extent. Yet most agreed that like Lynne and Pointer they deferred primarily to the precedents of the Supreme Court and the circuit court of appeals. Lynne's early civil rights decisions indicated a desire to try cases by existing precedent until the Supreme Court provided unequivocal doctrine. The Montgomery bus boycott and Ollie's Barbecue cases were the leading examples of this cautious approach. Once the Supreme Court acted, however, Lynne, Pointer, and most of the other judges neither pursued nor advocated an independent course.

CONCLUSION

During the decades following the Second World War, the pressures influencing routine and constitutional decisions changed. In keeping with the principles of strict scrutiny and ordered liberty the Court established in *Carolene Products* and *Palko*, constitutional litigation increasingly involved issues of individual rights. The federalization of more routine litigation increased procedural uniformity, which simultaneously enlarged the trial court's short-term autonomy while increasing its long-term dependency within a more nationally centralized institutional structure. Often, the political environment in which Alabama's federal judges decided these cases was more or less hostile. A judge's social, professional, and class background provided uncertain guidance as to the influence of conflict. At the same time, the local courtroom culture that in the past had offered considerable direction was undergoing decline. Thus at the very point the external political pressures facing the state's federal judges were greater than at any time since Reconstruction, the local institutions were steadily weakening. Meanwhile, the institutional influence of the national judicial system was becoming greater than ever. Ultimately, Alabama's federal judges deferred to national judicial control.

Individual Rights, Judicial Discretion, and Judge Frank M. Johnson, Jr.

INTRODUCTION

From the 1930s on, Americans' perception of the federal judiciary's defense of individual rights was ambiguous. The constitutional revolution the Supreme Court initiated in 1937 and extended during the decades following World War II subordinated the historically dominant defense of economic liberty to a new presumption favoring civil rights and liberties, particularly through the due process principle of selective incorporation and the doctrine of "strict scrutiny" that facilitated *Brown*.[1] Throughout the rest of the twentieth century, federal judges worked out the implications of the Court's action.[2] Ironically, as the nation's rights consciousness expanded, attacks on the federal courts' enforcement of rights claims grew apace.[3] Critics charged that federal judges and the Supreme Court were exercising unwarranted activism that violated traditional norms of judicial independence and discretion. Defenders accepted the activist characterization but argued that judicial intervention was necessary because state and federal authorities had defaulted on or refused to fulfill their duty to protect rights guarantees.[4] Thus, the public's enlarged rights consciousness failed to foster a consensus concerning the federal judiciary's formal constitutional role or its growing policy-making authority toward individual rights. Within the federal judicial establishment itself, there was the same tension between consensus and conflict.

Few judges suggested more directly the causes and consequences of this tension than Alabama's Frank M. Johnson, Jr. As a federal judge he helped to shape the changing course of individual rights in postwar America. Johnson was born in 1918; his appointment in 1955 as the nation's youngest federal district judge coincided with the beginnings of the white south's massive resistance to the civil rights movement. Until his move to senior status as a federal judge in 1991, Johnson successfully defended civil rights and liberties, overcoming first segregationist obstructionism and then public authority's continuing default on rights guarantees.[5] Johnson's origins and early professional career in an area where a Republican minority persisted among a Democratic majority mirrored the national triumph of New Deal liberalism during the middle of the twentieth century. His remarkable contribution to the rights revolution seemed consistent with the liberal tendencies of the postwar era to which the Supreme Court made such a significant contribution.[6] Like public opinion generally, however, the federal judiciary's response to the rights revolution was uneven, especially in the South. Some southern federal judges who shared Johnson's liberal political ideology but possessed different origins took the same stance, while southern pro–New Deal liberals supported the status quo. Thus neither Johnson's distinctive background nor the national liberal consensus within which he operated during much of his judicial career fully explain his creative defense of individual rights.

Johnson's innovative contribution to the rights revolution within the ongoing debate over judicial activism is instructive. Americans generally accepted Alexis de Tocqueville's perception that federal judges "almost always alone" decided the most important issues involving the nature and limits of governmental power, including conflicts over rights. A tension existed, however, between the popular respect for judicial authority and the federal judge's nonelective position, which seemed at odds with American democratic traditions. Explanations of Johnson's policy-making role that emphasized background and political ideology reflected a wider public discourse that criticized or defended judicial activism within terms consistent with Tocqueville's insight.[7] A focus on the political culture to which Johnson belonged suggested that, at least among partisan party loyalists, party ideology such as that reflected by the liberal consensus constituted a worldview that broadly influenced judges' decisions. Accordingly, activist judges such as Johnson were agents, not opponents, of democracy.[8]

Using Johnson's career to explore judicial innovation toward rights had further interpretive implications. Critics and defenders alike attributed much of Johnson's creative impulse to the character traits and values acquired from a strong family upbringing in the isolated mountains of northwest Alabama. This explanatory mode relied on the primacy of psychological motives and sociological influences identified with the theories of legal realists. As a formal pedagogical force, legal realism declined in importance by the 1940s. The popularized realist presumption that personality more than formal legal process and precedents shaped judicial decisions had considerable resonance, however, especially with the assertion that activist judges "made" law according to their personal predilections. As a result, the contention was, judges such as Johnson violated traditional judicial canons. Meanwhile, supporters of judicial activism followed

Frank M. Johnson, Jr. *Montgomery Advertiser*

realist assumptions by arguing that a strong personality was requisite for the judicial independence on which depended a vigorous defense of rights guarantees.[9]

Johnson's place in the activist-rights discourse had particular relevance also to understanding the civil rights struggle. Standard works on the conflict of course recognized the significance of *Brown v. Board of Education* (1954). The decision's invalidation of the separate but equal doctrine established in *Plessy v. Ferguson* (1896) was presented as a catalyst for change, including the white south's massive resistance and the response of the civil rights movement itself.[10] Recognized too was the vital support given the *Brown* ruling by a small number of southern federal judges, most of whom sat on the Fifth Circuit Court of Appeals. Johnson was one of even fewer southern federal district judges who vigorously enforced the *Brown* principle. Although most commentators acknowledged how important was this handful of judges to the implementation of *Brown*, explanations of their role relied essentially on quasi-realist assumptions concerning personal background, character, and the influence of political ideology. According to the prevailing interpretation, they were "unlikely heroes," possessing the courage to stand against the segregationist culture to which they belonged in order to attain the high ideal of equal justice.

Recent scholarship questioned the standard interpretation of *Brown* but failed to reconsider the role of Johnson and his colleagues. The central contribution of this scholarship was the well-documented argument that a determination of *Brown*'s significance required consideration of the "relative contribution to racial change of *Brown* as compared with the plethora of social, political, economic, and other forces."[11] Employing a comparative, multicausal analysis, this work revised the standard view of the short-term impact of *Brown*, arguing that the decision was a catalyst not only of massive resistance, but more particularly that "*Brown* both significantly exacerbated the level of . . . violence and rendered *officially-sanctioned* suppression politically profitable."[12] This argument relied on incisive treatments of such pivotal confrontations as the Montgomery bus boycott and the Selma march. Coincidentally, in these and other clashes Johnson's role was central. Nevertheless, the federal courts are treated as dependent rather than independent causal factors. As a result, no attempt is made to get beyond the heroic interpretation of Johnson and the few other federal judges who initially fought segregation.

Fuller treatment of the federal courts would have strengthened the revisionist treatment of *Brown's* short-term impact. The high level of violence associated with massive resistance was largely a result of southern public officials, and for a long time federal authorities as well, creating a law enforcement vacuum. State officials' defense of states' rights and the federal government's prolonged deference to local authority, moreover, legitimated opposition.[13] Public authority's response to *Brown* thus made "officially sanctioned suppression" of the civil rights movement "politically profitable" because state and to a lesser degree federal officials could gain political capital by blaming the need for change on the Supreme Court and federal judges such as Johnson.[14] The most successful practitioner of the blaming strategy was Alabama's Governor George Wallace, whose primary object of attack was, indeed, Johnson. The Eisenhower and Kennedy administrations did not formally pursue such a strategy, but their uneven and gradual support of the federal courts forced judges such as Johnson to decide between independent action and maintaining the status quo. Had not Johnson and his activist colleagues taken an independent course, the political advantages of resistance or delay would have been much diminished, but the status quo would have persisted even longer than it did.

Johnson's career thus highlighted tensions within rights-activism discourse, particularly interpretations of the civil rights struggle. Neither personal background nor political ideology alone adequately explained why federal judges such as Johnson aggressively defended individual rights. The issue was especially significant given revisionist treatments of *Brown*'s short-term consequences. It had even wider implications for understanding the primary relationship between judicial activism and rights guarantees during the second half of the twentieth century. This chapter explores these issues by considering first the primary influences identified with Johnson's origins and early career. It juxtaposes those influences on two African-American rights cases, one Johnson won during his brief tenure as federal attorney, the other his contribution as a new judge to the Montgomery boycott decision of 1956. Then we explore Johnson's innovative approach to judicial discretion and independence, particularly his pioneering use of remedial decrees. Finally, Johnson explains in his own words what core values informed his decision making, including what for him was the proper role of an "activist judge."

ORIGINS

Johnson's future as a judge was shaped in part by his past. He was born and grew up in a family and among people possessing a distinctive heritage associated with a special place. The strength of family bonds and the comparative isolation of the community instilled in Johnson values of independence, self-reliance, integrity, and self-sufficiency conditioned by a sensitivity to personal courage and human frailty. This experience fostered also a profound faith in fundamental fairness, especially involving racial or political minorities. University and legal education broadened Johnson's intellectual capabilities, which were tested to the fullest in a noteworthy criminal trial during his service in World War II. After the war, he earned a reputation as a skillful lawyer and active Republican, preparing him well for a career of public service.[15] Still, comparisons between Johnson and fellow Alabamian Richard T. Rives suggested that, at least initially, family background and the mode of law practice probably most influenced Johnson's attitude toward individual rights.[16]

Johnson's early youth profoundly shaped his instincts concerning right and wrong. Most public assessments and Johnson himself emphasized the importance of his Winston County origins. Winston and several neighboring counties in northwestern Alabama were the home of "mountain Republicans" whose ancestors had resisted secession and who well into the twentieth century retained an independent and unified political influence amidst the Democratic majority. Johnson's ancestors not only had fought on the Union side in the Civil War but also were respected local leaders, including his great-grandfather, James Wallace "Straight Edge" Johnson. According to family tradition, the local community so trusted the elder Johnson's integrity that neighbors often asked him to settle disputes instead of relying on the courts. The community maintained the same trust toward Johnson's father, electing him probate judge and finally, during the 1940s, the only Republican member of the Alabama legislature.[17]

Still, this intermingling of family and political tradition was an incomplete measure of the influence of place. Although Winston County was comparatively isolated and predominantly rural, the Illinois Central Railroad served the area. As a result of the railroad, Johnson acquired an image of individual African Americans that differed from that possessed by most white Alabamians. The fewer than one hundred blacks living in Winston County clustered principally in and around Haleyville, Johnson's hometown until he was fourteen. Here he played with black children whose fathers worked for the railroad. "They made good money. They lived in nice homes," he recalled. At the same time, he remembered that his own parents, although accepting the public and private separation racial orthodoxy imposed, "never did have any racial prejudice suggestive or overt or any other way." Indeed, Johnson's mother helped to establish the local school for blacks. Thus, unlike most other white Alabamians, Johnson's formative racial image combined legally imposed separation with economic independence, reasonable prosperity, and no formally articulated racism.[18]

The rural, small-town setting influenced Johnson's early life in other ways. Because Winston County was comparatively poor, the Johnsons, like many families, produced much of their own food. In addition, as the oldest son in a large family, Frank, Jr., was his mother's principal helper in all aspects of the family's life. "I changed diapers and everything else. Mamma was busy. I helped her everywhere. She never let me cook. I'd bring the wood in, build the fire, I'd help her run that old [hand-cranked] Maytag washing machine," he said. Johnson also worked with animals and plowed the fields. The limited local economy supported modest educational opportunities. Johnson's mother taught him to read and spell before he started the first grade. He remembered his mother as a "good teacher," who held "my ear to keep me from moving around and diverting my attention." His parents thus gave Johnson "a real consciousness that you don't get anything that you don't work for. And you can work and not get much if you don't get an education. And if you want to succeed, you get your education and work hard. You couldn't get it for nothing."[19]

Johnson's parents equated personal honesty and responsibility with strict regard for law. "They were very sensitive to their children being honest and not violating the law. You just didn't do it. And they set good examples in that respect all the way back to my grandfather and grandmother on both sides. I don't remember any of them getting into any trouble," he said. Similarly, Johnson's father, for much of the son's youth a local postmaster, "took great pride in the fact" that the annual postal inspections "never [found him] a penny short." In a small community, strict integrity and accountability were integral to maintaining the individual's and the family's respectability.[20]

Just as important, perhaps, his parents were firm but understanding during the exceptional instances when Johnson found himself on the wrong side of the law. For example, he assaulted one of his father's political opponents for making false accusations about the senior Johnson. His father advised him to plead guilty to disorderly conduct before the local magistrate, and that was the end of the matter. In a similar vein, the sixteen-year-old Johnson came in contact with bootleggers and the temptations of "wildcat whiskey." Fundamentally, the attitude Johnson absorbed from his parents concerning responsibility for one's conduct was consistent with the view stated by one of his closest friends: "We never got into any real trouble. We were mischievous, but we weren't mean. We didn't do destructive-type things." This attitude blended the belief in moral correctness with a practical appreciation of human nature, particularly a sense of family pride.[21]

The tensions between moral principle and human nature were suggested further by broader encounters with moonshine whiskey. In the "Free State of Winston," the illegal production and sale of moonshine was common. Equally widespread was the involvement of local law enforcement and elected

221

officials in the practice. At times elected authorities protected the moonshiners who voted for their party while these same officials prosecuted the producers who supported the opposing party. As Johnson confronted these moral and legal ambiguities, he instinctively embraced a faith in equality before the law, due process, and fairness. Discriminatory treatment of moonshiners, grounded as it was in political prejudice, offended Johnson more than violations of the tax code or moral concerns.[22]

This consciousness also shaped Johnson's awareness of unfair treatment and racial injustice. Watching his father handle the duties of a probate judge, Johnson learned respect for elemental procedural fairness. At some level, he probably perceived that this basic maintenance of due process was consistent with the firm but humane discipline prevailing in his home. In any case, Johnson's belief that fundamental fairness and respect for humanity were interdependent was already strong when he encountered for the first time blatant mistreatment of black convicts. After graduating from high school, Johnson worked carrying the rod for a surveyor's road crew. Black convict labor worked with this crew, too. Johnson became "sensitized" to the white guards' mistreatment of the black convicts "when, if they tried to escape, or if they were guilty of just blatantly disobeying an order, they'd get a certain number of licks with a whip. And no one would conduct a hearing to determine if it was appropriate or not. I got pretty sensitized to the fact that it wasn't right, that it wasn't just." He never forgot his repulsion. "I was nauseated. That one human being whipped another with a bullwhip. Nauseated."[23]

Johnson's belief in fundamental fairness also had spiritual and religious roots. "I have some strong, basic religious beliefs," he said. "Doing what's right and wrong to me is a religious belief. And doing what's fair instead of unfair to a fellow human being is a religious standard." Johnson prayed privately to God, usually "expressing appreciation, and some of the time asking for help and guidance." There was nonetheless a definite separation between the moral principles of the Bible and constitutional or legal principles. He was certain that American law or constitutional principles "should [not] be guided in any way by Biblical principles."[24]

The interplay of family and locale perhaps had its profoundest influence through the women in Johnson's life. In the isolated rural setting in which Johnson grew up, women, though working within domestic roles, were independent and strong. According to family tradition, Johnson's great-grandmother, Mrs. James Wallace Johnson, used a piece of firewood to defend her young grandson, Frank Johnson, Sr., from a buck deer that came too close to the child. A close friend described Johnson's mother, Alabama Long Johnson, as "a lovely lady . . . a woman of strong character, strong morals, strong convictions, the courage of her convictions—a strong, strong woman. And Frank inherited an awful lot of that. He has always shown the courage of his convictions—sometimes to a fault."[25]

Johnson married Ruth Jenkins, who was from the same locale and, like his mother and grandmother, possessed great inner strength. When Johnson decided to go to the University of Alabama School of Law, Ruth enrolled at the university, too. Johnson's mother vigorously supported the decision, saying, "If anybody goes to college, Ruth's going. She's smart."[26] During World War II she served in the Navy, attaining the rank of lieutenant commander. During the years of conflict and tragedy that eventually engulfed them, they complemented and supported each other. An intimate friend said, "theirs is a fantastic love story. Ruth provides ballast, security, and the leavening in [Frank's] . . . bread. And sometimes you see Ruth as the one who carries a long hat pin. If the balloon is going to get too big, Ruth doesn't have any hesitancy in puncturing it. It's drop-by-drop, day-by-day constant. Ruth will stay the course, whatever it is." They "disagree philosophically many times on something, but it never gets personal. They've learned to separate their ideas from their personal relationship." Both "learned to bring out the best that the other had. And ignore the worst."[27]

The qualities instilled in early manhood prepared Johnson for greater responsibilities and independent thought. While still in his early twenties, he supervised about forty men with diverse skills in a construction program under the joint authority of county health departments and the New Deal's Works Progress Administration. Whites and African Americans worked together in his crews on a non-segregated basis, receiving the same wage. The effectiveness of this operation strengthened Johnson's conviction that whites' belief in racial inferiority was "hogwash." Sensitive to the fact that most of the black workers possessed little formal education, Johnson found that given "proper guidance, supervision, and initiative" they were nonetheless as "effective in work" as the white workers. Also, he was "impressed how they cared about their families and making a living in an honest way if they got a chance to do so."[28]

Johnson strengthened these administrative and personnel skills when he entered the University of Alabama. He had received his initial education in the Winston County public schools and the Gulf Coast Military Academy; he then briefly attended Birmingham Southern College on a football scholarship before completing a one-year course at a business college in Birmingham. This mixed educational experience fostered Johnson's self-discipline and desire for learning. At the university, however, he confronted at "every turn" the "profound and shocking realization" of his "ignorance." Typically, he worked aggressively to overcome every educational deficiency. Feeling challenged by "outstanding professors," he "learned to extricate [him]self from errors in the thinking process that tend to darken one's intelligence and incapacitate a person from listening to and appreciating reason, learned to carefully avoid precipitancy and prejudice and, possibly above all, learned that a person—if he or she is to have a sense of contribution and fulfillment—must be an actor in life and not merely a spectator." As his facility to "reason, meditate, and reflect" grew, Johnson realized that all "one can achieve and all that one fails to achieve are the result of his own thoughts, that a person's weaknesses and strengths are his own—not another's and that these weaknesses and strengths are brought about by himself and can only be altered by himself." Johnson developed and sharpened his intelligence by taking both undergraduate and law school classes, which at the time was permitted as a combined course of study for the law degree.[29]

Johnson's success in law school reflected a blend of intellectual growth and personal background. Professor Leigh Harrison recalled that at the start of law school, Johnson "looked like a country boy when I first called on him, and I was surprised at the way he answered the question. I wouldn't have expected him to do as well as he did." He was "an exceptionally able student who evidently grew up with a sense of responsibility and integrity." Johnson was quickly able "to analyze facts and reach a solution based on legal principles," Harrison said. He also understood clearly that "for a lot of legal problems, there are no precise answers."[30] Johnson later emphasized that Harrison and his other teachers "did not limit their efforts to presenting the law in the traditional manner but challenged me to find truth, justice, common sense, and fairness in our country's law. . . . I learned to think, and through that process, learned to distinguish the true from the false. This is what education is all about."[31]

Intellectual acuity conditioned by life experience shaped Johnson's attitude toward the constitutional law governing race relations. The formative encounters with hardworking African Americans on the railroad in his hometown and as a WPA supervisor, along with the intense repulsion felt as to the whipping of black convicts on the road crews, engendered Johnson's belief that racial segregation was morally wrong. As a law student, this moral conviction in turn influenced his critical analysis of the Supreme Court's sanction of slavery in the *Dred Scott* case of 1857 and the affirmation of the South's system of apartheid through the separate-but-equal doctrine in *Plessy v. Ferguson* (1896). Johnson found Chief Justice Roger B. Taney's denial of the slaves' basic humanity in *Dred Scott* "scandalous." Likewise, he thought *Plessy* was "a terrible decision" that could not be the "law under our system of government." He was impressed, however, with Justice John Marshall Harlan's lone dissent in *Plessy*. "I think it was one of the finest opinions, even if it was a dissent. It took a lot of courage. And it was obvious that was the law, whether the Supreme Court was following it or not. It *had* to be the law if the Fourteenth Amendment meant anything," he said.[32]

At home, Johnson had learned to separate right and wrong, that through discipline and education one could live the right, that those in authority should treat everyone, including criminals, with fundamental fairness, sensitivity to human weakness, and a spiritual faith in personal accountability. This, along with a firm grasp of how legal institutions and the Constitution did in fact and ought to function, sustained his presumption that a "true" law or constitutional principle existed even if government agencies at any given time enforced an opposite and therefore "false" rule. Thus Johnson condemned *Plessy* not only because it sanctioned racial separation and a disrespect for individual dignity. The decision also was contrary to the fundamental principles on which the Constitution and America rested, regardless of what the Court had held.

This blend of perspicacity, practicality, and conviction guided Johnson's view of politics. Like Republicans across the nation and many Democrats in Alabama, Johnson considered much of Roosevelt's New Deal liberalism not only socialistic but also an unconstitutional aggrandizement of executive power. Along with many Alabamians, Johnson nonetheless supported the jobs the WPA and other New Deal programs created. Similarly, Johnson understood how his father, the lone Republican in the Alabama legislature, could successfully work with the more progressive National Democratic faction in support of economic and social programs benefiting north Alabama and the state as a whole against the generally dominant conservative Democratic majority. In the same vein, Johnson formed friendships with fellow law students, including George Wallace, who were politically active National Democrats associated with future governor James Folsom. Johnson was also a member of the Pi Kappa Alpha fraternity whose members included many of Alabama's aspiring or established National Democratic activists affiliated with Senator John Sparkman. Still, this practical understanding of party politics did not diminish Johnson's propensity to evaluate individual politicians in terms of whether their leadership was ultimately morally consistent with the spirit of America's basic constitutional principles.[33]

Wartime experience reinforced Johnson's character and legal values. He saw combat action in France and Germany; he was twice wounded, receiving a Purple Heart with an oak-leaf cluster and a Bronze Star. Transferred from the war zone to England to serve as a legal officer, he represented the defendants in one of the most publicized military trials of the war. Nine enlisted guards and two lieutenants were charged with mistreating prisoners at the Lichfield prison. Although inexperienced in criminal trial work, Johnson displayed skill and persistence in the conduct of the case. After lengthy proceedings, Johnson and experienced lead counsel, Clinton McGee (also from Alabama), proved that the brutal conditions in the prison were the result of the actions of superior officers. As a result, the principal enlisted man charged in the case received a minimum sentence. At one point an officer testified that Johnson had said that challenging senior officers did not concern him if it was necessary to protect the rights of the accused. In the process, Johnson recalled, "I filed motions . . . that the U.S. military had never heard of." The Lichfield case demonstrated Johnson's tenacious and creative use of legal process to defend the rights of vulnerable individuals threatened by higher authorities.[34]

After the war Johnson practiced law in the northwest Alabama town of Jasper. The three-man firm's general practice included corporations, probate, criminal work, and public bodies such as the county boards of education and revenue. Johnson handled the trial side while his partners advised business clients. From this mix of law practice, Johnson learned the financial exigencies of maintaining profitability through fee structures. Trying cases before juries, Johnson learned how a lawyer could tap the community's instinct for basic fairness; but he also came to understand that courts and attorneys could overcome this instinct by appealing to prejudice and fear. Ultimately, Johnson's success depended on overcoming such tactics, and among the fellow residents of the area he usually succeeded. He also returned to local politics, pushing a ticket-splitting strategy that enabled the Republicans to win an office or two from the dominant Democrats. In addition, Johnson resigned his membership in Rotary and other business groups when he learned that they excluded Jews.[35]

In one case, Johnson proved how local politics and criminal charges could get mixed up. He defended two brothers charged with murdering a county sheriff. The brothers' family, Johnson recalled, "had been in the [moonshine] whiskey business for years, farming on the side." They were Republicans in a Democratic area, and the sheriff had been politically involved with the most important banking and political family in the county, which included a long-serving member of the Alabama legislature. A local jury found the brothers guilty. On appeal to the Alabama Supreme Court, however, Johnson proved that the sheriff's allies exercised considerable economic and political influence over the jury selection process. In a four-to-three decision, the state Supreme Court reversed the conviction on legal technicalities. Eventually the case was dismissed and the brothers went free.[36]

226

The mountain Republicanism and strong family heritage identified with Johnson's Winston County origins taught him how interdependent were individual responsibility and community mores. The Johnson family and its forebears belonged to a political minority; their personal integrity and strength of character inspired sufficient trust and confidence, however, that various members of the family, especially Johnson's father, had active public careers. What balanced minority rights and community interests was the popular instinct for fundamental fairness. As a trial lawyer, Johnson's success resulted from his ability to overcome popular prejudices and fears and appeal to this basic instinct. The young Frank Johnson controlled these influences so effectively that he rejected the dominant culture's belief in white supremacy and racial segregation. Intellectual growth attained at college and law school equipped him, moreover, with the professional skills to become not only a successful lawyer but also one who often defended underdogs. Pursuing these career goals, he never forgot the lessons learned from his parents and reinforced by his marriage, that often human frailty conditioned moral principle.

Another Alabamian who during the civil rights era became one of the few federal judges vigorously defending individual rights lacked Johnson's distinctive origins. Richard T. Rives was a quintessential political and social insider from Montgomery, the heart of Alabama's firmly segregationist black belt. An active and influential National Democrat, he supported New Deal liberalism against the generally dominant conservative Democrats. Club memberships and social status clearly indicated furthermore that Rives belonged to the state's Establishment. At the same time, his law firm had a major trial practice that included representing white as well as black criminal defendants and plaintiffs before juries. Unlike most Montgomery firms, which shunned defending African Americans and other dispossessed individuals, Rives represented all clients. He resisted, moreover, the Boswell Amendment that imposed new devices to keep blacks disfranchised but defended black-belt registrars of voters when blacks attempted to defeat the traditional discriminatory methods. Rives explained that what other firms "gained in security they have often lost in the freedom and independence that come from representing many poor plaintiffs, rather than a few rich defendants."[37]

On the Fifth Circuit Court of Appeals, his respect for fundamental fairness set Rives apart. He was both "no radical . . . and a tradition-minded . . . Southern [National] Democrat," wrote one incisive observer. "At the same time, Rives was never committed to segregation as an item of faith, and he was a passionately fair man. The evidence of this in his years of practice was clear, and Rives maintained that this attitude came from his father. For him and for the

Left to right: Richard Rives, Robert E. Varner, and Frank M. Johnson, Jr. Varner (b. 1921), a Republican, has been a judge of the Middle District since 1971. *Montgomery Advertiser*

Judge, it was 'just an innate idea of what's right and wrong.' " Thus the interplay between the beliefs acquired from his family and the atypical jury trial practice that included outsiders and the dispossessed enabled Rives to become one of the very few southern federal judges who "rose above the received values of his [social and regional] background and established himself as one of the most courageous judges in our time."[38]

The commonalities Johnson and Rives shared were noteworthy. The locales from which they came profoundly differed, as did their social status and partisan political affiliation. To be sure, the National Democratic leadership often supported Johnson's father as the lone Republican in the Alabama legislature, but this was primarily because of shared economic and political values and associations inherent in the national liberal consensus. Alabama's conservative Democrats did not share this consensus. And even though both the National Democrats and the Eisenhower Republicans were relatively moderate on race, at least for Alabama, Rives's and Johnson's unusual personal rejection of white supremacy was due more to the influence of family than to political values or interests. The men's most conspicuous common experience was their law practice. Johnson and Rives not only represented poor and minority clients before all-white, middle-class male juries, they usually also won. Success reinforced the faith in fundamental fairness both men learned from their parents. Ultimately, however, this faith was inseparable from reliance on the institutional autonomy associated with the independent judiciary and the adversarial process itself.

POLITICAL AND JUDICIAL APPOINTMENTS

Johnson became a federal judge through ordinary politics, but the immediate results of his appointment were unpredictable. The active Republican partisanship of Johnson senior and junior, the personal connections the young Johnson had with Republican Attorney General Herbert Brownell and Alabama's National Democratic faction, the election to the presidency of the first Republican in twenty years, and the Supreme Court's growing support for civil rights converged to bring about Johnson's appointment, first as U.S. attorney and then as federal district judge. Neither the Eisenhower administration's moderate support for civil rights nor the inconsistent decisions of other Alabama federal judges who came from either Republican or National Democratic backgrounds suggested how distinctive would be Johnson's judicial career. His actions as U.S. attorney and judge revealed his independence, especially in the Montgomery

229

bus boycott case. Yet like Rives, Johnson's values and experiences, rooted in his family origins and lawyerly career, enabled him to use judicial independence and the adversarial process to achieve the basic outcome of fundamental fairness.[39]

The combination of lawyerly acumen and Republican activism won Johnson appointment as the United States attorney for northern Alabama. In 1944 and 1948, the senior Johnson actively supported New York governor Thomas Dewey as the Republican Party's presidential candidate. Johnson, Jr., was a Dewey loyalist, too. During the 1948 campaign, he met Warren Burger, Richard Nixon, and Herbert Brownell, Dewey's campaign manager. Alabama was split between the supporters of the more progressive National Democrats and the third-party Dixiecrats who defended racial segregation. Politically aligned with the National Democrats within the state were Governor James Folsom and his floor leader in the Alabama legislature, George Wallace. Dewey of course lost in 1948. But Brownell managed Dwight D. Eisenhower's successful campaign in 1952, a campaign Johnson actively worked for in Alabama. Appointed Eisenhower's attorney general, Brownell chose Johnson to be U.S. attorney for northern Alabama, with the support of the new assistant attorney general, Warren Burger. On race and various post–New Deal economic issues the Dewey-Eisenhower Republicans within Alabama were closer to the National Democrats affiliated with Senators Sparkman and Lister Hill, so the state's all-Democratic congressional delegation supported Johnson.[40]

Usually, U.S. attorneys principally administer the office, delegating to staff lawyers most of the trial work. Johnson, however, handled most trials himself. At the same time he significantly improved the office's administrative efficiency. He also learned how to use the investigative resources of the FBI. This commitment to trial advocacy and administrative effectiveness coincided with the judicial approach of the Northern District's two district judges, Seybourn H. Lynne and H. Hobart Grooms. Under Lynne's leadership especially, the Northern District of Alabama became one of the best-administered courts in the nation. Johnson displayed independence, however, declining to follow the court's standard regard for plea bargaining. Prosecutors often plea-bargained for a "lighter sentence than there should be just to avoid the work of prosecuting a case, or because of friendship with another lawyer, or political considerations." Johnson's experience in law school, as a legal officer in the Army, and in private practice convinced him that it was through a trial that justice was found.[41]

Johnson's equation of justice with trial due process was clear in a peonage case. The owner of a black funeral home in Sumter County, Alabama, sent Johnson a photograph of a beaten and mutilated African-American man's corpse. An accompanying letter said that whites had whipped the man to death. Johnson ordered an FBI investigation. The resulting evidence showed that on their plantation a family named Dial and local officials cooperated to entrap blacks in a debt system that the Dials exploited to maintain a captive labor force. The black man whose photograph Johnson received had tried to escape. Using dogs, the plantation owners tracked the man down, "brought him back and beat him with a bullwhip—and killed him." The Dials' counsel was the "best criminal defense lawyer in the south at the time." Nevertheless, Johnson skillfully brought out testimony that beatings were a common occurrence on the Dials' farm. The furious defense attorney called a recess and privately rebuked the testifier for admitting something "bad" about the Dials. The testifier told the lawyer that "whooping a nigger *ain't* bad in Sumter County." The jury returned verdicts of guilty.[42]

The peonage case coincided with the Supreme Court's *Brown* decision. Johnson's ability to win guilty verdicts from an all-white jury for whites' brutality against a black man impressed Brownell. Clearly, *Brown*'s overruling of *Plessy* and the separate-but-equal doctrine undercut the constitutional legitimacy of segregation, threatening massive resistance from the white south. Brownell not only strongly favored *Brown*, he also trusted that the peonage verdict indicated a willingness among most southern whites to obey the Supreme Court's decision. Judge Lynne, however, predicted that Johnson had a historic destiny because he would be the "last United States attorney . . . in the South to get a conviction for slavery, now that the Supreme Court's decided this *Brown* case."[43]

Success as U.S. attorney paved the way for Johnson's selection as a federal district judge. Trying cases before Lynne and Grooms "impressed" Johnson that the federal district court was "a very important place and a federal judge had tremendous authority and discretion. That's when I got interested in it. But getting interested in being a federal judge won't do it. You have to be where lightning strikes." Even so, Johnson's future was tied to *Brown*. After the *Brown* decision of 1954 the Court waited a year to formulate its implementation order. Brownell and the Justice Department perceived that the federal courts would bear the brunt of enforcing the decree the Court finally handed down in May 1955. During the same year, federal district judge Charles B. Kennamer of Alabama's Middle District suddenly died. The choice of a replacement was inseparable from the tensions surrounding the enforcement of *Brown*. Consistent with the tradition that judges should live in the areas of their court, Republicans and Democrats put forward candidates from Montgomery and south Alabama. Since *Brown* made civil rights a more volatile issue than ever, however, Brownell wanted Johnson in the Middle District because he had demonstrated a firm willingness to defend the rights of all regardless of race.[44]

Other factors worked in Johnson's favor. State Republican Party leaders selected Johnson because he and his father had been loyal to Dewey and Eisenhower. They were perhaps aware too that Kennamer had resided in north Alabama when Herbert Hoover appointed him to the Middle District in 1931. Meanwhile, Johnson was acceptable to the state's National Democrats, including Senators Lister Hill and John Sparkman, because he and his father were aligned with Governor Folsom and opposed to Alabama's Dixiecrat faction. Furthermore, some of the National Democrats' inner group had known and trusted Johnson since law school where they shared membership in the Pi Kappa Alpha fraternity.[45]

Ultimately, however, the determining factor was that Brownell wanted Johnson. Johnson's prosecution of the Sumter County peonage case demonstrated an ability to subordinate the express issue of race to the larger concern for humanity and fundamental fairness. This stance was consistent with the Eisenhower administration's moderate approach to the enforcement of school desegregation orders *Brown* spawned. Eisenhower himself publicly expressed doubts about the wisdom of the *Brown* decision. Accordingly, the administration's civil rights policy depended primarily on the discretion of federal judges. When two east Texas communities refused to desegregate public schools the federal government did nothing because the federal courts left matters in the hands of local officials. Somewhat later, the government intervened directly to enforce the lower court's desegregation order in Little Rock only after the Justice Department's secret negotiations with Arkansas Governor Orval Faubus failed and violence erupted. Thus Brownell probably realized that Johnson's appeal to fundamental fairness rather than racial justice per se in the peonage case corresponded to the government's reliance on the exercise of moderate judicial discretion in civil rights suits generally.[46]

Nevertheless, resistance to *Brown* became so extensive that Johnson could not avoid exercising expanded judicial discretion. Lynne's prediction that white public opinion in Alabama and the South generally would harden against civil rights was prophetic. On the local and state levels of government and within the congressional delegations, southern elected officials defended racial segregation and denied the authority of federal intervention, particularly through the federal courts. State and local authorities' defiance fostered brutal treatment of civil rights supporters; it also encouraged private terrorist attacks against nonviolent civil rights activists such as Martin Luther King, Jr., and Medgar Evers. The fundamental institutional fact was, however, that public officials in

Alabama and other southern states virtually never resisted to the point of going to jail. Instead these leaders politically exploited the federal courts, blaming them for actions that in fact resulted from the officials' own opposition and the refusal to comply with constitutional principles. As a result, they gained local political advantage but also forced increased federal intervention.

Thus federal judges either enforced constitutional principles creatively or indirectly permitted law and order to disintegrate. Shortly after Johnson received unanimous Senate confirmation, Judge Grooms faced mob disruption resulting from Autherine Lucy's enrollment at the University of Alabama in Tuscaloosa. When Lucy sought admission, Grooms granted a court order that overruled the university's racially exclusionary policy. But within days, continuing harassment of Lucy compelled university officials to suspend her in order to ensure her own safety and "the safety of the students and faculty members." Lucy's NAACP lawyers, Thurgood Marshall and Arthur Shores, filed suit seeking readmission, alleging that university officials and the mob had "conspired" to force her out. In court, however, they could present no evidence supporting the conspiracy charge. The university then formally expelled Lucy for making false claims, and Grooms upheld the university's action. Reportedly, Grooms admitted privately to Marshall and Shores that because of threats against his wife and two young children, ruling in Lucy's favor was increasingly dangerous. Grooms, like Johnson a Republican appointed by Eisenhower, received no help from the president, who said he hoped federal action could be avoided.[47]

The Autherine Lucy confrontation and Grooms's response revealed to Johnson the magnitude of the desegregation struggle. Federal judges were neither insulated from threats nor could they count on formal support from the executive. More particularly, a federal judge could decide how much or little discretion to employ. Grooms had used his authority courageously yet ultimately conservatively, initially defending Lucy's constitutional rights but then affirming her expulsion by the university when violence erupted. Unintentionally, Grooms's conservatism suggested to the public that disorder and violence could prevail over constitutional principle. The Lichfield trial and Alabama cases involving political or racial minorities convinced Johnson, however, that skillful and creative uses of legal process could protect individual rights despite public antagonism.[48]

Before 1956 ended, Johnson tested these perceptions in the Montgomery bus boycott case. Following Rosa Parks's arrest, Martin Luther King, Jr., led a bus boycott that significantly curtailed the operation of the city's transportation system. The NAACP challenged the ordinance before a federal panel of

Rives, Lynne, and Johnson. The NAACP's lawyers argued that the ordinance's constitutional basis was the separate-but-equal doctrine established in *Plessy*, which the Supreme Court had for all intents and purposes overturned in *Brown*. The city's counsel, which included the state's assistant attorney general, responded that *Brown* applied to public education, not public transportation; the three-judge court should not act, they said, until the Supreme Court decided that particular issue and provided clear precedent. Montgomery's mayor testified that ending segregation would engender "violence and bloodshed."[49] The prediction occurred against the background not only of the Autherine Lucy confrontation but also of the announcement of the Southern Manifesto, in which the southern states' congressional delegations declared *Brown* unconstitutional and called on state leaders to prevent its enforcement through "massive resistance."[50]

The federal court's approach to precedent in the case required discretion. In order for the three judge court to adopt the NAACP's theory, it would have to hold that *Brown* applied analogously, since the Supreme Court had not directly decided the status of segregated public transportation facilities under the *Plessy* doctrine. Such reasoning required a creative exercise of judicial authority. Following the state's wait-and-see argument engendered no such creativity, thereby limiting the scope of discretionary judgment. Rives and Johnson formed a majority extending *Brown* to overturn Montgomery's segregation ordinance. "We cannot in good conscience perform our duty as judges," Rives wrote, "by blindly following the precedent of *Plessy v. Ferguson* when . . . we think that *Plessy v. Ferguson* has been impliedly, though not explicitly, overruled." Accordingly, the ordinance violated the due process and equal protection clauses of the Fourteenth Amendment. In his first ever dissent, Lynne took a contrary view of precedent. Although Lynne shared with Rives a heritage of active involvement with Alabama's National Democrats, he rejected the majority's reasoning to extend the reach of *Brown*. It was his "simple belief that the laws which regulate the conduct, the affairs, and sometimes the emotions of our people should evidence not only the appearance but the spirit of stability." Lower courts should not decide new issues on the basis of some perceived "new doctrinal trend" emerging from the Supreme Court, but wait until the Court "in a proper case" overturned "established precedent . . . explicitly."[51]

Various factors may have influenced Johnson's vote supporting Rives's opinion. On one level, it followed logically from the negative view of the *Plessy* decision and the preference for Harlan's dissent that he had formed in law school. The state's formal imposition of racial separation was, he believed,

Harlan H. Grooms (b. 1900), Northern District judge from 1953 to 1991;
Republican. *Montgomery Advertiser*

contrary to American traditions and institutions embodied in the Constitution, including the Fourteenth Amendment. Undoubtedly shaping this view were the family values he absorbed and the positive racial encounters he had had growing up. Johnson's experience and formal legal education instilled a belief in basic norms of justice such as equality before the law, which were distinctively American. Courts declared and legislatures enacted legally binding measures that were often contrary to such norms. When in due course the Supreme Court chose to return to fundamental principle and overrule one of these particular measures, however, it was appropriate for lower federal courts to strike down similar measures through analogous reasoning. The Court's reaffirmation of elemental constitutional principle was so important that lower federal judges were bound by their oath to extend it into related areas where justice was being denied.[52]

A related but distinct factor was his faith in courts. Johnson's upbringing established a primary faith that courts were best equipped to treat fairly minority and other weak groups. In the peonage case, Johnson won from an all-white jury a guilty verdict in the death of an African American. This reliance on the courts to attain racial justice was consistent with the defense of the enlisted men from the wrongdoing of superior officers in the Lichfield case. It was noteworthy too that the mountain Republicans of northwest Alabama were a political minority that sometimes encountered discrimination from the local Democratic establishment. As a lawyer, Johnson overcame such discrimination through the legal process. In addition, the evenhanded way Johnson's father dispensed justice as a probate judge reinforced the belief that courts could best protect vulnerable groups.[53]

This faith in fundamental justice enforced through courts helped to explain Johnson's vote for Rives's opinion. Both Rives and Lynne appealed to conscience to justify their opposing approaches to precedent. The logic of Johnson's position also started from a conscientious conviction that any precedent that sanctioned segregation violated a core value of American constitutionalism. If through *Plessy* the Supreme Court had established a doctrine that was repugnant to the basic principle of equality before the law, the Court possessed the power to correct its error. Lynne did not deny the Court's authority to overturn even the most established precedent. What he dissented from was an exercise of discretion by the lower federal courts that through analogy in effect did the same thing. For Lynne this violated the federal courts' dependence within the judicial system. Johnson believed, however, that once the Supreme Court acknowledged its error the very fact of dependence imposed on federal judges the obligation to employ discretion on a scale commensurate with the problem requiring correction.[54]

Still, Johnson distinguished equality before the law from the moral principle that segregation was evil. He later told an interviewer that his vote for the plaintiffs in the boycott case "was not based on any personal feeling that segregation was wrong, it was based on the law, that the state imposing segregation violated my interpretation of the Constitution. . . . It wasn't for a judge to decide on the morality question, but rather the law."[55] In the Montgomery case, this meant extending the reach of *Brown* beyond education to include transportation facilities. Yet the court's creative assertion of authority in this instance left open the question whether the judicial process was equipped to eradicate discrimination on the enormous scale that existed.

Johnson's personal and professional experience fostered confidence in courts exercising broad discretion. Even so, political party affiliation was no assurance of how—or if—Alabama's federal judges would employ discretion to protect individual rights. The state's federal judges decided two of the most significant decisions of the early civil rights struggle. Autherine Lucy's unsuccessful attempt to desegregate the University of Alabama came before Grooms; the panel that heard the Montgomery bus boycott case included Rives, Lynne, and Johnson. Lynne and Rives had been active National Democrats, while Johnson and Grooms were Eisenhower Republicans possessing personal connections with that same Democratic faction. Thus, to the extent that these four men held a common political ideology it was reflected by the moderate approach to civil rights National Democrats and Eisenhower Republicans shared, which in turn was consistent with the nation's postwar liberal consensus. Yet when it came to reaching a result in either case, Grooms and Lynne were content to remain within the limits of moderation, whereas Rives and Johnson were not. Their creative use of precedent was explained more by institutional and jurisprudential values reinforced by personal background. In Johnson's case it was possible to identify the weight of both these influences with some precision. Indeed, he acknowledged that formal legal processes operating alongside institutional autonomy, rather than large social or political values, determined the outcome.

THE BOUNDARIES OF JUDICIAL DISCRETION

Throughout his career, Johnson tested the limits of governmental power. To Johnson's court of the Middle District of Alabama came many of the most controversial issues arising from the nation's continuing struggle with rights guarantees. Often these conflicts were more intense because they involved the protracted defiance of such public officials as George Wallace. The willingness of Wallace and other leaders to shift the responsibility for implementing policy choices to Johnson and other federal judges increased the federal courts' role in Alabama's public affairs.[56] The growing scale of this role compelled Johnson to formulate new tools to bring about compliance with constitutional principles. The coincident expansion of state resistance and judicial authority thus enlarged the demand for federal judicial action. Nevertheless, the outcomes were relatively moderate, consistent with the reliance on the adversarial process and an independent judiciary.

Johnson devoted much of his career to determining the appropriate boundaries of judicial discretion. Growing numbers of individual rights cases required balancing the state's prerogatives with the court's authority to prescribe constitutional principles and legal doctrines. In more routine civil and criminal cases, by contrast, the application of efficient standards of judicial administration determined the nature of the balance. For Johnson, justice delayed in such cases was justice denied. Over the years, the annual workload per judge in the Middle District exceeded the national average by more than forty cases. Yet there were years in which the Middle District led the nation in the rate of disposing of civil litigation. During one year, for example, the "median elapsed time from filing of the complaint to final disposition of a civil case . . . was four months, and in criminal cases the time was less than three months." In each category of litigation Johnson satisfied all those involved that the proceedings were handled fairly.[57] Indeed, George Wallace's longtime lawyer said that Johnson was "the finest judge I've ever seen. I always felt he was totally fair."[58]

Johnson's ability to treat even controversial issues efficiently and fairly was evident in school desegregation cases. In 1958, Birmingham civil rights activists challenged the city's Board of Education for failing to comply with *Brown*. The board argued that the state's pupil assignment law permitted administrative discretion in assigning students to schools. Without question, local officials could have used the law to maintain segregation. Rives and Johnson refused to act on that possibility, however, presuming instead that the law would be administered so as to achieve desegregation. The court nonetheless asserted that if it was later shown that the board had used the statute to preserve segregation, the judges would grant appropriate relief to the African-American plaintiffs. The Supreme Court affirmed this moderate approach.[59]

The federal court's presumption that Alabama's officials would act on good faith of course proved to be misplaced. In 1962, George Wallace campaigned for and won the office of governor on a strident segregationist platform. The next year, Johnson found that the Macon County School Board had used Alabama's pupil assignment law unconstitutionally to maintain segregation. Following the pattern established in Birmingham, Johnson declined to coerce the board immediately, giving it time to develop an appropriate desegregation plan. The school board responded with defiance. Approved by Wallace, state troopers kept blacks from the Macon County schools. Meanwhile, Wallace made available state patrol cars to transport white students to the all-white county schools and a new private school. At the same time, exercising authority as ex officio state Board of Education president, the governor got the board to close Tuskegee High School, the principal school under Johnson's desegregation decree. Wallace's intervention formally maintained racially segregated schools in defiance of Johnson's order. State and local authorities thus met the judge's patient moderation with intransigence.[60]

Johnson responded with the most creative use of judicial authority yet. On questionable formal authority he ordered the Justice Department to enter the case as a party. Following the practice of Judge Ronald N. Davies in the Little Rock desegregation case, Johnson employed the FBI to develop a strong record documenting the unconstitutional actions of Wallace and the school board. He then used this evidence and the federal court's discretionary authority to fashion injunctive relief reaching all of the state's public schools. Wallace had intervened to use state power to block desegregation; Johnson now relied on that same statewide authority to justify implementation of a comprehensive remedial order, not just for Macon County but all of Alabama. The order enjoined Wallace and state board members from preventing desegregation and employing state funds to maintain racially segregated schools. It also compelled state and local school authorities in more than one hundred school systems throughout Alabama to fashion "realistic" desegregation plans.[61]

Johnson's approach to injunctive relief in the Macon County schools desegregation case was pioneering. Historically, courts employed injunctions to remedy past grievances by providing prohibitory relief. The injunction Johnson ultimately fashioned was reparative in nature, intended to go beyond immediate prohibition to correct and prevent future wrongs through continuing judicial intervention.[62] "If we, as judges, have learned anything from *Brown v. Bd. of Education* and its progeny, it is that prohibitory relief alone affords but a hollow protection to the basic and fundamental rights of citizens to equal protection of the law," Johnson wrote. "Once a constitutional deprivation has been shown, it becomes the duty of the court to render a decree which will as far as possible eliminate the effects of the past deprivations as well as bar like deprivations in

239

the future. Because of the complexity and nature of the constitutional rights and issues involved the traditional forms of relief have proven totally inadequate."[63]

Johnson nonetheless administered the reparative injunction with moderation. Once the court issued the injunction, the reliance on facts continued as Johnson retained jurisdiction and required school authorities to provide ongoing progress reports. As a result, the injunction legitimated a continuous give-and-take between the court and all the parties, guaranteeing that change would proceed gradually. All interested groups had access and contributed to the decision-making process as long as they acted in good faith. Johnson's capable handling of this process solidified his reputation for fairness. Upholding Johnson's desegregation order for Montgomery schools, the Supreme Court's Justice Hugo L. Black said that the judge's "patience and wisdom" were "written for all to see and read on the pages of the five-year record."[64] Consistent with this moderation, too, was Johnson's dislike of busing. "In the school cases that I heard during the years of desegregation, the prime concern came down to the welfare of the children. In my mind, busing to achieve racial balance is simply not worth the price of the potential disruption both to the school system and the students themselves."[65]

Johnson's combination of activism and restraint gave school officials someone to blame for desegregation. According to Johnson, school authorities "would come in with their lawyers and say, 'Now judge, we know we are going to have to desegregate our school, but we have to have a court order to do it. We can't live in the community without a court order.' We'd give them a court order—get cussed for it. They would go back and implement it. I consistently through the years required reports to keep me advised."[66]

Johnson's pioneering uses of injunctive relief encouraged extended application. Once lawyers realized the potential reach of Johnson's remedial principles, they brought cases seeking to have state mental facilities provide patients adequate care and treatment. Initially, these suits involved racial discrimination in the administration of treatment. When Governor Wallace resisted the litigation, Johnson, again on technically questionable authority, brought in the federal government. Using its investigative resources, the government helped to establish a factual record of deplorable and often tragic conditions affecting all patients. Relying on this record and other data, Johnson employed a broad range of administrative approaches to settle the cases on the basis that handicapped and mental patients possessed fundamental constitutional rights under the Fourteenth Amendment. In the leading decision of *Wyatt v. Stickney*, Johnson employed the reparative injunction at a new level of sophistication. To monitor compliance with the order, he appointed a Human Rights Committee of Alabama citizens, which then reported to the court.[67]

During the 1970s, Johnson extended similarly complex injunctive relief to Alabama's prison system. In *Newman v. Alabama,* there was conclusive evidence that state officials had not provided prisoners with adequate medical care. Johnson employed a detailed order designed to enforce a prisoner's right to satisfactory medical treatment. Some years later, litigation produced undisputed evidence that overcrowding and other inhumane conditions were so extensive throughout the state's prison system as to constitute violation of the Eighth Amendment's prohibition against cruel and unusual punishment. Again there was opposition from Governor Wallace. Johnson extended the earlier decree to include operation of the whole penal system. To implement and monitor compliance with this order, Johnson again appointed a Human Rights Committee.[68]

The pioneering character of these large, institutional remedial decrees obscured their restrained administration and outcome. Of course Johnson had the opportunity to act initially because lawyers brought suits involving significant violations of individual rights, usually conditioned by resistance from Wallace and other public officials. He reacted to this challenge with marked creativity and innovation. Yet his remedies always followed a process that accepted the "delicate balance of power" between state and federal government. Accordingly, his decrees kept to a "minimum the disruption of state institutions and the intrusion into state functions." He readily conceded that his orders curtailed state officials' "autonomy and flexibility." He did so, however, only after those officials failed to respond effectively once the court held that a problem existed. And even after such default, Johnson maintained the involvement of all parties in order to legitimate remedial enforcement through what amounted to an ongoing process of negotiation.[69]

As a result, change not only proceeded at a gradual pace but was relatively moderate in scope. In both the desegregated public schools and the mental hospitals and prisons conditions were not "affirmatively good" but "merely better" under the reparative injunctions. This did not diminish the significance of the results. The wrongs were sufficiently great that the degree of improvement Johnson's orders achieved was noteworthy. Nevertheless, the scale of the change could not exceed the limits of judicial, as opposed to legislative or executive, enforcement. As one insightful commentator observed, the "issuance of an injunction only initiated a long term relationship in which Johnson intervened again and again with supplemental orders, relaxing deadlines and establishing new ones, in the course of shaping an institution's

241

operations into satisfactory order."[70] More profound change would have required a degree of community support that did not exist in Alabama. Put another way, judicial remedies were necessary because the state had defaulted on its policy-making role; yet the impact of judicial administration could only partially match the scale of that default.

Indeed, Johnson perceived his role within distinctly legal limits. Regarding the broad range of individual rights cases, he said that "I don't find them complex social issues. I don't regard them as societal issues. I regard them as legal issues."[71] A keen observer of the judge's reparative remedial decrees emphasized that "Johnson didn't begin where he wound up. I think it was a kind of education that he got sitting on the bench trying to do his job, being confronted with outright and open defiance time and time again." He did not start with a large social theory. Rather, he was "creative under the force of circumstance—he was understanding, he was responding to the necessities of the situation, and improvised and innovated. He didn't have a map of what he was doing." His creativity came from "a man of great integrity, of great courage, determined to do a difficult job. Just going back and doing the job sometimes forces you to sort of shatter old forms of law and create new ones. Every step that Johnson took was pushed by historic circumstances."[72]

Voting rights further suggested the legalistic limitations within which Johnson innovated. An initial clash with Wallace, who at the time was a local judge in Barbour County, set the tone for Johnson's handling of voting rights confrontations. When the U.S. Commission on Civil Rights ordered local voting records released, Wallace took a public stance of defiance. Johnson threatened Wallace with a contempt citation, whereupon Wallace transferred the records to the grand jury, which gave them to the commission. The incident convinced Johnson that patience combined with the threat of contempt could achieve public officials' compliance. At the same time, Johnson doubted whether actual use of the contempt power would achieve the desired results, because it could easily heighten popular support for the public official. Johnson was determined to compel state authorities to comply with constitutional principles. For him the central question was merely "how fast are we going to do it."[73]

The clash with Wallace preceded years of voter registration litigation in which Johnson developed the "freeze doctrine." From many cases the court fashioned the principle requiring voter registration boards to use the least qualified white voter to determine the qualification of any black applicant. The freeze doctrine became the Fifth and subsequently the Eleventh Circuit's basic standard in voter registration cases. Congress incorporated essentially the same standard into the Voting Rights Act of 1965.[74]

Earlier, however, Johnson had dissented from the claim that federal judges should intervene in voting rights issues. In Tuskegee, African-American litigants argued that white local leaders were gerrymandering voting districts to exclude the great majority of black voters. Supreme Court precedent held that voting was a "political thicket" from which federal courts were excluded. But these precedents did not raise a claim of racial discrimination. When the Tuskegee case came before Johnson, he followed precedent. He nonetheless suggested that the racial dimension of the case perhaps provided a basis for revising the established rule. Consistent with Johnson's intimation, the Supreme Court reversed and established a new doctrine permitting extensive federal judicial protection of African-American voting rights.[75] In 1964, Johnson was a member of the three-judge court that enlarged on this doctrine to recognize that the votes of all qualified voters, white and black, were of equal weight. Holding that the Fourteenth Amendment's equal protection clause required states to adhere to one person, one vote, the Court's decision of *Reynolds v. Sims* engendered the historic reapportionment of state legislatures in Alabama and across the nation.[76]

This mix of experience shaped Johnson's handling of the most dramatic episode of the voting rights struggle. In conjunction with brutal attacks by local law enforcement officials, Wallace interfered with Martin Luther King's famous Selma-to-Montgomery march, the protest that significantly influenced passage of the Voting Rights Act of 1965.[77] In this explosive environment, Johnson ordered that King could proceed only after he agreed in a hearing to comply with a court order regulating the course of the march. The court's order undercut Wallace's resistance, and the march progressed peacefully. King's march pitted the "right to petition one's government for the redress of grievances" against the "rights by other citizens to use the sidewalks, streets, and highways." Johnson conceded that "where, as here, minorities have been harassed, coerced and intimidated, group association may be the only realistic way of exercising such rights." He emphasized, however, that these rights were not "unrestricted" and it was the court's duty to determine the "constitutional boundary line."[78]

To draw that boundary line, Johnson employed the principle of proportionality. In civil and criminal law, the principle was used to provide "a larger award for a more serious personal injury, or a harsher penalty for a more serious crime."[79] Essentially, Johnson held that in constitutional conflicts proportional remedies too were permissible. It "seems basic to our constitutional principles that the extent of the right to assemble, demonstrate and march peaceably along the highways and streets in an orderly manner should be commensurate with the enormity of the wrongs that are being protested and petitioned against," Johnson's order stated. "In this case the wrongs are enormous. The extent of the right to demonstrate against these wrongs should be determined accordingly."[80]

Johnson's facility for adapting established principle to new purposes was controversial. The order not only put the authority of a federal court behind a peaceful demonstration, it also resulted in President Lyndon Johnson federalizing the National Guard to protect the marchers at a cost of $500,000. In addition, the plan the order embodied blocked off miles of a public highway so that the march could proceed according to the "highest standards of dignity and decorum." Even those who recognized the wisdom, innovativeness, and necessity of Johnson's remedy said that formal sanction through court order and federal government action of a protest march was "troublesome." Some of Johnson's keenest admirers, moreover, found the scale of the plan disturbing, particularly because it "didn't have any justification in the law whatsoever." Nevertheless, these and other observers conceded that given the massive resistance from Wallace and other public officials, anything less than Johnson's plan would have failed.[81]

In other cases involving individual rights, Johnson demonstrated remarkable skill in establishing a constitutional boundary line. He compelled both state and local officials and the freedom riders to comply with court orders regulating the course of protests. He refused to support civil rights demonstrations that did not comply with the sort of legal forms he had employed in the Selma case.[82] In the highly charged racial climate surrounding the march, Johnson inspired an all-white jury to return guilty verdicts against three Klansmen for violating Viola Liuzzo's civil rights by killing her while en route home from the march. Despite eyewitness testimony, white juries in state court had acquitted the Klansmen on murder charges.[83] In addition, Johnson used creatively the federal remedial power to overcome the Alabama state courts' exclusion of women from juries.[84] Meanwhile, in numerous cases involving state challenges to First Amendment rights, Johnson decided in favor of the individual.[85]

This skillful balancing included other creative uses of precedent. Employing the technique of analogizing precedent the court had used in the Montgomery bus boycott case, Johnson asserted a new right prohibiting sex discrimination, reading into the Fifth Amendment's due process clause the Fourteenth Amendment's equal protection clause. He stated the theory in dissent from a three-judge court's decision that held that the military's disparate treatment of the dependents of female armed services personnel was not unconstitutional. In *Frontiero v. Richardson* (1973), the Supreme Court voted eight to one to reverse the lower court, following in large part Johnson's theory.[86] The federal government's refusal to reimburse a court-ordered counsel for expenses in defending an indigent bootlegger also made new law. Ordering the bootlegger released from custody and the case dismissed, Johnson ruled that the Justice Department's action constituted a violation of the defendant's Sixth Amendment right to counsel. Within a year Congress changed the law in accord with Johnson's ruling.[87]

Resistance from Alabama's public officials influenced but did not determine the boundaries Johnson established for judicial discretion. Wallace and others exploited the federal courts for political gain, shifting from public officials to unelected federal judges the responsibility for remedying profound social problems. Thus resistance increased rather than diminished the federal court's involvement in Alabamians' lives. Yet Johnson's creative uses of injunctive relief and other devices mobilized a wide range of popular interests and values that gained new force when legitimated and protected by the federal judiciary's institutional autonomy. The balance struck between this autonomy and governmental authority confined remedial outcomes within relatively moderate limits. The enormity of social problems requiring remedy nonetheless meant that moderate gains were significant. Both the means and ends Johnson pursued were consistent with a faith in fundamental fairness enforced by lawyers and judges, conditioned by an understanding of human nature rooted in his past.

His Own Words

Johnson published many articles explaining the values and assumptions underlying his uses of judicial discretion. Consistent with his origins and family background, Johnson's core values were essentially conservative, embodying a view of America based on individual freedom defined in terms of equal opportunity and equality under law. Freedom depended in turn on rights guarantees enforced by an independent judiciary. Johnson's view of independence extended discretionary authority to flexible procedures and forms of relief that combined social science theory with a practical understanding of human nature and politics, including the resistance of public officials. The fundamental institutional goal to be attained through the entire judicial process was fairness, maintained through extending access to previously excluded groups by strengthening the incentives for lawyers to represent them. Thus, neither the federal judiciary's institutional autonomy nor creative injunctive remedies were sufficient to overcome the inertia or defiance of public authorities. The active role of lawyers was indispensable.

In an address to the Montgomery County Bar Association in 1990, Johnson stated some fundamental beliefs. He was sure that, despite innumerable problems and injustices, a distinctive commitment to basic rights characterized America. This singular regard for rights recognized that the "welfare of the individual is the final goal of group life," embodying "a basic moral principle: all persons are created equal as well as free." The principle established the "obligation to build social institutions designed to guarantee equality of opportunity to all citizens. Without this equality, freedom becomes an illusion. Thus, the only aristocracy that is consistent with our way of life in America is an aristocracy of talent and achievement."[88]

The "American heritage of equality" rejected the "totalitarian arrogance" that imposed "human uniformity or regimentation." Thus, Johnson said, "In our land, citizens are equal, but they are free to be different. From these very differences... has come the great human and national strength of America." Consistent with the Declaration of Independence, the Constitution, and the Bill of Rights, government was "denied ... power to abridge or interfere with certain personal rights and freedom." This same government nonetheless "must referee the clashes which arise among the freedoms of citizens and protect each citizen in the enjoyment of the maximum freedom to which he or she is entitled." From the nation's heritage, institutions, and formal pronouncements of rights flowed the fundamental right to safety and security of the person, to citizenship and its privileges, to freedom of conscience and expression, and of equality of opportunity. The persistent gap between the articulation and fulfillment of these rights did not diminish Johnson's conviction that they were what was "right with America."[89]

These convictions were consistent with other ideas articulated over forty years of judicial service. As early as 1962, in an address on juvenile delinquency given before federal probation authorities, he revealed a keen awareness of the multidimensional nature of individual character, responsibility, culpability, and accountability. Starting with a "knowledge of human nature" informed by advances in psychiatry, psychology, sociology, and social work, it was possible to formulate "basic concepts and philosophies" with which to analyze a given problem. There were "no ready made answers, no simple formulas, no firm rules." Instead, the combination of intuition and acquired formal knowledge, which shaped conceptual approaches, gave public officials the means to "analyze our procedures, analyze our authority for adequacy or inadequacy . . . in practical application of these concepts of philosophy."[90]

246

The goal was an objective comprehension of the facts of each individual's "story." Sentencing was "above all an individual problem." With facts gleaned from the professionals in the field, the judge could fashion a "fair and appropriate sentence." There should be "uniformity in objectives, yes; uniformity in philosophy, yes; uniformity in sentencing, no." Staff work provided the facts that enabled the judge to fashion a remedy that took into account extenuating circumstances such as a defendant's emotional state and social background. Defined in these terms, fairness helped to diffuse the defendant's resentment and to foster the public's faith in both the law and the judicial system.[91]

Johnson's core beliefs and sensitivity to the complexities underlying human conduct informed his view of judicial authority. Throughout his career Johnson confronted the criticism that he and other federal judges were activists, violating Blackstone's prescription that judges should do not more than "find" and "declare" law. Such total objectively was, Johnson believed, neither possible nor desirable. The constitutional and legal questions that came before courts demanded of judges "an openness of mind and a willingness to decide the issues solely on the particular facts and circumstances involved, not with any preconceived notion or philosophy regarding the outcome of the case." In constitutional cases especially, federal courts trod a middle course. "While a refusal to show proper deference to and respect for the acts and decisions of the coordinate branches of government is judicial intrusion and is, therefore, improper," he wrote, "a blind and unyielding deference to legislative and executive action is judicial abdication and is equally to be condemned."[92]

A court's obligation to decide cases that lawfully came before it made a degree of activism inevitable. The "duty" to uphold law meant that a court was not free to "shirk its sworn responsibility to uphold the Constitution and laws of the United States. The courts are bound to take jurisdiction and decide the issues—even though those decisions result in criticism." This role was not "usurped by the judiciary" but was "inextricably intertwined with its duty to interpret the Constitution" and laws generally. According to Johnson, moreover, the federal courts "have never acted directly on the states or assumed jurisdiction of mere political issues, but in cases involving individual rights and liberties, these courts are compelled to construe the law in order to determine such rights and liabilities."[93]

The judge's decisional obligation resulting from linking jurisdiction to rights was essentially "not activism at all." Given his own profound struggles with Wallace (which included labeling the judge "an integrating, scalawagging, carpet-bagging, race-mixing, bald-face liar" who should be given a "barbed-wire enema") and others, and such threats to Johnson's family as the bombing of his mother's house, Johnson could say with authority that judges "do not relish making such hard decisions and certainly do not encourage litigation on social or political problems." The difference between the critics' regard for judicial passivity and the approach taken by Johnson and others was that the exercise of discretion was "measured not by the end result, but how and under what circumstances the result is achieved." Thus decision making was the outcome of a process conditioned by context. For Johnson, the "basic strength of the federal judiciary" was "its independence from political and social pressures, its ability to rise above the influence of popular clamor." Ultimately, he believed that this removal from immediate popular influences gave the American people the basis for a sufficiently detached judgment "that decisions of the federal judiciary . . . [became] accepted and revered as monuments memorializing the strength and stability of this nation."[94]

Johnson's trust in the judicial process engendered a primary concern about access and relief. He was an early and active supporter of publicly funded legal aid for the poor and other dispossessed groups.[95] Still, the basic factor determining the degree of access was whether a financial incentive existed for lawyers to take on what were otherwise unremunerative suits. In addition, Congress and the judiciary itself liberalized standing and joinder requirements so that lawyers could effectively represent and courts adjudicate the "multiplicity of competing if not conflicting interests among members of the same class, among different classes, and among other parties and intervenors" that increasingly characterized litigation during the decades following World War II. Traditional code pleading involved one party suing another with the winner taking all. Judges employed this procedure principally in business or economic litigation, and the result was usually a simple award of damages and a prohibitory injunction. The parties in complex litigation that became common after the Second World War were social welfare or civil rights litigants whose suits required more than merely a prohibitory injunction to achieve relief. As a result, Johnson and others developed the structural injunction, a form of equity relief tailored to the needs of the particular case. Usually this type of remedy required the court to monitor compliance, often over a long period of time. In addition, the court often relied on experts and citizens' commissions whose members were drawn from the community. Involvement of citizens in the ongoing implementation of the remedial order further legitimated the process.[96]

Access to and remedies within the new process imposed wider social imperatives on lawyers. Johnson's overriding deference to the supremacy of law required that lawyers "be vigilant in keeping our institutions responsive to claims of injustice and voices of dissent." American lawyers were "not only legal technicians, but also . . . social generalists." Especially with regard to "combatting emotionalism and demagoguery, lawyers have an educational function."[97] "They must clarify and illumine the distinction between the constitutionally-protected rights of expression and violation of the law." The "most fundamental of social virtues" was "respect for law," the alternative to which was "violence and anarchy." And it was the lawyer's duty to "proclaim that the heart of our American system rests in obedience to the laws which protect the individual rights of our citizenry. No system can endure if each citizen is free to choose which laws he will obey. Obedience to the laws we like and defiance of those we dislike is the route to chaos."[98]

Johnson had neither sympathy nor respect for lawyers who abdicated what he believed was a solemn duty. "In times of riot and disrespect for judicial decisions, the lawyer must speak. To remain silent is not only a violation of his oath but is tantamount to cowardice and is a grievous injustice to the free society which men of law by conscience and sworn duty, are bound to maintain," he asserted. It was essential that the "voice of moderation" prevail over the "cries of the far left and far right." Both extremists favored "social and political freedoms, individual liberties and states' rights, [but] they were driven by fanaticism. They invariably espouse democracy, but did not begin to understand its very heart: supremacy of and respect for the law—whether we like it or not."[99]

Initially, at least, Johnson's position toward professional obligation placed lawyers in a difficult position. Even lawyers who defended legal aid and fee structures that enlarged judicial access noted how powerful were the factors working against the realization of Johnson's views. Most lawyers in Alabama belonged to small firms whose business depended significantly on personal recommendations from satisfied clients. Middle-class and propertied individuals provided the principal market for legal services for such firms. Moreover, these firms constituted a competitive market in which a lawyer's reputation was paramount. As a practical matter, richer clients often distrusted lawyers identified with the representation of the poor or of controversial groups, including civil rights activists. At the same time, the more marginal client market was usually insufficiently remunerative to offset the loss of the traditional clients.[100]

Ultimately Johnson's views prevailed because of, rather than despite, market considerations. The growth in public law litigation was rooted in the social and institutional conflicts that dominated the half century following the Second World War. These conflicts did not generate a client market that rivaled the traditional one, but it was grounded on such basic tensions that it was more likely to grow. As federal judges and Congress enlarged access through procedures, fee structures, and legal aid, moreover, there were sufficient financial incentives that even smaller firms had reason to develop this class of suits as part of their wider practice. Thus by the 1980s, throughout Alabama there were a moderate number of firms that had beaten the odds and achieved the goals Johnson and others had for so long advocated. Also, in conjunction with these changes, Alabama's state law and judicial establishment were increasingly more supportive of public interest litigation, further enhancing what nevertheless remained a secondary client market.[101]

Meanwhile, two extremes threatened the law's supremacy and the lawyer's role in sustaining it. The first was the "conduct of those leaders, both political and social, who are busily engaged in the frustration of the law for personal gain." Johnson's criticism extended not only to the self-serving obstructionism of such elected public leaders as George Wallace but also included the corruption of public authority identified with Watergate, in which so many lawyers broke the law. "When persons with public responsibility make a mockery of law by prostituting legal process and stultifying the forms of law in defiance of their sworn duty to uphold the Constitution and the laws of the land," Johnson said, "the attorney of integrity has a positive duty to intercede." Wallace and Watergate represented a "brutal attack . . . launched against such fundamentals of a democratic society as the administration of justice by impartial courts and the consensus of acceptance and respect for judicial decision." It was the legal profession's "sacred and unique responsibility . . . to quietly illuminate the path of reason and to loudly proclaim the supremacy of law."[102]

Civil disobedience, the other extreme, raised more complex challenges. If lawyers provided dispossessed and exploited groups adequate access to legal institutions, the "condition for justifiable civil disobedience [would] rarely, if ever, exist," Johnson believed. He distinguished between legitimate civil disobedience and revolution. Advocates of both broke the law. But proponents of civil disobedience strove to change the established legal order, whereas the revolutionary worked for the "total eradication of the existing legal system." The latter was fundamentally inconsistent with the supremacy of law. Under certain circumstances and to a point, however, civil disobedience and the legal order were reconcilable. The only legitimate form of civil disobedience was "an open, intentional violation of a law concededly valid, under a banner of morality or justice by one willing to accept punishment for the violation."[103]

He also conditioned his acceptance of civil disobedience on several pragmatic considerations. First, "a serious extensive, and apparently enduring breakdown in the responsiveness of our institutions must be a necessary condition of justified civil disobedience." In the "recent history" of America, "only the persistent and flagrant denial of the rights of our Negro citizens in certain sections of our country could be cited as an example of this kind of breakdown." Second, demonstrators employing a strategy of peaceful disobedience should gauge the risk of it turning into a "violent confrontation. One who is responsible for violence loses all possible justification for civil disobedience." Third, "basic principles must be at issue, the provocation must be extreme, and the evils likely to endure unless most vigorously combatted." Finally, he distinguished between the conduct of individuals and that of groups. The lone protester acts as the result of "a private assertion of personal conviction," whereas "large dissident groups" employ civil disobedience as a "tactic of political protest." The latter was more controversial than the former. American tradition sanctioned by the First Amendment's free exercise clause "deferr[ed] to the mandates of individual conscience," which had "virtually no risk of violence and the effect on attitudes toward law [was] likely to be slight." The nation "inherit[ed] this tradition of civil disobedience from men of the moral stature of Socrates, Jesus Christ, and St. Thomas More."[104]

Johnson's professed rationale for what others described as boundless judicial activism was fundamentally conservative. His expression of core values emphasized a patriotic vision of America resting not on pervasive social or class amalgamation or individual libertarianism, but on basic equality under law and equality of opportunity. Johnson thus defined rights guarantees enshrined in the Constitution and Bill of Rights as contrary to the mass social and political conformity imposed by "totalitarian arrogance," the opposite of which was a brand of individual liberty characterized by the fundamental right to personal security, opportunity, citizenship, and freedom of expression and conscience. Americans achieved this vision of equal rights through legal institutions, particularly an independent judiciary and access to the adversarial process. Fundamental fairness secured through institutional autonomy protected individual rights and deflected social and political struggle.

The circumscribed change attainable through the adversarial process was central, then, to Johnson's essentially conservative faith. Critics attacked Johnson's uses of judicial discretion primarily because he employed the remedial process—particularly injunctive relief—to vindicate rights by compelling public officials to act in policy areas where previously they had declined or refused to do so. Inferentially, Johnson's detractors also recognized that the process legitimated the rights of traditionally excluded groups. As a description of judicial activism, however, both criticisms obscured the comparatively moderate results Johnson's injunctive innovations actually achieved. Making rights the basis of remedies meant that inhuman and tragic institutional conditions were improved, but the problems underlying these conditions often were not

251

permanently solved. And that was exactly the point. Johnson applied institutionally autonomous judicial authority to force elected and appointed policy makers to confront social issues that had little or no ultimate solution. Like crime or the maintenance of highways, such social issues required ongoing attention so that the system of which they were a part functioned to a reasonably effective degree. Fundamentally Johnson got and held public officials' attention on matters that they preferred to ignore.

CONCLUSION

In rights-activism discourse, critics and defenders alike focused on Frank Johnson. Dismayed that numerous other courts had adopted Johnson's remedial innovations, one critic observed that "moral hubris and intellectual confusion has permitted judges to believe that 'the Constitution' requires a more pervasive set of social policies." The same commentator suggested that judges such as Johnson were "psychically" attracted to the "role of moralist and the job of social reformer." As a result, the activist judicial intrusion Johnson represented sapped the "vitality of self-government at the local level," which depended on "maintaining strong incentives for popular participation" that had "characterized the American political system since de Tocqueville's time."[105] Supporters of the policy-making role Johnson symbolized argued, by contrast, that within the democratic order itself were "passionate and vested commitments to uphold . . . the apparatus of the state that is supporting and buttressing . . . [an] illegal, unconstitutional order, and the question is, how do you transform . . . [and] reconstruct it." To meet this challenge, his defenders agreed, took courage. But the essence of Johnson's "legacy" had most "to do with the administration of law and how you make law real in practical affairs," which is the "paradigmatic job of a [federal] District judge."[106]

The debate followed quasi-realist assumptions involving individual motivation and causality. Since the nation's founding, the idea persisted that judges decided cases according to personal predilections rather than formal constitutional or legal standards and principles. Throughout most of American history, judges effectively discredited this idea by claiming some version of the Blackstonian view that courts found and declared rather than made law. Due in large part to the popularization of realist theories following World War II, however, most judges acknowledged that personal background and motivations shaped judicial decision making. A refinement of this view focused on the influence of political party ideology, particularly New Deal liberalism. The critics who ascribed Johnson's institutional innovations to psychological impulses and liberal reformist zeal thus assumed quasi-realist theories, as did his defenders' emphasis on personal courage.

Realist assumptions revealed an underlying irony of rights-activism discourse. During the 1930s, the Supreme Court initiated its rights revolution, establishing the basic constitutional principle governing the selective incorporation of the Bill of Rights into the Fourteenth Amendment's due process clause and the doctrine that held that courts would subject to "strict scrutiny" state policies involving "insular minorities." These policy standards and their progeny reflected the Court's affirmation of Americans' expanded rights consciousness that the increasing threat of worldwide totalitarian regimes fostered. Thus the Supreme Court's *Brown* decision and the few judges such as Johnson and Rives who defied the South's segregated culture to enforce it were agents of a growing national consensus; they supported rather than opposed democracy. Ironically, the federal judiciary's use of constitutional principle to legitimate the growing popular consensus toward individual rights resulted in the criticism that activist courts ignored or manipulated constitutional standards and defied democratic traditions. The quasi-realist assumption that personal background and values motivated decision making thus facilitated the critics' claim that the federal courts' support of rights guarantees was unwarranted, antidemocratic activism.

Others more sympathetic to judicial activism at least in part also accepted realist assumptions. Studies of rights-sustaining decision making by Supreme Court justices and the judges of the federal trial and appellate tribunals alike emphasized the vital influence of personal background and qualities. Many works argued further that the postwar liberal consensus shaped the opinions of not only such members of the Court as the Republican Earl Warren and Democrat Hugo L. Black but also of a Johnson or a Rives, who despite different party affiliations shared a faith in government's active support of humanitarian values. The revisionist interpretation of the *Brown* decision also was not inconsistent with realist assumptions. Acknowledging that *Brown* was undoubtedly the twentieth century's consummate example of judicial activism, the leading revisionist study said that its primary short-term impact was to exacerbate, and make politically profitable, officially sanctioned massive resistance. The interpretation neglected the role of Johnson and his colleagues in facilitating Wallace's and others' politically successful exploitation of a "blaming" strategy. But inferentially it accepted that the motivation for these few judges' stands against segregationist defiance was, essentially, personal courage.

Those working from quasi-realist assumptions nonetheless have missed important dimensions of Johnson's place within rights-activism discourse. The humanitarian individualism and integrity associated with Winston County origins did not alone explain Johnson's independent approach to rights struggles. Rives's social and community background contrasted sharply with Johnson's, yet they both rejected racist values. Similarly, despite differing party affiliation and partisan commitment, each man's association with Alabama's National Democrats indicated a general attachment to the postwar liberal consensus. Lynne and Grooms shared very much the same degree of bipartisan involvement with the National Democrats, however, and like most Alabamians belonging to that faction they did not vigorously challenge the racial status quo. Thus neither political values nor cultural origins necessarily determined the contribution judges made to America's expanding rights consciousness.

Deeper psychological motivations shaped Johnson's actions, but they were not moralistic or reformist. Like Rives, Johnson rejected white supremacy primarily because of an overriding faith in fundamental fairness. Both men acquired this faith from their families, though powerful personal encounters with African Americans reinforced it in Johnson's case. More, what both men shared was the atypical experience of successfully defending minorities in court. As a result of the linkage between conviction and career, both men had reason to believe that through the lawyer's adversarial process and judicial independence, fairness could prevail over prejudice. Yet outside the court system public officials seeking political advantage through democratic appeals prevented the triumph of fundamental fairness, and inadequate access and representation by lawyers or a judge's self-restraint impeded achieving it from within the judicial process. Nevertheless, it was apparent that what drove judges such as Johnson and Rives was not a "psychically" inspired reformist zeal and attachment to large moral philosophies but the narrower pursuit of basic fairness.

The goal of achieving fairness conditioned the impact of Johnson's institutional innovations on democratic institutions. Americans' reaction against diverse totalitarian threats fostered the eventual emergence of a majoritarian consciousness that favored rights guarantees in the abstract. The Court's constitutional legitimation of these guarantees broadly sustained the emerging democratic consensus. But Johnson's and other federal judges' actual enforcement of particular rights claims spawned resistance from, or aggravated the default of, public officials, who in turn justified their opposition by appealing to democratic values. Thus as the rights revolution proceeded, democracy was at war with itself. Johnson's analogical use of precedent, applications of the proportionality principle, and reparative injunctions generally represented the employment of the wide discretion judicial independence sanctioned to reconcile the tensions within the growing majoritarian consensus. Given the enormity of the challenge posed by George Wallace and other leaders following the *Brown* decision, Johnson's pursuit of fundamental fairness was an attainable goal, one consistent with the moderate results his institutional creativity actually achieved. Although the stand Johnson and other federal judges took was certainly courageous, the true life it gave to individual rights transcended personal accomplishment, strengthening rather than weakening American democracy.

V
Conclusion

The history of Alabama's federal courts suggested the federal judiciary's changing role within the nation. In 1842, a Mobile attorney described the state's federal courts as those tribunals in which "nonresidents" were "most interested." Paradoxically, the Union's federal judges were both constrained by and yet independent of state law. As a result, Tocqueville said, the federal judiciary decided the most significant issues involving American government, but they acted against state authority only "indirectly." At the turn of the century, a Birmingham lawyer indicated that the federal courts' formal dependence on state law had declined significantly. Increasingly, however, proliferating federal bureaucracies such as the Interstate Commerce Commission and antitrust complemented federal judicial authority. Accordingly, the lawyer observed, federal judges were known primarily only to the comparatively few attorneys practicing before them. Following the Second World War, in Alabama and other southern states, federal courts came under mounting criticism from public officials because of the civil rights struggle. The conflict was indicative of a growing national concern about individual rights, which eventually coincided with what was perceived as a new era of litigiousness. The federal courts in Alabama dealt with these changes within a national judicial establishment that more than ever was organizationally centralized.

In Alabama and other states, the tension between independence and dependence influenced the course of change. The Constitution's Article III established the judiciary's formal separation but left to Congress the determination of the size of the Supreme Court and the creation of the lower courts. The Judiciary Act of 1789 allotted district courts to each state and assigned circuit-riding duties to the Supreme Court justices. The act's section 25 gave the Supreme Court power to review the decisions of state high tribunals; section 34, however, bound federal courts to state law in cases where it applied. The law's other provisions further linked dependence to autonomy. The purpose of this dual system was to keep federal judges attuned to state law without undercutting their constitutional independence. From 1820 to 1861, Alabama's federal district judge and the circuit-riding justice, who was also a resident of the state, confronted this tension, primarily in commercial and property cases concerning citizens of the different states. Alabama's federal judges also addressed leading constitutional issues involving comity in the *Alabama Bank* cases, admiralty jurisdiction in the *Steamboat Magnolia*, and the enforcement of laws against the slave trade on the eve of the Civil War. The commercial and property decisions balanced national and local market values, but the constitutional opinions generally favored states' rights and local economic interests.

Following the Civil War, state authority became constitutionally subordinate to federal power, though only gradually. During Reconstruction, Congress strengthened the federal judiciary's independence by enlarging its jurisdiction to the constitutional limit, particularly in the Removal Act of 1875, which encouraged litigants to remove cases from state to federal court. In Alabama, federal judges initially used the new authority to protect individual rights under federal laws and the Fourteenth and Fifteenth amendments. Congressional Republicans and the North generally allowed Reconstruction to collapse and the South to win the peace. Alabama's federal courts nonetheless continued throughout the succeeding decades to apply their enlarged jurisdiction to defend various underdogs, including the African American whose case led to the Supreme Court's invalidation of peonage. On the whole, however, the federal courts did not interfere with the triumph of Jim Crow. Meanwhile, Alabama's federal judges broadly sustained the Interstate Commerce Commission's and state agencies' regulation of the railroads. Similarly, after World War I the state's federal courts limited and yet supported Prohibition and other national policies. But these courts showed no such sympathy for the early New Deal, striking down the NRA and TVA. Only after Franklin Roosevelt appointed a new judge in the Northern District did a major New Deal law receive constitutional sanction, the Social Security Act of 1935.

Alabama's propensity for testing the limits of federal judicial independence reached new heights after World War II. The Court's affirmation in *Palko v. Connecticut* (1937) of the selective incorporation of the Bill of Rights through the Fourteenth Amendment's due process clause and the formulation of a strict scrutiny standard governing laws involving individual rights in *Carolene Products* (1938) created a new constitutional preference for rights claims. The Supreme Court potentially enhanced federal dependence on state law by overturning the federal common law in *Erie Railroad v. Tompkins* (1938). The very next year, however, promulgation of the Federal Rules facilitated procedural discretion, thereby strengthening the federal judiciary's organizational autonomy. This autonomy, along with the new constitutional presumption favoring individual rights and the proliferation of federal, civil, and criminal jurisdiction initiated by Roosevelt liberalism, which reached a turning point in the Civil Rights Act of

1964 and Voting Rights Act of 1965, fostered the federal judiciary's increased administrative centralization. The resulting institutional independence came under enormous stress because of the civil rights struggle. Following *Brown v. Board of Education* (1954), Alabama's federal courts ended the Montgomery bus boycott, upheld the constitutionality of key provisions of the Civil Rights and Voting Rights laws, established the one person one vote standard in state legislative apportionment, brought about a peaceful end to state officials' assault on Martin Luther King, Jr.'s Selma march, pioneered new forms of injunctive relief to defend the rights of mental patients and prisoners, extended the rights of women, and defined the limits of affirmative action.

Federal judges overcame the pressures facilitating dependence through the exercise of discretion. Blackstone's theory that judges merely found and declared law influenced judicial decision making throughout American history. Nevertheless, before the Civil War, Alabama's federal courts employed other jurisprudential principles to fill legal and constitutional texts with extratextual meanings. In routine commercial and property cases arising under diversity-of-citizenship jurisdiction, federal judges asserted an independent judgment to draw on a general commercial law or to choose the appropriate doctrine from local property rules. The comity, admiralty, and slave-trade decisions reflected a similar interpretive independence toward constitutional questions. In the exceptional cases reviewed by the Supreme Court, the state's federal district and circuit courts usually prevailed in routine litigation. Regarding constitutional issues, however, these same courts usually lost. Even so, the Supreme Court's affirmation of the lower courts' judicial discretion in the far more numerous routine cases undoubtedly encouraged the persistent assertion of independence in the few but more controversial constitutional ones.

By 1900, federal judges increasingly conceded that the jurisprudential assumptions underlying the declaratory theory had been displaced. Although the failure of Reconstruction subjected the freedman to second-class citizenship, the expanded federal jurisdiction that resulted, particularly under the Removal Act and the Fourteenth Amendment, brought new economic and social issues to the federal courts. Consistent with ideas associated with sociological jurisprudence, federal judges in Alabama attempted to balance economic liberty and expanded government regulation. The growing concern about the social consequences of laws, identified with the Progressives, also explained the federal courts' willingness to ensure that moonshiners, women, assorted criminal defendants, and African Americans entrapped in the peonage labor system received fair treatment. From the 1930s on, the federal judiciary's search for balance was transformed, shaped by the popularization of legal realist theories.

259

The force of the realists' formal teachings dissipated by the 1940s, but the basic idea that social background and psychology influenced a judge's decisions became commonplace during the rest of the century. Interviews with most of Alabama's federal judges in 1990 and 1991 confirmed this: All but one judge described his process of decision making in terms that accepted quasi-realist assumptions. This recognition of a personal element influencing judicial outcomes confirmed the judges' common experience that applying legal rules and principles required discretionary judgment; yet the personal element was not separate from formal institutional factors as much as it interacted with them to shape results.

The jurisprudential basis of judicial discretion nonetheless operated within institutional limits, which also changed. From the beginning, the federal judicial establishment in Alabama was small. By 1860, only one federal district judge held court in the state's three districts. According to the Judiciary Act, a Supreme Court justice joined the district judge to hold the circuit court, but often distance, ill health, or various other factors compelled either judge to sit alone, exercising either jurisdictional authority as the case required. A single clerk handled the district's docket and other paperwork; there was also a U.S. attorney, a marshal, and usually a few attorneys administering bankruptcy proceedings. Judges wrote their own decisions without the assistance of clerks; they used only their own books because library resources were limited or nonexistent. The terms the courts held in each district or circuit averaged three to five days, though on the civil side, at least, about 20 to 25 percent of the cases were continued. Both routine and constitutional litigation usually involved business matters; criminal suits were exceptional. Jury trial was the norm, and jurors were drawn from the residents of the various counties making up a given district. Infrequent review by the Supreme Court strengthened the lower courts' jurisdictional autonomy within the locality.

From the Civil War to the end of the twentieth century, the federal judicial establishment grew apace. In 1891, there were two federal district judges in the state and one judge from Alabama sitting on the new Fifth Circuit Court of Appeals. As late as the 1950s, Alabama had only four district judges and the one circuit judge. By the 1990s, the system had been transformed. In the Northern District (the state's largest), there were seven active and three senior status judges; the Middle and Southern districts had three active judges each and a total of five judges on senior status. On the Eleventh Circuit, three active and two senior-status judges were from Alabama. Over four decades, then, the number of active district judges went from four to thirteen, and the number of circuit judges tripled. During the same period, each active judge gained a clerical staff, which by the 1990s included two recent law school graduates who helped research and write opinions. In addition, each district had its own clerk of the court and a research library. Within the state's three districts there was also a total of ten magistrate judges and numerous bankruptcy judges, each of whom had a staff. Each district also had a probation officer, U.S. attorney, and marshal, aided by a support staff. This state-based federal judicial establishment, in turn, belonged to the larger self-governing, organizationally centralized conference system operating within the circuit.

As the federal judiciary's size and organizational centralization increased, the institutional pressures shaping judicial discretion gradually altered. As long as federal district judges lacked staff and research support, and review of their decisions was unusual, the primary institutional factor influencing decision making was the local courthouse culture. Well into the twentieth century, the number of lawyers practicing before a federal judge in Alabama, both in real terms and as a proportion of the attorney and general population, was fairly small. In 1845, there were 664 lawyers registered to practice law in the state; the number admitted to the federal bar in the Northern District, at the time Alabama's least populated section, was 56. By 1930, there were approximately 1,307 lawyers in the state. At that point, the majority of Alabama's population had shifted to the northern section. Meanwhile, the number admitted to the federal bar in the Northern District had risen to just 88. Sixty years later, the state bar's total membership was 10,595, and the number admitted to federal practice in the Northern District was 2,298. Thus in 1845, the ratio of judge to lawyer in the Northern District was 1 to 23; eighty-five years later it was 1 to 44. During the 1980s, the ratio was 1 to 383.

The relation between the local federal bench and bar constituted a changing institutional culture influencing decision making. Perhaps two factors were determinative. First, the corresponding smallness of the bench and bar created an institutional intimacy that fostered predictability, both in terms of what the judge expected from the lawyer's expertise and what the lawyer might assume concerning the judge's decisions. Second, as long as judges lacked a deep support organization, their dependence on lawyers was greater. During the second half of the twentieth century, by contrast, the transformation in the ratio between attorney and judge increased the randomness governing the relationship between bench and bar while it decreased dependence. At the same time, the emergence of the support staff helped to insulate the judges from external pressures. Paradoxically, this increased local autonomy coincided with greater organizational centralization resulting from the conference system and the extended frequency of appellate review, which in turn heightened the lower federal court's dependence within the national judicial establishment itself.

The declining influence of the local courthouse culture coincided with a changing market for legal services. Throughout the nation's history, routine and constitutional litigation in federal court was a specialized practice. Even so, the nature of specialization gradually shifted from suits involving primarily interstate business controversies arising under diversity jurisdiction to cases in which rights and obligations defined by federal statute and constitutional provisions predominated, particularly federal crimes and rights claims. As litigation became federalized and therefore more identified with national law enforcement concerns, a modest but growing number of firms, at least in smaller, strongly-rural states like Alabama, gradually incorporated into their practice the specialized federal issues. The trend partially corresponded to the bar's general division between plaintiff and defense lawyers; it also reflected the state's declining market and cultural distinctiveness, as Alabama became more urban and suburban during the postwar era. As a result, there were more lawyers litigating more federal and constitutional issues before more federal judges, which subjected to growing randomness the informal institutional relationship between the local bench and bar and encouraged the organizationally-centralizing influence of the national judicial establishment.

External political tensions only indirectly influenced the federal judicial process. The history of Alabama's federal judicial appointments confirmed the importance of political exigencies. Yet despite noteworthy exceptions, national party partisanship determined judicial appointment less than local considerations. Throughout the nineteenth century, the dominant local political factors included the substate sectional rivalry between north and south Alabama. During the twentieth century, Democratic senators, particularly those affiliated with the pro–New Deal National Democrats and their successor Howell Heflin, significantly influenced the selection of judicial candidates from Alabama, including Republicans. Generally, informal, personal, or factional associations and shared cultural values either intermingled with or cut across party loyalties, diluting and diminishing the force of national political ideologies such as Jacksonian Democracy, Reconstruction Republicanism, Democratic conservatism, the post–World War II liberal consensus, or the Republican conservatism identified with Ronald Reagan.

Party ideology thus rarely threatened judicial independence and the exercise of discretion. In some instances it was possible to establish a close identification between party ideology and a court's particular decision, such as Campbell's circuit opinion supporting the Buchanan administration's prohibition of the slave trade, some of Wood's and Busteed's decisions defending Reconstruction, or the Davis opinion upholding the Roosevelt administration's Social Security Act. But such cases were exceptions. Usually internal institutional factors interacting with personal, nonparty values were the most important influences shaping a judge's decisions. The necessary distinction that needed to be made was between personal values derived from family and social background on the one hand and formal partisan party principles on the other. Accordingly, the judge's use of discretion to determine a particular decision reflected personal values and the federal judiciary's indigenous institutional culture.

Alabama's state motto is "We defend our rights." Throughout American history, the popular manifestations of that motto often touched the national experience, regularly precipitating the action of federal courts. The indigenous institutional culture and external political exigencies influencing the federal judiciary's response to formal litigation and public conflict within the state changed. As the pressures on judicial dependence and the exercise of discretion shifted, the federal judge's independence increased. In Alabama as in other states, political party affiliation usually determined a judge's appointment. But the interaction of institutional and personal values within the federal judicial establishment itself generally shaped judicial conduct and decision making, while in most cases it diffused whatever impact political ideology might have had. During the second half of the twentieth century, the growing organizational centralization of the national judiciary, evidenced by a greater incidence of appellate review, circumscribed the federal district court's autonomy. Over the same period, Alabama's public officials often resisted including weaker groups within the democratic process, justifying their position by attacking the federal courts in the name of democracy. Resistance facilitated the federal judiciary's intervention, and through the widened discretion national institutional autonomy sustained, federal judges strengthened the individual rights on which democracy depends.

Appendix A

Highlights of Alabama Federal Court History

1817   Alabama Territory separated from Mississippi Territory.

1819   Alabama admitted to the Union.

1820   District Court of Alabama created. Terms to be held at Mobile and Cahawba beginning in April 1821.

1824   Alabama divided into Northern and Southern districts. Northern District sessions held at Huntsville; Southern District sessions held at Cahawba and Mobile.

1826   Southern District terms at Cahawba abolished. Two terms to be held annually at Mobile.

1837   District courts assigned to Ninth Circuit. Circuit court to be held in Mobile in April and October and in Huntsville in June. Huntsville meetings of the circuit court were repealed in 1838 with provisions for handling Northern District appeals in circuit court sessions in Mobile. In 1842, this was repealed and provision was made for appeal directly to the U.S. Supreme Court from the district court of the Northern District in certain cases.

1839   Middle District created, terms to be held at Tuscaloosa. Appeals were to be taken to the circuit court in Mobile.

1842   Alabama federal courts transferred to Fifth Circuit.

1848   Terms of Middle District courts transferred from Tuscaloosa to Montgomery.

1873   Circuit court at Mobile given appeals jurisdiction from the district courts of the Northern and Middle districts. In 1874, circuit courts were provided for the Northern and Middle districts, with the Northern District term at Huntsville and Middle District term at Montgomery.

1886   Separate judgeship created for the Southern District. Incumbent judge becomes district judge for the Northern and Middle districts.

1903   Eastern division of Northern District created to hold court in Anniston.

1907   Additional judgeship created for Northern District.

1908   Middle District divided into northern and southern divisions, with sessions to be held at Montgomery and Dothan.

1909   Middle division of Northern District created, with sessions to be held in Gadsden.

1911   Northern division of Northern District split into northeastern and northwestern divisions. Jasper and western divisions created. Sessions of court held at Florence, Huntsville, Jasper, and Tuscaloosa.

1913   Southern District divided into northern and southern divisions, with court to be held at Selma and Mobile. Eastern division of Middle District created, with sessions to be held at Opelika.

1936   Separate judge assigned to Middle District, giving each district its own judge. Additional judgeships have been created periodically since 1936.

1981   Alabama federal courts transferred to Eleventh Circuit.

Appendix B

Federal Judges' Biographies

ACKER, WILLIAM MARSH, JR. Born October 25, 1928, Birmingham, Alabama; son of William Marsh and Estelle (Lampkin) Acker. Married Martha Walters, 1957. Children: William Marsh, III, Stacey Reed. B.A., Birmingham Southern College, 1949; LL.B., Yale Law School, 1952. U.S. Army, 1944–47; admitted to Alabama bar, 1952; practiced in Birmingham, 1952–82; delegate to Republican National Convention, 1972, 1976, 1980; former member Alabama Republican Executive Committee; appointed judge of U.S. District Court for the Northern District of Alabama, 1982, by President Reagan.

ALBRITTON, WILLIAM HAROLD. Born December 19, 1936, Andalusia, Alabama; son of Robert Bynum and Carrie Veal Albritton. Married Jane Rollins Howard, June 2, 1958. Children: William Harold, IV, Benjamin Howard, Thomas Bynum. B.A., University of Alabama, 1959; LL.B., University of Alabama, 1960. Admitted to Alabama bar, 1960; U.S. Army, Judge Advocate General Corps, 1960–62; private practice in Andalusia, 1962–91; appointed judge of U.S. District Court for the Middle District of Alabama, 1991, by President Bush. Republican. Presbyterian.

ALLGOOD, CLARENCE WILLIAM. Born September 12, 1902, Birmingham, Alabama; son of Robert Veneable and Patricia (Robinson) Allgood. Married Marie Maxwell, June 27, 1927. Child: Clarence William. Attended Howard College, 1921–23; B.S., Alabama Polytechnic Institute, 1926; LL.B., Birmingham School of Law, 1941. Admitted to Alabama bar, 1941; referee in bankruptcy, U.S. District Court for Northern District of Alabama, 1937–61; appointed U. S. district judge for Northern District of Alabama, 1962, by President Kennedy, assumed senior status January 9, 1973. Died November 30, 1991. Democrat.

BLACKBURN, SHARON LOVELACE. Born May 7, 1950; daughter of Barnes Flournoy and Barbara Blount Lovelace. Married Joseph W. Blackburn,

September 15, 1979. Children: Whit, Bob, Barbara. B.A., University of Alabama, 1973; J.D., Cumberland School of Law, Samford University, 1977. Law clerk for Robert Varner, U.S. District Court for the Middle District of Alabama, 1977–78; staff attorney, Birmingham Area Legal Services, 1979; assistant U.S. attorney, Birmingham, 1979–91; appointed judge of U.S. District Court for the Northern District of Alabama, 1991, by President Bush. Episcopalian.

BRUCE, JOHN. Born February 16, 1832, Sterlingshire, Scotland; son of James and Margaret (Liddell) Bruce. Married Anna Johnson Hamil, April 7, 1870. Five children. Emigrated in 1840, settling in Ohio. A.B., Franklin College, 1854. Read law with Samuel F. Miller, later associate justice of U.S. Supreme Court; admitted to bar of Iowa, 1856; private practice in Keokuk, Iowa, 1856–62; served in U.S. Army, infantry, 1862–64. Moved to Wilcox County, Alabama, in 1865. Representative to State legislature from Prairie Bluff, 1872–75; appointed judge of U.S. District Court for District of Alabama by President Grant in 1875 (appointment became judge of Northern and Middle districts in 1886); served until his death on October 1, 1901. Republican. Presbyterian.

BUSTEED, RICHARD. Born February 16, 1822, Cavan, Ireland; son of George Washington Busteed. Worked as publisher and printer in Canada, Ohio, Connecticut, and New York. Admitted to the bar of New York in 1846. Corporation counsel of New York City, 1856–59. Served in U.S. Army, 1861–63. Appointed U. S. district judge for Alabama by President Lincoln in 1864; resigned bench, 1874; practiced law in New York until his death, September 14, 1898. Democrat. Methodist.

BUTLER, CHARLES R., JR. Born March 28, 1940, New York, New York; son of Charles R. and Venetia Neville (Bacon) Butler. Married Jacqueline Warren, July 13, 1963. Children: Charles R. III, Michael W. B.A., Washington and Lee University, 1962; LL.B., University of Alabama, 1966. Admitted to Alabama bar, 1966; U.S. Army, 1962–64; private practice in Mobile, 1966–69 and 1975–88; assistant public defender of Mobile County, 1969–70; district attorney of Mobile County, 1971–75; adjunct professor, University of South Alabama, 1975–76; appointed judge of U.S. District Court for the Southern District of Alabama, 1988, by President Reagan. Episcopalian.

CARNES, EDWARD E. Born June 3, 1950, Albertville, Alabama; son of T. J. and Florine Carnes. Married Sarah Rebecca Boyd, August 13, 1972. Child: Julian Katherine. B.A., University of Alabama, 1972; J.D., Harvard Law School, 1975. Admitted to Alabama bar, 1975; assistant Alabama attorney general,

268

1975–92; appointed judge of the U.S. Eleventh Circuit Court of Appeals, 1992, by President Bush. Republican. Methodist.

CLAYTON, HENRY DeLAMAR. Born February 10, 1857, Barbour County, Alabama; son of Major General Henry DeLamar and Victoria V. (Hunter) Clayton. Married Virginia Ball Allen, 1882; Bettie Davis, 1910. Educated at University of Alabama (A.B.), 1877, (LL.B.), 1878. Entered practice 1878; register in chancery of Barbour County, 1880–84; practiced in Eufaula, Alabama, 1880–1914; member Alabama state legislature, 1890–91; U.S. district attorney for the Middle District of Alabama, 1893–96; member U.S. House of Representatives, 1897–1914; resigned Congress to accept appointment by President Wilson as U.S. district judge for the Middle District and Northern District of Alabama, 1914; served until 1929. Author of the Clayton Act. Died December 21, 1929. Democrat. Episcopalian.

CLEMON, U. W. Born April 9, 1943, Fairfield, Alabama; son of Mose and Addie Clemon. Married Barbara Lang, December 27, 1967. Children: Herman Issac, Addine Michele. B.A., Miles College, 1965; J.D., Columbia Law School, 1968. Admitted to Alabama bar, 1968; practiced in Birmingham, 1968–80; member Alabama State Senate, 1974–80; chairman of Senate Judiciary Committee; appointed judge of U.S. District Court for the Northern District of Alabama, 1980, by President Carter. Democrat.

COX, EMMETT RIPLEY. Born February 13, 1935, Cottonwood, Alabama; son of Emmett M. Cox, Jr. and Myra E. (Ripley) Stewart. Married Ann MacKay Haas, May 16, 1965. Children: John H., Catherine M. B.A., University of Alabama, 1957; LL.B., University of Alabama, 1959. Admitted to Alabama bar, 1959; practiced in Birmingham, 1959–64; practiced in Mobile, 1964–81; appointed judge of the U.S. District Court for the Southern District of Alabama, 1981, by President Reagan; appointed judge of the Eleventh Circuit Court of Appeals, 1988, by President Reagan.

CRAWFORD, WILLIAM H. Born 1784, Louisa County, Virginia. Married Temperance Winnifred Fitts, 1820. United States attorney for the Alabama Territory in 1817; entered private practice in St. Stephens, 1818; U.S. attorney for Alabama, 1820–26; candidate for United States Senate, 1822; member, Alabama State Senate, 1825–26; appointed federal district judge of Alabama, 1826, by John Quincy Adams; served on federal bench until his death in 1849 in Mobile, Alabama. Jeffersonian Democrat.

DAVIS, DAVID JACKSON. Born Wedowee, Alabama, October 15, 1878. Son of Dora Franklin and Callie Rebecca (Satterwhite) Davis. Married Mary Helm, May 1, 1912. Child: Marjorie Helm. Educated at Phillips Academy, Andover, Massachusetts, 1899–1901; LL.B. Yale, 1906. Admitted to Alabama bar, 1906. Practiced in Birmingham, 1906–35. One-time law partner of Hugo L. Black. Appointed U.S. District Court judge by President Franklin D. Roosevelt, 1935. Died December 7, 1938. Democrat.

DeMENT, IRA. Born December 21, 1931, Birmingham, Alabama; son of Ira Jr. and Helen (Sparks) DeMent. Married Ruth Lester Posey. Child: Charles Posey. B.A., University of Alabama, 1953; L.L.B., University of Alabama, 1958; J.D., University of Alabama, 1969. Admitted to Alabama bar, 1958; law clerk, Alabama Supreme Court, 1958–59; assistant attorney general, State of Alabama, 1959; assistant U.S. attorney, Montgomery, 1959–61; private practice, Montgomery, 1961–69; special assistant attorney general, State of Alabama, 1966–69, 1981–92; acting U.S. attorney, Middle District of Alabama, 1969; U.S. attorney, 1969–77; private practice, Montgomery, 1977–92; special counsel to governor, State of Alabama, 1980–88. Appointed judge of U.S. District Court for the Middle District of Alabama, 1992, by President Bush. Republican. Methodist.

DUBINA, JOEL F. Born 1947, Elkhart, Indiana. Married Elizabeth Gordy. Children: Britton E., Martha K., Mitchell F. B.S., University of Alabama, 1970; J.D., Cumberland School of Law, Samford University, 1973. Admitted to Alabama bar, 1973; law clerk for Robert Varner, U.S. District Court for the Middle District of Alabama, 1973–74; private practice in Montgomery, 1974–83; U.S. magistrate for the Middle District of Alabama, 1983–86; appointed judge of the U.S. District Court for the Middle District of Alabama, 1986, by President Reagan; appointed judge of the Eleventh Circuit Court of Appeals, 1990, by President Bush. Presbyterian.

ERVIN, ROBERT TAIT. Born May 27, 1863, Wilcox County, Alabama; son of Robert Hugh and Sarah A. (Tait) Ervin. Married Frances Patterson Pybas, June 8, 1897. Children: Frances Patterson, Robert Tait, Elinor McCarry. Studied law at University of Alabama (LL.B.), 1887. Admitted to the bar, 1887. Private practice in Mobile; appointed U.S. district judge for the Southern District of Alabama by President Wilson, 1917; served to 1935. Died 1949. Democrat. Baptist.

GAYLE, JOHN. Born September 11, 1792, Sumter, South Carolina; son of Matthew and Mary (Reese) Gayle. Married Sarah Ann Haynesworth, November 14, 1819; Clarissa Peck, November 1, 1839. Ten children. Educated at Newbery Academy and South Carolina College. Moved to Alabama and studied law under A. S. Lipscomb. Admitted to bar, 1818. Member of legislative council of Territorial legislature of Alabama, 1818; solicitor of First Judicial Circuit, 1819; representative from Monroe County to Alabama legislature, 1822; judge of 3rd Circuit Court of Alabama, 1823; appointed to Alabama Supreme Court, 1828; resigned court to serve as Greene County representative in state legislature, 1829; speaker of Alabama House, 1829–31; governor of Alabama, 1831–35; presidential elector, 1836 and 1840; elected to U.S. House of Representatives, 1847; appointed United States district judge of Alabama by President Taylor, 1849; served until his death on July 21, 1859, in Mobile, Alabama. Whig. Presbyterian.

GEWIN, WALTER PETTUS. Born December 9, 1908, Nanafalia, Alabama; son of John Walker and Julia (Crenshaw) Gewin. Married Anna Fidelia Sledge, December 5, 1936. Children: Walter Pettus, Jr., James William, Margaret Juliette. A.B., Birmingham Southern College, 1930; B.L.S., Emory University, 1932; LL.B., University of Alabama, 1935. Admitted to Alabama bar, 1935; practiced in Birmingham, 1935–36; practiced in Greensboro, 1936–51; member state legislature, 1938–42; deputy solicitor, Hale County, 1942–51; judge advocate general's office, 1944–45; state prosecutor in Tuscaloosa, 1951–61; appointed judge of the Fifth Circuit, U.S. Court of Appeals, 1961, by President Kennedy. Took senior status November 11, 1976; died May 15, 1981. Democrat. Presbyterian.

GODBOLD, JOHN COOPER. Born March 24, 1920, Coy, Alabama; son of Edwin Condie and Elsie (Williamson) Godbold. Married Elizabeth Showalter, July 18, 1942. Children: Susan, Richard, John C., Cornelia, Sally. B.S., Auburn University, 1940; J.D., Harvard Law School, 1948. U.S. Army, 1941–45; taught at Auburn University, 1946; private practice in Montgomery, 1948–66; appointed to the U.S. Court of Appeals for the Fifth Circuit, 1966, by President Johnson; became Eleventh Circuit judge, October 1, 1981; chief judge Eleventh Circuit Court of Appeals, 1981–86; assumed senior status, 1987. Democrat. Episcopalian.

GROOMS, HARLAN HOBART. Born November 7, 1900, Jeffersonville, Kentucky; son of John F. and Ida (Alfrey) Grooms. Married Angeline McCrocklin, May 3, 1930. Children: Harlan H., Jr., Ellen Elizabeth, John Franklin, Angeline M. Educated at University of Kentucky, 1920–26, LL.B., 1926. Admitted to practice in Alabama, 1926. Practiced in Birmingham, 1926–53;

U.S. Army Reserve, 1920–39; appointed U.S. district judge for the Northern District of Alabama by President Eisenhower, 1953; became senior judge, 1969. Republican. Baptist.

GRUBB, WILLIAM IRWIN. Born March 8, 1862, Cincinnati, Ohio; son of John and Sidney (Irwin) Grubb. Married Alice C. Vigo, June 18, 1906. Children: Katharine, Archibald Irwin, William Irwin. Graduated from Yale University (A.B.), 1883; attended Cincinnati Law School. Began legal practice in Cincinnati in 1884 and Birmingham, Alabama, 1888. Private practice, 1884–1909; appointed U.S. district judge for the Northern District of Alabama by President Taft, 1909; served until 1935. Died October 27, 1935. Democrat. Presbyterian.

GUIN, JUNIUS FOY, JR. Born February 2, 1924, Russellville, Alabama; son of Junius Foy and Ruby (Pace) Guin. Married Dorace Jean Caldwell, July 18, 1945. Children: Janet E., Judith A., Junius Foy, III, David J. Educated at Georgia Institute of Technology, 1940–41; B.A., University of Alabama; J.D., University of Alabama, 1947. Admitted to Alabama bar, 1948; private practice in Russellville, 1948–73; candidate for U.S. Senate, 1954; Republican county chairman, 1954–58 and 1971–72; Republican state finance chairman, 1972–73; lecturer, Cumberland School of Law, Samford University, University of Alabama School of Law; appointed U. S. district judge for the Northern District of Alabama, 1973, by President Nixon; assumed senior status in 1989. Church of Christ.

HALTOM, ELBERT BERTRAM, JR. Born December 26, 1922, Florence, Alabama; son of Elbert Bertram and Elva Mae (Simpson) Haltom. Married Constance Boyd Morris, August 19, 1949. Child: Emily. Educated at Florence State Teachers College, 1940–42 and 1945; LL.B., University of Alabama, 1948. Admitted to Alabama bar, 1948; practiced in Florence, 1948–80; member Alabama House of Representatives, 1954–58; member Alabama Senate, 1958–62; member, Alabama Democratic Executive Committee, 1966–80; candidate for lieutenant governor, 1962; appointed judge of the U.S. District Court for the Northern District of Alabama, 1980, by President Carter; assumed senior status December 31, 1991. Protestant.

HANCOCK, JAMES HUGHES. Born April 30, 1931, Montgomery, Alabama. Married, three children. B.S., University of Alabama, 1953; LL.B., University of Alabama, 1957; U.S. Army and reserve, 1953–55; admitted to Alabama bar, 1957; private practice in Birmingham, 1957–73; lecturer, Alabama Continuing Legal Education, 1968–72; appointed U. S. district judge for the Northern District of Alabama, 1973, by President Nixon.

HAND, WILLIAM BREVARD. Born January 18, 1924, Mobile, Alabama; son of Charles C. and Irma W. Hand. Married Allison Denby, June 17, 1948. Children: Jane C., Virginia A., Allison P. B.S., University of Alabama, 1947; J.D., University of Alabama, 1949. Admitted to Alabama bar, 1949; practiced in Mobile, 1949–71; appointed U. S. district judge for the Southern District of Alabama, 1971, by President Nixon, later chief judge; assumed senior judge status, 1989. Republican. Methodist.

HOBBS, TRUMAN M. Born February 8, 1921, Selma, Alabama; son of Sam F. and Sarah Ellen (Greene) Hobbs. Married Joyce Cummings, July 9, 1949. Children: Emilie C., Frances J., Dexter C., Truman M. B.A., University of North Carolina, 1942; LL.B., Yale Law School, 1948. Admitted to Alabama bar, 1948; law clerk to U.S. Supreme Court Justice Hugo Black, 1948–49; practiced in Birmingham, 1949–51; practiced in Montgomery, 1951–80; chairman, Alabama Unemployment Appeal Board, 1952–58; appointed U. S. district judge for the Middle District of Alabama, 1980, by President Carter; assumed senior status February 8, 1991. Democrat. Episcopalian.

HOWARD, ALEX TRAVIS, JR. Born July 9, 1924, Mobile, Alabama; son of Alexander Travis and Cecile Hunter Morrissette Howard. Married Ann Lesesne Boykin, January 5, 1952. Children: Alexander Travis, III, Catherine. Educated at University of Alabama, 1942 and 1946; Auburn University, 1942–43 and 1944; J.D., Vanderbilt University, 1950. U.S. Army, 1943–46; admitted to Alabama bar, 1950; U.S. probation officer, 1950–51; private practice in Mobile, 1951–86; U.S. commissioner, U.S. District Court for the Southern District of Alabama, 1956–70; appointed judge of the U.S. District Court for the Southern District of Alabama, 1986, by President Reagan; chief judge, 1989. Republican. Methodist.

HUNDLEY, OSCAR RICHARD. Born October 30, 1854, Limestone County, Alabama; son of Orville M. and Mary E. Hundley. Married Anna E. Thomas, February 1878; Bossie O'Brien, June 24, 1897. Attended Marietta College, Ohio, 1873–74; Vanderbilt University (LL.B.), 1877. Admitted to bar, 1878. Private practice in Huntsville, 1878–1907; city attorney of Huntsville, 1882–84; member of Alabama House of Representatives, 1886–90; member of state Senate, 1890–98; Republican nominee for Congress, Eighth Alabama District, 1907; appointed U.S. district judge for the Northern District of Alabama by President Theodore Roosevelt, 1907; retired from bench, May 1909. Died December 22, 1921. Democrat (until 1896), then Republican. Roman Catholic.

JOHNSON, FRANK MINIS, JR. Born October 30, 1918, Haleyville, Alabama; son of Frank M. and Alabama (Long) Johnson. Married Ruth Jenkins, January 16, 1938. Child: James Curtis. Educated at University of Alabama (LL.B.), 1943. Admitted to Alabama bar, 1943. U.S. Army, 1943–46; private practice in Haleyville and Jasper, Alabama, 1946–53; U.S. attorney for Northern District of Alabama, 1953–55; appointed U.S. district judge for the Middle District of Alabama by President Eisenhower, 1955; became chief judge, 1966; served on district court to 1979; appointed by U.S. Supreme Court Chief Justice Warren Burger to serve as judge of U.S. Temporary Emergency Court of Appeals, 1972–82; appointed judge of the U.S. Court of Appeals for the Fifth Circuit by President Carter; became Eleventh Circuit judge October 1, 1981; assumed senior status, 1991. Republican. Baptist.

JONES, THOMAS GOODE. Born November 25, 1844, Macon, Georgia; son of Samuel G. and Martha Ward (Goode) Jones. Married Georgena Bird, December 20, 1866. Thirteen children. Educated at Virginia Military Institute, 1859–62. Entered Confederate States Army, 1862, serving to 1865. Studied law while in winter quarters in the army and in the office of John A. Elmore. Admitted to Alabama bar, 1866. Newspaper editor, Montgomery, 1868; reporter of Alabama Supreme Court, 1870–80; alderman of the City of Montgomery, 1875–84; member Alabama legislature, 1884–88 (speaker, 1886–88); governor of Alabama, 1890–94; appointed federal district judge for the Northern District and Middle District of Alabama by President Theodore Roosevelt in 1901, serving until his death in 1914; delegate to Alabama constitutional convention, 1901. Died April 28, 1914, in Montgomery. Democrat. Episcopalian.

JONES, WILLIAM GILES. Born November 6, 1808, Powhatan County, Virginia. Married Miss Branch; Miss Hobson. Two sons. Educated at Hampden-Sidney College and the University of Virginia. Studied law under Attorney General John Robertson in Richmond, Virginia. Admitted to the bar, 1830. Practiced in Virginia, 1830–34. Moved to Alabama, 1834. Practiced Erie County and Greene County, 1836–43; representative of Greene County in Alabama legislature, 1843; practiced in Mobile, 1843–58; representative of Mobile County in Alabama legislature, 1849; chairman, Judiciary Committee. Appointed judge of the U.S. District Court for the Southern District of Alabama by President Buchanan, 1859; resigned upon secession of Alabama from the United States; appointed to same office by C.S.A. President Davis; served until fall of Confederacy; practiced in Mobile until his death in 1883. Whig, then Democrat.

KENNAMER, CHARLES BRENTS. Born November 25, 1874, Marshall County, Alabama; son of Seaborn F. and Nancy Elizabeth (Mitchell) Kennamer. Married Birdie Hooper, December 2, 1907. Children: Charles B., Ralph, Seaborn A., Rex, Mary Virginia. Studied law at Georgetown University. Entered practice in Guntersville, Alabama, 1903; county solicitor for Marshall County, 1905–06; assistant U.S. attorney for Northern District of Alabama, 1907–14; special assistant U.S. attorney for Northern District of Alabama, 1914–16; U.S. attorney for Northern District of Alabama, 1923–31; resigned U.S. attorney's office to accept President Hoover's appointment as judge of the U.S. District Court for the Northern District and Middle District of Alabama, 1931. Delegate to Republican National Convention, 1916, 1920, 1924, and 1928 (chairman of Alabama delegates, 1920, 1924, and 1928). Republican candidate for Congress, 7th Alabama District, 1906, 1919, and 1920. Died June 3, 1955.

LANE, GEORGE WASHINGTON. Born 1806, Cherokee County, Georgia; son of Jonathan and Elizabeth (Colley) Lane. Family moved to Limestone County, Alabama, in 1821. Read law under Judge Daniel Coleman. Entered practice of law in Athens. Representative in Alabama legislature, 1829 and 1832; elected judge of county court, 1832; elected circuit judge, 1834, serving for twelve years; resigned bench, 1846; practiced law in Huntsville, beginning in 1846. Appointed U.S. district judge by President Lincoln, March 28, 1861, but never assumed bench. Died in 1863 in Louisville, Kentucky.

LYNNE, SEYBOURN HARRIS. Born July 25, 1907, Decatur, Alabama; son of Seybourn Arthur and Annie Leigh (Harris) Lynne. Married Katherine Donaldson Brandau, June 16, 1937. Child: Katherine Roberta. B.S. degree, Alabama Polytechnic Institute, 1927; LL.B., University of Alabama, 1930. Admitted to practice in Alabama, 1930. Private practice in Decatur, Alabama, 1930–34; judge of Morgan County Court, 1934–41; judge Eighth Judicial Circuit of Alabama, 1941–42; U.S. Army, Judge Advocate General Department, 1942–46; appointed judge of the U.S. District Court for the Northern District of Alabama by President Truman, 1946; chief judge, 1953; became senior judge, 1973. Democrat. Baptist.

McCORD, LEON CLARENCE. Born June 21, 1878, Conyers, Georgia; son of William Henry and Ellen Grant (Davis) McCord. Married Bobbie Tanner, February 20, 1906. Studied law in a private law office, entering practice in Alabama, 1900. Secretary of the Supreme Court of Alabama, 1903–09; private practice in Montgomery, 1901–16; member Alabama Railroad Commission, 1911–15; judge of circuit court, 15th Judicial Circuit of Alabama, 1916–35; presiding judge, 1919–35; private practice, 1935–38; appointed judge of the U.S. Circuit Court of Appeals, Fifth Circuit, by President Franklin D. Roosevelt, 1938; retired from bench, 1951. Died February 11, 1952. Democrat. Presbyterian.

McDUFFIE, JOHN. Born September 25, 1883, River Ridge, Alabama; son of John and Virginia Marion (Lett) McDuffie. Married Cornelia Hixon, October 18, 1915; Mary Clarke Maxon, September 8, 1941. Child: Cornelia. Studied at Southern University, Greensboro, Alabama; Alabama Polytechnic Institute (B.S.), 1904; University of Alabama (LL.B.), 1908. Member, Alabama House of Representatives, 1907. Admitted to Alabama bar, 1908. Prosecuting attorney, 1st Judicial Circuit of Alabama, 1911–19; member U.S. House of Representatives from 1st Alabama District, 1920–35; resigned Congress to accept appointment of President Franklin D. Roosevelt as judge of the U.S. District Court of the Southern District of Alabama, 1935; served 1935–50. Died November 1, 1950. Democrat. Catholic.

McFADDEN, FRANK H. Born November 20, 1925, Oxford, Mississippi; son of John Angus and Ruby McFadden. Married, two children. B.A., University of Mississippi, 1950; LL.B., Yale Law School, 1955. Admitted to New York bar, 1956; admitted to Alabama bar, 1959; practiced in New York City, 1956–58; practiced in Birmingham, 1958–69; appointed U. S. district judge for the Northern District of Alabama, 1969, by President Nixon. Resigned January 1, 1982.

MULLINS, CLARENCE. Born March 16, 1895, Clanton, Alabama; son of Clement and Leila (Dawson) Mullins. Married Barbara Gonzales, March 28, 1922. Children: Clarence, Barbara Jean, Robert. Studied at University of Alabama (LL.B.), 1914. Private practice in Birmingham during 1914–1943. Appointed U.S. district court judge by President Franklin D. Roosevelt; served, 1943–53. Assumed senior status May 1953. Died 1957. Democrat. Baptist.

MURPHREE, THOMAS ALEXANDER. Born December 1, 1883, Blount County, Alabama; son of Lindsey Sylvester and Martha (Hendricks) Murphree. Married Helen Rosa Randolph, April 25, 1914. Child: Florence. Educated at University of Alabama (B.S.), 1910, (LL.B.), 1911. Admitted to Alabama bar, 1911. Private practice in Birmingham, 1911–38; appointed judge of the U.S.

District Court for the Northern District of Alabama by President Franklin D. Roosevelt, 1938. Died in office September 5, 1945. Democrat. Episcopalian.

NELSON, EDWIN L. Born February 10, 1940, Brewton, Alabama; son of John D. and Ruby Davis Nelson. Married Linda M. Nelson, December 27, 1965. Children: Patrick L., Susan A. Educated at University of Alabama, 1962–63; Samford University, 1965–66; LL.B., Cumberland School of Law, Samford University, 1969. Admitted to Alabama bar, 1969; U.S. Navy, 1958–62; private practice in Fort Payne, 1969–74; candidate for U.S. Congress, 1972; magistrate, U.S. District Court for the Northern District of Alabama, 1974–90; appointed judge of U.S. District Court for the Northern District of Alabama, 1990, by President Bush. Republican. Episcopalian.

PITTMAN, THOMAS VIRGIL. Born March 28, 1916, Enterprise, Alabama; son of Walter Oscar and Anne Lee (Logan) Pittman. Married Floy Lasseter, 1944. Children: Karen, Walter. B.S., University of Alabama, 1937; LL.B., University of Alabama, 1940. Admitted to Alabama bar, 1940. Special agent, FBI, 1940–44; U.S. Navy, 1944–46; private practice in Gadsden, Alabama, 1946–51; judge of Alabama Circuit Court for Sixteenth Judicial Circuit, 1951–66; lecturer, University of Alabama Center, Gadsden, 1951–66; appointed U. S. district judge by President Johnson, 1966; served on District Court of Middle and Southern Districts of Alabama, 1966–71; chief judge U.S. District Court for Southern District, 1971–81; assumed senior status, 1981. Democrat. Baptist.

POINTER, SAM CLYDE, JR. Born November 15, 1934, Birmingham, Alabama; son of Sam Clyde and Elizabeth Inzer (Brown) Pointer. Married Paula Purse, October 18, 1958. Children: Minge, Sam C., III. B.A., Vanderbilt University, 1955; J.D., University of Alabama, 1957; LL.M., New York University Graduate School of Law, 1958. Admitted to Alabama bar, 1957; private practice, 1958–70; vice chairman and general counsel, Alabama Republican Party, 1965–69; appointed U. S. district judge for Northern District of Alabama, 1970, by President Nixon; chief judge, 1983; appointed judge of the Temporary Emergency Court of Appeals of the United States, 1980, by U.S. Supreme Court Chief Justice Warren Burger, serving to 1987. Episcopalian.

PROPST, ROBERT B. Born July 13, 1931, Ohatchee, Alabama; son of Franklin Glen and Mildred Martha Propst. Married Elna Jo (Griffin), December 29, 1962. Children: Stephen G., David B., Joanne R. B.S., University of Alabama, 1953; LL.B., University of Alabama, 1957. U.S. Army, 1953–55;

admitted to Alabama bar, 1957; private practice in Anniston, 1957–80; appointed judge of the U.S. District Court for the Northern District of Alabama, 1980, by President Carter. Methodist.

RIVES, RICHARD TAYLOR. Born January 15, 1895, Montgomery, Alabama; son of William Henry and Alice Bloodworth (Taylor) Rives. Married Jessie Hall Daugherty, July 23, 1918. Children: Richard Taylor, Callie Daugherty. Attended Tulane University, 1911–12; studied law in the office of Hill, Hill, Whiting and Stern in Montgomery. Admitted to Alabama bar, 1914. Served in National Guard, Mexican border, 1915–16; Signal Corps, American Expeditionary Forces, 1918–19; general practice in Montgomery; delegate to Democratic Convention, 1940; appointed judge U.S. Court of Appeals, Fifth Circuit, by President Truman, 1951; chief judge, 1959–66. Assumed senior status, 1966; died October 27, 1982. Democrat. Presbyterian.

SHELBY, DAVID DAVIE. Born October 24, 1847, Madison County, Alabama; son of David and Mary Tabitha (Bouldin) Shelby. Married Annie Davis, August 8, 1872. No children. Studied law at Cumberland University. Admitted to Alabama bar, 1870; practiced in Huntsville, 1870–99; city attorney of Huntsville, 1874; member Alabama state Senate, 1882–86. Appointed U.S. circuit judge for the Fifth Circuit Court of Appeals by President McKinley, 1899. Died August 22, 1914, at Huntsville, Alabama. Republican.

TAIT, CHARLES. Born February 1, 1768, Louisa County, Virginia; son of James and Rebecca (Hudson) Tait. Married Mrs. Anne (Lucas) Simpson, January 3, 1790; Mrs. Sarah (Williamson) Griffin, 1822. Children: James Asbury, Charles Jefferson. Attended Wilkes Academy, Washington, Georgia, 1786–87; Cokesbury College, Abingdon, Maryland, 1788. Instructor, Cokesbury College, 1788–94, during which time he studied law. Admitted to bar, 1795. Headmaster of Richmond Academy, 1795–98; practiced law, Oglethorpe County, Georgia, 1798–1803; Judge, Superior Court for the Western District of Georgia, 1803–09; U.S. senator from Georgia, 1809–19; chairman, Committee on Naval Affairs, 1814–. Moved to Alabama, 1819; appointed as first federal district judge of Alabama by President Monroe, 1820; resigned bench, 1826. Died October 7, 1835, Wilcox County, Alabama. Jeffersonian Democrat.

THOMAS, DANIEL HOLCOMBE. Born August 25, 1906, Prattville, Alabama; son of Columbus Eugene and Augusta (Pratt) Thomas. Married Dorothy Manning Quina, September 26, 1936; Catharine J. Miller, October 25, 1979.

Children: Daniel Holcombe, Jr., Merrill P. Studied at University of Alabama (LL.B), 1928. Admitted to Alabama bar, 1929. Private practice in Mobile, 1929–43; assistant solicitor 13th Judicial Circuit, 1932–39; solicitor for Mobile County, 1943; United States Navy, 1943–45; private practice in Mobile, 1946–51; appointed judge U.S. District Court for the Southern District of Alabama by President Truman, 1951. Assumed senior status August 25, 1971. Democrat. Methodist.

THOMPSON, MYRON H. Born January 7, 1947, Tuskegee, Alabama; son of Lawrence Julius and Lillian Thompson. Married Ann Nichelle, May 5, 1979. B.A., Yale University, 1969; J.D., Yale Law School, 1972. Admitted to Alabama bar, 1972; assistant attorney general of the State of Alabama, 1972–74; private practice in Dothan and Montgomery, 1974–80; appointed judge of U.S. District Court for Middle District of Alabama, 1980, by President Carter; chief judge of Middle District, 1991. Democrat.

TOULMIN, HARRY THEOPHILUS. Born March 4, 1838, Mobile County, Alabama; son of Theophilus Lindsey and Amante (Juzan) Toulmin. Married Mary Montague Henshaw, May 4, 1869. Educated at University of Alabama, University of Virginia, and University of Louisiana. Admitted to Alabama bar, 1860. Practiced in Mobile, 1860–61; entered Confederate States Army, April 1861, serving until the end of the war; resumed practice in Mobile, 1865; presidential elector, 1868; Alabama state legislator, 1870–72; chairman, Committee on Judiciary; judge of Sixth (later First) Judicial Circuit Court of Alabama, 1874–82; resigned bench and resumed private practice, 1882; appointed U.S. district judge for the Southern District of Alabama by President Cleveland in 1886; served until his death, November 12, 1916. Democrat. Episcopalian.

VANCE, ROBERT S. Born Talladega, Alabama, May 10, 1931; son of Harrell Taylor and Mae (Smith) Vance. Married Helen Rainey, October 4, 1953. Children: Robert S., Charles R. B.S., University of Alabama, 1950; J.D., University of Alabama, 1952; LL.M., George Washington University, 1955. U.S. Army, 1952–54; private practice in Birmingham, 1956–77; lecturer, Cumberland School of Law, Samford University, 1967–69; chairman, Alabama Democratic Committee, 1966–67; appointed judge of U.S. Court of Appeals for the Fifth Circuit, 1978, by President Carter; became Eleventh Circuit judge, October 1, 1981. Died December 16, 1989.

VARNER, ROBERT EDWARD. Born June 11, 1921, Montgomery, Alabama; son of William and Georgia W. (Thomas) Varner. Married Carolyn H. Self; Children: Robert E., Jr., Carolyn. Married Jane Hannah, February 27, 1982. Educated at Auburn University, 1938–42; B.S., 1946; J.D., University of Alabama, 1949. Admitted to Alabama bar, 1949; practiced law in Tuskegee, 1949–54; city attorney, 1951; U.S. attorney for the Middle District of Alabama, 1954–58; practiced in Montgomery, 1958–71; appointed U. S. district judge for the Middle District of Alabama, 1971, by President Nixon; chief judge, 1979–84; assumed senior status, 1984. Republican. Methodist.

VOLLMER, RICHARD WADE, JR. Born March 7, 1926, St. Louis, Missouri; son of Richard W. and Beatrice (Burke) Vollmer. Married Marilyn S. Strikes, September 17, 1949. Educated at Springhill College, 1946–49; LL.B., University of Alabama, 1953; admitted to Alabama bar, 1953; claims representative, State Farm Mutual Automobile Insurance Company, 1953–56; private practice in Mobile, 1956–90; appointed judge of the U.S. District Court for the Southern District of Alabama, 1990, by President Bush. Roman Catholic.

WALKER, RICHARD WILDE. Born March 11, 1857, Florence, Alabama; son of Richard Wilde and Mary A. (Simpson) Walker. Married S. White, June 22, 1886. Attended Washington and Lee University, 1873–74; Princeton University (A.B.), 1877; Columbia University Law School. Admitted to Alabama bar, 1878. Practiced in St. Louis, New York City, and Huntsville; associate justice of Alabama Supreme Court, 1891–92; delegate to Alabama Constitutional Convention, 1901; member Alabama state legislature, 1903; presiding judge, Alabama Court of Appeals, 1911–14; appointed U.S. circuit judge for Fifth Circuit Court of Appeals by President Wilson, 1914; served as circuit judge until 1930. Died April 10, 1936. Democrat.

Appendix C

Federal District Court and Justice Department Personnel, 1820–1994

U.S. Attorneys, Northern District

William Crawford	1820
Frank Jones	1824–26
Harry J. Thornton	1826–29
Joseph Scott	1829–30
Byrd Brandon	1830–36
John D. Phelan	1836
Edwin R. Wallace	1836–39
Jermiah Clemens	1839–40
Joseph A.S. Acklin	1840–50
Jefferson F. Jackson	1850–53
George S. Welden	1853–59
M. J. Turnley	1859–60
Charles E. Mayer	1876–80
William H. Smith	1880–85
George H. Craig	1885
William H. Denson	1885–89
Lewis E. Parsons, Jr.	1889–93
Emmet O'Neal	1893–97
William Vaughn	1897–1902
Thomas R. Roulhac	1902–07
Oliver D. Street	1907–13
Robert N. Bell	1913–19
Erie Pettris	1919–22
Charles B. Kennamer	1922–31
Jim C. Smith	1931
John B. Isbell	1931–33

Jim C. Smith	1933–46
John D. Hill	1946–53
Frank M. Johnson, Jr.	1953–55
Atley A. Kitchings, Jr.	1955–56
William L. Langshore	1956–61
Macon L. Weaver	1961–69
Wayman G. Sherrer	1969–77
Jesse R. Brooks	1977–81
Frank W. Donaldson	1981–92
Claude Harris	1993–94
Jack Selden	1994–present

U.S. Attorneys, Middle District

John A. Minnis	1870–74
N. S. McAfee	1874–75
Charles E. Mayer	1876–80
William H. Smith	1880–85
George H. Craig	1885
William H. Denson	1885–89
Lewis E. Parsons, Jr.	1889–93
Henry D. Clayton, Jr.	1893–96
George F. Moore, Jr.	1896–97
Warren S. Reese, Jr.	1897–1906
Erastus J. Parsons	1906–13
Thomas D. Samford	1913–24
Grady Reynolds	1924–31
Arthur B. Chilton	1931–34
Thomas D. Samford	1934–42
Edward B. Parker	1942–53
Hartwell Davis	1953–62
Ben Hardeman	1962–69
Leon J. Hopper	1969
Ira DeMent	1969–77
Barry E. Teague	1977–81
John C. Bell	1981–87
James Eldon Wilson	1987–92
Charles Redding Pitt	1992–present

U.S. Attorneys, Southern District

Henry Hitchcock	1825–30

John Elliot	1830–35
John Forsyth, Jr.	1835–38
George W. Gayle	1838–42
George I. S. Walker	1842–46
Alexander B. Meek	1846–50
Peter Hamilton	1850
A. J. Requier	1850–58
John P. Southworth	1869
George M. Duskin	1877–85
John D. Burnett	1885–89
Morris D. Wickersham	1889–93
Joseph N. Miller	1893–97
Morris D. Wickersham	1897–1904
William H. Armbrecht	1904–12
James B. Sloan	1912–13
Alexander D. Pitts	1913–22
Aubrey Boyles	1922–26
Nicholas E. Stallworth	1926–27
Alexander C. Birch	1927–35
Francis H. Inge	1935–43
Albert J. Tully	1943–48
Percy C. Fountain	1948–56
Ralph Kennamer	1956–61
Vernol R. Jansen, Jr.	1961–69
Charles S. Spunner-White, Jr.	1969–77
William A. Kimbrough, Jr.	1977–81
William R. Favre, Jr.	1981
J. B. Sessions, III	1981–93
Edward J. Vulevich, Jr.	interim

U.S. Marshals, District of Alabama

David Files	1820
Taliaferro Livingston	1820–23
Francis W. Armstrong	1823

U.S. Marshals, Northern and Southern Districts

Francis W. Armstrong	1828
Benjamin F. Moore	1829

U.S. Marshals, Northern District

Benjamin Patteson	1830–50
Willis H. Gibson	1850–52
Benjamin Patteson	1852–60
Edward E. Douglass	1866–68
John W. Henley	1868–71
Zachariah E. Thomas	1871–75
Robert P. Baker	1875–79
Joseph H. Sloss	1879–82
Joseph M. Hinds	1882–85
Arthur H. Keller	1885–89
Charles C. Austin	1889–90
Alexander R. Nininger	1890–93
Judge C. Musgrove	1893–97
Daniel N. Cooper	1897–1905
Pope N. Long	1905–14
Henry A. Skeggs	1914–22
Thomas J. Kennamer	1922–35
Alex Smith	1935–39
Raymond E. Thomason	1939–53
Pervie Lee Dodd	1953–61
Rufus M. Lackie	1961
Peyton Norville, Jr.	1961–63
John D. Hill	1963–64
Roy L. Call	1964–70
Johnny M. Towns	1970–77
Ralph C. Bishop	1977–81
Thomas C. Greene	1981–present

U.S. Marshals, Southern and Middle Districts

Robert L. Crawford	1830–42*
William Armistead	1842–45
James G. Lyon	1845–50
Charles Bingham	1850–53
Cade M. Godbold	1853–60
John Hardy	1866–67
Robert W. Healy	1867–75

*Marshal for Southern District, 1830–39. When Middle District was created in 1839, the marshal performed duties in both districts.

Jerome J. Hinds	1875–76
George Turner	1876–80
Matthias C. Osborn	1880–83
Paul Strobach	1883–84
W. G. M. Golson	1884
Joseph H. Speed	1884–85
William W. Allen	1885–89
Benjamin W. Walker	1889–93

*U.S. Marshals, Middle District***

William H. Tisdale	1893–97
Leander J. Bryan	1897–1905
James H. Judkins	1905–10
Benjamin E. Walker	1910–14
McDuffie Cain	1914–23
Douglas Smith	1923–35
Walter Bragg Smith	1935–47
Benjamin F. Ellis	1947–54
Charles Swann Prescott	1954–61
William M. Parker, Jr.	1961
James T. Lunsford	1977
Rufus A. Lewis	1977–82
Melvin E. Jones	1982–89
Walter J. Bamberg	1989–present

U.S. Marshals, Southern District

Edward R. Morrissette	1893–97
Frank Simmons	1897–1903
Gilbert B. Deans	1903–14
Christopher C. Gewin	1914–23
John W. VanHeuvel	1923–28
James A. Stafford	1928–36
Roulhac Gewin	1936–49
Katherine Battle	1949
Vernon P. Burns	1949–53
James L. May	1953–61
George M. Stuart	1961
H. Stanley Fountain	1977

**Separate marshal authorized in 1893.

James M. Garrett	1977–79
Tyree Richburg	1979–82
Howard V. Adair	1982–93
Robert J. Moore	1994

Clerks, Northern District

Caswell R. Clifton	1824–36
Benjamin Tyson Moore	1836–60
John H. King	1865–75
A. W. McCullough	1875–90
Nathaniel W. Trimble	1890–99
Charles J. Allison	1899–1925
William S. Lovell	1925–36
Charles B. Crow	1936–53
Mary L. Tortorici (acting)	1953
William E. Davis	1953–75
James E. Vandegrift	1976–86
Charles T. Cliver	1987–90
Perry D. Mathis	1991–present

Clerks, Middle District

J. W. Dimmick	
Harvey E. Jones	1911–20
George Stuart	1920–31
O. D. Street, Jr.	1931–57
Robert C. Dobson	1957
Jane P. Gordon	1983
Thomas C. Caver	1983–present

Clerks, Southern District

Henry S. Skaats	1887
Richard Jones	1887–1917
Virgil C. Griffin	1917–46
John Foscue	1946–51
Tazewell T. Shepard	1951–53
William J. O'Connor	1953–81
John V. O'Brien	1982–present

U.S. Magistrates, Northern District

R. Macey Taylor	1971–86
Edwin L. Nelson	1974–90
James F. Reddoch, Jr.	1980–85
Elizabeth Todd Campbell	1986–present
T. Michael Putnam	1987–present
Paul W. Greene	1988–present
Robert R. Armstrong, Jr.	1991–present

U.S. Magistrates, Middle District

John V. Denson, II	1971
Marion L. Gwaltney	1975–86
Joel F. Dubina	1983–86
John L. Carroll	1987–present
Charles S. Coody	1987–present
Vanzetta Penn McPherson	1993–present

U.S. Magistrates, Southern District

Allan R. Cameron	1971–79
John H. Blanton	1975–86
David A. Bagwell	1979–85
Patrick H. Sims	1981–86
William E. Cassady	1985–present
Bert W. Milling, Jr.	1987–present
William H. Steele	1990–present

Personnel lists are as complete as possible based on available records.

Private Civil Cases, 1873–1990

	1873	1874	1875	1876	1877
N.D.	n.a.	2	5	59	109
M.D.	136	26	66	97	154
S.D.	156	54	80	93	111
National Mean	223[a]	174[a]	144[a]	334	423

	1878	1879	1880	1881	1882
N.D.	76	55	59	46	47
M.D.	134	111	99	82	98
S.D.	62	54	71	48	46
National Mean	483	487	610	542	452

	1883	1884	1885	1886	1887
N.D.	63	73	76	133	114
M.D.	103	99	152	92	137
S.D.	35	55	50	65	82
National Mean	523	567	547	594	555

	1888	1889	1890	1891	1892
N.D.	75	70	151	132	185
M.D.	111	86	109	115	102
S.D.	54	32	52	47	42
National Mean	608	652	700	727	758

Source: Data from *Annual Report of the Attorney General of the United States* (1873–1939); *Annual Report of the Administrative Office of the United States Courts* (1940–90).

Note: All dates represent fiscal years. The caseload figures represent the total cases terminated by the court in that year plus cases pending at the end of the year. The National Mean represents the total caseload of all federal courts divided by the number of federal judicial districts.

[a]Figures represent only cases terminated in the year.

	1893	1894	1895	1896	1897
N.D.	164	121	165	173	192
M.D.	80	75	70	64	66
S.D.	34	45	63	54	47
National Mean	750	806	747	731	739

	1898	1899	1900	1901	1902
N.D.	204	172	152	171	203
M.D.	59	52	43	49	63
S.D.	48	61	44	87	74
National Mean	746	728	747	631	610

	1903	1904	1905	1906	1907
N.D.	395	446	441	473	507
M.D.	71	84	110	99	89
S.D.	70	85	86	87	87
National Mean	598	633	653	689	707

	1908	1909	1910	1911	1912
N.D.	n.a.	n.a.	n.a.	n.a.	466
M.D.	92	108	76	83	80
S.D.	87	82	72	83	87
National Mean	662	615	628	628	766

	1913	1914	1915	1916	1917
N.D.	395	323	352	271	245
M.D.	76	78	108	72	66
S.D.	103	89	98	91	140
National Mean	760	765	727	844	784

	1918	1919	1920	1921	1922
N.D.	274	271	263	281	423
M.D.	80	89	65	89	131
S.D.	120	106	121	142	121
National Mean	724	594	530	633	668

	1923	1924	1925	1926	1927
N.D.	367	281	330	294	275
M.D.	100	106	85	94	83
S.D.	112	109	95	88	97
National Mean	683	697	705	680	679

	1928	1929	1930	1931	1932
N.D.	279	259	270	328	341
M.D.	75	115	142	240	250
S.D.	87	131	78	91	80
National Mean	681	662	669	672	693

	1933	1934	1935	1936	1937
N.D.	393	342	285	232	202
M.D.	260	277	107	155	127
S.D.	71	75	77	80	77
National Mean	700	704	554	640	582

	1938	1939	1940	1941	1942
N.D.	201	213	183	249	243
M.D.	83	62	56	73	58
S.D.	68	52	37	42	35
National Mean	540	499	469	453	429

	1943	1944	1945	1946	1947
N.D.	247	213	166	200	279
M.D.	33	35	29	26	40
S.D.	32	43	37	42	43
National Mean	377	350	355	413	528

	1948	1949	1950	1951	1952
N.D.	222	249	270	235	336
M.D.	71	77	61	73	78
S.D.	64	74	79	56	76
National Mean	606	659	702	713	757

	1953	1954	1955	1956	1957
N.D.	430	550	551	615	603
M.D.	82	81	75	96	117
S.D.	97	123	148	190	240
National Mean	837	881	904	943	940

	1958	1959	1960	1961	1962
N.D.	636	531	397	431	457
M.D.	159	110	95	111	113
S.D.	288	367	452	416	448
National Mean	974	940	906	919	980

	1963	1964	1965	1966	1967
N.D.	544	615	738	746	809
M.D.	150	207	251	371	324
S.D.	416	475	616	669	739
National Mean	1,013	1,054	1,097	1,146	1,176

	1968	1969	1970	1971	1972
N.D.	860	1,044	1,191	1,460	1,690
M.D.	297	377	399	454	526
S.D.	785	816	884	1,065	993
National Mean	1,222	1,284	1,391	1,517	1,583

	1973	1974	1975	1976	1977
N.D.	1,725	1,858	1,963	2,106	2,266
M.D.	605	588	697	789	838
S.D.	850	708	767	888	954
National Mean	1,604	1,658	1,813	1,961	2,088

	1978	1979	1980	1981	1982
N.D.	2,388	2,350	2,378	2,700	2,958
M.D.	823	988	1,072	1,302	1,540
S.D.	1,010	1,001	1,116	1,345	1,470
National Mean	2,163	2,293	2,388	2,591	2,786

	1983	1984	1985	1986	1987
N.D.	3,254	3,344	3,454	3,592	3,648
M.D.	1,774	1,778	1,405	1,431	1,507
S.D.	1,668	1,773	1,812	1,936	1,894
National Mean	3,122	3,315	3,457	3,612	3,737

	1988	1989	1990
N.D.	3,562	3,819	3,735
M.D.	1,892	1,991	2,105
S.D.	2,021	1,827	1,806
National Mean	3,826	3,840	3,736

Appendix E

Private Civil Cases, 1873–1932 (Dollars)

	1873[a]	1874[a]	1875[b]	1876[b]	1877[a]
N.D.	-	-	2,885	2,372	2,086
M.D.	14,855	-	100,418	157,311	1,479,145
S.D.	76,885	51,020	90,970	58,181	167,282

	1878[b]	1879[b]	1880[a]	1881[a]	1882[a]
N.D.	38,550	31,145	14,787	8,507	4,491
M.D.	205,941	155,612	44,881	359,624	210,216
S.D.	123,793	22,169	12,085	28,964	24,789

	1883[a]	1884[b]	1885[a]	1886[a]	1887[a]
N.D.	10,151	18,436	13,350	77,623	52,033
M.D.	61,748	41,384	74,277	49,383	35,134
S.D.	9, 134	34,082	11,776	42,884	27,719

	1888[b]	1889[a]	1890[a]	1891[b]	1892[b]
N.D.	31,604	20,892	146,761	39,401	164,972
M.D.	1,002,392	71,633	17,748	21,856	29,192
S.D.	12,491	58,438	51,869	2,950	1,425

Source: Data from *Annual Report of the Attorney General of the United States* (1873–1932).

Note: All dates represent fiscal year. Figures not available after 1932.

[a]Judgments for plaintiffs only.

[b]Aggregate judgements for plaintiffs and defendants.

	1893[b]	1894[a]	1895[a]	1896[a]	1897[b]
N.D.	84,849	11,023	19,513	23,295	1,008,682
M.D.	247,610	342,717	2,585,004	17,003	24,412
S.D.	2, 103	25,737	25,827	107,335	397,911

	1898[a]	1899[a]	1900[b]	1901[a]	1902[b]
N.D.	34,817	124,783	498,710	1,474,665	178,297
M.D.	377,250	57, 184	3,112	5,250	301,854
S.D.	678,988	7,689	3,823	14,385	24,195

	1903[b]	1904[a]	1905[b]	1906[a]	1907
N.D.	31,411	24,528	37,463	24,040	n.a.
M.D.	40,653	63,389	10,687	19,487	n.a.
S.D.	5,059	1,629	11,337	36,586	n.a.

	1908[a]	1909[b]	1910[b]	1911[a]	1912[b]
N.D.	-	-	-	-	59,491
M.D.	-	12,410	4,300	-	12,619
S.D.	105,731	58,998	4,474,657	47,484	82,020

	1913[a]	1914[a]	1915[a]	1916[a]	1917[a]
N.D.	55,816	82,633	57,895	114,836	115,313
M.D.	-	7,550	8,787	85,451	283,774
S.D.	18,652	46,969	299,944	26,106	26,326

	1918[a]	1919[b]	1920[a]	1921[b]	1922[b]
N.D.	77,953	271,708	294,553	238,229	196,064
M.D.	98,732	40,947	39,847	47,065	115,749
S.D.	16,044	73,763	104,406	53,729	67,143

	1923[b]	1924[a]	1925[b]	1926[b]	1927[b]
N.D.	2,315,484	179,339	352,789	885,622	468,373
M.D.	29,099	57,173	13,338	96,292	40,847
S.D.	174,587	153,727	135,555	12,484	71,328

	1928[a]	1929[a]	1930[a]	1931[b]	1932[a]
N.D.	207,225	946,919	166,187	359,550	446,994
M.D.	18,965	168,850	17,307	368,618	257,718
S.D.	90,085	53,734	38,641	26,192	56,527

Appendix F

Civil Suits, United States as a Party, 1873–1990

	1873	1874	1875	1876	1877
N.D.	57	63	169	113	46
M.D.	44	30	30	36	22
S.D.	79	10	24	20	15
National Mean	166	150	155	153	144

	1878	1879	1880	1881	1882
N.D.	70	28	407	134	69
M.D.	22	43	25	19	18
S.D.	19	37	41	39	14
National Mean	107	101	97	80	65

	1883	1884	1885	1886	1887
N.D.	32	19	129	104	117
M.D.	9	13	12	6	11
S.D.	25	113	69	89	113
National Mean	87	111	54	60	68

	1888	1889	1890	1891	1892
N.D.	195	345	396	21	55
M.D.	27	23	15	10	13
S.D.	101	76	53	14	11
National Mean	71	72	64	69	57

Source: Data from *Annual Report of the Attorney General of the United States* (1873–1939); *Annual Report of the Administrative Office of the United States Courts* (1940–90).

Note: All dates represent fiscal year. The caseload figures represent the total cases terminated by the court in that year plus cases pending at the end of the year. The National Mean represents the total caseload of all federal courts divided by the number of federal judicial districts.

	1893	1894	1895	1896	1897
N.D.	29	71	78	207	134
M.D.	14	46	68	31	28
S.D.	74	48	108	93	65
National Mean	51	52	70	144	133

	1898	1899	1900	1901	1902
N.D.	223	159	142	107	63
M.D.	74	24	24	47	43
S.D.	28	17	12	27	29
National Mean	121	60	102	82	82

	1903	1904	1905	1906	1907
N.D.	24	27	22	18	18
M.D.	45	42	9	9	15
S.D.	15	13	15	26	29
National Mean	62	55	55	51	60

	1908	1909	1910	1911	1912
N.D.	30	26	18	25	23
M.D.	16	26	19	23	48
S.D.	27	30	30	43	44
National Mean	81	89	87	91	104

	1913	1914	1915	1916	1917
N.D.	27	35	28	32	30
M.D.	28	27	20	14	19
S.D.	13	12	28	39	35
National Mean	110	330	385	343	180

	1918	1919	1920	1921	1922
N.D.	34	52	52	64	77
M.D.	22	22	18	20	16
S.D.	21	32	30	36	73
National Mean	138	142	136	184	229

	1923	1924	1925	1926	1927
N.D.	98	87	123	142	118
M.D.	21	59	50	60	40
S.D.	69	93	72	55	59
National Mean	266	308	365	406	404

	1928	1929	1930	1931	1932
N.D.	93	78	76	276	582
M.D.	47	36	97	135	276
S.D.	60	73	71	72	68
National Mean	408	472	506	513	609

	1933	1934	1935	1936	1937
N.D.	334	255	204	346	403
M.D.	295	148	162	127	68
S.D.	79	81	100	61	102
National Mean	572	371	318	313	261

	1938	1939	1940	1941	1942
N.D.	472	594	440	331	405
M.D.	63	79	86	118	83
S.D.	81	172	75	94	97
National Mean	260	253	250	277	297

	1943	1944	1945	1946	1947
N.D.	420	429	381	342	367
M.D.	105	108	119	95	98
S.D.	153	140	133	177	115
National Mean	332	385	638	747	610

	1948	1949	1950	1951	1952
N.D.	166	249	275	273	337
M.D.	83	83	82	66	59
S.D.	114	107	119	129	156
National Mean	448	445	468	428	451

	1953	1954	1955	1956	1957
N.D.	374	473	370	444	427
M.D.	91	178	122	146	156
S.D.	190	194	182	175	170
National Mean	486	463	456	453	400

	1958	1959	1960	1961	1962
N.D.	461	450	491	469	352
M.D.	127	106	120	117	86
S.D.	164	152	165	167	154
National Mean	403	400	390	394	405

	1963	1964	1965	1966	1967
N.D.	401	492	567	504	427
M.D.	113	128	120	110	102
S.D.	166	175	253	231	293
National Mean	418	425	424	451	438

	1968	1969	1970	1971	1972
N.D.	340	377	384	419	487
M.D.	90	111	99	130	185
S.D.	197	198	207	192	176
National Mean	406	433	476	490	504

	1973	1974	1975	1976	1977
N.D.	458	445	619	880	959
M.D.	144	140	129	133	187
S.D.	151	151	121	128	150
National Mean	519	522	576	702	793

	1978	1979	1980	1981	1982
N.D.	983	839	932	1,218	1,902
M.D.	201	301	266	281	568
S.D.	193	216	191	228	455
National Mean	914	1,087	1,260	1,269	1,371

	1983	1984	1985	1986	1987
N.D.	2,475	3,275	3,314	2,368	1,405
M.D.	732	1,056	1,267	876	491
S.D.	759	952	1,001	674	439
National Mean	1,636	1,934	2,117	1,802	1,382

	1988	1989	1990
N.D.	1,436	1,211	1,066
M.D.	527	482	469
S.D.	550	531	480
National Mean	1,312	1,241	1,118

Appendix G

Civil Cases, United States as a Party, 1873–1932 (Dollars)

	1873	1874	1875	1876	1877
N.D.	-	-	7,387	800	-
M.D.	307	-	2,555	1,005	2,309
S.D.	15,966	212	23,379	16,213	33,883

	1878	1879	1880	1881	1882
N.D.	4,682	-	12,359	7,066	7,210
M.D.	16,648	7,009	1,340	617	14,368
S.D.	5,974	6,033	3,539	21,104	1,413

	1883	1884	1885	1886	1887
N.D.	1,029	372	6,896	7,350	1,459
M.D.	-	58	500	-	80
S.D.	2,260	1,526	897	453	1,060

	1888	1889	1890	1891	1892
N.D.	15,018	22,882	38,455	-	2,627
M.D.	365	-	549	8,630	-
S.D.	9,203	2,425	849	262	-

	1893	1894	1895	1896	1897
N.D.	-	5,215	4,077	6,802	7,987
M.D.	-	193	298	-	-
S.D.	3,264	782	1,101	3,546	2,696

Source: Data from *Annual Report of the Attorney General of the United States* (1873–1932).

Note: All dates represent fiscal year. All figures are judgment amounts in favor of U.S.

	1898	1899	1900	1901	1902
N.D.	10,367	3,608	2,792	703	4,304
M.D.	-	2,629	775	2,665	621
S.D.	419	125	1,294	9,721	1,810

	1903	1904	1905	1906	1907
N.D.	3,884	1,199	727	8,076	500
M.D.	536	1,133	50	116	3,414
S.D.	1,899	840	188	108	97

	1908	1909	1910	1911	1912
N.D.	800	1,100	185	1,146	-
M.D.	-	5,807	1,119	3,194	3,992
S.D.	2,155	275	3,394	2,253	10,733

	1913	1914	1915	1916	1917
N.D.	2,845	1,970	1,259	567	1,702
M.D.	434	800	500	325	1,485
S.D.	1,778	46	2,883	8,605	4,625

	1918	1919	1920	1921	1922
N.D.	24,039	5,800	1,358	5,959	1,663
M.D.	739	643	800	446	1,844
S.D.	8,669	1,020	273	716	650

	1923	1924	1925	1926	1927
N.D.	8,645	1,079	15,895	15,781	7,466
M.D.	468	2,875	1,480	100	100
S.D.	2,045	1,509	5,407	1,359	5,760

	1928	1929	1930	1931	1932
N.D.	44,839	48,693	4,072	218,145	1,006
M.D.	780	2,924	700	4,884	4,306
S.D.	1,126	10,570	26,971	36,260	39,004

Appendix H

Criminal Prosecutions, 1873–1990

	1873	1874	1875	1876	1877
N.D.		94	124	231	419
M.D.	80	71	174	175	387
S.D.	21	70	88	58	56
National Mean	200	192	208	220	222

	1878	1879	1880	1881	1882
N.D.	572	587	532	260	191
M.D.	480	388	266	303	306
S.D.	150	126	140	176	222
National Mean	275	312	245	260	167

	1883	1884	1885	1886	1887
N.D.	282	342	310	558	605
M.D.	391	466	400	389	413
S.D.	242	229	136	516	716
National Mean	196	261	225	287	289

	1888	1889	1890	1891	1892
N.D.	746	713	643	587	635
M.D.	511	706	424	474	369
S.D.	640	396	402	280	311
National Mean	307	303	338	387	384

Source: Data from *Annual Report of the Attorney General of the United States* (1873–1939); *Annual Report of the Administrative Office of the United States Courts* (1940–90).

Note: All dates represent fiscal year. The caseload figures represent the total cases terminated by the court in that year plus cases pending at the end of the year. The National Mean represents the total caseload of all federal courts divided by the number of federal judicial districts.

	1893	1894	1895	1896	1897
N.D.	1,223	860	1033	902	837
M.D.	414	664	918	851	848
S.D.	181	258	256	225	197
National Mean	424	440	506	500	383

	1898	1899	1900	1901	1902
N.D.	704	516	652	563	559
M.D.	506	400	273	306	276
S.D.	156	81	74	75	68
National Mean	355	363	356	327	309

	1903	1904	1905	1906	1907
N.D.	397	317	352	356	245
M.D.	362	303	318	223	276
S.D.	76	75	85	41	81
National Mean	315	343	362	346	369

	1908	1909	1910	1911	1912
N.D.	256	213	244	253	299
M.D.	145	92	128	189	264
S.D.	140	155	82	86	143
National Mean	264	281	286	283	298

	1913	1914	1915	1916	1917
N.D.	279	303	359	450	366
M.D.	466	382	315	280	295
S.D.	67	56	122	133	157
National Mean	307	333	343	354	348

	1918	1919	1920	1921	1922
N.D.	437	597	1,094	1,594	1,570
M.D.	473	455	274	172	147
S.D.	183	195	247	293	280
National Mean	549	738	968	1,200	1,351

	1923	1924	1925	1926	1927
N.D.	1,380	1,489	1,420	1,156	724
M.D.	179	221	328	381	215
S.D.	533	524	579	394	412
National Mean	1,560	1,580	1,584	1,311	1,141

	1928	1929	1930	1931	1932
N.D.	629	606	597	629	758
M.D.	253	238	254	430	751
S.D.	488	463	519	624	704
National Mean	1,305	1,284	1,302	1,314	1,319

	1933	1934	1935	1936	1937
N.D.	915	624	613	881	806
M.D.	974	223	295	317	380
S.D.	645	268	236	258	375
National Mean	1,161	605	491	521	500

	1938	1939	1940	1941	1942
N.D.	901	1,097	1,072	881	808
M.D.	228	309	282	292	320
S.D.	403	376	343	273	271
National Mean	486	491	467	445	457

	1943	1944	1945	1946	1947
N.D.	609	565	799	575	544
M.D.	204	215	261	303	236
S.D.	247	240	351	299	281
National Mean	516	552	542	475	468

	1948	1949	1950	1951	1952
N.D.	510	499	587	524	537
M.D.	197	198	170	158	164
S.D.	225	174	221	196	183
National Mean	445	468	490	511	497

	1953	1954	1955	1956	1957
N.D.	456	534	537	446	465
M.D.	175	152	202	173	165
S.D.	256	195	185	248	195
National Mean	503	561	502	418	397

	1958	1959	1960	1961	1962
N.D.	521	499	452	482	737
M.D.	161	159	209	189	172
S.D.	161	145	164	159	271
National Mean	407	405	395	417	540

	1963	1964	1965	1966	1967
N.D.	619	434	423	494	508
M.D.	238	193	180	204	201
S.D.	311	181	196	209	232
National Mean	552	446	466	465	472

	1968	1969	1970	1971	1972
N.D.	605	493	442	500	563
M.D.	206	218	276	261	347
S.D.	219	227	186	189	188
National Mean	496	540	621	689	782

	1973	1974	1975	1976	1977
N.D.	559	574	633	741	739
M.D.	364	308	320	266	307
S.D.	182	175	185	215	214
National Mean	722	683	701	675	651

	1978	1979	1980	1981	1982
N.D.	822	630	531	516	548
M.D.	346	289	254	318	385
S.D.	177	138	96	102	153
National Mean	559	511	464	485	511

	1983	1984	1985	1986	1987
N.D.	616	510	447	443	427
M.D.	338	334	292	271	322
S.D.	129	165	234	249	240
National Mean	559	590	632	679	721

	1988	1989	1990
N.D.	445	425	414
M.D.	359	381	478
S.D.	274	296	307
National Mean	743	784	849

Appendix I

Criminal Fines, Forfeitures, and Penalties, 1873–1932 (Dollars)

	1873	1874	1875	1876	1877
N.D.	n.a.	n.a.	-	2,800	13,500
M.D.	n.a.	n.a.	-	1,950	8,750
S.D.	n.a.	n.a.	494	2,246	847

	1878	1879	1880	1881	1882
N.D.	5,085	7,002	8,444	2,000	-
M.D.	3,333	7,195	2,840	2,514	6,542
S.D.	2,174	527	2,188	511	2,129

	1883	1884	1885	1886	1887
N.D.	3,230	7,461	20,562	15,000	14,653
M.D.	2,641	2,062	8,124	3,671	13,437
S.D.	944	2,177	42	2,597	6,442

	1888	1889	1890	1891	1892
N.D.	40,410	25,053	9,820	31,653	39,425
M.D.	23,392	23,940	8,436	10,570	11,458
S.D.	10,019	6,454	13,901	8,762	15,017

	1893	1894	1895	1896	1897
N.D.	23,075	28,500	34,013	10,950	10,933
M.D.	5,181	11,510	13,000	15,900	12,800
S.D.	1,990	5,484	2,617	11,660	8,671

Source: Data from *Annual Report of the Attorney General of the United States* (1873–1932).

Note: All dates represent fiscal year.

	1898	1899	1900	1901	1902
N.D.	15,100	15,510	35,125	9,841	14,092
M.D.	4,198	16,720	4,900	5,125	12,706
S.D.	14,716	4,937	6,484	6,951	7,349

	1903	1904	1905	1906	1907
N.D.	3,707	22,859	17,011	7,794	4,443
M.D.	18,375	42,731	14,865	5,200	46,052
S.D.	7,545	3,503	5,184	2,656	262,182

	1908	1909	1910	1911	1912
N.D.	9,884	7,775	8,885	6,767	13,737
M.D.	16,637	7,501	8,150	-	16,125
S.D.	7,766	8,767	2,095	4,070	2,399

	1913	1914	1915	1916	1917
N.D.	14,650	17,026	7,875	15,461	13,005
M.D.	26,286	7,175	8,806	9,850	7,750
S.D.	2,551	2,522	6,836	4,212	3,988

	1918	1919	1920	1921	1922
N.D.	13,134	15,686	25,322	75,270	39,261
M.D.	17,579	10,298	10,460	7,735	3,086
S.D.	2,460	3,733	7,221	4,876	4,278

	1923	1924	1925	1926	1927
N.D.	36,752	37,340	25,514	53,402	31,239
M.D.	4,246	2,470	4,175	8,067	1,715
S.D.	23,770	22,771	22,215	24,187	23,953

	1928	1929	1930	1931	1932
N.D.	34,205	27,871	19,224	47,089	12,506
M.D.	12,236	7,662	8,302	14,015	16,998
S.D.	36,678	31,442	18,394	23,638	21,099

Appendix J

Appeals to Court of Appeals, 1873–1990

	1873	1874	1875	1876	1877
N.D.	-	-	-	-	-
M.D.	-	-	-	-	-
S.D.	-	-	-	-	-

	1878	1879	1880	1881	1882
N.D.	-	-	-	-	-
M.D.	-	-	-	-	-
S.D.	-	1	-	-	-

	1883	1884	1885	1886	1887
N.D.	-	-	-	-	-
M.D.	-	-	-	-	-
S.D.	-	-	-	-	-

	1888	1889	1890	1891	1892
N.D.	-	-	-	-	-
M.D.	-	-	-	-	-
S.D.	1	2	1[a]	-	1[b]

Source: Data from *Annual Report of the Attorney General of the United States* (1873–1939); *Annual Report of the Administrative Office of the United States Courts* (1940–90).

Note: All dates represent fiscal year. Due to different reporting methods, comparable Total D.C. Appeals and Total for Circuit statistics are available only beginning in 1939.

[a]Appealed from District to Supreme Court.

[b]Appealed from Circuit to Circuit Court of Appeals.

	1893	1894	1895	1896	1897[c]
N.D.	-	-	-	1	2
M.D.	-	1	-	-	5
S.D.	-	-	-	-	-

	1898[c]	1899	1900	1901[c]	1902
N.D.	19	-	-	-	-
M.D.	1	-	-	1	-
S.D.	-	-	-	-	-

	1903	1904	1905	1906	1907
N.D.	-	-	1	-	-
M.D.	-	-	-	-	-
S.D.	-	-	-	-	-

	1908	1909	1910	1911	1912
N.D.	-	-	-	-	-
M.D.	-	1	-	-	-
S.D.	1	-	-	-	1

	1913	1914	1915	1916	1917
N.D.	-	-	-	-	-
M.D.	-	-	-	-	-
S.D.	-	1	-	1	1

	1918	1919	1920	1921	1922
N.D.	-	-	-	-	-
M.D.	-	-	-	-	-
S.D.	-	-	-	-	1

	1923	1924	1925	1926	1927
N.D.	-	2	1	1	1
M.D.	-	-	-	-	-
S.D.	1	-	-	-	-

[c]Appealed to Circuit Court or Circuit Court of Appeals.

	1928	1929	1930	1931	1932
N.D.	2	1	3	1	1
M.D.	1	-	-	-	-
S.D.	-	2	3	1	-

	1933	1934	1935	1936	1937
N.D.	n.a.	n.a.	n.a.	n.a.	n.a.
M.D.	n.a.	n.a.	n.a.	n.a.	n.a.
S.D.	n.a.	n.a.	n.a.	n.a.	n.a.

	1938	1939	1940	1941	1942
N.D.	n.a.	7	20	15	8
M.D.	n.a.	1	3	6	4
S.D.	n.a.	7	5	8	6
Total D.C. Appeals[d]		272	337	306	291
Total for Circuit[e]		327	398	406	382

	1943	1944	1945	1946	1947
N.D.	13	18	15	13	22
M.D.	3	3	4	8	3
S.D.	5	6	6	3	5
Total D.C. Appeals	261	262	261	257	274
Total for Circuit	347	354	329	301	324

	1948	1949	1950	1951	1952
N.D.	14	15	8	7	17
M.D.	2	5	5	5	8
S.D.	7	6	4	1	8
Total D.C. Appeals	352	358	322	340	384
Total for Circuit	394	453	408	421	452

[d]Appeals from District Courts.

[e]Appeals from all District Courts, Tax Courts, NLRB, and other boards and commissions, as well as original proceedings filed in Court of Appeals.

	1953	1954	1955	1956	1957
N.D.	22	19	19	17	15
M.D.	1	5	6	3	7
S.D.	2	4	8	5	8
Total D.C. Appeals	404	418	463	407	468
Total for Circuit	481	510	527	511	595

	1958	1959	1960	1961	1962
N.D.	17	18	23	22	22
M.D.	9	10	7	18	12
S.D.	9	5	14	15	16
Total D.C. Appeals	441	470	468	526	562
Total for Circuit	530	555	577	630	715

	1963	1964	1965	1966	1967
N.D.	22	32	29	38	59
M.D.	16	31	21	20	20
S.D.	26	22	31	36	30
Total D.C. Appeals	722	869	926	935	1,023
Total for Circuit	874	1,033	1,065	1,093	1,173

	1968	1969	1970	1971	1972
N.D.	59	64	83	92	107
M.D.	37	27	42	31	49
S.D.	41	42	50	74	84
Total D.C. Appeals	1,214	1,504	1,832	2,116	2,576
Total for Circuit	1,378	1,763	2,014	2,316	2,864

	1973	1974	1975	1976	1977
N.D.	90	144	145	173	158
M.D.	74	70	72	87	72
S.D.	67	84	63	55	60
Total D.C. Appeals	2,746	2,981	2,964	3,196	3,040
Total for Circuit	2,964	3,079	3,292	3,629	3,563

	1978	1979	1980	1981	1982[f]
N.D.	177	175	168	210	210
M.D.	83	69	56	80	69
S.D.	63	79	94	126	93
Total D.C. Appeals	3,026	3,229	3,682	4,206	2,326
Total for Circuit	3,507	3,854	4,225	4,914	2,556

	1983	1984	1985	1986	1987
N.D.	300	321	407	414	466
M.D.	143	202	175	183	184
S.D.	128	203	174	184	181
Total D.C. Appeals	2,818	3,205	3,620	3,617	3,578
Total for Circuit	3,078	3,489	3,923	3,929	3,875

	1988	1989	1990
N.D.	379	421	408
M.D.	182	188	243
S.D.	156	191	221
Total D.C. Appeals	3,648	4,006	4,234
Total for Circuit	3,924	4,346	4,476

[f]Prior to 1982, statistics are for 5th Circuit; from 1982 statistics are for 11th Circuit.

Appendix K

Bankruptcy Caseload, 1908–1990

	1908	1909	1910	1911	1912
N.D.	848	1,306	19[a]	2,721	3,591
M.D.	502	452	484	394	404
S.D.	188	214	218	215	235

	1913	1914	1915	1916	1917
N.D.	3,925	3,936	4,245	4,338	5,069
M.D.	422	423	525	518	768
S.D.	308	320	401	434	294

	1918	1919	1920	1921	1922
N.D.	5,446	4,761	4,327	4,858	3,941
M.D.	625	520	505	576	682
S.D.	248	102	137	201	265

	1923	1924	1925	1926	1927
N.D.	3,683	3,807	4,166	4,501	4,211
M.D.	685	773	745	694	824
S.D.	276	342	324	298	309

Source: Data from *Annual Report of the Attorney General of the United States* (1873–1939); *Annual Report of the Administrative Office of the United States Courts* (1940–90).

Note: All dates represent fiscal year. Figures represent the total cases terminated by the court in that year plus cases pending at the end of the year.

[a]Reporting incomplete.

	1928	1929	1930	1931	1932
N.D.	4,314	4,806	6,494	7,271	6,706
M.D.	793	865	986	987	749
S.D.	323	356	445	568	519

	1933	1934	1935	1936	1937
N.D.	5,017	4,176	4,375	4,925	5,907
M.D.	602	468	637	721	730
S.D.	446	343	305	264	251

	1938	1939	1940	1941	1942
N.D.	8,320	10,170	11,378	13,532	15,056
M.D.	668	644	540	529	462
S.D.	258	328	251	322	355

	1943	1944	1945	1946	1947
N.D.	13,936	11,840	10,435	9,463	9,081
M.D.	356	251	227	287	395
S.D.	340	201	143	140	143

	1948	1949	1950	1951	1952
N.D.	11,045	14,921	15,681	18,475	18,863
M.D.	522	698	965	1,097	1,448
S.D.	128	190	263	302	361

	1953	1954	1955	1956	1957
N.D.	16,404	16,254	16,732	16,723	16,695
M.D.	1,092	1,222	1,238	1,119	1,014
S.D.	675	1,322	1,796	2,118	2,337

	1958	1959	1960	1961	1962
N.D.	16,831	16,548	14,815	15,233	15,505
M.D.	1,150	1,226	1,150	1,661	2,457
S.D.	2,402	2,566	2,176	2,781	3,477

	1963	1964	1965	1966	1967
N.D.	16,953	16,979	16,631	16,147	16,067
M.D.	2,966	3,377	3,695	3,921	3,996
S.D.	4,033	4,564	4,302	4,186	4,367

	1968	1969	1970	1971	1972
N.D.	16,071	15,707	15,778	15,188	13,946
M.D.	4,279	4,075	4,224	4,413	4,220
S.D.	4,363	4,259	4,147	4,236	3,876

	1973	1974	1975	1976	1977
N.D.	13,465	12,688	13,433	13,315	12,782
M.D.	3,810	3,639	4,050	3,982	3,905
S.D.	3,567	3,708	4,052	3,948	3,667

	1978	1979	1980	1981[b]	1982
N.D.	12,816	13,454	10,230	20,407	23,969
M.D.	3,695	3,719	2,756	6,115	7,497
S.D.	3,395	3,304	2,152	3,572	4,011

	1983	1984	1985	1986	1987
N.D.	26,563	20,927	21,970	24,737	28,643
M.D.	7,646	5,164	5,259	6,226	7,093
S.D.	4,499	3,416	3,761	4,238	4,938

	1988	1989	1990
N.D.	30,273	33,349	38,524
M.D.	8,246	9,740	11,347
S.D.	5,690	5,748	5,424

[b]From 1981, statistics reflect number of cases originally filed under the Bankruptcy Act and reopened after Bankruptcy Reform Act of 1978.

Notes

Preface

1. Erwin C. Surrency, *A History of the Federal Courts* (New York, 1987); Russell R. Wheeler and Cynthia Harrison, *Creating the Federal Judicial System* (Washington, D.C., 1989); Kermit L. Hall, *The Politics of Justice: Lower Federal Judicial Selection and the Second Party System, 1829–61* (Lincoln, Neb., 1979); Erwin C. Surrency, "Federal District Court Judges and the History of Their Courts," 40 F.R.D. 139 (1967); Tony Freyer, *Forums of Order: The Federal Courts and Business in American History* (Greenwich, Conn., 1979); Robert A. Carp and C. K. Rowland, *Policymaking and Politics in the Federal District Courts* (Knoxville, 1983); Richard A. Posner, *The Federal Courts: Crisis and Reform* (Cambridge, 1985).
2. Kermit L. Hall, *The Magic Mirror: Law in American History* (New York, 1989); Lawrence M. Friedman, *A History of American Law* (New York, 1985).
3. Edward A. Purcell, Jr., *Litigation and Inequality: Federal Diversity Jurisdiction in Industrial America, 1870–1958* (New York, 1992); Tony Freyer, *Harmony & Dissonance: The Swift & Erie Cases in American Federalism* (New York, 1981); Freyer, *Forums of Order*; Tony Freyer, *The Little Rock Crisis: A Constitutional Interpretation* (Westport, Conn., 1984).
4. For the federal appellate courts, see Jeffrey B. Morris, *Federal Justice in the Second Circuit: A History of the United States Courts in New York, Connecticut, and Vermont, 1787–1987* (New York, 1987); Marvin Schick, *Learned Hand's Court* (Baltimore, 1970); J. Woodford Howard, *Courts of Appeals in the Federal Judicial System: A Study of the Second, Fifth, and District of Columbia Circuits* (Princeton, 1981), and *History of the United States Court of Appeals for the District of Columbia Circuit in the Country's Bicentennial Year* (Washington, D.C., 1977); Stephen B. Presser, *Studies in the History of the United States Courts of the Third Circuit* (Washington, D.C., 1982); Harvey C. Couch, *A History of the Fifth Circuit, 1891–1981* (Washington, D.C., 1984); Judicial Conference of the United States, *A History of the United States Court of Appeals for the Eighth Circuit* (Washington, D.C., 1977). On the establishment of the Eleventh Circuit, see Deborah J. Barrow and Thomas G. Walker, *A Court Divided: The Fifth Circuit Court of Appeals and the Politics of Judicial Reform* (New Haven, 1988). On specialized federal courts, see Henry J. Bourguinon, *The First Federal Court: The Federal Appellate Prize Court of the American Revolution, 1775–1787* (Philadelphia, 1977); Giles S. Rich, *A Brief History of the United States Court of Customs and Patent Appeals* (Washington, D.C., 1980); Marion T. Bennett, Wilson Cowen, and Philip Nichols, Jr., *The United States Court of Claims: A History*, 2 vols.

(Washington, D.C., 1976–1978). On the federal district courts, see Kermit L. Hall and Eric W. Rise, *From Local Courts to National Tribunals: The Federal District Courts of Florida, 1821–1990* (Brooklyn, 1991); Charles M. Hough, *The United States District Court for the Southern District of New York* (New York, 1934); George Cosgrave, *Early California Justice: The History of the United States District Court of California* (San Francisco, 1948); Matthew F. McGuire, *An Anecdotal History of the United States District Court for the District of Columbia* (Washington, D.C., 1977); Richard C. Heaton, "A Study of the Federal Courts for North Dakota," *Dakota Law Review* 4 (December 1932): 133–74; Calvin Chestnut, "The Work of the Federal Court of Maryland," *Maryland Historical Magazine* 37 (December 1942): 361–77; Irwin S. Rhodes, "The History of the United States District Court for the Southern District of Ohio," *University of Cincinnati Law Review* 24 (Summer 1955): 338–54; George Templar, "The Federal Judiciary of Kansas," *Kansas Historical Quarterly* 37 (Spring 1971): 1–14; Rebecca W. Thomson, "The Federal District Court in Wyoming, 1890–1982," *Annals of Wyoming* 54 (Spring 1982): 10–25; Mary K. Bonsteel Tachau, *Federal Courts in the Early Republic: Kentucky, 1789–1816* (Princeton, 1978); Dwight F. Henderson, *Courts for a New Nation* (Washington, D.C., 1971); Curtis P. Nettels, "The Mississippi Valley and the Federal Judiciary, 1807–1837," *Mississippi Valley Historical Review* 12 (September 1925): 202–26; Richard E. Ellis, *The Jeffersonian Crisis: Courts and Politics in the Young Republic* (New York, 1971); James W. Hulse, "Making Law in the Great Basin: The Evolution of the Federal Law in Nevada, 1855–1905," *Western Legal History* 1 (Summer-Fall 1988): 135–62; Monique C. Lillard, "The Federal Court in Idaho, 1889–1907: The Appointment and Tenure of James H. Beatty, Idaho's First Federal District Court Judge," *Western Legal History* 2 (Winter-Spring 1989): 34–78. Also see John S. Goff, "The Organization of the Federal District Court in Arizona," *American Journal of Legal History* 8 (April 1964): 172–79; David S. Clark, "Adjudication to Administration: A Statistical Analysis of Federal District Courts in the Twentieth Century," *Southern California Law Review* 55 (November 1981): 69–152; J. W. Peltason, *Fifty-Eight Lonely Men: Southern Federal Judges and School Desegregation* (New York, 1961); Tinsley E. Yarborough, *A Passion for Justice: J. Waties Waring and Civil Rights* (New York, 1987); Staff of the National Archives Regional Archives System, "Fighting Words: Finding the First Amendment in Lower Federal Court Records," *Journal of American History* 78 (June 1991): 240–48; Charles L. Zeldon, *Justice Lies in the District, the U.S. District Court, Southern District of Texas, 1902–1960* (College Station, Texas, 1993); Frank R. Kemerer, *William Wayne Justice: A Judicial Biography* (Austin, Texas, 1991); Jack Bass, *Taming the Storm: The Life and Times of Judge Frank M. Johnson, Jr. and the South's Fight over Civil Rights* (New York, 1993); Tinsley E. Yarborough, *Judge Frank Johnson and Human Rights in Alabama* (Tuscaloosa, 1981); Frank Sikora, *The Judge: The Life and Opinions of Alabama's Frank M. Johnson, Jr.* (Montgomery, 1992); Robert F. Kennedy, Jr., *Judge Frank M. Johnson, Jr.* (New York, 1978); Christian G. Fritz, *Federal Justice in California: The Court of Ogden Hoffman, 1851–1891* (Lincoln, Neb., 1991).

Chapter I

1. Alexis de Tocqueville, *Democracy in America* (New York, 1969), 276.
2. Carp and Rowland, *Policymaking and Politics;* Harold W. Chase, *Federal Judges: The Appointing Process* (Minneapolis, 1972); Martin H. Redish, *The Federal Courts in the Political Order Judicial Jurisdiction and American Political Theory* (Durham, North Carolina, 1991); Freyer, *Forums of Order;* Freyer, *Harmony & Dissonance;* Hall, *The Magic Mirror,* 75–76, 233–35, 282–84, 306–07; Hall, *The Politics of Justice;* Friedman, *A History of American Law,* 138–39, 142, 668–70; Christian G. Fritz, *Federal Justice in California: The Court of Ogden Hoffman, 1851–1891* (Lincoln, Neb., 1991); James Willard Hurst, *The Growth of American Law: The Law Makers* (Boston, 1950).
3. Tocqueville, *Democracy in America,* 143, 148, 149, 99.
4. Redish, *Federal Courts in the Political Order;* Freyer, *Forums of Order;* Carp and Rowland, *Policymaking and Politics.*
5. Hall, *Politics of Justice;* Kermit L. Hall, "The Children of the Cabins: The Lower Federal Judiciary, Modernization, and the Political Culture, 1789–1899," in Kermit L. Hall, ed., *The Judiciary in American Life: Major Historical Interpretations* (New York, 1987), 163–211.
6. Hall, *Politics of Justice,* 156.
7. As quoted, Carp and Rowland, *Policymaking and Politics,* 29.
8. Ibid., 29, 51, 84, 87, 89, 90.
9. Ibid., 1–24, 145–71.
10. Herbert M. Kritzer, *The Justice Broker: Lawyers and Ordinary Litigation* (New York, 1990), 13, 14, 15.
11. Hall, *Politics of Justice,* 82–83, 121, 145–47.
12. Ibid.; Swisher, *Taney Period,* 248–49, 251, 255–56, 267.
13. J. Mills Thornton, III, *Register of Lawyers United States District Court for Middle District of Alabama For Period of About 1835–1866* (Montgomery, 1979), i-v, copy located in Law Library, University of Alabama School of Law; *Journal,* Federal District and Circuit Court of the Northern District of Alabama, 1820–1888. Original in possession of the clerk of the United States Court, Northern District of Alabama.
14. For the jurisprudential assumptions, see G. Edward White, *The Marshall Court and Cultural Change, 1815–35: A History of the Supreme Court of the United States,* 11 vols. (New York, 1988), Vols. III-IV.
15. Hall, *Politics of Justice,* 173. See also Hall, "Children of the Cabins," 163–211.
16. General works on Alabama that provide the contextual setting of legal culture are Joseph G. Baldwin, *The Flush Times of Alabama and Mississippi* (New York, 1957); Thomas Perkins Abernethy, *The Formative Period in Alabama, 1815–1828* (Tuscaloosa, 1990); J. Mills Thornton, III, *Politics and Power in a Slave Society, Alabama, 1800–1860* (Baton Rouge, 1978). The basic biographical material is taken from Thomas McAdory Owen, *History of Alabama and Dictionary of Alabama Biography,* 4 vols. (Birmingham, 1888).
17. Abernethy, *Formative Period,* 58–63, 172; Thornton, *Politics and Power,* 10–11, 14; Owen, *History of Alabama,* 4:1640.

18. Abernethy, *Formative Period*, 60; Hall, *Politics of Justice*, 82–83; Owen, *History of Alabama*, 3:420–21.

19. Hall, *Politics of Justice*, 82–83; Owen, *History of Alabama*, 3:646–47; Thornton, *Politics and Power*, 28–31, 34, 43, 55, 87, 110, 113, 126, 244.

20. Thornton, *Politics and Power*; Hall, *Politics of Justice*; Owen, *History of Alabama*.

21. Thornton, *Politics and Power*, 138, 173n, 176, 254–56, 259, 261, 455; Hall, *Politics of Justice*, 121, 122, 145, 146; William Gillette, "John Campbell," in Leon Friedman and Fred L. Israel, eds., *The Justices of the United States Supreme Court 1789–1969, Their Lives and Major Opinions*, 4 vols. (New York, 1969), 2:927–62.

22. Hall, *Politics of Justice*, 144–47; Owen, *History of Alabama*, 4:945, 947.

23. Hall, *Politics of Justice*, as quoted, 145.

24. Ibid., as quoted, 146; Owen, *History of Alabama*, vol. 4.

25. Hall, *Politics of Justice*; Hall, "Children of the Cabins," 163–228.

26. Baldwin, *Flush Times*; Abernethy, *Formative Period*; Thornton, *Politics and Power*; Owen, *History of Alabama*.

27. Owen, *History of Alabama*, 1:249, 252; 2:926, 1024. See also Thornton, *Politics and Power*.

28. Baldwin, *Flush Times*; Abernethy, *Formative Period*; Thornton, *Politics and Power*; Owen, *History of Alabama*; Hall, *Politics of Justice*; Hall, "Children of the Cabins."

29. Baldwin, *Flush Times*; Abernethy, *Formative Period*; Thornton, *Politics and Power*; Owen, *History of Alabama*; Hall, *Politics of Justice*; Hall, "Children of the Cabins."

30. Baldwin, *Flush Times*; Abernethy, *Formative Period*; Thornton, *Politics and Power*; Owen, *History of Alabama*; Hall, *Politics of Justice*; Hall, "Children of the Cabins."

31. Compare Thornton, *Politics and Power* generally, and Hall, *Politics of Power*, 82–83, 121, 144–47.

32. Baldwin, *Flush Times*; Abernethy, *Formative Period*; Owen, *History of Alabama*; Hall, *Politics of Justice*; Gillette, "John Campbell"; Frank Otto Gattell, "John McKinley," in Friedman and Israel, *Supreme Court Justices*, 1:769–77; Carl B. Swisher, *The Taney Period 1836–1864: History of the Supreme Court of the United States*, 11 vols. (New York, 1974), 22–26, 31–36, 58–64, 225, 248–74, 637, 825–30, 837; Thornton, *Politics and Power*, 18, 22, 23, 26, 31, 126.

33. Baldwin, *Flush Times*; Abernethy, *Formative Period*; Owen, *History of Alabama*; Hall, *Politics of Justice*; Gillette, "John Campbell"; Frank Otto Gattell, "John McKinley," in Friedman and Israel, *Supreme Court Justices*, 1:769–77; Carl B. Swisher, *The Taney Period 1836–1864: History of the Supreme Court of the United States*, 11 vols. (New York, 1974), 22–26, 31–36, 58–64, 225, 248–74, 637, 825–30, 837; Thornton, *Politics and Power*, 18; 22, 23, 26, 31, 126.

34. Gattell, "McKinley," 769–77; Swisher, *Taney Period*, 249–65, 272, the assessment of McKinley is quoted at 242.

35. Campbell to Calhoun quoted in Swisher, *Taney Period*, 242–43; Gillette, "Campbell," 927–39.

36. Wythe Holt, " 'To Establish Justice': Politics, the Judiciary Act of 1789, and the Invention of the Federal Courts," *Duke Law Journal* (December 1989), 1421–1531.

37. Quoted in Gattell, "McKinley," 773; "Petition of John McKinley Praying an alteration in the Judicial Circuits of the United States," S. Doc. no. 99, 27th Cong., 2d sess. 3 (1842); *Cong. Globe*, 27th Cong., 2d sess. 781 (1842); Swisher, *Taney Period*, 248–49, 251, 255–56, 267; S. Rep. no. 50, 25th Cong., 3d sess. 35 (1839).
38. *Cong. Globe*, 27th Cong., 2d sess. 781 (1842); "Petition of McKinley" 3.
39. Swisher, *Taney Period*, 271–72, 289–91.
40. Ibid., as quoted, 290.
41. Gattell, "McKinley"; "Petition of McKinley"; Swisher, *Taney Period*.
42. Swisher, *Taney Period*.
43. Gattell, "McKinley"; "Petition of McKinley"; Swisher, *Taney Period*. See also Hall, *Politics of Justice*, 144–47.
44. Holt, " 'To Establish Justice.' " See also Freyer, *Forums of Order*, 53–98; Freyer, *Harmony & Dissonance*, 1–43.
45. Thornton, *Register of Lawyers; Journal*, 1820–1888.
46. White, *Marshall Court*, 77–156, 927–75; Freyer, *Harmony & Dissonance*, 1–43.
47. Freyer, *Harmony & Dissonance*, 1–43; White, *Marshall Court*, 77–156, 927–75.
48. As quoted in Freyer, *Harmony & Dissonance*, 24–25.
49. Ibid.
50. Quoted in White, *Marshall Court*, 742.
51. Ibid.
52. *Journal*, Northern District.
53. White, *Marshall Court*; Freyer, *Harmony & Dissonance*; Swisher, *Taney Period*, 271–72, 289–91.
54. Holt, " 'To Establish Justice' "; Freyer, *Forums of Order*; Freyer, *Harmony & Dissonance*.
55. As quoted in Swisher, *Taney Period*, 272.
56. Benjamin Porter, "Law of Debtor and Creditor in Alabama," *Hunt's Merchants' Magazine* 15 (December 1846): 580.
57. Benjamin Porter, "The Law of Bankruptcy," *Hunt's Merchants' Magazine* 28 (April 1853): 67.
58. For the ultimately unsettled status of the law of commercial paper in Alabama, see *Fenoville v. Hamilton*, 35 Ala. 319 (1859); *Bank of Mobile v. Hall*, 6 Ala. 639 (1844). For analogical evidence, see Jerome A. Hoffman, "Alabama's Scintilla Rule," *Alabama Law Review* 28 (Summer 1977): 592–640.
59. *Journal*, Northern District.
60. Baldwin, *Flush Times*, 176.
61. Figures drawn from an analysis of docket books for the federal district and circuit court of the Southern District for the years 1822, 1824, 1825, 1834, 1837, 1846, 1856, located at National Archives, Southeast Region, East Point, Georgia, Record Group 21. We thank Peter Wonders for his assistance, as well as the guidance of the archive's Mary Hawkins.
62. Ibid., compare to the less systematic record of the *Journal*, Northern District; Josiah Bond, "Laws Relative To Debtor and Creditor," *Hunt's Merchants' Magazine* 6 (February 1842): 155, 156.

63. Docket books, Southern District.
64. Ibid.
65. Porter, "Law of Debtor and Creditor" and "Law of Bankruptcy."
66. William E. Davis, "Brief History Outline of United States District Court Northern District of Alabama" (unpublished manuscript, 1975), located in the office of the court's clerk. See also "History of Federal Courts, Alabama," 40 *Federal Rules Decision*, 153–57; Mary Hawkins, "History of the Southern District of Alabama" and "History of the Middle District of Alabama" (unpublished manuscripts), National Archives, Southeast Region, East Point, Georgia.
67. For theoretical framework of courtroom work group, see Kritzer, *Justice Broker*, 68–76; Thornton, *Register of Lawyers*; *Journal*, Northern District; Baldwin, *Flush Times*, 175–76.
68. Bond, "Debtor and Creditor," 155, 156.
69. Davis, "Brief History Outline"; "History of Federal Courts"; Hawkins, "History of Southern District"; Hawkins, "History of Middle District."
70. Davis, "Brief History Outline"; "History of Federal Courts"; Hawkins, "History of Southern District"; Hawkins, "History of Middle District."
71. As quoted, Swisher, *Taney Period*, 248–49.
72. Ibid.; White, *Marshall Court*; Freyer, *Harmony & Dissonance*.
73. Thornton, *Register of Lawyers*; *Journal*, Northern District.
74. Baldwin, *Flush Times*, 175.
75. H. Rep., no. 69, 17th Cong., 2d sess. 87 (1823), quote at 3.
76. Ibid.
77. Ibid., 2.
78. Ibid., 2, 3.
79. Davis, "Brief History Outline"; "History of Federal Courts"; Hawkins, "History of Southern District"; Hawkins, "History of Middle District."
80. See *U.S. v. Six Boxes Claret Wine* (1819); *Browner v. Flinn* (1822); *Bledzoo v. Cook* (1824); *U.S. v. Barney* (1837); *Hunt v. Brack* (1846); *Gaines v. Hennen* (1856). These are manuscript case files located in Record Group 21, National Archives, Southeast Region, East Point, Georgia.
81. White *Marshall Court*, 427–740; Swisher, *Taney Period*.
82. White, *Marshall Court*, 427–84; Swisher, *Taney Period*, 112, 427–84, 866–70.
83. Swisher, *Taney Period*; White, *Marshall Court*.
84. 12 How. 443 (1851). For the debate over the interpretation of the 1845 statute and the impact of *Genesee Chief*, see Swisher, *Taney Period*, 444–47. The market implication can be inferred, I think; see Freyer, *Forums of Order*, 1–35.
85. The *Steamer Oregon v. Rocca*, 18 How. 570 (1855).
86. White, *Marshall Court*; Swisher, *Taney Period*.
87. 20 How. 296 (1857).
88. Ibid., 296, 321.
89. Ibid., 341.
90. Baldwin, *Flush Times*; Abernethy, *Formative Period*; Thornton, *Politics and Power*; Owen, *History of Alabama*.

91. White, *Marshall Court*; Freyer, *Harmony & Dissonance*.
92. White, *Marshall Court*, 677–703, 739–40, 971; Swisher, *Taney Period*, 691–707.
93. Swisher, *Taney Period*; White, *Marshall Court*.
94. *The Merino*, 9 Wheaton 391 (1824).
95. Ibid.
96. *The Emily and the Caroline*, 9 Wheaton 391 (1824); *The St. Jago de Cuba*, 9 Wheaton 408 (1824); White, *Marshall Court*, 677–703, 739–40, 971.
97. Hall, *Politics of Justice*, 144–47.
98. 25 Fed. Cas. 1375 (No. 15239) (D.C. S.D. Ala. 1860), 1376.
99. Ibid., 1378–79.
100. 12 How. 443 (1851); Swisher, *Taney Period*; Freyer, *Forums of Order*; 18 How. 570 (1855); White, *Marshall Court*; 20 How. 296 (1857).
101. For the ratio of slaves and free blacks to whites in Alabama generally, see Gary Mills, "Slavery in Alabama," in Randall M. Miller and John David Smith, eds., *Dictionary of Afro-American Slavery* (New York, 1988), 38–45. For Mobile, see Owen, *History of Alabama*.
102. 26 Fed. Cas. 227 (No. 15, 329) (C.C.S.D. Ala. 1860), 230–31.
103. Ibid. For larger issues, see Swisher, *Taney Period*, 691–707.
104. Compare White, *Marshall Court*, 677–703, 739–40 on national trends to Abernethy, *Formative Period*, 52–63, 103–10, and Thornton, *Politics and Power*, 1–57, on state trends.
105. Hall, *Politics of Justice*, 144–46; Swisher, *Taney Period* 691–707.
106. Thornton, *Politics and Power*; Hall, *Politics of Justice*; Gillette, "John Campbell"; Swisher, *Taney Period*.
107. *Fenoville v. Hamilton* (1859) and *Bank of Mobile v. Hall* (1844) suggest the local orientation of Alabama's state courts, and Freyer, *Forums of Order*, 1–72, indicates the extent to which the same held true elsewhere. What deserves attention here is the degree to which the states' protectionist policies and action existed amid a network of credit transactions among local and out-of-state debtors and creditors. The extent of this interstate credit network is suggested by the manuscript case files cited earlier, and the U.S. Supreme Court cases discussed below. Bond, "Debtor and Creditor," and Baldwin, *Flush Times*, suggest further the scope of this network, which can be inferred also from Abernethy, *Formative Period*, 72–119, and Thornton, *Politics and Power*, 268–89. The point is that although provincialism often prevailed in state law, it coexisted with counterpressures favoring the persistence of the interstate credit network. Thus the commercial cases suggest that the federal courts' response reflected a tension among competing interests rather than equivocal support for either local or national interests.
108. *Journal*, Northern District; White, *Marshall Court*, 593–673, 896–98; Swisher, *Taney Period*, 172–73, 333–34, 746–809.
109. The "dominance" of local factors must be understood within the context of conflicting pressures, so that in such areas as the credit network, local and interstate interests often may be seen as coincident or complementary, rather than opposed to each other.

110. *Bank of Augusta v. Earle*, 13 Pet. 519 (1839). Swisher, *Taney Period*, 115–21, 464–72; Freyer, *Forums of Order*, 28–30, are useful overviews of the litigation and its impact.
111. *Tombigbee R.R. Co. v. Kneeland*, 4 How. 16 (1846).
112. 13 Pet 519 (1839), 592.
113. *Tombigbee R.R. Co. v. Kneeland.*
114. Gattell, "McKinley"; Swisher, *Taney Period.*
115. As Crawford's decision in the *Tombigbee R.R. Co.* case suggested, Alabama continued its protectionist policy, despite the Supreme Court's decision in *Bank of Augusta v. Earle*. See generally James Crawford King, Jr., " 'Content with Being': Nineteenth-Century Southern Attitudes Toward Economic Development" (Ph.D. thesis, University of Alabama, 1985), 97–143.
116. White, *Marshall Court*, 794–829; Freyer, *Forums of Order*, 36–98; Freyer, *Harmony & Dissonance*, 1–43; Swisher, *Taney Period*, 320–38.
117. The manuscript case files indicate the degree to which Alabama's local debtors and creditors who sued in federal court were part of a credit network that extended across state borders. This network made it difficult if not impossible to distinguish local from nonlocal interests, at least insofar as strict market imperatives were concerned. The local lawyers representing and the federal judges adjudicating these interests undoubtedly viewed the interests in the same way.
118. Freyer, *Forums of Order*, 36–52.
119. Ibid., 36–72.
120. Ibid., 53–98; Freyer, *Harmony & Dissonance*, 1–43; *Swift v. Tyson*, 16 Pet. 1 (1842).
121. *Fenoville v. Hamilton; Bank of Mobile v. Hall;* Hoffman, "Alabama's Scintilla Rule."
122. *Parish v. Murphee*, 13 How. 92 (1851); *Harris v. Robinson*, 4 How. 336 (1846); *Dennistown v. Stewart*, 18 How. 565 (1855); *Hinkle v. Wanzer*, 17 How. 353 (1854); *Smyth v. Strader Pevine & Co.*, 12 How. 327 (1851); *Rogers v. Lindsey*, 13 How. 441 (1851); *Smyth v. Strader*, 4 How. 404 (1846); *Matheson's Adms. v. Grant's Adm.*, 2 How. 263 (1844); *Ellis v. Taylor's Administrator*, 1 How. 197 (1843); *Brander v. Phillips*, 16 Pet. 121 (1842); *Fowler v. Brantly*, 14 Pet. 318 (1840); *Edmonds v. Crenshaw*, 14 Pet. 166 (1840); *Withers v. Greene*, 9 How. 213 (1850).
123. 16 Pet. 121.
124. 1 How. 197.
125. 9 How. 213.
126. Freyer, *Harmony & Dissonance*, 20–36, 45–50.
127. 9 How. 226.
128. Ibid., 222.
129. 9 How. 220. Compare *Fenoville v. Hamilton* and *Bank of Mobile v. Hall.*
130. For this consensus reflected by the justices of the Supreme Court who decided *Swift* and the wider legal culture, see Freyer, *Harmony & Dissonance*, 1–43.
131. Ibid., 4, 14–16, 18–23, 26, 30, 31, 33–43.
132. Ibid., Peter DuPonceau, as quoted, 35.
133. Ibid., John William Wallace, as quoted, 20–21.
134. Kritzer, *Justice Broker;* Thornton, *Register of Lawyers; Journal*, Northern District; case files, Southeast Region.

135. Freyer, *Harmony & Dissonance*.
136. White, *Marshall Court*, 741–94; Swisher, *Taney Period*, 172–73, 333–34, 746–809; Freyer, *Harmony & Dissonance*, 28–30. These works acknowledge the significance of Marshall Court's decision in *Wayman v. Southard*, 10 Wheat. 1 (1825), which affirmed a wide-ranging discretion on the part of federal judges in issues of process and procedure, technical judgments that were often vital in property cases.
137. Abernethy, *Formative Period*, 64–71; Thornton, *Politics and Power*, 7, 10, 15, 29–30, 332, 334–35. See White, *Marshall Court*, 296–97, 410, 716, 730–40, 773–74, 785, for the struggle between Jackson and Marshall in *Worcester v. Georgia*, 6 Pet. 515 (1832). See Swisher, *Taney Period*, 751–53, for discussion and case citations to the lengthy litigation involving the legal status of the Spanish cession land in Alabama.
138. *Journal*, Northern District.
139. *De La Croix v. Chamberlain*, 12 Wheat. 599 (1827).
140. Abernethy, *Formative Period*; Thornton, *Politics and Power*; White, *Marshall Court*; Swisher, *Taney Period*.
141. Baldwin, *Flush Times*, 173–76.
142. 9 How. 407, 412.
143. 9 How. 415.
144. 10 How. 187.
145. Ibid., 188–89.
146. Freyer, *Forums of Order*; Freyer, *Harmony & Dissonance*.

Chapter II

1. For Reconstruction in Alabama, see Walter L. Fleming, *Civil War and Reconstruction in Alabama* (Spartanburg, S.C., 1978); Sarah Woolfolk Wiggins, *The Scalawag in Alabama Politics, 1865–1881*. These works should be considered in light of Eric Foner, *Reconstruction: America's Unfinished Revolution, 1863–1877* (New York, 1988). For the continuing influence of Reconstruction, see Allen Johnston Going, *Bourbon Democracy in Alabama, 1874–1890* (Tuscaloosa, 1951); William Warren Rogers, *The One-Gallused Rebellion: Agrarianism in Alabama, 1865–1896* (Baton Rouge, 1979). For the general constitutional and legal dimensions of the story, see William E. Nelson, *The Fourteenth Amendment from Political Principle to Judicial Doctrine* (Cambridge, 1988). For early twentieth-century developments in Alabama, see Tony Freyer, *Hugo L. Black and the Dilemma of American Liberalism* (Glenview, Ill., 1990), 1–72; Sheldon Hackney, *Populism to Progressivism in Alabama* (Baton Rouge, 1969); Virginia Van der Veer Hamilton, *Hugo Black: The Alabama Years* (Tuscaloosa, 1972). For the wider national story, see Morton Keller, *Affairs of State, Public Life in Late Nineteenth Century America* (Cambridge, 1977), and *Regulating a New Economy: Public Policy and Economic Change in America, 1900–1933* (Cambridge, 1990).
2. General works tracing the expansion of federal jurisdiction are Freyer, *Harmony & Dissonance*; Freyer, *Forums of Order*, Hall, *Magic Mirror*, 75–76, 233–35, 306–07;

Hall and Rise, *From Local Courts to National Tribunals*; Couch, *A History of the Fifth Circuit*.

3. Except where indicated otherwise, the basic biographical material is taken from Davis, "Brief History Outline." See also "History of Federal Courts, Alabama," 40 *Federal Rules Decision:* 153–57; Hawkins, "History of the Sourthern District of Alabama" and "History of the Middle District of Alabama"; and Owen, *History of Alabama*.

4. *First, Second, and Third Annual Meetings*, 57, 224, 271–74 and unpaged "Officers of Association, 1882"; Davis, "Brief History"; Kennamer, "Federal Judiciary in Alabama," 312–15; *Alabama Official and Statistical Register 1947* (Montgomery, 1947), 357.

5. Kritzer, *Justice Broker Lawyers*, 13–15.

6. The scholarly material on Busteed reveals the complexity of Reconstruction politics. Alabama Scalawags spearheaded the impeachment campaign against Busteed on the grounds that the New York Democrat was collaborating with the local Alabama Democrats. Although there may have been substance to this claim, a careful reading of the records accumulated by the House investigating committee suggests that Busteed's basic failure to serve the interests of the local bar was the deeper reason for the campaign's success. Indeed, Bruce, Busteed's successor, was chosen against the wishes of Alabama's Scalawags, apparently more because of his legal qualifications than his political ones. Wiggins, *Scalawag*, 52, 75, 90–95, 119–20, 139–44, 150. For a more tradiational view see Fleming, *Civil War and Reconstruction*, 511, 744, 774. In light of these considerations the Congressional reports are illuminating: "Impeachment of Judge Busteed," 430 Cong., 1st sess., June 20, 1874, Report no. 773, 1–8; 430 Cong., 2d sess. January 7, 1774, 324–26. Kennamer, "Federal Judiciary in Alabama," 319; Owen, *History of Alabama*, 3:710, 869; 4:1541; Louis R. Harlan, *Booker T. Washington: The Wizard of Tuskegee, 1901–1915* (New York, 1983), 9–10, 240–51, 300–13; *To the President and Senate of the United States: Lawyers of the Northern District of Alabama . . . reasons . . . given why Oscar R. Hundley should not be appointed* (Birmingham, 1909, privately printed); E. L. Russell, "Address [lauding appointment of Judge Jones]," *Proceedings of 25th Annual Meeting Alabama State Bar Association* (Montgomery, 1902), 33–35; Freyer, *Hugo L. Black*, 14–33.

7. See especially Couch, *Fifth Circuit*, 51.

8. Ibid., 30; Peter Graham Fish, *The Politics of Federal Judicial Administration*, (Princeton, 1973), n. 26.

9. *Annual Report of the Attorney General of the United States* (Washington, D.C., 1877).

10. Davis, "Brief History," Chaps. I, III.

11. Ibid., Chap. III; Owen, *History of Alabama*, 3:239, 272, 1805; Kennamer, "The Federal Judiciary in Alabama," 313.

12. Davis, "Brief History," Chaps. III, IV; Owen, *History of Alabama*, 3:710, 869, 942, 1677; Kennamer, "Federal Judiciary in Alabama," 315–16.

13. Kennamer, "Federal Judiciary in Alabama."

14. Ibid.

15. Ibid.
16. Davis, "Brief History," Chaps. III, IV; Owen, *History of Alabama*, 3:239, 272, 710, 869, 942, 1677, 1805; Kennamer, "Federal Judiciary in Alabama," 313–16; Freyer, *Hugo L. Black*, 3–6.
17. Davis, "Brief History," Chaps. III, IV; Owen, *History of Alabama*, 3:239, 272, 710, 869, 942, 1677, 1805; Kennamer, "Federal Judiciary in Alabama," 313–16.
18. *To the President*, 1–16, quote at 14 [cited in full, above, note 6].
19. Ibid., 15; Thomas G. Jones, "Report of the Committee on Judicial Administration and Remedial Procedure," *Report of the First, Second, and Third Annual Meetings of the Alabama State Bar Association* (Montgomery, 1882), 226.
20. *First, Second, and Third Annual Meetings*, 57, 224, and unpaged "Officers of Association, 1882"; Davis, "Brief History"; Kennamer, "Federal Judiciary in Alabama," 312–15. Until the Bar Association succeeded during the 1920s in requiring association membership in order to practice law in Alabama, only about one-third of the state's lawyers bothered to join. We are grateful to Reginald T. Hamner, executive director of the Alabama State Bar, for this point; see also *36th Annual Meeting* (Montgomery, 1913), 71–72.
21. Perry D. Mathis, Clerk, U.S.D.C. N.D. Ala., to Tony Freyer, February 18, 1992; *First, Second, and Third Annual Meetings*, 271–74; *Alabama Official and Statistical Register 1947* (Montgomery, 1947), 357.
22. Freyer, *Hugo L. Black*, 13, 17–23.
23. Ibid., 17–23.
24. *First, Second, and Third Annual Meetings*, 233, 234, 236.
25. Ibid., 240, 241.
26. Freyer, *Hugo L. Black*, 21–30.
27. *36th Annual Meeting* (1913), 121.
28. *37th Annual Meeting* (1914), 62–63.
29. *First, Second, and Third Annual Meetings*, 228.
30. *37th Annual Meeting*, 193; *Second and Third Annual Meetings*, 237.
31. For this point we are indebted to Judge Seybourn H. Lynne.
32. *Alabama Official and Statistical Register 1947* (Montgomery, 1947), 357.
33. Compare Freyer, *Hugo L. Black*, 1–71, and Keller's companion studies, *Affairs of State* and *Regulating a New Economy*.
34. Freyer, *Hugo L. Black*, 14–48.
35. Ibid.
36. Ibid.
37. Ibid.
38. Ibid., 6, 44–45.
39. Ibid.
40. Ibid., 7–9, 32, 34–35, 46.
41. Ibid., 9, 11, 20–21, 49.
42. Ibid., 1–71; Keller, *Affairs of State* and *Regulating a New Economy*.
43. Freyer, *Harmony & Dissonance*, 55–100; Freyer, *Forums of Order*, 45–101.
44. Couch, *Fifth Circuit*, 19–37. The reference to Bruce and Toulmin is based on the *Federal Reporter*; the reference to Grubb is Couch, *Fifth Circuit*, 51.

45. John V. Orth, *The Judicial Power of the United States: The Eleventh Amendment in American History* (New York, 1987), 145.
46. Freyer, *Harmony & Dissonance*, 55, 56, 75–76, 78.
47. Henry D. Clayton, "Necessity for Federal Legislation," *Alabama State Bar Association Meetings 1925–1928*, 79–92.
48. See Tony Freyer, "Federalism," *Encyclopedia of the American Judicial System*, ed. Robert J. Janosik, 3 vols. (New York, 1987), 3:1095–1100.
49. Freyer, *Hugo L. Black*, 49–87.
50. Ibid. 72–87.
51. Freyer, *Harmony & Dissonance*, 101–54; *40th Meeting State Bar Association* (Montgomery, 1917), 78.
52. Couch, *Fifth Circuit*, 51.
53. Fish, *Federal Judicial Administration*, n. 26, 30–39.
54. *Annual Report of the Attorney General of the United States* (Washington, D.C., 1877), 14, 16, 18, 20, 22, 24.
55. Ibid., 18, 20, 22, 24.
56. Ibid., 29, 33.
57. Ibid., 58.
58. *Annual Report of the Attorney General of the United States* (Washington, D.C., 1938), 234, 235.
59. Ibid., 218, 221.
60. Ibid., 228.
61. Ibid., 264, 270, 271, 274, 275.
62. Ibid., 179, 264, 274.
63. Ibid., 234, 240, 243.
64. Ibid., 251.
65. Edward A. Purcell, Jr., *The Crisis of Democratic Theory, Scientific Naturalism & the Problem of Value* (Lexington, Ky., 1973), 74–94, 159–78.
66. *First, Second and Third Annual Meetings*, 224–41; Henry D. Clayton, *47th and 48th Annual Meetings State Bar Association* (Montgomery, 1924–1925), 105–29; *40th Annual Meeting* (Montgomery, 1917), 74–78; Henry D. Clayton, *48th, 49th, 50th, 51st Annual Meetings* (Montgomery, 1925–1928), 79–92; Leon McCord, "Address," *52nd–54th Annual Meetings* (Montgomery, 1929–1931), 70–78.
67. *47th and 48th Annual Meetings*, 129.
68. Ibid., 115.
69. *40th Annual Meeting*, 76.
70. *47th and 48th Annual Meetings*, 107.
71. *48th, 49th, 50th, 51st Annual Meetings*, 83, 84.
72. *52nd–54th Annual Meetings*, 71, 73, 74, 75, 77.
73. *47th Annual Meeting*, 76.
74. *47th and 48th Annual Meetings*, 110, 129.
75. Davis, "Brief History," Chaps. III, IV; Owen, *History of Alabama*, 3:239, 272, 869, 942, 1677, 1805; Kennamer, "Federal Judiciary in Alabama."

76. Davis, "Brief History," Chaps. III, IV; Owen, *History of Alabama*, 3:239, 272, 869, 942, 1677, 1805; Kennamer, "Federal Judiciary in Alabama."

77. Keller, *Affairs of State*, 223.

78. Ibid., 203. Significantly, although white supremacy was the dominant value accepted by the Alabama State Bar Association, Jones and others recognized a greater need for the protection of civil rights. See the view of future governor Emmet O'Neal in *32nd Annual Meeting* (Montgomery, 1909), at 39: "It was the bar of Alabama that planted deep and permanent in the fundamental law of the State that forever in this commonwealth it should be ruled by men of our own race." Compare the view of Jones discussed below in the section on the peonage cases.

79. 92 U.S. 214 (1876).

80. Keller, *Affairs of State*, 223.

81. The Court remained equivocal on the defense of voting rights in federal elections until the triumph of the white primary. See Freyer, *Hugo L. Black*, 6, 39–40; *U.S. v. Gale*, 109 U.S. 65 (1883); *Ex parte Yarborough*, 110 U.S. 651 (1884); *Ex parte Siebold*, 100 U.S. 371 (1880); *Ex parte Clark*, 100 U.S. 399 (1880).

82. *Ex parte Turner, Ex parte Mayer*, 24 Fed. Cas. (C.C.M.D. Ala. 1879, No. 14, 246), 334, 336, 337.

83. *U.S. v. Baldridge*, 11 Fed. Rep. 552, 557 (1882).

84. *U.S. v. Hall*, 26 Fed. Cas. (C.C.S.D. Ala. 1871, No. 15, 282), 79, 80, 81, 82.

85. 16 Wallace 36 (1873).

86. *U.S. v. Cruikshank*, 25 Fed. Rep. 707 (1874).

87. 106 U.S. 629 (1883).

88. Harold M. Hyman and William M. Wiecek, *Equal Justice Under Law: Constitutional Development 1835–1875* (New York, 1982), 373–81, 379, 483–84.

89. *In re Shorter*, 22 Fed. Cas. (D.C. Ala. 1865, No. 12, 811), 16.

90. Ibid., 20.

91. Compare *Smith v. Wilson*, 22 Fed. Cas. (D.C.S.D. Ala. 1872, No. 13, 128), 700; *U.S. v. King*, 23 Fed. Rep. 138 (1885); *The Lizzie Frank*, 31 Fed. Rep. 477 (1887).

92. Compare Busteed's opinion in *In re Haley*, 11 Fed. Cas. (D.C.N.D. Ala. 1868) to Wood's opinion in *Bailey v. Loeb*, 2 Fed. Cas. (C.C.M.D. Ala. 1875) and Bruce's opinion in *Barnewall v. Jones*, 2 Fed. Cas. (D.C.S.D. Ala. 1876).

93. *U.S. v. Hall*, 26 Fed. Cas. (C.C.S.D. Ala. 1871, No. 15, 282), 20, 79.

94. Davis, "Brief History," Chap. III; Owen, *History of Alabama*, 3:239, 272, 1805; Kennamer, "Federal Judiciary in Alabama," 313.

95. Keller, *Affairs of State*, 220–21.

96. 55 Fed. Rep. 58 (1892).

97. 35 Fed. Rep. 493 (1888), 494, 495.

98. *U.S. v. Ollinger*, 55 Fed. Rep. 959 (1893).

99. 23 Fed. Rep. 138 (1885).

100. 31 Fed. Rep. 477 (1887).

101. *Smith v. Wilson*, 22 Fed. Cas. (D.C.S.D. Ala. 1872, No. 13, 128), 700, 702, 703.

102. *Deposit Sav. Ass'n. v. Mayer*, 7 Fed. Cas. (C.C.S.D. Ala. 1876, No. 3, 813), 504, 506.

103. Stephen Cresswell, *Mormons, Cowboys, Moonshiners & Klansmen: Federal Law Enforcement in the South & West, 1870–1893* (Tuscaloosa, 1991), 135.
104. *U.S. v. Ducournau*, 54 Fed. Rep. 138 (1891).
105. *U.S. v. Imsand*, 26 Fed. Cas. (C.C.S.D. Ala. 1869, No. 15, 439), 465, 467.
106. Cresswell, *Moonshiners*, 135.
107. Ibid., 133–80, quote at 135.
108. Ibid., 156.
109. William F. Holmes, "Moonshiners and Whitecaps in Alabama, 1893," *The Alabama Review* 34 (January 1981): 31–47.
110. Freyer, *Harmony & Dissonance*, 1–43.
111. *Copley v. Grover & Baker Sewing Machine Co.*, 6 Fed. Cas. (C.C.S.D. Ala. 1875, No. 3, 213), 517, 518, 519.
112. *Mitchell v. Lippincott*, 17 Fed. Cas. (C.C.S.D. Ala. 1874, No. 9, 665), 503; *Lippincott v. Mitchell*, 94 U.S. 767 (1876).
113. *Buford v. Holley*, 23 Fed. Rep. 680 (1886), 685.
114. Freyer, *Harmony & Dissonance*, 56–63.
115. *Clews v. Lee County*, 5 Fed. Cas. (C.C.S.D. Ala. 1874, No. 2, 892), 1048.
116. *Sibley v. Mobile*, 22 Fed. Cas., (C.C.S.D. Ala. 1876, No. 12, 828), 57.
117. *Amy & Co. v. City of Selma*, 12 Fed Rep. 414 (1882).
118. *Chisholm v. Montgomery*, 5 Fed. Cas. (C.C.M.D. Ala. 1875), 635, 636.
119. 35 Fed. Rep. 496 (1888).
120. Freyer, *Harmony & Dissonance*, 101–53.
121. Freyer, *Hugo L. Black*, 30–31, 36–38, 43, 48, 54, 56.
122. Stephen B. Coleman, Jr. and Stephen B. Coleman, Sr., *Judge Clarence Allgood, His Brothers' Keeper* (Birmingham, 1991), 19–23.
123. Freyer, *Hugo L. Black*, 38, 40.
124. Ibid., 37–38.
125. Perry D. Mathis to Tony Freyer, February 18, 1992.
126. Keller, *Affairs of State*, 423–25, 427–30.
127. *Bigbee & Warrior Rivers Packet Co. v. Mobile & O.R. Co.*, 60 Fed. Rep. 545 (1893).
128. *ICC v. Alabama Midland Ry. Co.*, 69 Fed. Rep. 227 (1895).
129. *ICC v. Alabama Midland Ry. Co.*, 21 C.C.A. Reports 51 (1896).
130. *ICC v. Alabama M. R. Co.*, 168 U.S. 144 (1897), 177.
131. James F. Doster, *Railroads in Alabama Politics, 1875–1914* (Tuscaloosa, 1957), 102–11.
132. James F. Doster, "The Conflict over Railroad Regulation in Alabama," *Business History Review* 28, 4 (December 1954): 335.
133. Doster, *Railroads*, 26, 37–38.
134. Keller, *Affairs of State*, 221, 233; Doster, *Railroads*, 62–76, 87–101, 337.
135. Doster, *Railroads*, 79–80.
136. Ibid., 87–101, 337, for Comer's group. The note on Grubb is inferred from his prominence as a lawyer in Birmingham, Freyer, *Hugo L. Black*, 22; and Owen, *History of Alabama*, 3:710–11.
137. Doster, *Railroads*, 199.

138. Ibid., 112–45.

139. Ibid., 85, 215; 169 U.S. 466.

140. Doster, *Railroads*, 341.

141. Ibid., 157–219.

142. Ibid., 187–88.

143. *R R Commission of Alabama v. Central Georgia Ry. Co.*, 95 C.C.A. 117 (1909). See also Doster, *Railroads*, 198–99.

144. Doster, *Railroads*, 202, 209–10.

145. Ibid., 214–20; *L&N R. Co. v. R. Commission of Alabama*, 208 Fed. Rep. 35 (1913). *The Minnesota Rate Case* is at 230 U.S. 352 (1913).

146. Pete Daniel, *The Shadow of Slavery: Peonage in the South, 1901–1969* (Urbana, 1990), x–xi; William Cohen, *At Freedom's Edge: Black Mobility and the Southern White Quest for Racial Control, 1861–1915* (Baton Rouge, 1991), 23–43, 274–98; Alexander M. Bickel and Benno C. Schmidt, Jr., *The Judiciary and Responsible Government, 1910–21* (New York, 1984), 820–907.

147. Daniel, *Shadow of Slavery*, 22–23.

148. Ibid., as quoted, 31, 33, 35.

149. Ibid., as quoted, 25, 27.

150. Freyer, *Hugo L. Black*, 24–27, 32.

151. Daniel, *Shadow of Slavery*, 43; Harlan, *Washington*, 301.

152. Harlan, *Washington*, 308–12.

153. Daniel, *Shadow of Slavery*, as quoted 44–45.

154. Ibid., as quoted, 46–47.

155. Ibid., as quoted, 48.

156. Ibid., as quoted, 53.

157. Ibid., 61.

158. Ibid., as quoted, 63–64.

159. Ibid., 66.

160. Ibid., as quoted, 67.

161. Ibid.

162. Ibid., as quoted, 66.

163. Ibid., 68–71, 73–79; Owen, *History of Alabama*, 4:1663.

164. Daniel, *Shadow of Slavery*, 68–71, 73–79.

165. Ibid., as quoted, 69.

166. Ibid., 70–71.

167. Ibid., 73–79; Bickel and Schmidt, *Judiciary and Responsible Government*, 820–907; *Bailey v. Alabama*, 211 U.S. 452 (1908); *Bailey v. Alabama*, 219 U.S. 219 (1911).

168. 219 U.S. 219, 232–42.

169. Ibid., 231, 236, 245–50.

170. Cohen, *Freedom's Edge*, 276–77, 287–90; Daniel, *Shadow of Slavery*, 79–80, 180; Bickel and Schmidt, *Judiciary and Responsible Government*, 820–907; *U.S. v. Reynolds*, 235 U.S. 133 (1914).

171. Owen, *History of Alabama*, 4:1663.

172. *Annual Report of the Attorney General* (1938), 81

173. Daniel, *Shadow of Slavery*, 86–94.
174. Bickel and Schmidt, *Judiciary and Responsible Government*, 877.
175. Ibid., as quoted, 878–79.
176. Ibid.
177. Ibid., as quoted, 878.
178. Peter H. Irons, *The New Deal Lawyers* (Princeton, 1982), 75–79; *W. E. Belcher v. National Industrial Recovery Act*, Memorandum #539, B/17/28, June 1934, Criminal Case Files, Record Group 21, Western Division, Northern District of Alabama, National Archives, East Point, Georgia.
179. Irons, *New Deal Lawyers*, 77–82.
180. Ibid., 77–78; *Belcher v. NIRA*.
181. Irons, *New Deal Lawyers*, 77–107.
182. Freyer, *Hugo L. Black*, 56, 57, 59, 71.
183. *Aetna Coal Co. et al. v. TVA*, Memorandum, Record Group 21, Equity #810 B/17/14, 1935, U.S.D.C. N.D. Ala., B'ham., Div., National Archives.
184. *Ashwander v. TVA*, 8 F. Supp. 893 (1934).
185. Ibid., 897.
186. *TVA v. Ashwander*, 78 F.(2d) 578 (1935); *Ashwander v. TVA*, 297 U.S. 288 (1936).
187. Freyer, *Hugo L. Black*, 72–87.
188. *Steward Mach. Co. v. Davis*, 89 F.(2d) 207 (1937); *Steward Mach. Co. v. Davis*, 301 U.S. 548 (1937).
189. Kennamer, "Federal Judiciary in Alabama," 316–17.
190. Freyer, *Hugo L. Black*, 72–87.
191. Perry D. Mathis to Tony Freyer, February 18, 1992.
192. *Aetna Coal Co. v. TVA*.

Chapter III

1. Studies focusing on the postwar era are Peltason, *Fifty-Eight Lonely Men*; Bass, *Taming the Storm*; John M. Spivack, *Race, Civil Rights and the United States Court of Appeals for the Fifth Judicial Circuit* (New York, 1990); Barrow and Walker, *A Court Divided*; Zelden, *Justice Lies in the District*; Fish, *Politics of Judicial Administration*; Freyer, *The Little Rock Crisis*. A concise overview summarizing further works is Michael J. Klarman, "*Brown*, Racial Change, and the Civil Rights Movement," *Virginia Law Review* 80, 1 (February 1994): 7–150.
2. For an overview of development in Alabama, essays by Howard Ball, Sheldon Hackney, Virginia Van der Veer Hamilton, Paul L. Murphy, David A. Shannon, J. Mills Thornton III, Bertram Wyatt-Brown, and Tony Freyer in Tony Freyer, ed., *Justice Hugo Black and Modern America* (Tuscaloosa, 1990). See also Freyer, *Hugo L. Black*; Klarman, "*Brown*"; Bass, *Taming the Storm*.
3. Purcell, *Litigation and Inequality*; Couch, *Fifth Circuit*; Freyer, *Forums of Order*; Zelden, *Justice*.
4. A useful overview of the relation of National Democrats to federal judicial appointments is Coleman and Coleman, *Judge Clarence Allgood*.

5. Bass, *Taming the Storm*, 16–17, 78, 33; "Alabama GOP Splits Over New Judge [H. H. Grooms]," May 11, 1953, copy in Special Collections, University of Alabama School of Law (hereafter SC).

6. Bass, *Taming the Storm*, 86–91; "Nomination of Harlan Hobart Grooms of Alabama, To Be United States District Judge for the Northern District of Alabama, Vice Clarence Mullins, Retired," July 30, 1953, *Hearings before the Committee on the Judiciary*, United States Senate, 1–3.

7. Judge John C. Godbold, interview by Paul J. DeMarco, copy of transcript in possession of the author.

8. "Nomination of Grooms," Hearings, 1–3. Compare "On Confirmation of Nomination of Hon. Richard T. Rives of Alabama," Hearings, Subcommittee on the Judiciary, U.S. Senate, Volume 1, April 30, 1951; "On Confirmation of Nomination of Daniel H. Thomas," Hearings before Committee on the Judiciary, U.S. Senate, Volume 1, February 27, 1951; "Nomination of Clarence W. Allgood," Report of Proceedings, Subcommittee on Nominations of the Committee on the Judiciary, January 24, 1962.

9. Godbold interview.

10. "Senators' wants differ on U.S. judiciary changes in state," April 15, 1973; "GOP to recommend 3 for U.S. Judges," December 19, 1972; "Samford's Donaldson after GOP backing to put him in federal judge's post," November 22, 1973; "Touchy judgeship question is passed to Washington by Alabama GOP leaders," December 22, 1972; "Hancock, Sherrer, Guin recommended for judgeships," January 12, 1973; "Nixon announces two nominations," March 21, 1973; "McFadden takes Oath," September 13, 1969; "McFadden nomination advances," August 8, 1969, all in SC.

11. Sparkman quoted in "Senators' wants differ on U.S. judiciary changes in state"; "Nixon announces two nominations"; "Bob Vance judge," November 6, 1977; "70,000 job open, but rush to fill it, fails to develop," January 24, 1982, SC.

12. "Samford's Donaldson after GOP backing to put him in federal judge's post," SC.

13. "Judge [Guin] is grateful for an opportunity to sit on bench," May 16, 1973; "Varner says lack of judges might close up civil courts," July 22, 1979; "Nixon nominates Brevard Hand to be U.S. judge," July 27, 1971, SC; Robert Varner, interview with author.

14. "Judge's land purchase linked to case," July 5, 1975; "Birmingham lawyer Pointer will be appointed U.S. judge," September 17, 1970; "Logic intrigues youngest judge," October 9, 1970; "Wallace, Allen denounce order," September 25, 1971; "Group here wants Judge Pointer moved," October 18, 1972, SC.

15. "Heflin caught between 2 powerful groups," January 21, 1980; "Federal judgeships selection process causes rift," July 9, 1979; "Every appointment will make someone mad," May 28, 1979, SC.

16. "'Merit' choice of judges," February 25, 1980; "Every appointment will make someone mad"; "Heflin caught between 2 powerful groups"; "Federal judgeships selection process causes rift"; "Unlikely that woman will get a judgeship," May 11, 1979; "Federal judge selection politically hot issue," March 3, 1979, SC.

17. "Senators to push for quiet confirmation of Hobbs as U.S. Judge," February 29, 1980; "Hobbs confirmed," April 4, 1980; "Court giants' hang in nominee's office," February 12, 1980; "Vance confirmed," December 16, 1977; "Bob Vance Judge," November 6, 1977, SC; Bass, *Taming the Storm*, 408–28.

18. "Propst described as bright, well-prepared, innovative," February 11, 1980; "Haltom known as meticulous lawyer," February. 14, 1980, SC.

19. "Judge candidate's civil rights record marred by charges," June 21, 1979; "Hobbs hearing is like love feast," March 20, 1980; "Heflin reported seeking to dump Gray," August 2, 1980; "Blacks still wary of Davis' appointment," August 24, 1980; "Myron Who? is top contender for fed," August 24, 1980; "Heflin gives Thompson 50–50 odds," September 18, 1980; "With Heflin pushing all the way, Senate confirms Thompson," September 27, 1980, SC.

20. "Blacks still wary of Davis' appointment"; "Clemon responds to opposition," February 14, 1980; "ABA objection on Clemon was lien and attitude on income tax," May 19, 1980; "Clemon approval seems assured, 'will serve with distinction,' Heflin says," June 20, 1980; "Clemon gets 14–0 vote for confirmation," June 24, 1980; "Clemon unanimously confirmed by Senate," June 27, 1980; "Double Standard seen in judicial ratings," April 19, 1980, SC.

21. Birmingham Bar Association, "Resolution," 28 May 1980, copy in U. W. Clemon file, SC.

22. "Judge candidate's civil rights record marred by charges,"; "Hobbs hearing is like love feast,"; "Heflin reported seeking to dump Gray,"; "Blacks still wary of Davis' appointment,"; "Myron Who? is top contender for fed,"; "Heflin gives Thompson 50–50 odds,"; "With Heflin pushing all the way, Senate confirms Thompson,"; "Clemon responds to opposition,"; "ABA objection on Clemon was lien and attitude on income tax,"; "Clemon approval seems assured, 'will serve with distinction,' Heflin says,"; "Clemon gets 14–0 vote for confirmation,"; "Clemon unanimously confirmed by Senate,"; "Double Standard seen in judicial ratings,".

23. Godbold interview.

24. "Denton gets crossfire over vacant federal judgeship," July 22, 1981; "Judge Pittman's move surprises Denton," April 11, 1981; "Field is said down to three for successor to Judge Pittman," July 4, 1981, SC. See also Emmett Ripley Cox, Alex T. Howard, Joel B. Dubina, William M. Acker, Jr., U. W. Clemon, and Robert Propst interviews with the author. See also Judge Myron Thompson interview by Kelvin D. Jones, III, April 6, 1992, in possession of the author.

25. Cox and Howard interviews.

26. Unless otherwise noted, the discussion of jurisprudence is drawn from the author's interviews with the federal judges. For legal realism, see Grant Gilmore, *The Ages of American Law* (New Haven, 1977), 77–92; Laura Kalman, *Legal Realism at Yale* (Chapel Hill, N.C., 1986).

27. Author's interviews with Judges Clarence Allgood, Seybourn Lynne, and Daniel H. Thomas. See also Bass, *Taming the Storm*, 48, 113; Godbold interview; "Richard Rives, Judge helped breakdown racial barriers," April 19, 1981; "Rives nominated as U.S. judge, April 12, 1951; "Retired judge pleased at progress," April 9, 1975, SC; Hamilton, "Lister Hill," 94–95, Freyer, *Justice Hugo Black*, 142.

28. Freyer, *Justice Hugo Black*, 142; see also Judge Pittman interview with author.
29. Acker and Dubina interviews.
30. Judges' interviews. For the Republicans' accommodation of the New Deal's economic and social welfare programs, see Samuel Lubell, *The Future of American Politics* (New York, 1965), 221–28, esp. 227.
31. Lynne, Allgood, Thomas, Pittman, Frank M. Johnson, Jr. interviews; H. H. Grooms, "Segregation, Desegregation, Integration, Desegregation" (unpublished manuscript, in author's possession).
32. Barrow and Walker, *Court Divided*.
33. Cox, Howard, Dubina, Acker, Clemon, Propst, and Thompson interviews.
34. Ibid.
35. Herman Belz, *Equality Transformed: A Quarter Century of Affirmative Action* (New Brunswick, N.J., 1991).
36. Ibid.
37. Ibid.; see also author's interviews with judges.
38. Barry Cushman, "Rethinking the New Deal Court," *Virginia Law Review* 80, 1 (February 1994): 201–61; Gilmore, *Ages of American Law*; Kalman, *Legal Realism*; Bass, *Taming the Storm*.
39. Thompson, Godbold, Howard, Cox, Hand, Propst, Johnson, Lynne, Allgood, Haltom, Guin, Clemon, Thomas, Acker, Pittman, Pointer, and Dubina interviews.
40. 302 U.S. 319 (1937); 304 U.S. 144 (1938); Cushman, "Rethinking the New Deal Court"; Gilmore, *Ages of American Law*; Kalman, *Legal Realism*; Bass, *Taming the Storm*.
41. Merlin Owen Newton, " 'Preach the Gospel Unto Every Creature': Jehovah's Witnesses, Alabama, and the U.S. Supreme Court, 1939–1946" (Ph.D. dissertation, University of Alabama).
42. 347 U.S. 483 (1954); *Brown* II, 349 U.S. 294 (1955).
43. *The New Yorker*, as quoted; Freyer, *Hugo L. Black*, 153.
44. Ibid.; Guin interview.
45. Propst interview; Lee W. Borden, "Profile of Judge Robert B. Propst," *Birmingham Bar Magazine*, March 1981, 20.
46. Ibid.; "Propst described as bright, well-prepared, innovative."
47. Acker interview.
48. Clemon interview.
49. Guin interview.
50. Haltom and Pittman interviews.
51. Dubina interview.
52. Godbold, Thompson, Howard, Cox, Hand, Propst, Johnson, Lynne, Allgood, Haltom, Guin, Clemon, Thomas, Acker, Pittman, Pointer, and Dubina interviews.
53. Ibid.
54. Quote from Lynne interview; Johnson, Thompson, and Clemon interviews.
55. Acker, Thompson, and Godbold interviews.
56. Thompson interview.
57. Ibid.
58. Ibid.

59. Cox, Johnson, and Godbold interviews.
60. University of Alabama School of Law graduates: Thomas A. Murphree; John McDuffie; Clarence Mullins; Seybourn H. Lynne; Daniel H. Thomas; Frank M. Johnson, Jr.; Walter P. Gewin; Thomas V. Pittman; Sam C. Pointer; Robert E. Varner; William B. Hand; James H. Hancock; Junius F. Guin, Jr.; Robert S. Vance; Robert B. Propst; Elbert B. Haltom, Jr.; Emmett R. Cox; Charles R. Butler; Richard W. Vollmer; William H. Albritton; Ira Dement. Yale: McFadden, Hobbs, Thompson, and Acker; Vanderbilt: Alex T. Howard, Jr.; Harvard: Godbold and Carnes; Columbia: Clemon; Cumberland: Dubina, Nelson, Blackburn; Kentucky: Grooms; night school: Allgood.
61. Allgood Interview; Coleman and Coleman, *Judge Allgood*; "Debtors court in city called largest in U.S.," February 22, 1962; "Judgeship just new challenge," May 15, 1961, SC.
62. Acker, Clemon, Godbold, and Thompson interviews.
63. Lynne, Johnson, Thompson, Clemon, Acker, Godbold, Guin, Propst, Haltom, Allgood, Pittman, Dubina, Howard, Cox, Hand, and Pointer interviews; see also, Bass, *Taming the Storm*, 55.
64. Lynne, Johnson, Thompson, Clemon, Acker, Godbold, Guin, Propst, Haltom, Allgood, Pittman, Dubina, Howard, Cox, Hand, and Pointer interviews.
65. For the politicization of state judicial institutions, see Harry N. Scheiber, "Innovation, Resistance, and Change: A History of Judicial Reform and the California Courts, 1960–1990," *Southern California Law Review* 66, 5 (July 1993): 2049–2120, 2051, 2053. For the national institutional developments, see Fish, *Federal Judicial Administration*; Barrow and Walker, *A Court Divided*; Spivack, *Race, Civil Rights*; Couch, *Fifth Circuit*. For external political pressures, see Bass, *Taming the Storm*; Klarman, *"Brown."*
66. Purcell, *Litigation and Inequality*, 217–91; *Report of the Federal Courts Study Committee*, April 2, 1990; "Tentative Recommendations for Public Comment," *The Federal Courts Study Committee*, December 22, 1989; "National Conference on State-Federal Judicial Relationships," *Virginia Law Review* 78, 8 (November 1992): 1655–1902.
67. Purcell, *Litigation and Inequality*, 218, 220, 227; Freyer, *Harmony & Dissonance*; Lynne and Thomas interviews.
68. Purcell, *Litigation and Inequality*, 220–24, 386 n. 26, 387 n. 43.
69. Ibid., 239–44.
70. William H. Rehnquist, "Welcoming Remarks," *Virginia Law Review* 78 (November 1992): 1660.
71. Frank M. Johnson, Jr., "Equal Access to Justice," *Alabama Law Review* 41, 1 (Fall 1989): 1–2; Bass, *Taming the Storm*, 384; Thompson interview.
72. Johnson, "Equal Access," 11.
73. Bass, *Taming the Storm*, 234–35, 277–78; Larry W. Yackle, *Reform and Regret: The Story of Federal Judicial Involvement in the Alabama Prison System* (New York, 1989).
74. Johnson, "Equal Access"; Bass, *Taming the Storm*; Yackle, *Reform and Regret*.
75. Rehnquist, "Welcoming Remarks," 1659.
76. Hall, *Magic Mirror*, 214–15, 221, 225, 228, 259, 289.

77. Quoted in Malcolm M. Lucas, "Keynote Address: National Conference on State-Federal Judicial Relationships," *Virginia Law Review* 78 (November 1992): 1669.

78. Fish, *Federal Judicial Administration*, 125–27.

79. Ibid., 151, 369, 374.

80. Ibid., 162, 395; see also Fish, *Federal Judicial Administration*, 453; Lynne, Johnson, and Godbold interviews.

81. *Alabama Official and Statistical Register* (Montgomery, 1947), 357, 360–63; U.S. Bureau of the Census, *State and Metropolitan Area Data Book*, 1991 (Washington, D.C., 1991), 204; 1990 Census of Population and Housing, *Population and Housing Characteristics for Census Tracts and Block Numbering Areas, Montgomery, AL*, 1; 1990 Census of Population and Housing, *Population and Housing Characteristics for Census Block Numbering Areas, Mobile, AL*, 1; *The Book of the States*, Vol. 29 (Lexington, Ky., 1992–93), 418.

82. "Varner says lack of judges might close up civil courts," July 22, 1979, SC. See also author's interviews with federal judges.

83. Reginald T. Hamner, executive director, Alabama State Bar, to Tony Freyer, January 30, 1992, in possession of the author.

84. Perry D. Mathis, Clerk, U.S. District Court, Northern District of Alabama, to Tony Freyer, February 18, 1992, in possession of the author.

85. Ibid.

86. Thomas and Pointer interviews.

87. Judges' interviews.

88. Fish, *Federal Judicial Administration*, as quoted, 193, 281.

89. William D. Quarles, *Summary Adjudication: Dispotive Motions and Summary Trials* (New York, 1991), 9; John J. Coleman, "Summary Judgement in Alabama," *Cumberland Law Review* 20 (1989): 1; Stephen A. Bullington, "Justice Delayed is Justice Denied," 30 *Arizona Law Review* (1988): 171, 174. The Court cases are *Matsushita Electrical Industrial Co. v. Zenith Radio Corp.*, 475 U.S. 574 (1986); *Celotex Corp. v. Catrett*, 477 U.S. 317 (1986); *Anderson v. Liberty Lobby, Inc.*, 477 U.S. 242 (1986).

90. *Sanders et al. v. F. W. Woolworth Co.*, 339 F. Supp. 777 (S.D. Ala. 1972); *Sanders v. Shockly*, 468 F.2d 88 (5th Cir. 1972).

91. *Phillips v. Unijax, Inc.*, 462 F. Supp. 942 (S.D. Ala. 1980); 625 F.2d 54 (5th Cir. 1980).

92. IRS cases: *McLeod v. United States*, 276 F. Supp. 213 (S.D. Ala. 1967); *Chamberlain v. Alexander*, 419 F. Supp. 235 (S.D. Ala. 1976); *Chamberlain v. Kurtz*, 589 F.2d 827 (5th Cir. 1976); cert. denied 444 U.S. 842 (1979). Insurance cases: *Dancy v. State Farm*, 324 F. Supp. 964 (S.D. Ala. 1971); *Adams v. State Farm Life Insurance Co.*, 324 F. Supp. 648 (S.D. Ala. 1971); reversed 453 F.2d 224 (5th Cir. 1971); *Radcliff v. Stuyvesant Insurance Co.*, 298 F. Supp. 917 (S.D. Ala. 1968).

93. *Overstreet v. Cohen*, 303 F. Supp. 6 (S.D. Ala. 1969); *Tarleton v. Finch*, 303 F. Supp. 12 (S.D. Ala. 1969); *Williams v. Finch*, 307 F. Supp. 1357 (S.D. Ala. 1969).

94. *McLaughlin v. Callaway*, 30 Fair Empl. Prac. Cas. 724 (S.D. Ala. 1975); *Puckett v. Mobile City Commission*, 380 F. Supp. 593 (S.D. Ala. 1974); *McMeans v. Schwartz*, 330 F. Supp. 1397 (S.D. Ala. 1971).

95. *Wright v. United States*, 311 F. Supp. 693 (S.D. Ala. 1970); *United States v. Powell*, 310 F. Supp. 379 (S.D. Ala. 1970).

96. *Dickerson v. Simpson*, 298 F. Supp. 915 (S.D. Ala. 1969); *White v. Sullivan*, 368 F. Supp. 292 (S.D. Ala. 1973); *Jones v. Hale*, 278 F. Supp. 166 (S.D. Ala. 1967); *McCarroll v. Alabama*, 422 F. Supp. 137 (S.D. Ala. 1976); *Dickinson v. Gallion*, 301 F. Supp. 1307 (S.D. Ala. 1969). But see *Kircheis v. Long*, 425 F. Supp. 505 (S.D. Ala. 1976); affirmed 564 F.2d 414 (5th Cir. 1977).

97. Pittman interview.

98. Ibid.

99. Judges' interviews.

100. Mark Sabel, "The Jurisprudence Proclivities of Judge William Acker and Judge Myron Thompson" (unpublished paper, 1992), in possession of the author.

101. Ibid.

102. Ibid.

103. *United States v. Handley*, 591 F. Supp. 1257 (N.D. Ala. 1984); order reversed 763 F.2d 1401 (11th Cir. 1985); stay denied sub nom *Handley v. United States*, 474 U.S. 916; cert. denied 474 U.S. 951 (1985); on remand sub nom *United States v. Handley*, 644 F. Supp. 1165 (N.D. Ala. 1986); cert. denied sub nom *Handley v. United States*, 488 U.S. 984 (1988).

104. *Liao v. Dean*, 658 F. Supp. 1554 (N.D. Ala. 1987); rev'd. 867 F.2d 1366 (11th Cir. 1989); cert. denied 494 U.S. 1078 (1990). Johnson case is at 480 U.S. 616 (1987). Quote from Acker interview.

105. *Tull v. U.S.*, 481 U.S. 412 (1987).

106. *Beasley v. Hartford Fire Insurance Co.*, 723 F. Supp. 635 (N.D. Ala. 1989); *Walton v. Cowen Equipment Co.*, 733 F. Supp. 327 (N.D. Ala. 1990); vacated 930 F.2d 924 (11th Cir.); cert. denied 112 S.Ct. 86; on remand 774 F. Supp. 1343 (N.D. Ala. 1991); aff'd. 974 F.2d 1348 (11th Cir. 1992). The Supreme Court opinion is *Yellow Freight Systems, Inc. v. Donnelly*, 110 S. Ct. 1566 (1990). The Eleventh Circuit precedent is *Wilson v. City of Aliceville*, 779 F.2d 631 (11th Cir. 1986).

107. *Pennsylvania v. Delaware Valley Citizens Counsel for Clean Air*, 107 S.Ct. 3078, 3091 (1987).

108. 681 F. Supp. 752, 757 (M.D. Ala. 1988).

109. Ibid., 758–59.

110. *NAACP v. Allen*, 493 F.2d 614, 618, 621 (5th Cir. 1974).

111. *Paradise v. Shoemaker*, 470 F. Supp. 439, 442 (M.D. Ala. 1979); *Paradise v. Prescott*, 585 F. Supp. 72 (M.D. Ala. 1983); aff'd. 767 F.2d 1514 (11th Cir. 1985); aff'd. *United States v. Paradise*, 480 U.S. 149 (1987).

112. Sabel, "Jurisprudence Proclivities."

113. *Browder v. Gayle*, 142 F. Supp. 707 (M.D. Ala.); aff'd. sub nom *Gayle v. Browder*, 352 U.S. 903, (1956); *Brown v. Board of Education*, 349 U.S. 294 (1954); remedial decree, 349 U.S. 294 (1955).

114. *Gainer v. School Bd. of Jefferson Cty.*, 135 F. Supp. 559 (N.D. Ala. 1958).

115. *Armstrong v. Bd. of Educ. of the City of Birmingham*, 220 F. Supp. 217 (N.D. Ala. 1963); order vacated in part 333 F.2d 47 (5th Cir. 1964). The Rives opinion was

Shuttlesworth v. Birmingham Bd. of Educ., 162 F. Supp. 372 (N.D. Ala. 1958); aff'd. 358 U.S. 101 (1958). See also *Carson v. Warlick*, 238 F.2d 724 (4th Cir. 1956); cert. denied 353 U.S. 910 (1957).

116. *Armstrong v. Bd. of Ed. of Birmingham*, 323 F.2d 333 (5th Cir. 1963).

117. Commerce clause cases: *Wickard v. Filburn*, 317 U.S. 111 (1942); *Bob-Lo Excursion Co. v. Michigan*, 333 U.S. 28 (1948); *Henderson v. United States*, 339 U.S. 816 (1950).

118. *McClung v. Katzenbach*, 233 F. Supp. 815 (N.D. Ala.); probable jurisdiction noted sub nom *Katzenbach v. McClung*, 379 U.S. 802; rev'd. 379 U.S. 294 (1964).

119. Employment cases: *Hardy v. U.S. Steel Corp.*, 289 F. Supp. 200 (N.D. Ala. 1967); *Pettway v. American Cast Iron Pipe Co.*, 332 F. Supp. 811 (N.D. Ala. 1970); rev'd. 494 F.2d 211 (5th Cir. 1974). Voting apportionment: *Moody v. Flowers*, 256 F. Supp. 195 (N.D. Ala. 1966); vacated 387 U.S. 97 (1967). See also *Grey v. Saunders*, 372 U.S. 368 (1963); *Reynolds v. Sims*, 377 U.S. 533 (1964); *Baker v. Carr*, 369 U.S. 186 (1962). The cemetery case is *Terry v. Elmwood*, 307 F. Supp. 369 (N.D. Ala. 1969).

120. "Lecture and Open Forum, Honorable Seybourn H. Lynne, Senior United States District Judge to UAB Class, *The South Since 1945*," April 23, 1987, Birmingham, Alabama (unpublished transcript, Federal Courthouse Building).

121. Ibid.

122. Ibid.

123. Ibid.

124. Ibid.

125. Ibid.

126. "Wallace, Allen denounce order," September 25, 1971; "Group here wants Judge Pointer moved," October 18, 1972; "Lawyers' stories indicate Pointer became jail expert before order," n.d., SC. See *United States v. Bd. of Trustees of Crosby Indep. School Dist.*, 424 F.2d 625 (5th Cir. Tex. 1970); *Swann v. Charlotte-Mecklenberg Bd. of Ed.*, 402 U.S. 1 (1971); *Brown v. Bessemer Bd. of Ed.*, 464 F.2d 382 (5th Cir.); cert. denied sub nom *Bessemer Bd. of Ed. v. Brown*, 409 U.S. 981 (1972). See also *Youngblood v. Board of Public Instruction of Bay Co.*, 430 F.2d 625 (5th Cir. Fla. 1970); cert. denied sub nom *Board of Public Instruction of Bay Co. v. Youngblood*, 402 U.S. 943 (1971).

127. *E.E.O.C. v. Union Oil Co. of California*, 369 F. Supp. 579 (N.D. Ala. 1974); *Edmondson v. U.S. Steel*, 20 Fair Empl. Prac. Cas. 1745 (1979); *Hughes v. Jim Walter Resources Inc.*, 29 Fair Empl. Prac. Cas. 825 (1981).

128. Ingrid Kindred, "I call them as I see them," n.d., SC.

129. Ibid.; Pointer interview.

130. "Legal experts call Pointer one of the best judges in nation," "Pointer named 1 of 11 best federal judges," June 20, 1980, SC.

131. Pointer interview.

Chapter IV

1. *Palko v. Connecticut*, 302 U.S. 319 (1937); *U.S. v. Carolene Products Co.*, 304 U.S. 144, 152 n.4 (1938); Cushman, "Rethinking the New Deal Court"; Freyer, *Hugo*

L. Black, 72–166; G. Edward White, The American Judicial Tradition: Profiles of Leading American Judges (New York, 1976), 178–250; Klarman, "Brown," 7–150; Michael Kammen, A Machine That Would Go of Itself: The Constitution in American Culture (New York, 1987), 315–401.

2. Peltason, Fifty-Eight Lonely Men; Spivack, Race, Civil Rights; Jack Bass, Unlikely Heroes (New York, 1981); Frank T. Read and Lucy S. McGough, Let Them Be Judged: The Judicial Interpretation of the Deep South (Metuchen, N.J., 1978); Michael R. Belknap, Federal Law and Social Order: Racial Violence and Constitutional Conflict in the Post-Brown South (Athens, Ga., 1987); David J. Bodenhamer and James W. Ely, Jr., eds., The Bill of Rights in Modern America After 200 Years (Bloomington, Ind., 1993); Tony A. Freyer, "A Precarious Path: The Bill of Rights After 200 Years," Vanderbilt Law Review, 47 (April 1994): 757–94; Hall and Rise, From Local Courts to National Tribunals; Kemerer, William Wayne Justice; Zeldon, Justice Lies in the District; Tony Freyer and Timothy Dixon, Democracy and Judicial Independence: A History of the Federal Courts of Alabama, 1820–1994.

3. Herbert McClosky and Alida Brill, Dimensions of Tolerance: What Americans Believe About Civil Liberties (New York, 1983); Mary L. Dudziak, "Desegregation as a Cold War Imperative," Stanford Law Review, 41 (November 1988): 61–120; Kammen, A Machine, 315–401; Robert M. Cover, "The Origins of Judicial Activism in the Protection of Minorities," Yale Law Journal, 91 (June 1982): 1287–1316; Klarman, "Brown," 14–30; Freyer, "Precarious Path," 757–794.

4. "A Symposium on Judicial Activism: Problems and Responses," Harvard Journal of Law and Public Policy 7 (Winter 1984), 1–176; Charles L. Black, Jr., The People and the Court: Judicial Review in a Democracy (Englewood Cliffs, N.J., 1960).

5. Yarborough, Judge Frank Johnson; Bass, Taming the Storm; Sikora, The Judge; Kennedy, Judge Frank M. Johnson; Bass, Unlikely Heroes; Read and McGough, Let Them Be Judged; Yackle, Reform and Regret; Robert F. Nagel, "Controlling the Structural Injunction," Harvard Journal of Law and Public Policy 7 (Winter 1984): 395–411; Freyer and Dixon, Democracy and Judicial Independence, Chapters III and IV; "Judge [Frank Johnson] Interpreter in the Front Line," Time, May 12, 1967.

6. Bass, Taming the Storm, 12–79; Freyer and Dixon, Democracy and Judicial Independence, Chapter III; G. Edward White, Earl Warren: A Public Life (New York, 1982); Lubell, Future of American Politics.

7. Tocqueville, Democracy in America, 276 n. 7; Freyer, "Paradox."

8. Freyer, "Paradox"; Malcolm Feeley, "Another Look at the 'Party Variable' in Judicial Decision Making: An Analysis of the Michigan Supreme Court," Policy 4 (1971): 91, 93.

9. Gilmore, Ages of American Law, 68–111; Purcell, Crisis of Democratic Theory, 74–94, 159–78; William W. Fisher III, Morton J. Horwitz, and Thomas A. Reed, American Legal Realism (New York, 1993); Morton J. Horwitz, The Transformation of American Law 1870–1960: The Crisis in Legal Orthodoxy (New York, 1992); Kalman, Legal Realism; Duncan Kennedy, "Toward an Historical Understanding of Legal Consciousness: The Case of Classical Legal Thought in America, 1850–1940," Research in Law and Sociology 3 (1980): 3–150. See Nagel, "Controlling

the Structural Injunction," 395–411; Freyer and Dixon, *Democracy and Judicial Independence*, Chapter III.

10. Klarman, "*Brown*"; David R. Goldfield, *Black, White and Southern: Race Relations and Southern Culture, 1940 to the Present* (Baton Rouge, 1990); Belknap, *Federal Law and Social Order*; Freyer, *Little Rock Crisis*; Juan Williams, *Eyes on the Prize: America's Civil Rights Years, 1954–1965* (New York, 1987); Taylor Branch, *Parting the Waters: America in the King Years, 1954–63* (New York, 1988); Richard Kluger, *Simple Justice* (New York, 1976); Bass, *Unlikely Heroes*.
11. Klarman, "*Brown*," 185.
12. Ibid., 194.
13. Compare Freyer, *Little Rock Crisis*; Klarman, "*Brown*."
14. Freyer, *Little Rock Crisis*; Klarman, "*Brown*."
15. Yarborough, *Judge Frank Johnson*, Bass, *Taming the Storm*, and Sikora, *The Judge* give valuable discussions of Johnson's origins. I rely primarily on *Taming the Storm*, since it is the most recent work.
16. Spivack, *Race*.
17. Bass, *Taming the Storm*, 12–57; "Judge—the Law and Frank Johnson," *Bill Moyers's Journal*, transcript of program aired July 24, 1980; Johnson interview with Tony Freyer.
18. Moyers, "Judge"; Bass, *Taming the Storm*, as quoted, 17.
19. Bass, *Taming the Storm*, as quoted, 19.
20. Ibid., as quoted 20. On the importance of respectability in another small-town mountain community, Clay County, Alabama, birthplace and early home of Hugo Black, see Freyer, *Black*, 1–13.
21. Bass, *Taming the Storm*, as quoted, 32.
22. Ibid., 74–76.
23. Ibid., as quoted, 37.
24. Ibid., as quoted, 28.
25. Ibid., as quoted, 23.
26. Ibid., as quoted, 44.
27. Ibid., as quoted, 462–63.
28. Ibid., as quoted, 41.
29. Ibid., as quoted, 46–47. For the reference to the combined law school/undergraduate curriculum, we are indebted to Rufus Beale, former legal counsel, University of Alabama, and member of the law school class of 1942.
30. Bass, *Taming the Storm*, as quoted, 55.
31. Ibid., as quoted, 52.
32. Ibid., as quoted, 52, 53, 55.
33. Ibid., 48–51; Moyers, "Judge"; Johnson interview.
34. Bass, *Taming the Storm*, as quoted, 60, 61.
35. Ibid., 68–79.
36. Ibid., as quoted, 74–76.
37. Spivack, *Race*, 55–56, 139–50, quote at 141.
38. Ibid., as quoted, 145, 139.

39. Bass, *Taming the Storm*, 80–117; Spivack, *Race*, 55–56, 139–50.

40. Bass, *Taming the Storm*, 80–117; Virginia Van der Veer Hamilton, "Lister Hill, Hugo Black, and the Albatross of Race," and J. Mills Thornton, III, "Hugo Black and the Golden Age," in Freyer, ed., *Justice Black*, 85–100, 139–56.

41. Bass, *Taming the Storm*, 80–95, as quoted, 82.

42. Ibid., passages quoted directly and as quoted, 83.

43. Ibid., as quoted, 85.

44. Ibid., 80–95, and phrase as quoted, 81.

45. On Kennamer, see Freyer and Dixon, *Democracy and Judicial Independence*, Chapter II.

46. Bass, *Taming the Storm*, 87; Freyer, *Little Rock Crisis*; Robert Fredrick Burk, *The Eisenhower Administration and Black Civil Rights* (Knoxville, 1984).

47. Bass, *Taming the Storm*, 104–06; Burk, *Eisenhower Administration*; E. Culpepper Clark, *The Schoolhouse Door: Segregation's Last Stand at the University of Alabama* (New York, 1993).

48. Bass, *Taming the Storm*, 106.

49. Ibid., 107–17.

50. Ibid., 109; Freyer, *Little Rock Crisis*, 75; Goldfield, *Black, White and, Southern*, 84, 85; Burk, *Eisenhower Administration*, 161–62.

51. *Browder v. Gayle*, 142 F.Supp. 707 (M.D. Ala. 1956); *Gayle v. Browder*, 352 U.S. 903 (1956).

52. Bass, *Taming the Storm*, 113.

53. Ibid.

54. Ibid., 107–17.

55. Sikora, *The Judge*, as quoted, 37.

56. In Alabama, this shifting of responsibility was known by a football metaphor, the "punting syndrome." A label popularized by publicists captured the enforcement side or executive implications of Johnson's decisions: Steven Brill called him "The Real Governor of Alabama," *New York*, April 26, 1976, 37–41. These characterizations neglect the contribution Johnson made to the fairer operation of democratic institutions.

57. Bass, *Taming the Storm*, 455, 458.

58. Yackle, *Reform and Regret*, as quoted, 16.

59. Ibid., 18; *Shuttlesworth v. Birmingham Board of Education*, 162 F. Supp. 372 (N.D. Ala. 1958); *Shuttlesworth v. Birmingham*, 373 U.S. 262 (1963). See also Sikora, *The Judge*, 232.

60. Bass, *Taming the Storm*, 207, 208, 209–18, 229–35; Yackle, *Reform and Regret*, 18–20; *Lee v. Macon County Bd. of Educ.*, 221 F. Supp. 297 (M.D. Ala. 1963); *Lee v. Macon County Bd. of Educ.*, 231 F. Supp. 743 (M.D. Ala. 1964).

61. Bass, *Taming the Storm*, 456. Concerning the use of the FBI, see Yackle, *Reform and Regret*, 19; Freyer, *Little Rock Crisis*, 102, 104–09, 118–26, 140.

62. Yackle, *Reform and Regret*, 20.

63. Bass, *Taming the Storm*, as quoted passages, 91, 232, 234.

64. Yackle, *Reform and Regret*, 21–22; *U.S. v. Montgomery Bd. of Educ.*, 395 U.S. 225, 236 (1969).

65. Bass, *Taming the Storm*, as quoted, 265.

66. Ibid., 231.

67. Yackle, *Reform and Regret*, 22–29; *Stockton v. Alabama Indust. School for Negro Children*, Civ. Action No. 2834–N (M.D. Ala. 1969); *Alabama v. Finch* and *Marable v. Alabama Mental Health Board*, 297 F. Supp. 291 (M.D. Ala. 1969); *Wyatt v. Stickney*, 334 F. Supp. 1341 (M.D. Ala. 1971); *Wyatt v. Stickney*, 325 F. Supp. 781 (M.D. Ala. 1971); *Wyatt v. Aderholt*, 503 F.2d 1305 (5th Cir. 1974).

68. Yackle, *Reform and Regret*; *Newman v. Alabama*, 349 F. Supp. 278 (M.D. Ala. 1972); *James v. Wallace*, 406 F. Supp. 318 (M.D. Ala. 1976).

69. Yackle, *Reform and Regret*, as quoted, 17. But see Nagel, "Controlling the Structural Injunction," 395–411.

70. Yackle, *Reform and Regret*, 20, 259.

71. Bass, *Taming the Storm*, as quoted, 90.

72. Ibid., as quoted.

73. Bass, *Taming the Storm*, 184–94; as quoted, Yackle, *Reform and Regret*, 18; *In re Wallace*, 171 F. Supp. 720 (M.D. Ala. 1959).

74. Bass, *Taming the Storm*, 153–55, 254–55; *U.S. v. Alabama*, 171 F. Supp. 720 (M.D. Ala. 1959) (dismissed case against voting registrars and state because registrars had resigned); aff'd. 267 F.2d 808 (5th Cir. 1959); rev'd. 362 U.S. 602 (ordered reinstatement of State of Alabama as defendant); 188 F. Supp. 759 (M.D. Ala. 1960) (overruled motion to dismiss by State of Alabama); 192 F. Supp. 677 (1961) (granted injunction against refusal to register black voters); *U.S. v. Duke*, 332 F.2d 759 (5th Cir. 1964); Pub. L. No. 89–110, 79 Stat. 437 (1965).

75. *Gomillion v. Lightfoot*, 167 F. Supp. 405 (M.D. Ala. 1958); *Gomillion v. Lightfoot*, 364 U.S. 339 (1960).

76. *Sims v. Fink*, 205 F. Supp. 245 (M.D. Ala. 1962); 208 F. Supp. 431 (M.D. Ala. 1962); *Reynolds v. Sims*, 377 U.S. 533 (1964).

77. The precise nature of Wallace's role in bringing on the violence of "Bloody Sunday" at Edmund Pettus Bridge is unclear. See Klarman, *"Brown,"* 128. For general discussion of Selma, see Goldfield, *Black, White and Southern*, 163–67; David J. Garrow, *Protest at Selma: Martin Luther King, Jr., and the Voting Rights Act of 1965* (New Haven, 1978).

78. Bass, *Taming the Storm*, 250; *Williams v. Wallace*, 240 F. Supp. 100 (M.D. Ala. 1965).

79. Bass, *Taming the Storm*, 252.

80. *Williams v. Wallace.*

81. Bass, *Taming the Storm*, as quoted, 251–53.

82. Yarborough, *Judge Frank Johnson*, 80–83; *U.S. v. U.S. Klans*, CA 1718 N (1961), on file, U.S. District Court, Middle District of Alabama, Montgomery.

83. Yarborough, *Judge Frank Johnson*, 125–27; *U.S. v. Eaton*, criminal case 11736-N (1965), on file, U.S. District Court, Middle District of Alabama, Montgomery.

84. *White v. Crook*, 251 F. Supp. 401 (M.D. Ala. 1966).

85. Yarborough, *Judge Frank Johnson*, 145–47; *Dickey v. Alabama State Board of Education*, 273 F. Supp. 613 (M.D. Ala. 1967); *Griffin v. Tatum*, 300 F. Supp. 60 (M.D. Ala. 1969); *Brooks v. Auburn University*, 296 F. Supp. 188 (M.D. Ala. 1969); *Parducci v. Rutland*, 316 F. Supp. 352 (M.D. Ala. 1970); *Drake v. Covington Board of Education*, 371 F. Supp. 974 (M.D. Ala. 1974). But see *Dixon v. Alabama State Board of Education*, 186 F. Supp. 945 (M.D. Ala. 1960); *Rowe v. Forrester*, 368 F. Supp. 1355 (M.D. Ala. 1974).

86. *Frontiero v. Laird*, 341 F. Supp. 201 (M.D. Ala. 1972); 411 U.S. 677 (1973).

87. *U.S. v. Germany*, 32 F.R.D. 343 and 421 (M.D. Ala. 1963); Bass, *Taming the Storm*, 389.

88. Frank M. Johnson, Jr., "What Is Right With America," address delivered at the Montgomery County Bar Association, Law Day, May 2, 1990. Tony Freyer thanks Judge Johnson for permission to quote from this manuscript.

89. Ibid.

90. Frank M. Johnson, Jr., "With A Juvenile Delinquent, A Youth Offender, or A Young Adult Offender?," 30 F.R.D. 185, 258, 259, 260 (1962).

91. Ibid.

92. Frank M. Johnson, Jr., "The Role of the Judiciary With Respect to the Other Branches of Government," *Georgia Law Review* 11 (Spring 1977): 468–69.

93. Ibid., 469.

94. Ibid., 474–75.

95. Frank M. Johnson, Jr., "The Role of the Organized Bar In Providing Legal Services," *The Alabama Lawyer* 36 (January 1975): 11–16.

96. Frank M. Johnson, Jr., "Role of Judiciary," *Georgia Law Review* 11 (Spring 1977): 469–74; see also Johnson "Equal Access to Justice," 1–12.

97. Frank M. Johnson, Jr., "Supremacy of the Law," *The Alabama Lawyer* 30 (July 1969): 295.

98. Frank M. Johnson, Jr., "The Attorney and the Supremacy of Law," *Georgia Law Review* 1 (Fall 1966): 41, 42.

99. Ibid., 42.

100. Bass, *Taming the Storm*, 127–29; Freyer and Dixon, *Democracy and Judicial Independence*, Chap. III.

101. Freyer and Dixon, *Democracy and Judicial Independence*, Chap. III.

102. Johnson, "The Attorney and the Supremacy of Law"; Frank M. Johnson, Jr., "Responsibility For Integrity In Government," *The Alabama Lawyer* 35 (January 1974): 12–18.

103. Frank M. Johnson, Jr., "Civil Disobedience and the Law," *Tulane Law Review* 44 (December 1969): 12, 6, 8.

104. Ibid., 8, 9.

105. Nagel, "Controlling the Structural Injunction," 401, 400, 399.

106. Bass, *Taming the Storm*, as quoted, 90.

Index

Acker, William Marsh, Jr.
  affirmative action and, 201
  appellate review and, 197–99, 202
  appointment of (as federal judge),
    153, 154
  biography of, 267
  employment discrimination and, 199
  Howell Heflin and, 165
  on judicial decision making, 171, 174
  Ku Klux Klan and, 198
  legal realism and, 177
  precedent and, 202
  right to jury trial and, 199, 202
  summary judgment and, 198
Acklin, Joseph A. S., 281
Activism
  legal realism and, 253
  public view of, 252–53
  on rights issues, 215
  See also Conservative-activist
    jurisprudence; Social
    jurisprudence
Adair, Howard V., 286
Adams, John Quincy
  William Crawford (of Alabama)
    appointment and, 8, 11
Adams-Onis Treaty of 1819
  seizure of the *Merino* and, 37
Administrative Office Act of 1939
  judicial self-governance and, 185–86
Admiralty jurisdiction
  Richard Busteed and, 98
  changing patterns in, 108, 109
  cotton economy and, 34

English precedent and, 31, 41
expansion of, 39, 100–102
local interests and, 56, 108
navigability of waterways and,
  31–36
sectional tensions and, 17
slave-trade prosecution and, 36, 40
universal principles and, 37
Affirmative action
  quota relief and, 201
  reverse discrimination and, 201
  voluntary programs and, 199, 201–2
African Americans
  Constitution of 1901 and, 78
  convict-lease system and, 73–74
  judicial appointments and, 147,
    148–52
  jury selection and, 73
  Ku Klux Klan and, 198
  peonage and, 117–25
Agricultural Adjustment Act
  John H. Bankhead and, 84
  Hugo Black and, 84
Alabama
  description of federal litigation in
    (1824–1860), 5–6, 21–26, 28
  economy of, 59, 62, 77
  legal realism and, 168–69
  as one-party state, 78–79
  population of, 59, 66, 76–78, 187–89
  religions of, 79
  sectionalism and, 187
  as two-party state, 161–62
  urbanization and, 76–77, 187, 188